SLOW DEATH
BRITISH INDUSTRY

THE

SLOW DEATH

OF

BRITISH INDUSTRY

—

A SIXTY-YEAR SUICIDE
1952–2012

—

NICHOLAS COMFORT

Biteback Publishing

This edition published in Great Britain in 2013 by
Biteback Publishing Ltd
Westminster Tower
3 Albert Embankment
London SE1 7SP
Copyright © Nicholas Comfort 2012

First published in Great Britain in 2012.

ISBN 978-1-84954-463-4

10 9 8 7 6 5 4 3 2 1

A CIP catalogue record for this book is available from the British Library.

Set in Caslon and ChunkFive

Printed and bound in Great Britain by
CPI Group (UK) Ltd, Croydon CR0 4YY

CONTENTS

PREFACE

The story outlined in this book is one I have lived through, and at times been close to. As a schoolboy in the 1950s I marvelled at the new technologies Britain was developing in aerospace, nuclear energy, computing and much more. As a young reporter I covered politics and industry in Sheffield (just after steel was renationalised) and in Birmingham, where I witnessed the travails of Birmingham Small Arms (BSA), British Leyland and the Meriden motorcycle co-operative. In Fleet Street I experienced at first hand the debilitating effects of poor management and industrial anarchy on an industry. As a Lobby correspondent over two decades I rubbed shoulders with the ministers who were framing the policies that impacted on industry. I was close to their efforts to keep Chrysler and British Leyland afloat, and to a number of catastrophic defence procurements, notably the Nimrod early warning aircraft. My involvement with the Scottish media – and later the Scotland Office – brought me close to the Ravenscraig saga and the struggles to keep Scotland's last shipyards going. I worked in the Department of Trade and Industry, alongside civil servants doing their best to encourage British industry and secure a fair deal for it in Europe, and then for QinetiQ, one of Britain's greatest sources of technological innovation, after it was floated out of the Ministry of Defence. And in each of these capacities I found myself asking the same question: 'Why don't we, as a country, want to make things any more?'

The threads finally came together when I started writing obituaries for the *Daily Telegraph*. While the news pages daily reported the collapse of one once-proud British industry after another, the yellowing files of cuttings I was going through from the 1950s and 1960s trumpeted optimism and success, frequently for these very same companies. This book is intended to explore how things went so badly wrong, and give some indications as to why.

Some of the instances I give come from my own contacts with industry, government and trade unionism. Others come from what is charitably termed 'desk research'. Quite a few of the statistics, and some of the examples, are taken from Sir Geoffrey Owen's 1999 book *From Empire to Europe*, which chronicles the same process of decline but draws a more optimistic conclusion than I can accept – or than he would have drawn had he written it now. I am also grateful to many friends and contacts for highlighting and explaining particular episodes along the way, notably David Adams, Jeremy Candfield, John Cockcroft, Neil Fisher, Roland Gribben, Mike Hayle, Robert Hollidge, James Miller, Louisa-Jayne O'Neill, Jeanette Owens, Theo Steel, Gus Tilley and Jim Wilson. Yet the opinions expressed are my own, and any factual inaccuracies are my responsibility.

I am especially grateful to Sean Magee for encouraging me in this project and paving the way for publication, to Sam Carter for his expertise in editing my manuscript, and to the electors of Norfolk North for convincing Iain Dale that his future lay in publishing rather than in the House of Commons, the consequence being the launch of Biteback Publishing, under whose imprint this book appears.

Nicholas Comfort
London, January 2013

1

AN UNTHINKABLE DECLINE

When Queen Elizabeth II came to the throne in 1952, the talk was of a New Elizabethan Age of British economic and technological achievement, founded on the fruits of ground-breaking wartime research and backed by the financial might of the City. Britain was about to launch the world's first jet airliner. She was on the verge of becoming the first nation to generate nuclear power; a close second to the United States in the development of the computer. Her factories were working flat out producing the cars, ships, buses, lorries, aircraft, electrical goods, clothes, chemicals and construction materials demanded by a society on the verge of prosperity after the pain of rationing and post-war reconstruction.

One half of the working population was employed in manufacturing, from massive plants to tiny workshops; unemployment was negligible. Despite the depredations of war, Britain's share of the world's manufactured exports was higher than when it broke out, at a heady 25.4 per cent in 1950. The industrial colossi of Germany and Japan had yet to recover from devastating military defeats and posed no immediate threat. It appeared that Britain's slide in international competitiveness, which had begun as far back as the 1870s, had been arrested. Britain's export markets in what was still known as the Empire seemed secure. The risk of nuclear war with the Soviet Union apart, there was scarcely a cloud on the horizon.

Sixty years on, having recently celebrated the Diamond Jubilee, the picture is unrecognisable. Entire sectors of British industry have vanished. Household names from the 1950s and more recently have gone, and most that remain are a shadow of their former selves or under foreign ownership – or both. From having a plethora of forward-looking plane makers, Britain now scarcely has the capacity to manufacture an airframe. Our nuclear engineering industry – the world's first – stayed on its home turf, suffered from the 1970s as domestic nuclear power station construction ground to a halt, and now requires Japanese assistance as a second generation of stations is needed. Most of our car makers from the 1950s have gone out of business after losing the battle with imports, and although production has partly recovered, today's volume plants are in Japanese hands and even the most British of marques like Jaguar and Rolls-Royce are under foreign ownership. Our mainframe computer industry barely got off the ground, and American and Japanese technologies now predominate. We invented television, but Britain's last (Japanese-owned) television factory closed in 2009. Our truck and bus industry, once a world leader, has largely evaporated. It is of little wonder that by 2009 our share of world-manufactured trade had shrunk to just 2.9 per cent. As Labour's Business Secretary Peter Mandelson lamented in 2010, 'We have forgotten how to make things.'

To some, this does not matter. One hears the argument that Britain is still a world leader in defence industries, aero engines, pharmaceuticals and other niche markets (though as I started writing this, Pfizer announced the closure of its UK Research and Development (R&D) facility with the loss of 2,400 jobs). We have been told – particularly by Gordon Brown when Chancellor – that Britain's economic future rests with a powerful and well-regulated financial services sector; the near-collapse of the banks in 2008–9 took care of that. We are told that the balance of payments, which terrified ministers in the 1960s, no longer matters, and that sterling can thrive despite massive trade deficits only partly offset by 'invisibles' like insurance. We are told that globalisation has stripped every country of its national champions as corporations in manufacturing, as in all other spheres of activity, operate across borders, so it does not matter if British-based and controlled companies no longer manufacture goods in bulk. Above all, we are told that Britain no longer needs to be a manufacturing nation because other countries can do it cheaper and better; in short, we have moved on and should be thankful.

It is beyond question that Britain could not have continued to produce a quarter of the world's internationally traded goods; challengers were bound to come forward and gain market share. It is self-evident that some of the items Britain made for the world up to the 1950s, like steam locomotives, would become obsolete (the Chinese produced their last in 1988). And as demand for items from the mangle to the radio valve and the typewriter died out, the skills needed to produce them were also no longer necessary. It was inevitable that the vast, tribal smokestack plants where heavy industrial production – and trade union organisation – was once concentrated, would be replaced by more flexible facilities with smaller and more productive workforces. Inevitable, too, that the shift in production of cheap goods from Britain to the developing world, which had started well before the Second World War with textiles and toys, would continue.

Yet, had the present situation been visible from those heady days of 1952, it would have been viewed as a disaster – and, probably, a betrayal. How is it that Germany retains a Siemens and France an Alstom, but there is no longer a British General Electric Company (GEC)? (Alstom, ironically, was originally Alsace Thomson, the subsidiary of a British firm that eventually became part of GEC.) Why are there booming shipyards in Italy, but not in Britain? Why have Austin, Morris, Standard, Triumph, Hillman and many other British car marques disappeared while Renault and Volkswagen have survived? How can France boast an independent aircraft maker in Dassault as well as EADS when apart from BAE Systems – which now regards itself primarily as a contractor to the Pentagon – all British equivalents have gone to the wall? How, for that matter, has France managed to thwart foreign bids for the likes of Danone while Cadbury dropped into Kraft's hands like a ripe fruit? All this without even considering the success – and inroads made in British markets – of competitors from Japan, Korea, China and, increasingly, India.

Nor has this change been driven by the consumer. In 1952 the British public not only expected to buy British; except for items at the very top and bottom of the market, it had no choice. As a greater variety of goods, including imports, came into the shops, some British manufacturers inevitably paid the price for complacency or uncompetitive pricing. Yet by 2012 the British consumer would be hard pressed to find any household articles produced in the United Kingdom. The Coronation souvenirs of 1952 were almost entirely British-made, but the vast majority of those for the Diamond Jubilee have been manufactured in China.

Even products that convey the essence of Britishness are now made overseas: Slazenger's official Wimbledon tennis ball in the Philippines, Terry's Chocolate Orange in Poland, HP Sauce at a Euro-glop factory in Holland and Smarties – just one of Nestlé's 6,000 global brands – in Germany. The Dunlop Rubber Company no longer makes tyres; Tate & Lyle – targeted for nationalisation as a strategic industry *circa* 1950 – has given up refining sugar. These decisions were not taken by the consumer, but by managements who had lost the will to take manufacturing forward in the United Kingdom, or saw no commercial interest in doing so.

Today, of Britain's 20 leading companies by market capitalisation, just five (GlaxoSmithKline, British American Tobacco, AstraZeneca [in part a spinoff from ICI], Diageo and Reckitt Benckiser) manufacture anything at all in the United Kingdom. And intriguingly, just eight of the 20 have a British-born chairman. To some, the fact that many of the remnants of Britain's manufacturing sector are in overseas ownership – or even, as with BAE Systems, have predominantly foreign shareholders – does not matter: jobs are jobs. Yet when a British plant is doing well, the profits flow overseas – and when it does badly, there is nothing to stop the owners closing it down or transferring production somewhere cheaper. Decisions on where and whether to invest – and, of equal importance, to continue to invest – are taken abroad.

Some blame the City. The City of the 1950s was even more powerful in the world economy than today, with sterling the dominant global currency after the dollar, and extremely influential in preserving domestic economic stability. There was no hint of the role that investment banks and other institutions would play in making gargantuan sums of money to be pocketed by their most speculative employees, with manufacturing firms – and jobs – treated as casino chips. To the City pages of the 1950s, manufacturing was the bedrock of the economy, and featured largely in unexciting columns of company results reflecting steady returns for shareholders, small and – increasingly – institutional. Nowadays manufacturing features almost solely as a takeover target or because of the announcement of closures – or, less frequently, investment – by an owner based overseas.

Then, as now, the City and the banks were seen by many in industry as a brake on productive investment: over-cautious and dominated by short-term considerations. Yet the strength of British manufacturing and exports was an essential ingredient of the City's own stability and success, reflected in manufacturing's dominance of the 30 companies tracked by the FT Ordinary share index, the barometer of the stock market until the advent of the 100-company Footsie in 1984. And the changes in that index tell us much about what has happened to British manufacturing.

The FT index of 1952 was a roll-call of the companies driving the British economy; indeed the dominance of manufacturing was understated because it would take most of the 1950s to unscramble the steel industry nationalised by Labour. The 30 companies were: Associated Portland Cement (later Blue Circle), Bass (brewers), British Motor Corporation, Coats (thread makers), Wm Cory (transport), Courtaulds Textiles, Distillers (drinks and pharmaceutical), Dunlop Rubber, EMI, Lancashire Cotton, GEC, Leyland Motors, Guest Keen & Nettlefolds (GKN), Harrods, Hawker Siddeley (aircraft), Imperial Chemical Industries (ICI), Imperial Tobacco, London Brick, Murex (metallurgical services), P&O, Patons & Baldwins (textiles), Pinchin Johnson (textiles), Rolls-Royce, Spillers (animal feed), Swan Hunter (shipbuilding), Tate & Lyle, Tube Investments (specialised engineering), Vickers (aircraft and armaments), Watney Combe & Reid (brewers) and FW Woolworth. Twenty-six manufacturers – in the broadest sense – out of 30.

Sixty years on, just five of these companies are still trading as British entities: Cory Environmental, GKN, Imperial Tobacco,

Rolls-Royce and Tate & Lyle (having exited from its refining business in 2010). Distillers merged with Guinness to become Diageo, Hawker Siddeley and Vickers were merged into British Aerospace (now BAE Systems), London Brick survives as part of the now German-owned Hanson, Murex was acquired by BOC (also now under German ownership), TI became part of the Smiths Group, Watney disappeared after merging into Grand Metropolitan Hotels. These companies' continuing activities are generally on a much smaller scale and many of their plants have been closed. Bass is now owned by Molson-Coors and Anheuser-Busch, Blue Circle is part of the French company Lafarge, Courtaulds Textiles – having been a division of Sara Lee – is owned by a private Hong Kong company, Dunlop Tyres is owned by Goodyear and Sumitomo, Harrods by Qatar Holdings, Murex (as part of BOC) by the Linde Group, P&O by Dubai's DP World and Spillers by Nestlé. What is left of EMI has been split between France's Vivendi and a consortium headed by Sony. But, most dramatically, GEC, ICI, BMC/Leyland Motors – all industrial giants – and Woolworth, are simply no more.

Look at the FT 30 index today. Just two companies from 1952 still feature: GKN and Tate & Lyle. Privatised utilities and service companies are well represented: British Gas, British Airways, British Telecom, National Grid. So is financial services: 3i, Lloyd's Bank, Man Group, Prudential, Royal and Sun Alliance, Royal Bank of Scotland. Retail also figures (Marks & Spencer, Tesco), as do petroleum (BP), catering (Compass), broadcasting (ITV), gambling (Ladbrokes), property (Land Securities), telecoms (BT and Vodafone), IT and consulting (Logica) and advertising (WPP). All indicators of a modern economy, even if RBS had to be rescued from collapse by the taxpayer. But what of manufacturing? BAE Systems, British American Tobacco, Diageo, GKN, GlaxoSmithKline, Invensys, Reckitt Benckiser, Smiths Group, Tate & Lyle and (peripherally) Wolseley. Ten out of 30, if anything over-representing the sector.

There are model manufacturing companies who have consistently performed, and their enterprise, sound management and continuing commercial success without a change of ownership should be recognised; the Anglo-Dutch food-to-detergents giant Unilever is a fine example of a company that has avoided the temptations and pitfalls of global business. JCB has demonstrated, and continues to, that a British manufacturer with a world-beating product and a clear strategic focus can succeed against the toughest of competition; it is one of the few major family firms not to have floated on the stock market, exposing itself as a takeover target. Martin-Baker, another family-run firm, has become the supplier of ejector seats to 93 of the world's air forces, with over 7,630 lives saved to date. GKN, which with the eclipse of Wedgwood took over the crown as Britain's oldest quoted industrial company, has successfully reinvented itself from a maker of nuts and bolts to a high-quality automotive and aerospace component maker. And the Glasgow-based Weir Group, a specialised engineering firm quoted on the Stock Exchange since 1947, has maintained both its product quality and its independence. But sadly these are the exception rather than the rule.

Companies may indeed be organisms which are born, grow, mature and die; but in British manufacturing the number being taken over or giving-up-the-ghost over the past 60 years has consistently exceeded the number of new entrants, and it is hard today to detect a future generation of giants. It is true that corporate death occurs even in the healthiest of economies; witness the demise of AEG in Germany and great American airlines like PanAm and TWA. But Britain's graveyard is by far the largest.

For long it was argued that Britain's relative – and absolute – industrial decline was the fault of fuddy-duddy management, failure to invest, outdated working practices and head-in-the-sand trade unions, the loss of guaranteed markets in the Commonwealth and the success of Germany and Japan in rebuilding their industrial bases. And there was, especially in the 1950s and 1960s, a good deal of validity to these arguments.

Yet there have been many more factors at play: an arrogant belief by management and labour that the British public and the world beyond should be grateful for what they were producing regardless of its quality or relevance; the importing of cheap labour when the need was for higher productivity; short-termism in the City and the Treasury; near-suicidal exchange rate policies; inadequate market size at home; failure to make a commercial success of British inventions; the sterile and destructive cycle up to the 1980s of nationalisation and privatisation; an obsession with size; failure or refusal to adapt to obvious trends in the market; the reckless transfer of technology to overseas competitors; collaborative projects in which Britain surrendered the initiative; poor decision-making by government (not least over procurement); plagiarism by foreign competitors; takeovers – notably of companies in the United States – driven by boardroom egos and financed by unsustainable borrowing; other takeovers of specialist businesses by conglomerates who took no interest in them; the loss or transfer of jobs to the developing world and (since the collapse of Soviet communism) the former Iron Curtain countries; reliance on 'inward investment' projects that vanished overnight; treatment of Europe as a handicap rather than an opportunity; increasing boardroom disdain for manufacturing as such; the tendency of investment banks and the ultra-rich, in recent years, to treat strategically important companies as their playthings as the influence of even institutional shareholders declined; the lure of Wall Street; corporate greed; sheer bad luck – and good old fashioned incompetence.

Each of these factors has played a part in the decline of British industry over what could have been 60 glorious years. There are exceptions, and there have been shining examples of enterprise, but much hard work has been in vain and manufacturing now accounts for just 12 per cent of GDP, with well under 3 million workers employed in the sector. While some British exporters do fly the flag for excellent products, our overall record in manufacturing in recent decades is frankly one to be ashamed of. The chapters that follow look more deeply into how this came about; with luck, there may yet be some lessons we can learn.

2

CONFIDENCE AND COMPLACENCY: 1952-64

The first dozen years of the new reign, coinciding almost exactly with the Conservative governments of Churchill, Eden and Macmillan, were a time of rising prosperity, full employment and confidence that Britain would remain a global industrial force, not least through the new technologies of jet aircraft, computing and nuclear power. These were the icing on an apparently appetising industrial cake, with a powerful motor industry the prime ingredient and Britain's steel, chemical and other base industries working at full throttle. It was no coincidence that the launch of the BMC Mini in 1959 coincided with Harold Macmillan's assertion that 'You've never had it so good.'

During these years of optimism and stability the structure of British manufacturing changed little, as reflected in the membership of the FT 30 index. It was 1959 before any change took place: Coats, Cory and Harrods were replaced by Bowater (paper), Alfred Herbert (machine tools) and House of Fraser. The next year Pinchin Johnson was taken over by Courtaulds, replaced by the denationalised United Steel. Then in 1964 Courtaulds hoovered up Patons and Lancashire Cotton, with Glaxo (pharmaceuticals) and United Drapery Stores taking their place. The giants of industry, with ICI a model of strength as it regrouped and shed some of its bureaucracy under the leadership of Paul Chambers, cruised on.

Yet Britain's competitiveness was already weakening. By 1961 its share of global trade in manufactures had already fallen back to

16.2 per cent, a decline of one-third in just eleven years and not solely through the revival of old competitors. One factor was a failure in immediate post-war years to develop clear priorities for key sectors of the economy, as did France, or a long-term strategy for export-based manufacturing, as Japan was working towards with ruthless single-mindedness. Distracted by the headaches and challenges of trying to remain a great power and carry the burdens of enforcing the peace, Britain gave its highest priorities to housing the people of its devastated cities and building on technological advances made in wartime.

At the dawn of the new Elizabethan era, nowhere was Britain's confidence more apparently justified than in the air; each Farnborough Air Show was a showcase for fresh British innovations and exciting new types of aircraft. Building on the wartime achievements of Britain's aircraft industry, post-war governments concentrated their R&D spending on developing new generations of military and civil aircraft (in preference to electrical products and chemicals, identified as promising sectors by Germany and Japan). Moreover, the industry was boosted by the Korean War and the orders for military planes that followed, taking on an extra 100,000 workers between 1950 and 1954 for its workforce to peak at 279,000 – a level held into the 1960s.

The jewel in the crown was the De Havilland Comet, the world's first jet airliner. Built at Hatfield and first flown in 1949, it made its inaugural commercial flight – to Johannesburg for the British Overseas Airways Corporation (BOAC) – in May 1952, just three months into the new reign. The advent of jet airliners would be revolutionary for the thousands living near airports as well as for the initially tiny number of passengers; until the Comet, most of the complaints of noise around Heathrow concerned the airport's public address system. Despite having only 36 seats, the Comet was expected to turn a profit when less than half full, and Britain's primacy in aircraft manufacture seemed assured as orders poured in, not just from across the Empire but from Air France, Japan Air Lines and three carriers in the United States.

The Comet's order book was still growing, despite three crashes on take-off, when in January 1954 BOAC's Comet Yoke Peter broke up in flight and crashed into the Mediterranean off the isle of Elba. No explanation for the plane's disintegration had been found when that October a second Comet on charter to South African Airways plummeted into the sea near Naples, again with no survivors. Production was halted, and all Comets grounded. Exhaustive tests at Farnborough ascertained that metal fatigue was to blame: cracks caused by repeated pressurisation and depressurisation had spread from a rivet hole around a small fibreglass window, leading the entire fuselage to rip open. Modifications were made and a much improved Comet 4 returned to commercial service in October 1958, initially on the New York run.

That four-year delay cost Britain its lead as America's plane makers learned – and profited – from the Comet experience; they admitted that had they been first, they could have suffered the same misfortune. The same month that the Comet 4 entered service, the Boeing 707 – with a capacity of over 100 – made its transatlantic debut, followed soon after by the Douglas DC8. (This was a challenge not only for De Havilland, but for Rolls-Royce who saw General Electric and Pratt & Whitney erode its head start in developing jet engines.) By then, BOAC had reluctantly placed an order with Boeing; over 1,000 707s would be built for airlines worldwide. The Comet lingered on into the 1970s on secondary routes despite further embarrassing crashes (one to the Saudi King Saud's personal aircraft in 1963, fortunately without him on board). Orders faded away, and despite the technical success of the next-generation VC10, developed by Vickers at its own expense and first flown by BOAC in 1964, America cornered the market for long-haul airliners until the advent of Airbus, in which Britain made itself a junior partner. After the VC10, Britain never again produced a long-haul airliner alone: Concorde would be a joint venture with France; the Airbus has only its wings, some engines and a few other components manufactured in Britain.

Though the Comet was a ground-breaking aircraft in many respects, there was nothing technological in the way it was constructed. Like the excellent aircraft that had won the war in the air, the Comet and other post-war British planes were designed by engineers with slide rules working in imperial measure; Britain's first metric aircraft would be the Anglo-French Jaguar ground-attack jet which made its debut in 1968.

As the Comet morphed into the Nimrod maritime surveillance aircraft, flown by the RAF until 2011, engineers noted that no two of the airframes had exactly the same dimensions. (Nimrod would feature in two defence procurement disasters: the early warning version in the mid-1980s and the MRA4 upgrade a generation later. Each was abandoned by ministers with billions of pounds spent and with the project years behind schedule, and with the cancellation of the MRA4 in 2010, Britain lost the capacity to manufacture a large airframe.)

Astonishingly, Britain's plane makers continued with the same handmade approach even to aircraft whose numbers would suggest mass production. A case in point was the BAC One-Eleven, the highly successful short-haul jet airliner which entered service in 1963 and of which 244 were built up to 1987, the last few in Romania. When a tea trolley damaged the wing tip of a One-Eleven under mainte-nance at British United Airways, the British Aircraft Corporation (BAC) at Weybridge was unable to provide a replacement part with screw-holes in the same places, and eventually the airline's engineers knocked the damaged wing tip back into shape.

Britain's aircraft industry in the 1950s seemed in good heart overall, with a plethora of companies developing a wide range of products. The state-owned airlines BOAC and British European Airways (BEA), through (at times over-precise) joint work on development and the placing of orders, determined which of the civil aircraft in blueprint form should go into production; for military planes the decision rested with the RAF (and the Fleet Air Arm). Many concepts did not make it into production, and several military variants of a civil airliner were stillborn.

The turbo-prop Vickers Viscount, seating up to 48 passengers, was Britain's most successful civil aircraft of the day, indeed Europe's most successful pre-Airbus: 445 were built between 1948 and 1963, the last for the People's Republic of China. Less successful was the longer-haul turbo-prop Bristol Britannia, which suffered repeated delays as

BOAC changed its specifications, eventually entering service in 1957; it was eclipsed by the 707 and only 85 were built. There was also the cautionary tale of the De Havilland 121, opted for by British European Airways in 1959 as De Havilland merged into Hawker Siddeley. BEA was reluctant to operate jet aircraft at all, and insisted that the three-engined DH121 – better known as the Trident – be developed to fill a very particular niche, with limits imposed on its range and payload. The effect of this was to ensure that the Trident – first flown in 1962 – was only of interest to BEA, limiting the number produced of what could otherwise have been a commercially successful aircraft to 117. By contrast the DH Dove, a small two-engined commuter aircraft, sold steadily between 1948 and 1967, with 542 being produced, while the DH125 – a mid-sized turbine-powered business jet – would arguably become Britain's most successful civil aircraft. First flown in 1962 (as the HS 125), two a month on average would roll off the production line into the next century with its later cousin the Hawker 850, well over a thousand entering service around the world.

By the early 1960s, however, concerns were surfacing that Britain's plane makers were growing complacent about key export markets. The Conservative MP Brian Harrison, an advocate of closer trading links with his native Australia, sold the Commons of a salesman sent there who was incapable of answering basic technical questions from Qantas, and of two airline executives who for three days were given the run-around by a British aircraft manufacturer between Farnborough and the company's headquarters in an abortive attempt to secure the technical data on which they would decide whether to place an order. For good measure, he added, military aircraft ordered by the Royal Australian Navy had been delivered late.

Military aircraft production was even heavier as the RAF re-equipped with jets and new threats emerged: from 1949 1,972 Hawker Hunter fighters were built for the RAF and 19 other air forces, 901 English Electric Canberra high-level bombers (plus 478 in the United States and Australia), 436 Gloster Javelin interceptors and 337 English Electric Lightnings (the only all-British Mach 2 fighter), plus a wide range of transport, reconnaissance and training aircraft. No fewer than 136 Avro Vulcan bombers with a delta-wing looking ahead to Concorde were constructed for the RAF between 1951 and 1964. Intended to drop atomic bombs on targets in the Soviet Union, they thankfully never saw action in this role, though Vulcans did attempt to crater the runway at Port Stanley during the Falklands War of 1982. Moreover, there was strength in depth: Shorts of Belfast were commissioned in the early 1950s to design and build the Sperrin, to go into production if there were a delay in getting the V-bombers operational.

There was every reason to believe that Britain would remain a global force in aircraft production and development; only the United States had a stronger industry, with France and possibly Canada the only credible competition. The Soviet Union was playing catch-up, helped by the post-war Labour government's decision to hand over Rolls-Royce's technology for the Nene jet engine; RAF pilots shot down during the Korean War by Mig-15s powered by the Soviet version of the Nene had particular reason to curse this generosity.

Nor was Britain's technological advance in the air at an end. Barnes Wallis, mastermind of the Dam Busters' bouncing bomb, was developing new swing-wing aircraft designs. Readers of schoolboy comics and the imperialist *Daily Express* were treated to the prospect of supersonic flight to Australia. In the Coronation year of 1953 Rolls-Royce first flew what became known as the 'flying bedstead' – a test rig on which was developed the vertical and short take-off (VSTOL) technology that would in 1969 make its debut as the world-beating Hawker Siddeley Harrier. For several years the 'bedstead' was a star attraction at Farnborough … and visible proof that British technology led the world. And in March 1956 the Fairey Delta 2 supersonic-research aircraft, with the test pilot Peter Twiss at the controls, set a new world speed record for level flight of 1,132 mph – 300 mph faster than the previous best set by the Americans – at the price of broken windows across a swathe of southern England.

Then there was the Hovercraft, invented by Sir Christopher Cockerell and first flown in 1959 after each of the armed services had rejected it as a threat to its independence. Developed by

Saunders-Roe with a raft of British aircraft and shipbuilding firms also seizing the opportunity, the hovercraft found niche applications around the world, from ferries – notably across the Channel – and lifeboats to military craft. Yet a combination of factors from higher fuel prices to the Channel Tunnel would limit long-term hovercraft development worldwide – though Britain would continue to develop and export smaller versions, often for military use.

During the 1950s it became increasingly obvious that Britain could not accommodate so many competing design teams and constructors, none of whom could generate economies of scale at a time when the RAF was shedding global commitments and America was taking ever more aircraft orders in what had become the Commonwealth. Several plane makers slipped out of business or diversified into other areas, and in 1960 a first step towards rationalisation was taken with the formation of the British Aircraft Corporation, a government-inspired merger of the aircraft interests of English Electric and Vickers-Armstrong with the Bristol Aeroplane Company and Hunting Aircraft. Its first project was to be the TSR-2 strike and reconnaissance aircraft ... of which more will come later. Soon afterwards, Armstrong Whitworth, Avro and Gloster (whose works runway was too short for fully constructed aircraft to take off) merged into Hawker Siddeley, who had earlier acquired Folland and Blackburn. Vickers's Supermarine operation, which had produced the Spitfire, was not taken on by BAC and closed in 1963.

France also rationalised its aircraft industry, promoting the privately owned Dassault and Breguet (which would later merge) and the state-owned Sud-Aviation and Nord-Aviation as airframe manufacturers, with the state-owned Snecma producing engines. Its flagships were the Caravelle airliner, flown by Air France from 1958, and Dassault's Mystère (1951) and Mirage (1955) jet fighters. From the early 1960s France also, significantly, co-operated with Germany on two military planes: the Atlantic patrol aircraft and Transall transport. Under de Gaulle, France would see aircraft manufacture as a field in which it could project itself as a global force – and would succeed as Britain hesitated.

One factor that frustrated the progress of Britain's aircraft industry during this period was the decision by defence chiefs to develop rocketry for military use (and, as a secondary consideration, for a space programme). It led to a switch of R&D funding and resources into missile development, only for most of these projects to be abandoned one after another, as the Macmillan government – having given up a purely British solution in favour of a co-operative project – was forced to adopt America's Polaris submarine-launched nuclear deterrent.

The rise and fall of British missile development is encapsulated in Blue Streak. This intermediate-range ballistic missile was developed by De Havilland and Rolls-Royce as a possible replacement for the V-bombers. Its development for military purposes was cancelled in 1960, in favour of America's aircraft-launched Skybolt, with Britain taking a stake in that programme. To avoid costly compensation to the Australian government (Blue Streak was tested at Woomera, now a detention centre for asylum-seekers) the rocket was retained as the first stage of the European satellite launcher Europa. The project expired in 1972.

Britain joined the Douglas-led Skybolt programme intending to equip its V-bombers with the missile. Having put most of its deterrent eggs in one basket, the government was livid when the Kennedy administration in 1962 unilaterally cancelled the project. A series of frosty meetings culminated in the Bermuda agreement between Kennedy and Macmillan, under which the Royal Navy was given Polaris; Britain built the *Resolution* class of submarines to carry them, but the missiles were made in America. Britain developed a satellite launch programme through its Ariel and Falstaff rockets, but launches from Woomera ceased in 1979. Becoming a junior partner in the European Space Agency, Britain played little part in the production of rockets now launched from French Guiana or Baikonur in Kazakhstan.

British firms would, however, enjoy some commercial success with shorter-range and ground-defence missiles. The Bloodhound, developed by Bristol and Ferranti, was deployed by the RAF and foreign air forces from 1958 to 1991, providing their successor companies with a useful revenue stream as 783 were manufactured and deployed.

Another field in which New Elizabethan Britain looked set to lead the world was nuclear power. Though it was a by-product of the atomic weapons programme embarked on in 1947, Whitehall and industry grasped the potential for electricity generated though a controlled reaction even though coal remained king. Calder Hall on the Windscale/Sellafield site was the first nuclear power station in the world to deliver electricity in commercial quantities; it came on stream in August 1956, the Queen officially opening it that October. Despite a fire a year later in one of the Windscale reactors devoted to producing weapons-grade plutonium, in which catastrophe was only narrowly averted, a major programme for constructing Magnox power stations modelled on Calder Hall went ahead, with nine in operation by 1966. This provided a major work stream for construction firms like Taylor Woodrow, heavy engineering companies like Babcock & Wilcox and – as the demand for warship turbines subsided – the turbine manufacturers CA Parsons. Parsons also had a full order book providing generating machinery for Britain's new conventional power stations, and well into the 1960s was exporting them as far afield as Poland and Alabama. Further possibilities for nuclear power were explored at Dounreay, on the north coast of Scotland near Thurso, where five experimental fast breeder reactors were installed, the first – surrounded by an iconic 60m giant steel sphere nicknamed 'Fred the golf ball' – going critical in 1958; a second began supplying the National Grid four years later. Initially all nuclear reactor development was under the auspices of the defence ministries and their partner the Ministry of Supply, but in 1954 responsbility for nuclear power was hived off from the MoS to the UK Atomic Energy Authority, reducing the level of co-ordination with defence programmes.

Development of the computer was another area in which Britain seemed a world leader. The first 'Turing-complete' computer had been developed by Germany's Konrad Zuse in 1941, and his patents were taken up by IBM soon after the war. By contrast, not only was the pioneering work on computers to break codes at Bletchley Park still an official secret, but the Colossus machine developed there in 1943 was destroyed at the end of the war on orders from the top – a staggering decision however one looks at it. However Britain – largely through work at Cambridge and Manchester Universities – was not far behind America in striving to produce a serious mainframe, even if the first prototypes took up a space the size of a house and the received wisdom was that half a dozen computers might be the most the world would ever need. Cambridge's EDSAC ran its first program in 1949.

Commercial computer production in Britain dates from 1951, when the first Ferranti Mark 1 was installed at Manchester University; at least eight more such machines were constructed up to 1957, mainly to universities but also to Shell in Amsterdam. Later in 1951, the caterers J. Lyons & Co. built their own LEO 1 computer based on a Cambridge machine, to do their weekly bakery valuations – the first routine office computer task undertaken. In 1953 Manchester University developed the first computer using transistors instead of valves but it would be the 1970s before a further leap forward would come with the development of microprocessors.

Meanwhile in America, the first Remington Rand Univac computer was delivered to the US Census Bureau, and in 1952 IBM announced its IBM 701 data processing machine, the world's first mainframe. The less bulky IBM 650 of 1954 weighed barely 2½ tonnes with its power supply, taking up two cabinets of 4 cubic metres each; for decades, however, rooms full of cooling equipment would be needed. The year 1956 brought the first IBM machine with magnetic disks of random access memory (RAM). By 1960, IBM had captured one third of the world market in computers, other US manufacturers having most of the rest.

Among British manufacturers, Ferranti was first out of the trap, working out of a former steam locomotive factory in Manchester to produce its Mark 1 in 1951, the Pegasus in 1956 and an upgraded

Mark 1, the Mercury, in 1957; 66 in all were sold. Ferranti's next generation of machines was launched with the Atlas in 1962 – rated at the time the world's most powerful – and subsequently the Titan, which became the backbone of Cambridge University's mathematical laboratory. Then the pace of development stalled as senior management lost interest; Ferranti-Packard of Canada produced its 6000 model based on work done in Britain, then in 1963 Ferranti's business computer division – though not its military capability – was merged into International Computers and Tabulators (ICT). Lyons stayed in computing until that year when it merged its LEO business with English Electric's computer operation, going on to sell its stake to Marconi; this merged company gravitated into ICT.

ICT was formed from the merger in 1959 of the British Tabulating Machine Company (BTM) and Powers-Samas, both of whose roots were in punch-card data systems rather than electronics. BTM had manufactured and installed Hollerith card systems, and during the war designed and manufactured the 'bombe' machine at Bletchley Park conceived by Alan Turing. BTM stayed in computing after the war as Hollerith developed machines in the United States. The creation of ICT was intended to concentrate research and prevent the gap between IBM and Britain's computer industry widening further. But it took the absorption of Ferranti's – and subsequently EMI's – computer division to give it anything like critical mass and win a credible volume of export business. EMI's Emidec machines (initially very similar to Lyons's LEO) were by the mid-1960s in commercial use with EMI itself, Boots, London Transport, Lloyds Bank and the Admiralty. ICT's 1100 model was based on the Emidec, the 1201 on a Hollerith machine, the 1300 series launched in 1962 was developed in-house, the 1500 on technology licensed from RCA and the highly successful 1900 series on the Ferranti-Packard 6000.

ICT did not, however, embrace industrial and military computing. Ferranti continued development in these fields, especially for the RAF's ongoing Nimrod programme and the Royal Navy, with some upgraded Ferranti 1600s still in service today on the high seas. Moreover in 1959 Automatic Telephone and Electric (taken over soon after by Plessey) was named as prime contractor for the Linesman air defence system. Linesman was developed under strict secrecy at a factory in the centre of Liverpool, and its computer room occupying 4,186 square metres was located with equal anonymity in the middle of a council estate at West Drayton. The project made Plessey a leader in world computer design in the 1960s – but this, too, had to remain a secret and compatible further orders were limited.

Britain's wider electronics industry had come out of the war in good shape, and the pace of innovation continued. Decca's navigation systems acquired world-wide markets, and in 1954 its engineers developed a stereophonic recording system for large orchestras. Ferranti was leading the way in the development of airborne radar from its Crewe Toll, Edinburgh site, and produced, in 1955, Europe's first silicon diode. Cossor, which had pioneered the development of radar, introduced the first commercial aircraft radar systems to guide planes into airports. It was one of several well-established electronics companies to relocate from London to Harlow New Town, in 1958. However, losses following disputes over the cost of its contract for the Fylingdales early warning station forced its takeover in 1961 by America's Raytheon, with which it had built up a wartime partnership rolling out radar systems.

Mullard produced early semiconductors, and in 1957 set up the Mullard Radio Astronomy Laboratory at Cambridge University. Pye developed the first British transistor in 1956, though its faults in its V14 television seriously damaged the business. Plessey in 1957 produced an integrated circuit ahead of Texas Instruments and Fairchild in the United States. Through shrewd acquisitions Standard Telephones and Cables, owned by America's ITT, became the world leader in high-quality submarine telephone cables from its Southampton factory, opened in 1956. And Racal, started from scratch in 1950, began its growth into a worldwide electronics company, employing over 30,000 people, by making an iconic radio receiver of its own – the RA17 – after being prevented by an American company from producing an existing model under licence for the Royal Navy.

At the same time, the conglomerates that had grown up thanks to wartime demands on the electrical industry began to regroup. In 1955 English Electric (EE) took over the Vulcan Foundry and Robert Stephenson & Hawthorns (producers of steam locomotives for a century) as it geared up to supply the modernised railways; when the West Coast Main Line was electrified in the early 1960s, EE supplied the motive power. The formation of BAC took EE out of aircraft manufacture, and in 1963 it sold its guided weapons division to BAC. In 1961 Plessey acquired British Ericsson and AT&E to become Britain's largest manufacturer of telecoms equipment. And then there was GEC.

Having attempted to become a rival to Siemens between the wars, GEC in the 1950s was a sleeping giant: despite investing substantially in heavy engineering and nuclear power and benefiting from the boom in electrical consumer goods, it atrophied internally and its profits began to slip. Then in 1961 GEC acquired Sir Michael Sobell's Radio & Allied Industries, and two years later Sobell's son-in-law, Arnold Weinstock, became its managing director. In a generation, he would create arguably Britain's most successful and solidly-based company. Weinstock started by rejuvenating GEC internally, cutting out deadwood and playing to its strengths, then as profitability returned he prepared to reorganise the entire British electrical industry.

The industry was held back in one important respect: by the Post Office's determination to replace its ageing Strowger system of telephone switchgear with a totally electronic system – which did not yet exist. This hamstrung the 'ring' of five suppliers who had shared the Post Office's orders without competition since the 1920s: GEC, Siemens, STC, AT&E and Ericsson. In the 1950s overseas networks were switching to Crossbar, an intermediate system devised by Bell, and export orders were starting to be lost as the Post Office waited for something better. The manufacturers pressed for the adoption of Crossbar, which they could then gear up to deliver; but creation of an electronic system proved painful and, as an interim measure, small-scale orders were placed for Crossbar and, even, more Strowger equipment. Manufacturing capacity contracted, and by 1964 mergers had reduced the 'ring' to STC, GEC and Plessey.

Britain's television manufacturers – Thorn, GEC, Philips and Rank were the largest – had a strong and growing market as the number of licence holders soared from 1.4 million in 1952 to 15.1 million in 1968. They also had the edge over foreign producers: until the mid-1960s the BBC (and independent television) broadcast solely on a 405-line system not used in other countries – and for years they could depend on bulk orders from TV rental companies. Cossor, who had manufactured the very first television sets before the war, failed to replicate its success and in 1958 sold its radio and television business to Philips.

Bush, almost alone among British manufacturers, was able for a time to compete with Japanese radio imports through its TR82 transistor set, styled by Ogle Design and launched in 1959. Other manufacturers concentrated on producing valve-based sets in cabinets, or heavy portables, well after Sony in 1955 launched the first integrated transistor set; by 1959 several Japanese companies were producing radios that would fit into a good-sized pocket, and demand for conventional British-made sets plummeted.

The makers of record players, too, were thriving – there was no more popular household good in late 1950s Britain than the Dansette record player. Launched in 1952 by the Margolin family, whose factory at its peak employed several hundred workers, the Dansette sold over a million as rock'n'roll was born. The vinyl 45 rpm single succeeded the shellac 78, first outselling it in 1958 as Cliff Richard joined Elvis Presley in the hit parade and record sales boomed. Teenage girls could now jive at home to records of their choice instead of catching the occasional pop programme on the radio; for many the Dansette's best feature was its auto-change facility, enabling six singles to be loaded at a time to give 18 minutes' dancing or swooning instead of just three.

Throughout the 1950s, Britain's factories were kept fully stretched as the country re-equipped after six years of war. Steelworks ran at full stretch to meet demand for vehicles, ships, white goods and much more. Steel, indeed, was effectively rationed; it was 1955 before John Lewis was allowed, after several refusals, the construction steel it needed to rebuild its bombed-out Oxford Street store. Heavy electrical plants were kept busy with demand for their products across the piece. Brickworks ran at capacity as Harold Macmillan fulfilled his pledge to build 300,000 new houses a year, prompting a search by government and the building industry for alternative materials which led to the architectural disasters of 1960s 'system building' and subsequent corruption scandals. Massey-Ferguson (using an old Standard car plant at Coventry) and Ford – who opened a new factory at Basildon in 1964 – upped tractor production for the home market and by the end of the 1950s were also the world's leading exporters. Leyland, AEC, Bristol and other chassis manufacturers (plus a host of coachbuilding firms) worked flat out to replace superannuated fleets of buses and trams. Between 1947 and 1954 nearly 7,700 buses were built for London alone – almost all by AEC and Leyland – and in the decade from 1958, 2,876 of the iconic Routemaster were produced, predominantly by AEC. Orders on this scale could not continue indefinitely (particularly as the public began switching to their cars). A slowing in the pace was reflected in Leyland's acquisition of AEC in 1962 and Guy's cessation of bus production in 1964 after being taken over by Jaguar. But Leyland's Atlantean (produced from 1956 to 1986) was a commercial success and orders from the Commonwealth held up. One controversial order for Leyland, in 1964, came from Cuba; the East German ship carrying the buses to Havana sank in the Thames, allegedly sabotaged by the CIA.

Britain's HGV manufacturers were also doing well, helped by the nationalised British Road Services placing large orders with the likes of Leyland and Seddon, and British Railways basing its road deliveries on the Scammell Scarab 'mechanical horse'. General Motors' Bedford marque won big military contracts, developed the iconic 1955 'Green Goddess' fire engine and provided the most popular coach chassis for the lower end of the market. In 1962 Foden launched the first British-built mass-produced tilting cab. Yet even with the road-haulage market expanding fast, consolidation was in the air with Leyland acquiring Scammell in 1955 and AEC – with orders from Iran and Iraq to Argentina and the Caribbean – taking over Thornycroft in 1961, a year before its merger with Leyland.

British Railways, severely run down during the war, also began to modernise. A new generation of 'Standard' steam locomotives was developed, the last being produced at Swindon in 1960. But in 1954 a 'modernisation plan' with a switch to diesel traction at its core was announced. In the rush to get rid of steam, numerous types of diesel locomotive were produced, many in plants that had previously made steam locos. Not all were successful, and several well-known companies from the age of steam went under – starting with North British, Glasgow, in 1962, after pioneering a disastrous hydraulic transmission. BR belatedly concentrated on a few standard types, as it had with steam, and carriage and wagon makers found orders drying up as existing stock was used more efficiently. Metro-Cammell closed one of its two Birmingham plants in 1962, and four years later took over Cravens, which had recently completed a large order for Underground trains; Cravens Sheffield plant did not last much longer. In the years that followed, BR's own workshops from Brighton to Darlington in which steam engines had been constructed, went steadily to the wall. The 2012 Olympics were staged on the site of the former Great Eastern Railway Stratford works, dating from 1848, which once built a locomotive in under ten hours. It serviced its last steam engine in 1963, when the main site closed; a part stayed open maintaining diesels up to 1991.

Britain was the cradle of not only the locomotive but the modern ship, and at the start of the new reign shipbuilding looked set to remain one of its premier industries. With the shipyards of most competing nations (America apart) devastated by war, Britain's enjoyed full order books as booming world trade fuelled a demand for new ships, though the requirements of the Royal Navy eased. In 1950, British yards launched 1.324 million tons of new merchant vessels, 37.9 per cent of the world's total.

However, they were still employing construction methods little changed from the years before 1914, when Britain had built more than half the world's entire tonnage. Technology of almost any sort was absent, the judgment of craftsmen being rigidly preferred to the numerical control of modern machine tools. Methods harnessed by America in wartime to build 'Liberty ships' in vast numbers were taken up by Britain's competitors as they rebuilt; indeed America's National Bulk Carriers, under contract to the Japanese government, brought the technology to the former Imperial Naval Yard at Kure, and trained technicians from other yards such as Hitachi's at Chiba and Mitsubishi's at Nagasaki. It was the Japanese, however, who devised the reorganisation of shipyards as production lines with a central 'building dock'.

Japan's modernised yards concentrated in the 1950s on producing ever larger tankers and bulk carriers while British yards failed to cash in on the booming tanker market, instead concentrating on building freighters one by one by traditional methods and chasing orders for bespoke ocean liners. These dried up with the advent of the Boeing 707, P&O's last great liners for carrying passengers (rather than cruising) being the *Oriana*, built by Vickers-Armstrong at Barrow, which entered service in 1959, and the *Canberra* (1961) built in Belfast by Harland & Wolff. Around this time Harland & Wolff closed its three yards on the British mainland.

Ironically the *Oriana* left Barrow just as the Italian government was setting up a combine – Fincanteri – that by the new century would be Europe's premier builder of cruise liners, with the UK out of the running. Headquartered at Trieste, two of Fincanteri's yards – at Genoa and La Spezia – continued to build warships. Six more – at Gorizia, Venice, Genoa, Ancona, Naples and Palermo – produced merchant ships and, eventually, fleets of liners for the Carnival, Princess and Grimaldi lines, and Cunard's *Queen Victoria* and new-generation *Queen Elizabeth*. Fincanteri remained under government ownership throughout.

By 1958 both Japan and West Germany were building more new tonnage than Britain, harnessing modular methods of construction; Denmark and Sweden too were making inroads into the British yards' traditional order base of British, Greek and Norwegian shipowners.

Moreover, British owners regarded the charter market for tankers as too risky to invest in, and 'flagging out' as the major owners registered their ships under 'flags of convenience', removed the synergy of British construction and registration. A world recession in shipbuilding from that year hit yards around the world. But as demand returned in 1961 it was Britain's shipbuilders – some by now belatedly re-equipping – who continued to suffer, continuing as they did to chase their traditional markets. And while global production surged, Britain's remained stuck at just over 1 million tons per annum.

The industry was not helped by its archaic working practices and abysmal industrial relations, at a time when West Germany and Japan had reorganised their key industries on the basis of consensus management. Each task was the province of a particular group of craftsmen, often with their own separate union; it was said that 'it takes 21 unions to build a ship'. Moreover, each union had its own agenda. The Boilermakers deliberately kept down the number of apprentices to keep members' wages up; their leader, Ted Hill, would boast that there wasn't a boilermaker in Gateshead under 58. Such restrictive practices were common among skilled workers determined to preserve their craft, and management knew that resisting them, let alone modernising working practices, would trigger damaging strikes. For the yards were also afflicted by a bloody-mindedness that led to the saying: 'When the tulips come out, the Cammell Laird workers strike in sympathy.' Hardly a day passed by without a demarcation – 'who does what?' – dispute in one yard or another, usually with the Boilermakers and the Shipwrights pitted against each other; a tension that had lasted for a century since boilermakers were brought in to weld together the iron hulls that superseded the wooden vessels of the age of sail, constructed by shipwrights. Quality suffered, and – even more damagingly – costs and delivery times. By early 1957, when yards throughout Britain were halted by a strike in support of a 10 per cent pay claim, major shipowners like Stavros Niarchos were starting to place follow-up orders in the Netherlands, Germany or Japan, reckoning Britain's shipyards simply too unreliable.

Some traditional industries did modernise and consolidate. Wedgwood under the enlightened Josiah Wedgwood, its managing director for 38 years, thrived, introducing a profit-sharing scheme for 400 senior staff and workers; between 1949 and 1965 after-tax profits quadrupled, and it began buying up compatible competitors. That the pottery industry overall had some way to go in adopting new working methods was demonstrated on the television panel game *What's My Line?*, where the celebrities failed lamentably to recognise the technique of a saggar maker's bottom knocker. Saggars were used to hold and protect pottery during kiln-firing. Producing them to the correct specifications was a skilled job and the saggar maker also needed a bottom knocker to make the bottom of the saggar by placing clay in a metal hoop and literally knocking it into shape.

Through Pilkington – and Triplex, which it gradually acquired – Britain was a leader in the development of safety glass, and in the float glass process invented at St Helens in the 1950s by Alastair Pilkington and Keith Bickerstaff, had a technology for producing plate glass over a bath of molten tin which was produced under licence around the world.

The furniture industry performed strongly on the back of the government's wartime utility scheme which embraced most of its output – the more so from 1951 when it was allowed to advertise again, and as the advent of hire purchase boosted demand. Companies like Ercol and Parker Knoll – who opened a new factory at Chipping Norton in 1962 – brought in innovative designs that saw product quality rise. Gomme launched its G-Plan and Lebus, which had produced the Horsa glider for D-Day alongside utility furniture, performed strongly in the mass market from its Tottenham factory. In High Wycombe, where chair making had long been the dominant trade, there were moves to concentrate manufacture, but in 1960 there were still over 100 firms and much of their work outsourced to local villages.

Britain's white goods industry – gas and electric cookers, vacuum cleaners, fridges and washing machines and new, more adventurous appliances produced by Hoover, GEC's Hotpoint, Pressed Steel (Prestcold), Thorn, Colston, the Swedish-owned Electrolux and the like – flourished into the 1960s. This market boomed as hire purchase made its products available to the masses, but was thus vulnerable to the hire purchase restrictions ('credit squeezes') imposed by successive Chancellors as they tried to stop the economy overheating. Parts of the market remained monopolistic – it would be almost impossible to buy a gas cooker except from a state-owned showroom until the late 1980s – but others were highly entrepreneurial, notably the direct selling by the tycoon John Bloom of Rolls Razor's 'affordable' twin-tub washing machine. Bloom caught the nation's imagination, but Rolls Razor was built on sand and came to grief in 1964 after a postal strike prevented buyers sending in their coupons.

In the 1950s the pharmaceutical sector was almost a sideshow. Glaxo – founded as a dairy company in Bunnythorpe, New Zealand in 1904 – was still a minnow despite its revenue stream from the discovery and development of penicillin. Pharmaceuticals remained a tiny fraction of ICI's business despite its development of new anaesthetics and, later, betablockers – though it did in 1957 open the Alderley Park laboratories in Cheshire which are today the nerve centre of AstraZeneca. In 1959 Beecham's scientists discovered the penicillin nucleus, paving the way for the development of semi-synthetic penicillins; global demand for Penbritin (ampicillin), launched two years later, so far exceeded productive capacity that a new complex was developed at Worthing to produce the semi-synthetic base. Wellcome, another heavy investor in research, gained critical mass with the launch of drugs to combat disorders ranging from migraine to hookworm, and in the 1960s Septrin, used in the treatment of bacterial infections. It also did groundbreaking work on the polio vaccine, and in veterinary medicine. Yet Britain continued to punch below its weight. By 1963 its share of world pharmaceutical exports was just 14 per cent, the same as Germany's and Switzerland's; America had 25 per cent of the market. Moreover most of the drugs supplied to the NHS came from US- or Swiss-owned companies – one reason why persistent criticism from Labour of their pricing did not lead to nationalisation. May & Baker, based at Dagenham, had been owned by Rhone-Poulenc since the 1920s, while America's Pfizer built up a presence from the 1950s. Of the 20 leading suppliers to the NHS, only Glaxo, Beecham, Allen & Hanburys (who merged with Glaxo in 1958) and Wellcome were British-owned.

If the Farnborough Air Show of the 1950s perennially displayed the confidence of Britain's aircraft industry, the Motor Show at Earl's Court reflected the optimism of Britain's car makers, manifested in a host of new models – usually with a pretty girl on the bonnet. (Mandy Rice-Davies, the most decorative player in the Profumo Affair, first made an impact as a 16-year-old Miss Austin at the 1960 show). The end of petrol rationing in 1950 (it was briefly reintroduced after the Suez debacle of 1956) was followed by a surge in demand for new cars, and almost every vehicle on the road was British; in 1955 just 2.2 per cent of cars sold were imported. In 1950 Britain was the world's second largest car producer after the United States, and accounted for 52 per cent of the world's automotive exports: 75 per cent of the cars produced and 50 per cent of vans. In that year 523,000 cars and a further 263,000 commercial vehicles rolled off the production lines. With home demand still not strong and petrol rationed, British factories had been working flat out to produce cars for export; not just for the Empire but for the United States, whose own plants could not in the short term keep up with post-war demand. Indeed a post-war Labour government desperate for exports imposed a 75 per cent export quota that obliged domestic buyers to wait. But in the early 1950s, while Britain's competitors were investing, the focus was on maximising output from existing capacity. For the mass producers, there was an end – over time – of the production of car bodies and chassis by different companies in separate plants. And a growing concentration on scale led to many smaller marques, such as Armstrong Siddeley and Jowett, going to the wall.

There was the odd newcomer, though: in 1952 Colin Chapman set up Lotus Engineering to make sports and racing cars in an old stables behind a pub in Hornsey; his minimalist Lotus Seven, launched in 1957, is still in production (by Caterham) today. Its sister company Team Lotus won its first Formula 1 grand prix at Monaco in 1960 with Stirling Moss at the wheel, and in 1963 won the first of seven F1 constructors' championships. Most car-making capacity in 1952 was British-owned, but Ford (itself then with UK shareholders) and Vauxhall (General Motors) between them had 29 per cent of the home market – the former with the Anglia, Popular, Prefect, Consul and Zephyr and the latter with the Velox and Wyvern. Ford's Dagenham plant was the largest in Britain, its workforce peaking at 40,000 in 1953 – one of the powerhouses of British manufacturing. Located on a 500-acre riverside site, it imported iron ore and exported finished vehicles, boasting its own blast furnace (which awed me as a 12-year-old visitor as a close approximation to Hell) and power station. Yet Dagenham in the 1950s was just the largest of 27 Ford plants around the country and, astonishingly, was not a monolith but several autonomous factories: Kelsey Hayes made the wheels for Ford until taken over in 1951, and Briggs the bodies. Briggs Bodies was absorbed in 1953 on the death of its founder, bringing with it the Southampton plant where Ford vans are made to this day, and a factory at Doncaster, making bodies for other cars such as Jowett, which later gravitated to BMC. Briggs Bodies was best known to the public for its turbulent industrial relations during the five years between the takeover by Ford, and the shop stewards signing a 'standardisation' agreement on pay and conditions with the parent company which they had done all they could to resist.

To create a counterweight to Ford, Lord Nuffield in 1953 merged his Oxford-based Morris Motors with Austin (centred on Birmingham) to create the British Motor Corporation (BMC). The merged company soon followed Ford's example and bought out the bodymakers Fisher & Ludlow who supplied Austin (and some bodies for Standard) – though not for another decade Pressed Steel who made bodies for Morris. With such marques as Austin, Morris, MG,

Riley and Wolseley, BMC started life with 40 per cent of the home market. Most of the remainder came from Rootes (with the Hillman Husky and Minx) and Standard-Triumph (the Standard Vanguard), with still-independent Rover and Jaguar leading the niche producers.

It did not help that BMC was initially headed by Leonard Lord, a former Austin production man renowned for his bullying methods, foul language and lack of vision. By retaining all five of BMC's marques and allowing them to compete with each other, Lord kept production and marketing costs high and limited the scope for investment in new capacity and models. When Lord showed the Duke of Edinburgh BMC's model range in 1955, the Duke urged him to rethink, saying with characteristic bluntness: 'I am not sure these are up to the foreign competition.' It was also Lord who insisted that the Mini should retail for £500 so as to undercut the Ford Anglia – when each vehicle cost £535 to produce. And apart from the launch of the Mini, little improved under Lord's calmer successor and protégé George Harriman.

By 1960 – the year it received a fillip from the introduction of the MoT test which took thousands of 'old bangers' off the road – Britain's motor industry had almost tripled its production to 1,811,000 units a year; 1,353,000 of them cars. BMC, with revolutionary designs from Issigonis (the Mini) and Farina (the Austin A40), looked a match for the futuristic concepts emerging from the likes of Citroën, while Ford – whose parent company bought out its 46 per cent of British shareholders in 1961 – was about to launch the iconic Cortina. The year 1963 saw Vauxhall launch the Viva, and Rootes the rear-engined Hillman Imp, while at the sporty end of the market the E-type Jaguar (1961) was a show-stopper.

Britain's motor industry may have been growing, but its overseas rivals were growing faster: in 1956 German car production overtook that of Britain – largely through the global success of the Volkswagen Beetle, brought about by a British officer, Major Ivan Hurst, after Sir William Rootes had written it off as 'too ugly and too noisy' to be worth taking as reparations (French and American manufacturers rejected it too). A year later the first serious importing of cars to

Britain since the war began, with the Renault Dauphine, bought in bulk for the launch of minicabs in London; most of the British public were not yet psychologically ready for a German or a Japanese car.

The industry was unprepared for a challenge. It had run up waiting lists for most models – an insurance policy for complacent manufacturers against sudden falls in demand or interruptions to the supply chain. When my grandfather looked in 1957 to replace his pre-war Austin, a call to his BMC dealer brought the response that he would have to wait a couple of months; he rang Renault and a car was outside that afternoon. He bought the Renault – and so did thousands of other British motorists.

It took a while for the industry's increasing lack of competitiveness to register; home demand was supplemented by continuing near-guaranteed sales in much of the former Empire, the 'mother country's advantage reinforced by the import duties imposed throughout on non-Commonwealth goods. In *Dr No*, filmed in Jamaica in 1961 on the eve of independence, James Bond rents a Sunbeam Alpine convertible with most British makes of car visible in the background – plus several American imports and, ominously, a couple of Volkswagen 'Beetles'. But the British motor industry's unit costs were markedly higher than those of the recovering manufacturers overseas – and as Britain's colonies became independent, the door opened to them; today Jamaica imports large numbers of used cars from Japan. India went down a different road: the Hindustan Ambassador, essentially a 1956 Morris Oxford manufactured under licence from BMC, is still in production today after half a century as the subcontinent's iconic car.

When the 5 millionth Mini was produced in the 1990s, it was calculated that the most successful British car ever had generated a profit of barely £5 per vehicle. The Mini's early costs were increased by BMC's insistence on producing not only the Mini Traveller, a tiny shooting brake, and the iconic Mini Cooper, but also separately-badged Austin and Morris Minis and nostalgic variants like the Riley Elf and Wolseley Hornet. Likewise BMC's previous star seller, the Morris Minor/Traveller, produced by craftsman engineers with everything hand tooled, reputedly barely broke even despite 1.3 million being sold over 23 years. And these were the company's successful models. Moreover, the Austin and Morris wings of BMC continued to develop competing model ranges, militating further against the economies of scale the merger had been supposed to achieve.

In the decades after the war, Lucas was the largest and best known of the plethora of motor component companies, employing 92,000 people at its peak. By the 1950s Lucas was manufacturing lamps, batteries, fuel injection systems, brake systems, clutches, shock absorbers, magnetos and heavy duty equipment for commercial vehicles; a virtual monopoly supplier of electrical equipment. With its eye on new technologies, it now also started making rectifiers and transistors. A major competitor had been Smiths, but before the war the two companies had agreed to stay out of each other's markets and Smiths, diversifying from its once lucrative clock and watchmaking business, set up aviation and marine divisions in 1958. The long-standing engineering conglomerate GKN was also thriving: it was producing the chassis for the new Triumph Herald, and in 1962 launched the FV432 armoured personnel carrier which is still in service with the Army today. Its Sankey plant at Wellington was turning out millions of wheels a year, and in 1963 it took over the Sheffield crankshaft maker Ambrose Shardlow, despite a series of strikes blamed on its Communist shop stewards (workers there were known in adjoining factories as 'Shardlow's millionnaires').

Countries rebuilding their motor industries after the war had the advantage of being able to adopt new production methods from the outset. Attempts to introduce them in Britain led to wildcat strikes and – in the case of Standard-Triumph which pressed ahead regardless as it launched the Triumph Herald – bankruptcy in 1960 and a takeover by the bus and truck builders Leyland Motors. Germany, in particular, also benefited from the post-war reform of its trade union structure, ironically by the British, with workers organised on an industry rather than a craft basis and centralised pay bargaining. For the decade of the *wirtschaftswunder* and beyond, each manfacturing company could reach binding agreements with one trade union – IG Metall – in the expectation that they would stick at all levels.

British car and component makers, by contrast, had to deal with several unions with at times conflicting interests – plus scope for tensions over recruitment and recognition between the Transport & General Workers' Union (T&G), which dominated the industry in the Midlands, and the Amalgamated Engineering Union which was strong in certain plants. Wartime 'joint production committees' to boost output had given shop stewards a stake in running their plants, and once that positive role was removed they became a focus for non-co-operation and disruption. Across British industry generally, wartime machinery for co-operation was being dismantled – primarily because employers wanted freedom to manage – while in Germany, at Britain's instigation, such structures were being put in place.

Both in the major car plants and right down a lengthy supply chain to countless 'metal-bashing' workshops, Britain's motor industry was plagued increasingly from the 1950s by strikes, most called not by national union leaders or across a company, but by shop stewards in individual plants or workshops. The Coventry Tool Room Agreement of 1941, which set pay differentials for the next 30 years, created the scope for numerous disputes over maintaining them when skills were in short supply. Shop stewards were ruggedly independent, with local grievances and interests making national and company-wide agreements academic. Since the Taff Vale judgment of 1906, agreements between employers and trades unions had not been legally enforcible, and holding shop stewards to account through disciplinary action merely triggered more strikes.

Some strikes, as in the shipyards, were over demarcation – notably between the T&G and the National Union of Vehicle Builders – and over craftsmen's work allegedly given to the less skilled; toolmakers and draughtsmen were particularly sensitive. At least as common, though, were disputes over differentials, with workers striking to regain a wage advantage they believed they had previously enjoyed over a group below them in the pecking order. The wave of mergers in the industry exacerbated this problem, creating more and more pockets of workers convinced that others with the same employer were being paid more for doing the same job. Any strike anywhere in the industry, even by a relatively small number of workers, could cut off the flow of essential components and bring production to a halt, laying off thousands.

Although the 1959 Boulting Brothers comedy *I'm All Right Jack* was ostensibly set in a missile factory, its target was the motor industry. Trade unionists and bosses alike were depicted as incompetent and/or corrupt. The quality of British industrial management in postwar years was patchy, but the chinless, useless boss's nephew (Ian Carmichael) who was put on the shop floor after failing all his job interviews, was correctly observed in only one respect: many managers with a public school background started on the shop floor to make sure they understood the business. Yet the Communist shop steward Fred Kite, played by Peter Sellers, waxing lyrical about the 'ballet and cornfields' of the Soviet Union as one pretext after another was found to bring the workers out, was generally perceived as only a marginal exaggeration. (In most strikes at that time, however, bloodymindedness was a far more powerful driving force than Communism, though the Party tried hard to maximise and boast of its influence in the unions; many Communist union officials spent long hours trying to persuade their striking members to go back).

The most damaging strikes in the 1950s were on the railways, on London's buses and in Fleet Street, where powerful unions had a stranglehold. Also in the docks, where an archaic system of casual labour and rivalries between dockers and stevedores – from the Portugese *estevador*: the man who stuffs – led to near-anarchy. The total number of days lost through strikes was, at the peak of industrial unrest in 1957, barely one-third of what it would be in the early 1970s and 1980s – and consistently less than in Italy. Yet by 1959 unofficial strikes in the motor industry were prompting demands from Conservative MPs for legislation setting out the rights and responsibilities of employers and labour. The Labour Party felt sufficiently vulnerable over the issue for Harold Wilson to dissociate himself from unofficial strikes in his first broadcast after being elected party leader in 1963. Wilson, during the following year's election campaign, claimed that an unofficial strike at the universal joint makers Hardy

Spicer, which was causing widespread layoffs, had been generated on behalf of the Conservatives to damage Labour's chances – a charge that brought a writ for libel from the company.

The first week of February 1960 provides a snapshot of the way small, unrelated disputes could wreak havoc in the motor industry, with three out of six major car manufacturers – all in the Midlands – seriously affected. A strike by 55 electricians at BMC's transmissions factory at Washwood Heath, Birmingham, halted all production at Longbridge, with 32,000 workers laid off there and at other sites, and only one car – the Wolseley 6/99 – still in production. The dispute, belatedly made official by the Electrical Trades Union, arose from the rejection by electricians' mates of a bonus scheme accepted by all other workers several months before. The damage caused by the strike led the Confederation of Shipbuilding and Engineering Unions to call a national conference to discuss its widening effects and the loss of earnings suffered by workers who were not involved. All car production by Standard-Triumph was at a standstill, with 11,000 workers idle, because of an unexplained walkout by 600 members of the National Union of Vehicle Builders at the company's Birmingham body-making subsidiary of Mulliners. Days after that dispute was settled, 300 workers at Mulliners walked out again over the use of components from Motor Panels Ltd of Coventry which had been 'blacked' because 22 NUVB members there were on strike over union recognition. Meanwhile Land Rover production at Solihull had been halted by a strike by 39 welders at Rover's Coventry factory over the recruitment of a replacement welder to whom they objected. And these were only the disputes that made the newspapers.

The one car maker to crack down on shop floor militancy was Ford. In 1957 it sacked the Dagenham shop steward Johnny McLoughlin – known as 'the bellringer' because of his technique for calling the workers out – who had led the five-year fight to exempt former Briggs Bodies workers from signing up to Ford's national pay and conditions. The ensuing dispute led to a Court of Inquiry under Lord Cameron which heard that there had been 234 stoppages at Ford over this period – frequently without warning – and that the shop stewards had operated as a 'union within a union'. McLoughlin stayed sacked and resistance crumbled. Five years later, in what union activists termed Ford's 'October Revolution', the company summarily dismissed 17 shop stewards, including two convenors, in a bid to end disruption at Dagenham.

A House of Lords judgment in 1963 started the long process that would lead to the legislative clipping of the wildcats' wings – two decades later and after incalculable damage to Britain's manufacturing capability and to jobs. The case was *Rookes* v. *Barnard*, concerning a non-union member sacked because the relevant union at BOAC (the Association of Shipbuilding and Engineering Draughtsmen) was threatening to strike to maintain a closed shop. The Lords upheld his claim for damages against the union branch secretary, leaving in doubt the unions' legal immunities which had been unchallenged since 1906. Both main parties went into the 1964 election committed to reviewing trade union law, in Labour's case by legislating to reverse the judgment.

Britain's motorcycle industry led the world in the 1950s, despite Victorian production methods. BSA, Triumph, Norton, AJS Motorcycles and others were formidable brands that thrived, basking in the glamour of Speedway – arguably the most popular national spectator sport after football – heavily sponsored motorcycle racing and the Manx TT. Production peaked in 1959 at 127,000 machines, with exports strong. British bikes did especially well in the United States, Harley Davidson was unchallengeable, but lighter-weight machines from BSA and Triumph put America's other main producer, Indian, out of business in 1953.

The industry saw petrolheads as its market; Donald Heather, a director of Norton, said: 'Most motorcyclists love to spend their Sunday mornings taking off the cylinder head and re-seating the valves.' But to many, at home and abroad, the motorcycle was a means of transport, and had to prove itself against others. At home, the challenge came from Italy in the shape of the motor scooter. The Piaggio Vespa, first produced in 1946, and the Lambretta, launched a year later, became in the late 1950s, along with various mainly German makes of 'bubble car', the coolest way to get around town for people who would never have dreamed of donning leathers and revving up a motorbike.

Far more damaging to the industry's long-term prospects, though, was the invasion of its export markets by lightweight two-stroke Japanese machines from Honda in 1955, Suzuki soon after, and mopeds from Germany's NSU. Soichiro Honda had grasped the potential of the basic motorised bicycle in 1948 when he strapped a secondhand US Army generator to a cycle frame; a world-beating industry was born with Yamaha and Kawasaki also entering the field. British manufacturers ignored, or did not notice, the thirst in the developing world for lighter, cheaper, less high-powered and less complex means of two-wheel transport than the heavy, throbbing machines they produced. They should have. BSA's most successful post-war model was the 125cc Bantam, but little was done to develop less powerful models. Within a decade, these simple and cheap machines were the staple form of personal transport in the teeming cities of developing Asia and beyond, meeting a need to which high-performance British motorcycles had little relevance. Before long, the Japanese would also conquer America with high-performance machines.

For the moment, however, Britain's motorcycle makers seemed to be doing well. One figure in the industry was visibly doing very well indeed: Sir Bernard Docker. His father Sir Dudley had joined the board of BSA – which also produced rifles, machine tools and bicycles – half a century before and helped turn it into a world-beater. By 1940 Bernard Docker was the company's chairman, also going on to chair its Daimler subsidiary. In 1949 he married Norah Turner, a former showgirl with extravagant tastes who had buried two well-heeled husbands (the heads of Henekeys wine merchants and Fortnum & Mason). In the still-austere Britain of the early 1950s, Sir Bernard and Lady Docker were a godsend to the tabloids as they embarked on an extravagant lifestyle, whose tastelessness even today's celebrities would struggle to match. If Fred Kite was the caricature of a militant shop steward, Sir Bernard came to epitomise – with grotesque unfairness to his hard-working and enterprising counterparts across British industry – the industrialist who was happier at play. He devoted his time increasingly to producing show cars, such as the 'Golden Daimler'. Meanwhile his wife kept in the headlines by dancing the hornpipe aboard their yacht for a group of miners – provocatively at a time when Britons could take just £25 abroad with them – and flaunting her wealth in Monaco, where she was ostracised for dancing on the national flag. Lady Docker was unrepentant at showing off her mink coats and jewellery, and changing the decor in her customised Daimler from gold plate to lizard skin to crocodile leather to zebra, saying: 'We bring glamour and happiness into drab lives. The working class loves everything I do.'

BSA's shareholders – then for the most part private individuals, not pension funds – did not. By 1956 profits were slipping, but the Dockers continued to finance their lifestyle from the company and Lady Docker's $20,000 gold dress (set against expenses) to match the Daimler being launched in Paris was the last straw. After an acrimonious dispute conducted in the media, BSA's board removed Sir Bernard and its decision was upheld by the shareholders. The Dockers retired to tax exile in Jersey. The next year, BSA sold its bicycle business to Raleigh, but confidence had returned by the time it celebrated its centenary in in 1961. One acquisition BSA made under Sir Bernard, in 1954, did wash its face commercially: Carbodies, the Coventry coach builders who since 1948 had been producing the iconic FX4 London black cab under contract from Austin.

Tube Investments was a rising star, particularly after acquiring British Aluminium in 1959 following a bruising takeover battle. The next year it merged its British Cycle Corporation subsidiary with Nottingham-based Raleigh to create the world's largest bicycle manufacturer. With 75 per cent of the home market, its range stretched from semi-custom Carlton bikes made at Worksop through the then household names of Hercules, Rudge and BSA to the cheapest TI-Raleigh bikes. TI also owned Brooks, who made saddles, Sturmey-Archer, pioneer of the 3-speed gear, and the tube maker Reynolds.

Over the dozen years to 1964, companies like English Electric which had become conglomerates – in part due to functions required of them during the war – disposed of what they considered fringe activities and concentrated on the core business. The textile industry, facing deadly competition from the developing world, regrouped, with Courtaulds becoming the dominant player. It had enjoyed a boom up to the end of 1952, but the end of the Korean War and America's drive for freer world trade also brought an end to the bar on Japanese textile exports to Britain and its colonies, and to tariffs that had benefited Lancashire's cotton mills in particular. Commonwealth preference still offered benefits to India, Pakistan and Hong Kong, and during the 1950s they began exporting heavily to Britain. Meanwhile the Continental market – both before and after the creation of the Common Market in 1958 – was essentially barred to them by tariffs, imports taking 35 per cent of the British market against 5 per cent on the Continent. In 1957 Germany's spun cotton output overtook Britain's, and by the end of the decade Britain was a net importer of cotton cloth for the first time since the Industrial Revolution – just as the rag trade was switching to man-made fibres. Macmillan's government adopted a double approach to the slump in demand: it pressed Commonwealth producers to curb their exports to Britain, and brought in incentives to scrap surplus capacity. Most mills had failed to modernise, but the pressures were such that decline was inevitable.

Some manufacturers managed to buck the trend with niche products. One of the most publicised was Gannex, the waterproof material produced at Elland, Yorkshire, from 1951 by Joseph (later Lord) Kagan, an intimate of Harold Wilson who wore one of Kagan's raincoats on a world tour on 1956. Gannex raincoats were worn by the Queen, her corgis and Prince Philip, by President Johnson, Chairman

Mao and Nikita Khruschev; demand soared, Gannex becoming Elland's largest employer and Kagan a multi-millionaire.

Another driver of reorganisation in the textile industry was the entrepreneur Joe Hyman, whose Viyella International became a household name. Starting in 1957 with a knitwear company, Hyman engineered a takeover of the company producing Viyella, a wool/cotton mix patented in 1894; a move into Lancashire with backing from ICI to develop polyester/cotton blends paid off, Viyella's Dorma sheets becoming a big seller.

In man-made fibres ICI had most of the market with polyesters, but Courtaulds had developed new acrylic fibres – Courtelle and Crimplene – and in 1957 took over British Celanese, with its huge plant outside Derby, to increase its product range. In 1960 ICI's new chairman Paul Chambers suggested to Courtaulds that the companies merge; nothing came of the approach, but tensions grew and at the end of 1961 ICI launched a hostile takeover bid. Frank Kearton, an up-and-coming director of Courtaulds, rallied the opposition and ICI was defeated, and left with an embarrassing 38 per cent stake in Courtaulds. When the Commons debated the issue, the Conservative MP Brian Harrison warned that ICI would be a 'dead hand' on innovation; Courtaulds had produced four or five new synthetic fibres since the war, but ICI had failed to come up with any.

Courtaulds now embarked on a plan to rescue the Lancashire cotton industry and make it more competitive through heavy investment, with ICI agreeing to take a minority stake. A merger with Lancashire's largest cotton spinners broke down, but in 1963 English Sewing Cotton and Tootal merged, and the next year saw Courtaulds take over Lancashire Cotton, Fine Spinners and Doublers.

Britain's footwear industry, during these years, combined the continuance of traditional production with innovations that gave it a future. Its base was Northamptonshire, where in 1956 there were still 12 tanneries employing 1,518 people to serve the local boot and shoe manufacturers. One – Satra of Kettering – produced the innovative water- and frostproof boot worn by John Hunt's expedition as they conquered Everest on the eve of the Coronation. Another, R Griggs, secured the rights to manufacture and improve the air-cushioned mountaineering boot developed by the Wehrmacht medic Klaus Märtens; launched in 1960, the Doc Marten became a classic and is still in production today. Away from Northamptonshire, Bata's factory at East Tilbury (designed by the father of the BBC's John Tusa) and the model village surrounding it survived the imposition of communism on its Czech parent to produce a popular brand for British and export markets. Clarks of Street, Somerset (another Quaker family firm) dominated the children's shoe market and predated the Doc Marten with their Desert Boot, launched in 1950. Etough's of Burton upon Trent introduced the first washable children's sandal in 1957, and in 1960 the Bolton running shoe makers J. W. Foster changed their name to Reebok.

One British industry that boomed from the early 1950s was confectionery. Petrol rationing may have ended in 1949 but, while chocolate came off ration the same year, it was February 1953 before the entire range of sweets could be freely purchased, paving the way for a surge in demand. Pre-war favourites quickly filled the shelves along with new varieties of chocolates and candies. Before long Cadbury's Mild Dessert and Almond Dessert chocolate, and Terry's chocolate apple disappeared from the market to be replaced by Caramac in 1959, Cadbury's chocolate buttons the following year and Toffee Crisp in 1963. The advent of commercial television in 1954 gave a powerful boost to Murray Mints ('the too good to hurry mints'), Maltesers ('the chocolates with the less fattening centres') and Treets ('melt in your mouth, not in your hand'). Sales soared, but while well-established firms expanded – particularly Cadbury who opened several new plants – an industry that was largely still family owned saw few structural changes.

The brewing industry had come out of the war looking little different from half a century previously, with large-scale but ageing breweries in London and Burton and hundreds of smaller ones throughout the country, each serving their own chains of pubs. Many of these excluded women, few served food, wine was widely regarded as a drink for homosexuals and the normal choice of beverage was confined to mild, bitter, pale ale, stout or cider. Lager was rarely to be seen, though Ind Coope shrewdly saw its potential and in 1949 took over the lager brewery at Wrexham which had struggled to interest the drinking public since the 1880s.

Given the fragmented nature of the industry and the inelastic public demand for beer, it was inevitable that breweries would merge. The 1950s saw Courage merge in turn with Barclay, Perkins and Simonds of Reading, creating – with further acquisitions – a chain of 5,000 pubs. The year 1958 saw the creation of Watney Mann from a merger of Watney, Combe Reid and Mann, Crossman & Paulin. Scottish Brewers merged with Newcastle Breweries in 1960 to create Scottish & Newcastle. Bass remained the market leader with its 1961 takeover of Mitchells & Butlers. The same year, Ansell's, Ind Coope and Tetleys joined forces as Allied Breweries. Whitbread during the 1960s took over no fewer than 23 other brewing companies. Yet brewing itself remained fragmented.

Despite the apparent, and in many respects, real success of British industry during the 1950s, there was an impression abroad among the general public that it was not trying hard enough. Prince Philip summed it up when he said it was time for Britain as an exporting nation, to 'take its finger out'. His comment did not play well with the Federation of British Industry, and generated an Osbert Lancaster cartoon in the *Daily Express* of a dowager asking: 'What exactly is it that Prince Philip would like us to take our finger out of?' But there was, more seriously, a growing frustration, especially in government, at the reluctance of industry to invest in new plant and processes.

Industry's willingness to make do with what it had would remain an issue for quite some time. In 1961 half of Britain's metal-using industries and 43 per cent of firms in paper and printing were still using machinery dating from before 1948, and in the 1950s a giant rolling mill engine built in 1905 to make armour plate for Dreadnought battleships was installed at Sheffield's River Don Works to shape nuclear reactor shields. As late as the 1970s some Sheffield engineering firms would still be using machine tools taken from the Germans as reparations after the Great War. By then, of course, the Germans had re-equipped twice over. The lack of ambition shown by British manufacturers in re-equipping also handicapped the machine tool industry; Germany's had a platform for developing more innovative products, and Britain's share of global machine tool exports fell steadily in the decade from 1955. Nevertheless machinery of all kinds remained the staple of Britain's exports: £7,215 million worth in 1960/61 compared with £6,086 million worth of chemicals, £5,062 million worth of vehicles, £3,837 million of electrical machinery and instruments, and £1,551 million of aircraft. Yet the government's R&D budget remained heavily skewed towards the aircraft sector.

Despite its commitment to private enterprise, the 'Butskellist' one-nation Conservative government did exert considerable pressure – and offer incentives – for heavy industry to invest. This it did in the context of regional policy, steering new plants to areas of high unemployment rather than allowing companies – by issuing the Industrial Development Certificates required – the more profitable option of building on success where they stood; they may have realised that this would be the only way some manufacturers would install new plants. Scotland and Merseyside were the main beneficiaries, though the North East and South Wales also gained valuable jobs and capacity. The just-denationalised Colvilles opened an integrated steelworks at Ravenscraig, near Motherwell, in 1954; Vauxhall and Standard Triumph new plants on Merseyside at Ellesmere Port and Speke respectively, in 1960; BMC a commercial vehicle plant at Bathgate, West Lothian in 1961; the Spencer steelworks at Llanwern, South Wales, started production in 1962; Rootes at Linwood, Renfrewshire in 1963 to launch the Hillman Imp, with Ford at Halewood on Merseyside that same year – shop stewards at Dagenham bringing workers there out on strike to make sure their Halewood counterparts were paid the same; Wiggins Teape a paper mill at Fort William – which struggled even to open despite a special Act of Parliament authorising it and cash from successive governments – and others besides. It was a brave strategy for locating skilled jobs where local economies needed them, but government initiative was followed by poor performance by plants at the end of elongated lines of supply and often lacking experienced or motivated workforces. One manufacturer who managed to evade the policy was Jaguar, who in 1960 acquired Daimler for its Coventry plant.

If many of these plants in the regions are now household names, it is largely because of the fuss surrounding the closure of most of them; only Ellesmere Port, Llanwern and Halewood (under new ownership) are still in business. Any long-term political kudos the Conservatives may have hoped for was eradicated by the electorate's eventual anger at the closure of iconic plants such as Ravenscraig. And industrialists increasingly came to argue that there would have been greater, and longer-term, economic gains for the nation had the companies been allowed to expand in their home areas, and that the direction of industry could not overturn the laws of economics. Moreover when a decision was needed in 1957 on where to site a fourth strip mill, Macmillan decided on two smaller ones, beside the existing plant at Ravenscraig and on a greenfield site at Llanwern. The economics of both were thus rendered shaky from the outset.

The nationalised Iron & Steel Corporation had been operating for less than a year when, at the end of 1951, a Conservative government committed to denationalisation was elected. It was duly returned to the private sector between 1953 and 1957 – except for Richard Thomas & Baldwins which was encumbered by heavy investment on new plant – but under the supervision of an Iron and Steel Board which controlled prices and attempted to co-ordinate investment. Steel industry managers reported back from visits to America in 1952/53 that Britain's steelworks were overmanned by a factor of two or three; ironically the practice was worst at the Port Talbot strip mill, opened only in 1951. They found productivity was further impaired by the smallness of many British plants, and by the readiness of American steel craftsmen to multi-task; in Britain there were 14 separate craft unions, all religiously guarding their mysteries. Overmanning in the steel industry may have been above the average, but too many workers for the job in hand was a widespread feature of British industry at the time. Bowater in the early 1960s discovered that it was using 50 per cent more labour at its Mersey paper mill than to do an identical job at Corner Brook, Newfoundland.

It is easy to criticise managements for not having taken a tougher line over working practices and productivity, but those who tried frequently ended with a bloody nose. Attempts to speed up work or reduce manning to rational levels were met by a flat 'No' or an immediate walkout. When the *Daily Mail circa* 1963 tried to install a machine that would count and bale newspapers automatically and deposit them in a van, the print union Natsopa (the National Society of Operative Printers and Assistants) demanded that every single man displaced should be found a job within the process. This could only be done by employing one man to count the bundles, another to cut the string of every twelfth bundle, a third to pick the papers up from the floor and a fourth to put them back on the conveyor belt to be bundled up...

The pressure to increase productivity and free-up under-utilised workers for jobs that urgently needed doing should have been all the greater because UK unemployment between 1950 and 1966 was running at a historic low; in 1954 it dipped below 2 per cent to under 300,000, which effectively meant that everyone wanting a job had one. Serious labour shortages began to develop, particularly in public transport, the NHS and the textile industry, but in other sectors too, putting pressure on wages and leading ministers to start worrying about inflation for the first time since the 1920s. France and Germany had a large surplus of agricultural labour that their industries could absorb, but this was not an option available to a Britain where most of the drift from the land had happened in the previous century. The classic response would have been to increase productivity through investment and more efficient use of labour, but the reluctance of some industrialists to invest and of the unions – especially at plant level – to co-operate prompted employers to look for a less painful solution.

They found one in the importation of cheap labour from the Commonwealth. While the first 492 immigrants from Jamaica on the *Empire Windrush* in 1948 had come to Britain under their own steam to better themselves, it was not long before employers struggling to fill their less attractive vacancies began to encourage the process. From the mid-1950s London Transport and the NHS – encouraged ironically from 1960 by Enoch Powell as Health Minister – were actively recruiting bus conductors, cleaners and ancillary staff in English-speaking Commonwealth countries; immigration surged as the word got round. The textile industry – cotton in Lancashire, woollen in Yorkshire, knitwear mainly in the East Midlands – found it ever harder to recruit millhands as it struggled to compete; its total workforce of 858,100 in 1954 was only 10 per cent down on the level in the 1920s, though more were employed in hosiery and knitwear at the expense of wool and worsted. Textile employers identified an alternative and cheaper source of (male) labour in the more backward areas of Pakistan – a country which by the end of the century would become the world's second largest exporter of clothing. Most of the men who came to work in Britain stayed despite poor housing, racial discrimination and frequent hostility from white workers who saw them as a threat – and before long they were sending for their wives and children. Immigration in numerical terms was far smaller than it was to become – the Home Office put the total net intake of Commonwealth citizens between 1955 and 1962 at 472,000 (or 59,000 a year) – but its social and economic impact in London, Birmingham, Bradford and other cities was considerable and they struggled to cope, not least as new arrivals from the Caribbean and the subcontinent tended – partly on economic grounds, partly because of racist landlords – to gravitate to run-down housing that had been earmarked for demolition so that new council flats could be built. The Commonwealth Immigrants Act of 1962, fought every inch of the way by liberals, did little to slow it, curbs on 'primary' immigration being offset by a growing number of dependants as men sent for their families.

While most immigrant labour headed for the public sector, there was both a direct and a knock-on effect for manufacturing. In particular sectors, migrant labour took on jobs indigenous workers were no longer eager to fill: not just in textiles but, for example, in the hottest and grubbiest parts of steelworks where Somalis carved out an early presence as labourers. London Brick only maintained production at its works round Peterborough in the 1950s by importing 3,000 workers from southern Italy; initially housed in old prisoner-of-war camps, they were joined later by their wives and became a strong local community.

Immigration trends were already well established when pressure on the workforce was eased by more women taking jobs instead of staying at home. This reduced the pressure on employers to grasp the nettles of overmanning and archaic working practices among white males who either had a craft to protect or were being paid to have a job rather than to do it. Some of the craft unions which had defended those practices most intransigently hardened their attitudes further as black workers began to appear in unskilled jobs in the same plants and wonder why the ladder to becoming a craftsman was closed to them.

While British industry remained largely complacent, giants were stirring across the water. Post-war France had gone down the route of economic planning, from which emerged 'concertation' between industry and the State under which the interests of both are treated as identical. Helped by a system of higher education that produced an élite who would move effortlessly between the public and private sectors as the distinction between them blurred, 'concertation' would, over the decades, prove highly successful both in terms of advancing the interests of flagship French firms as if they were arms of the State, and in consequence those of France itself. In the short term, post-war recovery was the aim, but by the late 1950s France was emerging as a technological challenger.

West Germany and Japan had emerged from the war with large parts of their productive capacities laid waste, but it did not take long for the organising genius of both countries to start planning a recovery that would pose a long-term threat, not just to Britain's traditional markets around the world, but to the home market and the UK manufacturing base.

Neither defeated Axis power looked a serious threat by 1952, but Germany appeared the more likely to compete, despite the dismantling of its heavy industries by the Allies – which reduced its steel production capacity alone by 6.7 million tons – and France's occupation (until 1957) of the coal and steel region of the Saar. Germany's manufacturing capacity (not to mention its economy) had also been disrupted by partition, which left more than a quarter of its industry in Communist hands and isolated Berlin. Up to the war, Germany had not only been Britain's principal industrial competitor in Europe but for over half a century had been pulling ahead in terms of competitiveness. To the chagrin of Britain's captains of industry, the recovery in German manufacturing was abetted not only by British-inspired reforms to its trade unions and the adoption from 1952 of a degree of industrial democracy, but by sizeable injections of American cash through the Marshall Plan.

In the short term, British industry benefited from sophisticated German equipment taken as reparations, but over time the transfer was counterproductive: forced to re-equip, West German firms installed newer and even more productive machinery, giving a flying post-war start to the country's machine tool industry. A further stimulus was the high regard in which the German educational system held manufacturing – in marked contrast to its British counterpart – as reflected in the training, in the immediate post-war years and since, of a highly skilled and respected corps of industrial managers. As a briefly demilitarised nation, West Germany also benefited from the Korean War which forced Britain, among others, to divert resources from civilian manufacturing into armaments – and in Britain's case reduced home demand through a round of fiscal belt-tightening which not only hastened the defeat of the Labour government at the end of 1951, but proved after the event to have been largely unnecessary. Germany's workforce was also readier than Britain's to work for low wages until productivity had risen, keeping down unit costs and thus gaining a competitive advantage. Subsequent German success was underpinned by the revival of confidence stemming from the introduction in 1948 of the Deutschmark, the fulcrum of a package of reforms which the future federal chancellor Ludwig Erhard had started devising – illegally – under the Nazis.

West Germany's 'economic miracle' took off in 1950, with a 25 per cent increase in industrial production; the following year it grew a further 18.1 per cent. Over the decade, production increased two and a half times, to a far higher level than the output of the whole of pre-war Germany (including not just the East, but the Saar and sizeable areas incorporated into Poland and even the Soviet Union). GDP rose by two-thirds, manufacturing employment by a half (those two statistics bespeaking a steady increase in productivity) and unemployment plunged from 10.3 per cent to 1.2 per cent. Underpinning the 'miracle' further was the establishment in 1957 of a strong central Bundesbank; preventing a return to hyperinflation became its enduring priority. Growth slowed a little after 1961, when the construction of the Berlin Wall cut off the supply of labour from the East (Turkey filling the vacuum) and the Bundesbank tightened the money supply to prevent the economy overheating. But by then West Germany was a formidable competitor.

The fightback was typefied by Germany's steel giants, Krupp and Thyssen. Alfried Krupp's steel and arms-making empire had been dismantled by the Allies, the Russians making off with the formula for tungsten steel. Krupp himself was sentenced to 12 years for using slave labour, and ordered to forfeit all his possessions. Then, in 1951, the Americans granted him an amnesty provided he renounced arms manufacturing, just as limits on steel production were removed. Krupp cut out unprofitable businesses and established a relationship with Chancellor Konrad Adenauer which bore fruit in approvals to build jet fighters in Bremen and a nuclear reactor at Jülich. He persuaded foreign leaders to welcome German equipment and engineering expertise, targeting in particular former British colonies and Iron Curtain countries. Krupp built rolling mills in Mexico, paper mills in Egypt, refineries in Greece, a vegetable oil processing plant in the Sudan and a steel plant in Brazil. Alfried Krupp had undertaken to sell off his mining and steel making interests by then, but no other German industrialist would bid for them. He then got round the Allies' policy of decartelisation by using a Swedish shell company to buy his strongest competitor, leaving the Common Market – which Sweden did not belong to – powerless to intervene. By 1959 Krupp was Europe's fourth largest company, with 125,000 employees, and Alfried Krupp the richest man in Europe.

Thyssen made an equally dramatic recovery. The Allies had ordered the company's liquidation because of its role in the Nazi war economy, and it was 1963 before a new August Thyssen-Hütte AG was formed in Duisburg, gradually absorbing former Thyssen steel mills. Further shrewd acquisitions soon made the company Europe's largest crude steel producer, and the fifth largest in the world.

Britain's iron and steel industry, by contrast, was hamstrung from 1951 by the lengthy process of denationalisation, without any rationalisation having been made of the 80 companies and their plants that had been taken over, at a time when Germany's steelmakers were innovating and achieving economies of scale. In the decade leading up to 1960, Britain's steel production did rise from 16.6 million to 24.7 million tons, but this compared with 12.1 million to 34.1 million for Germany (and 10.6 million to 17.3 million for France). Over the same period Britain's share of world steel exports fell from 15.1 per cent to 7.9 per cent, while Germany's rose from 11 per cent to 20 per cent. In 1950 France, the US and Britain had been the leading exporters of steel; ten years later Germany, France and Britain had the highest exports, but with Japan coming up fast on the rails. Moreover, in Britain the industry's return on capital declined from 1960 as post-war reconstruction came to an end and imports began to make an impact, and management responded by belatedly trying to raise productivity.

West Germany's heavy electrical industry also made a strong recovery. AEG's headquarters in Berlin had been flattened, so its revival after losing important plants in the East was orchestrated from Frankfurt. Kassel was chosen as a centre of excellence, and by the early 1960s 5,000 workers there were producing high voltage switchgear, refrigerators and ticket printers. As demand and production rose, AEG's workforce increased from 55,400 in 1957 to 127,000 in 1962, the year AEG's Telefunken subsidiary devised the PAL system of colour television.

Siemens – which like Bosch survived a US-inspired move to break it up – paid a heavy price for its role in 'Nazifying' the economy; almost 100,000 concentration camp inmates had worked at a Siemens factory inside Auschwitz. But it too regrouped, and in the 1950s, from a new base in Bavaria, Siemens began to manufacture computers, washing machines and – later – semiconductors and heart pacemakers.

West Germany's chemical industry, backed by its government as a strategic sector, made an equally strong recovery after the notorious IG Farben was split into three. Bayer, Hoechst and BASF all emerged in the 1950s as forces able to hold their ground in competition with Du Pont and ICI, which had opened its giant Wilton plant on Teesside in 1952.

Its automotive industry performed patchily, the success of the VW 'Beetle' being offset by the near-collapse of BMW. The 'Beetle', with its rear engine and rear-wheel drive, may have been spurned by the Allies' motor industries, but Major Hurst kept the company going after its chairman was sent to prison. The functional car with its low price tag went on to become the totem of German penetration of markets around the world, with 21 million sold before production finally ceased at Puebla, Mexico in 2003. The millionth 'Beetle' rolled off the Wolfsburg production line in 1955, and only in 1961 – by which time Volkswagens were becoming popular in Britain and its traditional overseas markets – did VW broaden its model range. VW also spawned Porsche – the first model, the 356, being built by the VW chairman Ferdinand Porsche's son Perry because he could not find a car he liked. The 356 went into production in 1952, evolving steadily until the 911 was launched in 1964 to replace it.

General Motors had thought twice about taking back control of Opel after the war, but in 1948 took the inspired decision to put in charge Ed Zdunek, an experienced and highly popular motor industry executive; over the next 13 years he positioned Opel to take advantage of West Germany's economic boom. Lacking the tools to relaunch its mass-market Kadett until 1962, Opel fitted naturally into the mid-market between Mercedes and VW, and in 1964 produced 167,650 cars from a completely rebuilt plant.

At the top of the range, Daimler-Benz (Mercedes) reasserted its primacy with the graceful 'Adenauer Mercedes' – the 300 – of 1951. Fewer than 9,000 were sold, but subsequent models were a success not just at home but in export markets. By contrast, Auto Union struggled to rebuild, being taken over by Daimler-Benz in 1959 then discarded; the first Audi did not appear until 1965. And in 1959 BMW's automotive division came within a whisker of going into liquidation; it was only saved by the Quandt family taking a controlling interest, and by a decision to produce the Italian Isetta bubble car under licence.

Japan owed its post-war recovery to careful government planning, but the Korean War was the turning point. Prior to then America, through the military administration headed by General Douglas Macarthur, had stimulated the economy out of a belief that the inflation, unemployment and shortages facing the defeated country would fuel the re-emergence of militarism (or even communism). After war broke out in Korea, America handed back full sovereignty to the government of Japan. Despite British objections they insisted on Japan's admission to the world trade organisation GATT (the General Agreement on Tarifs and Trade) and paid the country handsomely for 'special procurement' – 27 per cent of its total income from exports, in such key areas as vehicles and machinery. Surviving the recession caused when these payments ceased, Japan then began two decades of astounding economic recovery.

The strategy was simple, and ruthless: stimulate private sector growth, develop a strong home market – not least through protectionism – then use this as a launching pad for aggressive growth in exports. At its heart was the Ministry of International Trade and Industry (MITI), founded in 1949. MITI began by co-ordinating industry's efforts to overcome the effects of US-inspired deflation, developing such close co-operation that before long the whole of industry was attuned to respond to its requirements, entwining national production goals with industrialists' private interests. MITI targeted imports of foreign technology that could be more effectively harnessed by Japanese industry, taking powers in 1950 to negotiate import prices and conditions for promising industries as productivity rose through new equipment, good management and standardisation. In 1951 MITI set up the Japan Development Bank, which directed 83 per cent of its support into strategic industries – shipbuilding, electric power, coal and steel production – and doubled the size of the construction sector; a year later it gained the ability to regulate all imports.

From 1954 Hayato Ikeda – first as Minister for MITI and from 1960 as prime minister – drove a programme of heavy industrialisation. His aim was annual GDP growth of 7.2 per cent, but by his departure in 1964 it was 13.9 per cent. Manufacturers were encouraged to borrow beyond their capacity to repay, giving the Bank of Japan the whip hand over local lenders. Import controls were introduced, and investment in plant based on foreign exchange allocations to encourage export and prevent 'dumping' – except by Japanese exporters. Restrictions on monopolies were relaxed, leading to the emergence of the keiretsu: new conglomerates, mirroring those that had driven Japan's war economy, which could both complete globally and reinforce protectionism. Critical to the success of the keiretsu was a willingness to accept low profits in the short term at the expense of dividends to shareholders.

Barriers to imports even started to come down, until Ikeda met fierce opposition from overborrowed industrialists and a nationalist public who feared takeovers by foreign firms. He was only allowed to liberalise a little, after devising regulations to give Japanese products and firms an inbuilt advantage. Ikeda also mollified his critics with an 'income-doubling plan': interest rates and taxes were cut to stimulate demand, while the government invested heavily in highways, the Shinkansen 'bullet train' (launched in 1964), airports, harbours, dams and the country's previously neglected communications sector.

MITI's strategy for the Japanese automotive industry was typical: import foreign technology, manufacture under licence, improve, then export. In 1952 Nissan signed an agreement with Austin to assemble and market 2,000 A40s, and three years later it launched its own A50, made – as the British company had agreed – with local parts. After producing 20,855 Austins up to 1959, Nissan began producing cars that were entirely its own – leveraging the Austin patents to develop a more advanced engine that would power the Datsun, with which Nissan would begin its penetration of the British market. Toyota, by contrast, stayed outside the MITI strategy. It developed its home-grown Toyopet range from 1947, launching it on the American market ten years later.

The first Japanese product to conquer the world was the transistor radio. The first transistor was demonstrated in America by Bell Laboratories in 1947, and Texas Instruments launched the first production transistor radio in 1954. Raytheon followed the next year, but American manufacturers were soon undercut price-wise by Sony, whose founder Masura Ibuka had in 1952 persuaded MITI to spend $25,000 on a licence from AT&T to develop transistors. Sony had a radio in production by 1954, and the next year its TR-55 was launched in the United States. Other Japanese companies followed suit and their transistor radio production and exports around the world grew exponentially: by 1959, Japan was exporting 6 million radios a year to the United States – and proportionally as many to Britain.

Japan by the mid-1960s had re-established itself as a major economic power, and was challenging Britain in the markets for some consumer goods – and in the case of transistor radios making a serious dent in the business of home producers. But its growth was generally seen as an isolated phenomenon. In 1962, however, the Japanese author Kaname Akamatsu, with great foresight, put forward the 'Flying Geese Paradigm': that Asian nations would catch up with the West, forming a regional hierarchy (with Japan as lead goose), the production of goods continuously moving from the more advanced countries to those developing later. Japan would soon not be the only Asian country targeting Western markets.

3

LOSING OUR WAY: 1964-79

Britain, as Harold Wilson led Labour to power in 1964, seemed in good economic health. Its people were increasingly prosperous, GDP growth at 3.1 per cent per annum was comfortable – if below that of key competitors – profits were rising, unemployment was modest and industrial relations were generally calm with days lost through strikes near a post-war low. Wilson's commitment to a Britain 'forged in the white heat of technology' was music to the ears of scientists and managers who, while conscious that British industry and technology no longer claimed global primacy, remained confident that the country had the economic and intellectual resource base – and the products – to compete. On the face of it, good times lay ahead.

Other indicators, though, were telling a different story. Productivity growth was lower than in France or Germany, so the gap in competitiveness was widening. Handicapped by an overvalued currency, Britain was losing ground in export markets; between 1962 and 1966 the country's share of world manufactured exports fell again from 16.2 per cent to 12.1 per cent. Moreover foreign manufacturers were starting to gain a toehold in key home consumer markets, hence Wilson's warning as he came to power that Britain faced a deteriorating balance of payments.

The 15 years that followed would see three changes of government – two of them precipitated by industrial unrest – the devaluation of sterling, the nationalisation of key industries by Labour and Conservative governments alike, rocketing inflation and unemployment, an upsurge in shop floor militancy, increasing penetration of British markets by more efficient and enterprising competitors, and a loss of national self-confidence to the point where a military coup was rumoured and the question seriously raised as to whether Britain was governable. From all of this, British industry came out demonstrably weaker, with employment in manufacturing by 1979 down to 6.16 million, half what it had been in 1952 and – as worrying in terms of the future skills base – a near-halving in the number of apprenticeships. And in Whitehall, the 'white heat of technology' had given way to 'the management of decline'.

Many would put the tipping point at 1969, when Barbara Castle's *In Place of Strife* trade union reform package was killed by an alliance of conservative rather than militant union leaders, and Cabinet opponents of change led by James Callaghan. Wilson's government had responded to the *Rookes* v. *Barnard* judgment by legislating in 1965 to restore the unions' immunities, but had also set up a Royal Commission under Lord Donovan into the broader issue of industrial relations. Its report, delivered in 1968, rejected employers' arguments that collective agreements should be legally binding; it highlighted the discrepancy between national agreements and deals struck at plant level, recommending that shop stewards be brought into the negotiating machinery, but did not address specifically the issue of unofficial strikes. To remedy this, Mrs Castle produced *In Place of Strife*, which among other things proposed to make strike ballots compulsory and set up an Industrial Board to make settlements stick.

Regardless of its merits, the defeat of *In Place of Strife* handed the initiative to the unions, who from then until the early 1980s were able to bring governments to heel. Jack Jones, leader of the Transport & General Workers' Union from 1968 to 1978 and an advocate of devolving power to shop stewards, would be rated more influential than the Prime Minister in a 1977 Gallup poll. Resentment at successive governments' prices and incomes policies, rank-and-file opposition to the Heath government's Industrial Relations Act, the success of the work-in at Upper Clyde Shipbuilders and Heath's defeat in the 'who governs Britain?' election called early in 1974 with the miners on strike, brought the power of the unions to its height. There had been as many strikes during the 1960s as there were during the 1970s, but they involved far smaller numbers of workers and consequently did much less damage. It may be no coincidence that between 1973 and 1979, growth in manufacturing productivity dropped from an average 4.1 per cent per annum to just 1 per cent, before returning to trend. While Wilson, Callaghan and Denis Healey persuaded the unions for a time to accept pay restraint as inflation headed toward 30 per cent, civilities broke down again with the 'Winter of Discontent'. In 1979 – the year the number of days lost through strikes throughout the economy peaked at a staggering 29,474,000 with trade union membership at 13.3 million, up from 9.3 million in 1950 – Margaret Thatcher came to power with a mandate to bring the unions to heel. By the time she had, Britain's manufacturing base was a shadow of its former self.

While the unions – or rather their shop stewards and activist rank-and-file members – accentuated the problems of many firms through an assumption that the well-being or even the survival of their employer was no concern of theirs, the blame for this sharp reversal in fortunes is not theirs alone. The attitude of the City toward manufacturing – and other sectors of the economy – was starting to come under question. Accusations of sharp or unfair practice during takeover bids – notably the Sheffield engineering firm Millspaugh by Hadfields after a bitter struggle that involved some shareholders receiving twice the amount paid to others – led to the establishment of the Takeover Panel as early as 1968. The early 1970s brought the rise of asset-stripping, with speculators taking over a struggling company, selling off parts that were profitable and discarding the rest; John Bentley and Slater Walker became household names, especially when the secondary banking crisis broke in 1975. It was, moreover, a Conservative prime minister – Heath – who railed against the 'unacceptable face of capitalism'. Heath had himself espoused an industrial policy under which 'lame ducks' were allowed to go under until a strategic company – Rolls-Royce – got into such difficulties that it had to be rescued.

Industry during this period had much to contend with, over and above the business of winning orders against competition that stiff-ened after Britain joined the Common Market in 1973. The 'wasted years' of 1952 to 1964 seem an era of progress and certainty when measured against the turbulence of the manufacturing sector in the subsequent 15 years, as reflected in the composition of the FT 30 index. In 1966 the telecoms equipment manufacturer Plessey replaced the shipbuilder Swan Hunter, and British Oxygen the nationalised United Steel. Beecham took the place of the declining Murex and Boots succeeded Leyland Motors when it merged with BMC to become British Leyland (BL). Rolls-Royce's troubles took it out of the index; the travails of the machine tool maker Alfred Herbert let in John Brown. In 1975, the motor component manufacturer Lucas took the place of BL, when the sprawling conglomerate's problems became too grave for it to handle and the government stepped in to rescue it. Ironically, the fortunes of Lucas and BL were closely bound up.

Nowhere is the reversal in the fortunes of British manufacturing during this period more vivid than in the automotive sector. In 1964 Britain could boast successful mass car manufacturers in BMC, Ford and Vauxhall, a strong commercial vehicle and car manufacturer in Leyland Motors, smaller but still viable car producers in the Rootes group and Jaguar plus several low-volume prestige car makers. Popular new models were rolling off the production tracks: the Hillman Hunter in 1966, the Ford Escort in 1968, the Ford Capri in 1969, the Range Rover and Hillman Avenger in 1970. UK car production continued to increase steadily, peaking in 1972 at 1,921,311 (plus some 450,000 lorries and vans). And the downturn that followed could, at least at first, be excused as a consequence of falling demand brought about by the energy crisis of 1973 and the nation's subsequent economic travails.

Yet beneath the surface all was not well, record production being achieved despite an increasingly obvious lack of competitiveness resulting from high unit costs. These in turn stemmed from a duplication of models (especially at BMC/BL), inefficient production methods, deteriorating industrial relations and overmanning.

The brand-new Rootes plant at Linwood was a microcosm of these problems. Compelled by the Macmillan government to base production of the ground-breaking Hillman Imp in the west of Scotland rather than at Ryton, the company invested £23 million in a modern plant, but had to recruit a workforce largely comprised of former shipyard workers with no experience of automobile production and a streak of 'Red Clydeside' militancy. Linwood was at the end of a lengthy supply chain – most components still coming from the Midlands – and half-finished engine castings had to make the 600-mile round trip to Ryton for machining. The plant's shaky economics were compounded by strikes, and by quality and reliability problems that cost Rootes a fortune in warranty repayments, and by the time the Imp was truly competitive Rootes – drained of the funds it needed for new models – had sold out to Chrysler, a process completed in 1967. The Imp was killed off in 1976, management having lost interest in it, and when the Avenger went out of production in 1981 Linwood closed its gates.

Linwood was not the only Scottish automotive plant with problems. In 1966 the Labour MP Tam Dalyell warned workers at BMC's five-year-old Bathgate commercial vehicle plant in his constituency that unless they stopped striking and 'systematically sleeping on the night shift', they could say 'Cheerio' to the jobs it offered. (When the plant did close 15 years later, Dalyell kicked up such a fuss in the Commons that the Speaker had to be hauled out of a dinner with the Prince and Princess of Wales.)

Chrysler made a success of the Avenger, and its British designers showed their flair in the Talbot Solara and Chrysler/Simca Horizon, both named European Car of the Year. But by 1974 Chrysler UK was struggling, and turned to the government for help. This was only granted after Sir Peter Carey, permanent secretary at the Department of Industry, overcame the misgivings of his political master Eric Varley by clinching a deal with John Riccardo, head of the American parent company. The loan was to be paid in tranches as landmarks were reached, and before long Varley was complaining to me of the 'tranche warfare' this was leading to over whether conditions had been met. In 1979 Chrysler Europe collapsed, and the British operation was sold on to Peugeot, rebranded Peugeot-Talbot for home consumption. In the same year production of the Hillman Hunter ended, the machinery being shipped to Iran where it was manufactured as the Paykan until 2005.

During this period, American-owned Ford and Vauxhall each underwent changes that would shift decision-making and model development away from Britain to the Continent. Ford's model range remained popular, the Fiesta being launched in 1976, but the absorption of the Ford Motor Company (England) into Ford Europe in 1967 had long-term strategic implications that were not grasped at the time – the more so as Ford Europe was initially headquartered at Dagenham, only moving later to Cologne. From the launch of the Mk IV Cortina in 1976, Ford cars produced in Britain replicated those designed for its continental plants.

With its insistence on centralised bargaining, Ford experienced growing disruption at its UK plants, briefly reduced following its agreement after a major strike in 1969 to involve shop stewards in collective bargaining. The most celebrated stoppage was the walk-out at Dagenham's River plant by women machinists whose work was classified as 'unskilled' and who demanded pay parity with the men. The strike gave Labour's Employment Secretary Barbara Castle the leverage she needed to bring in equal pay legislation in 1970 – commemorated in the 2010 movie *Made in Dagenham* (released in Germany as *We Want Sex!*).

Continuing disputes – particularly a three-month stoppage at Dagenham in 1971 – poor product quality and uncertainties over delivery, led Ford increasingly to supply its export markets from its German plants and in times of shortage to start importing cars from Germany to Britain. Yet Ford continued to be regarded by government as British to the core, and the bellwether for the engineering industry as a whole; hence Labour ministers' efforts in 1978 (thwarted by its lack of a parliamentary majority) to impose legal sanctions on the company for breaking their pay guidelines.

Vauxhall's successful Viva had been designed in Britain, then replicated by Opel. The General Motors-owned company lost ground, then in an important shift of gravity was reinvigorated in 1976 with the launch of two models originating from GM's German operation: the Chevette and the Cavalier – which became Britain's most popular large family saloon. Vauxhall overtook Chrysler in terms of vehicles sold and by 1979, when the Astra was launched, was closing on Ford and British Leyland. But as with Ford, frequent strikes, especially at its Ellesmere Port plant where shop stewards were less willing to work with management than at Luton, led to cars being imported from Germany to meet demand, exports drying up. For both Ford and General Motors, Germany and Spain became more attractive countries to invest in than Britain.

Leyland Motors looked in a strong position when the dynamic Donald Stokes took over as chief executive in 1964. Triumph was doing well, and in 1967 Leyland acquired Rover (which had in turn taken over Alvis – who would soon stop producing cars to concentrate on military vehicles – in 1965). Meanwhile, BMC had absorbed Jaguar and Pressed Steel – originally a joint venture with an American bank which had manufactured Morris car bodies, Prestcold refrigerators and the odd light aircraft – to become British Motor Holdings in 1966. But the merged company lost money and continued to show a corporate lack of direction that contrasted sharply with Stokes's clearheadedness.

To Tony Benn, Minister of Technology from 1966, the opportunity was clear: if you merged BMH with Leyland Motors, you would create a world-beater with a highly rated management that would draw on the resources of both to develop a new car range, using capital-intensive production methods. As the fifth largest automotive company in the world and Britain's largest exporter, it was bound to punch its weight. The deal was struck early in 1968, the crucial talks taking place at Benn's Holland Park home, and British Leyland was launched.

In fairness to Benn, BMH looked less of a basket case than Stokes

– who had resisted the merger – found it to be. Indeed, in its 1100/1300 range of saloons, it could boast Britain's best-selling cars. But merging a tightly-managed truck and bus making company which also produced sporty cars with a sprawling giant whose most successful models barely turned a profit was at best risky, and as things turned out a recipe for disaster, the good being dragged down by the bad.

Stokes set to work with a will, reorganising the 100 or so companies he inherited into seven divisions. He was horrified that while BMH had a plethora of ageing models (the Morris 1000 went back to 1948) it had no serious plans for new ones. While the Morris Marina, launched in 1971, and even more the Austin Allegro of 1973, have been much maligned, their development was driven through by Stokes as the only way of getting a competitive new model into production in a realistic timeframe, and for a time the Marina sold. Stokes vetoed a hatchback version of the Mini, saying it would upset the unions without greatly increasing sales; it would be the new century before a hatchback Mini would be produced … by BMW.

British Leyland's biggest problem, though, was one of cultures. BMC/BMH had been dogged by internal rivalries as each plant and marque fought its corner, and these now spilled over into the larger organisation as Stokes endeavoured to streamline it and make it more productive. There were also tensions between old hands from the two merged groups and executives brought in from Ford by the group's new finance director Jon Barber. A combination of declining sales of tired models, quality issues – an increasing problem for most British car makers from the late 1960s, not helped by a slippage in the quality of home-produced steel – problems with suppliers, the inefficient use of what new equipment had been installed and increasingly frequent and bitter industrial disputes, all contributed to lower profits which in turn jeopardised the investment on which BL's future hinged.

The company's market share at home began to slip – from 40 per cent in 1971 to 32 per cent in 1973 – and the remarkable thing in retrospect was that Stokes kept trying to keep BL afloat for seven gruelling years before finally admitting defeat. Overseas, the picture was mixed. Stokes endeavoured to increase production at the

Innocenti plant in Milan, and in 1972 was decorated by King Baudoin of Belgium when he opened an extension to BL's factory at Seneffe; but in 1974 the company stopped producing cars in Australia. Jaguar increased production to 60,000 in 1973 with an eye on the American market, only to be caught on the hop when the US economy turned down. Overall during the 1970s, exports of BL cars more than halved, from 368,000 to 158,000. This was not altogether surprising; when a new Rover was shipped to Tokyo for its launch by Heath's trade minister Sir Geoffrey Howe at a British trade fair, BL sent a left-hand drive version, apparently unaware that right-hand drive is the norm in Japan. Moreover, after Britain's African possessions became independent, the governing class adopted the Mercedes-Benz as a sign of prestige; indeed in southern Africa the political élite came to be jokingly referred to as a separate tribe: the WaBenzi.

With hindsight, Stokes's mistake was to run BL with the same expansionist optimism that had characterised his success at Leyland Motors. While BL looked to many bloated and underproductive, Stokes's recipe was not to cut or rationalise, but to keep the labour force intact and boost production and sales. But even had the company been producing models that could have increased its market share at home and abroad, the level of demand on which Stokes based his strategy probably did not exist even before the global downturn of 1974.

When Stokes departed in 1975, handing over to Alex Park, the company at home was producing just over four cars per employee per annum, against seven for Ford's UK plants, and almost 23 for Honda in Japan and 36 for Toyota. Not all of its problems were inherited from BMH. Early on, Triumph managers refused to accept a Rover engine in their new Stag, resulting in costly duplication. As late as 1976, Triumph workers in Coventry struck after three of them were sent home for refusing to handle components from another BL plant. And the biggest headache was the modern Speke II plant, constructed as an act of faith in 1970 and given over in its entirety soon after to production of the TR7 two-seater, aimed at the American market: US drivers were thirsting for an open-top British roadster at a time when their own manufacturers had stopped making convertibles so, inevitably, BL developed the TR7 as a hard-top. When the TR7 flopped in the US market, it was relaunched in Britain, Princess Anne taking one. If her car was reliable it was an exception; the TR7 test-driven by *Motor* needed a new gearbox after 2,000 miles and other major components soon after.

Operations at Speke were governed by a 'mutuality agreement', under which management had effectively abdicated responsibility to the shop stewards. Not that management was blameless for the plant's performance: workers once had to be laid off for three days when Coventry sent 5,000 left-hand front wings after being asked for right-hand. Overmanning was so rampant that in some sections there were two entire workforces who swapped over in mid-shift, playing cards the rest of the time. Absenteeism was the worst at any BL plant; up to 25 per cent on Mondays and Fridays. Strikes at Speke over the flimsiest pretexts were rife; the workers fed cats on the shop floor from their lunch boxes, then walked out when Liverpool were playing at home claiming those same cats had fleas, and again when Everton were playing because the management had had the cats put down.

Belatedly BL tried to reassert its authority, but when management sought elimination of jobs through natural wastage and a speeding-up of the track, the shop stewards – convinced BL was bluffing with its talk of closure – called a 17-week strike. Soon after, in 1978, the company pulled the plug in its first major plant closure; shop stewards tried to call a further strike against the compensation terms, but were voted down at a mass meeting. Production of the TR7 was moved to the former Standard plant at Canley, Coventry, which in turn closed in 1980.

British Leyland was not the only company to experience labour problems at Speke. A distribution depot at Speke was in 1975 the scene of one of the only two strikes in the history of the John Lewis Partnership. And just after the Standard Triumph closure, Dunlop shut its tyre factory there with a further heavy loss of jobs. Management blamed overcapacity worldwide and the persistent failure of its Liverpool workforce to knuckle down to the job; the unions accused Dunlop of investing millions in new machinery overseas, including the Soviet Union, while expecting Speke to meet its targets with 'new' machinery which in one case had been written off in the accounts in 1936.

The TR7 was not the only new model from BL whose prospects were sabotaged by industrial strife. The V8-engined Rover 3500, which replaced the Rover P6 and Triumph 2000, was named European Car of the Year for 1977; but its export launch coincided with a toolmakers' strike at several BL plants and a dispute involving bodyshell makers at Castle Bromwich that left dealers without any left-hand drive cars to sell.

British Leyland first sought government help in 1974 at the same time as Chrysler; there was even talk of a merger, which the incoming Labour government wisely rejected. It is fair to note, though, that because of the state of the economy 100 other firms were also seeking assistance. Ministers set up an inquiry under Sir Don Ryder, the dynamic managing director of Reed who was shifting his company's emphasis from its traditional business of making paper into magazine publishing, as imports made home-produced paper increasingly uncompetitive. Ryder's recipe for BL was ambitious: he concluded that the company's strategy was sound but that huge government investment was needed to raise productivity through mechanisation, with better labour relations crucial. He came under fire from MPs for pinning much of the blame for BL's travails on Jon Barber.

The next year, with the economic downturn at its trough, BL – the last major British-owned car maker – effectively went bankrupt and was nationalised, and in 1977 the energetic South African Michael Edwardes took the helm; his first action was to halve the size of the company's board. He closed plants, reduced the workforce of 250,000 by 18,000 in 18 months, split up BL's car division to separate volume from prestige models and strove to centralise management. Meanwhile Varley underwrote a wholesale refit of BL's flagship plant at Longbridge. Yet its fortunes did not recover, good businesses being thrown to the wolves in a vain attempt to maintain BL (and specifically the Longbridge operation) as a competitive volume car producer.

In the view of Geoffrey Robinson, the youthful former Jaguar managing director elected a Labour MP for Coventry in 1976 – and briefly a Cabinet minister under Tony Blair – BL's problems were caused by 'mistaken management decisions, and wasteful and unnecessary redundancy and sales promotion programmes'. Management throughout BL clearly did have much to answer for, but to the car-buying British public the company – save for the increasingly suspect quality of some of its products – was best known for its abysmal industrial relations. And just as Sir Bernard and Lady Docker had personified the worst of British management in the 1950s, it was Derek Robinson – 'Red Robbo' – who in the 1970s came to symbolise all that was most destructive in motor industry trade unionism.

The 6ft son of a Black Country chainmaker, Derek Robinson went to work at Austin's Longbridge plant as a toolroom apprentice at the age of 14, and by the late 1940s was an Amalgamated Engineering Union shop steward and a member of the Communist Party. A decade later he was a member of the shop stewards' committee that dominated the plant, and in 1974 he took over as convenor from his mentor Dick Etheridge, despite representing the smaller of the two main unions at Longbridge which then employed some 18,000 workers. He became the main spokesman for the BL shop stewards' combine committee, which with each fresh merger had extended its influence until it could call workers out at no fewer than 42 factories. Within the combine, power was divided between the Communists, centred on Longbridge, and the more militant Trotskyists whose stronghold was the former Morris plant at Cowley, Oxford – ironically one of the few BL plants surviving today (though with production on an adjacent site).

Robinson was not a total Luddite: he supported the replacement of the archaic piecework system by the measured day work system, and was ready to wear Edwardes's reorganisation plans if there was a large enough role for the shop stewards. But it soon became plain that the reorganisation would involve sacrifices they would not stomach – including 25,000 more job losses and 13 more plant closures as BL got itself into shape to launch the Metro – and a wave of strikes began, purportedly against 'mismanagement'. Night after night, the nation saw on the news mass meetings at factory gates and in car parks at which a decision to strike was taken on a show of hands – with a strong suspicion of intimidation, no checks on who was voting and sometimes with Robinson declaring a vote carried when more hands seemed to have been raised against.

When Edwardes arrived at BL, one-sixth of its car production was being lost through strikes. How many Robinson encouraged can only be guessed at – Edwardes said there had been 523 walk-outs at Longbridge alone in three years, cutting production by 62,000 cars and 113,000 engines and costing £200 million in lost revenue. BL's competitors rubbed their hands: Fiat's advertising agency prepared a campaign around the slogan 'Built by robots, not by Robbos', only for the client to reject such obvious gloating.

Robinson had two stated aims: to halt the repeated walkouts by small groups of workers which brought the entire plant to a halt and hit thousands of wage packets, but create the climate for a strike right across BL that would compel the company and the government to guarantee the continuance of plants and jobs and give the shop stewards control over working methods and manning levels. He failed in both – though his efforts to persuade wildcat strikers to go back were rendered less credible by his extravagant rhetoric about the management which triggered further walkouts.

To a management used to dealing with Dick Etheridge – who had been a firebrand in the 1950s but mellowed to the point where Donald Stokes gave him a retirement party and left it with one of Mrs Etheridge's Christmas puddings – the portents were alarming. Edwardes concluded that as long as Robinson was trying to paralyse the company there would be no Metro, and his political masters (Varley and – from May 1979 – Margaret Thatcher and Sir Keith Joseph) remained determined not to give an inch. When that November Robinson co-signed a pamphlet from the shop stewards' combine attacking the management, BL sacked him. Decisive to Edwardes was that its text closely resembled the minutes of a meeting between 16

Longbridge shop stewards and Mick Costello, industrial organiser of the Communist Party, which had been passed to him by MI5.

Longbridge was largely a Transport & General Workers' Union plant whose shop stewards called an immediate strike. But Robinson's own union, the AEU, was under right-wing leadership and its president Terry Duffy – normally not the sharpest tool in the box – skilfully shunted the issue off to an independent inquiry, which sat on it for months before giving Robinson's case the weakest possible endorsement. When a vote was eventually called, with the *Birmingham Evening Mail* declaring: 'The choice is your job or Red Robbo', Longbridge workers voted 14,000 to 600 not to strike; a crucial factor was the disclosure on the eve of the vote that BL's market share had crashed to an all-time low of 15 per cent. BL went on to sack Alan 'The Mole' Thornett, an equally disruptive Trotskyist shop steward at Cowley; stoppages at both plants sharply reduced.

BL went on, after months of deadlock with the unions, to impose working arrangements under its recovery plan; resistance crumbled. Edwardes said this breakthrough gave the company a 'fighting chance of being competitive', but could BL recover? Indeed, what was the future for Britain's car makers as a whole, when production by 1979 was down to just over 1 million, barely half the total of seven years before?

During the 1970s foreign-made cars increased their share of the UK market from 14.4 per cent to a staggering 56.7 per cent. Volkswagen had gained a strong presence from the late 1960s with the 'Beetle' and the Microbus, many of which are still on the roads decades later. (Indeed VW's concentration on the Beetle and its failure to develop popular enough new models landed it in a crisis in the mid-1970s which forced 33,000 redundancies.) Peugeot and Citroën followed Renault in establishing a bridgehead, but from the early 1970s the greatest threat came from Japan. Datsuns from Nissan flooded onto the roads, Mazda also making inroads with more up-market models. It was not long before Britain's car makers were crying 'foul'; there was no way of keeping out imports from continental Europe after Britain joined the Common Market in 1973, so they concentrated on pressing for limits on imports from Japan.

When embarrassed British ministers raised the issue in Tokyo, they found the Japanese ready to exercise a degree of voluntary restraint; formal import quotas would have been an admission that Britain could no longer compete – a serious loss of face. Not that even such quotas were foolproof: when the Conservative MP Peter Viggers (later of duckhouse fame) visited a textile factory in Taiwan in 1979, he found half the output labelled 'Made in Huddersfield'. Nevertheless, curbs on imports through tariffs or quotas appealed to a range of manufacturers who were unable to compete with Japan (and increasingly Hong Kong, Taiwan and South Korea) on price or quality.

One of Britain's manufacturing strengths remained its truck and bus industry, in which Leyland Motors through the quality of its products, global reach and strategic acquisitions played the dominant role throughout the 1960s. Leyland ended production of double-deck buses under the AEC marque in 1968 and on the formation of the National Bus Company in 1969 bought a half-share in Bristol, the chassis builder that had been the automatic supplier to state-owned regional bus operators, and its bodybuilders Eastern Coach Works. The Leyland Atlantean, then from 1979 the Olympian, was the group's flagship double-deck offering, but it also offered the tinnier Daimler Fleetline, moving production from Coventry to Lancashire in 1973. London Transport took 2,646 Fleetlines for its quieter routes – but did not keep them long. Sensing a weakness, Guildford-based Dennis re-entered the double-deck market after a decade in 1977 with its Dominator rear-engined chassis, which would stay in production until 1996.

In 1972 the Leyland National single-deck bus was launched. Styled by Giovanni Michelotti – who had worked wonders at Triumph and built at a new plant at Workington (again a fruit of government regional policy) – it set a fine example to BL's car making side by replacing no fewer than five obsolescent Leyland, AEC, Daimler and Bristol models. In the short term, the Leyland National was a commercial success, but already operators who had a choice were starting to place orders for bus chassis from the likes of Scania.

Leyland Trucks remained dominant, through its various marques, in most of its export markets – though AEC's markets were quickly lost. When Arab states started boycotting companies trading with Israel in the mid-1970s, nimble footwork by Leyland executives led to one side being sent Leyland trucks and the other identical vehicles badged Scammell; honour was satisfied. However, both Leyland and Bedford lost out heavily in the Caribbean as from the mid-1960s newly-independent former British colonies repealed tariffs which had almost guaranteed them a market, letting in a rush of American imports. Yet at home there were strains; British Leyland closed three truck and van plants between 1969 and 1972, the merged Seddon Atkinson company was acquired by International Harvester in 1974, and Foden had to be bailed out with military contracts when the same year its development of a new greenfield plant landed it in financial difficulties.

The first serious challenge came from Sweden in the shape of the Volvo F88 (launched in 1964) and the Scania 110 (1968). These started penetrating the British market *circa* 1970 with the rise of the independent haulier at the expense of the still-nationalised British Road Services (BRS), impressing with their comfort and reliability during a period when Leyland was struggling to perfect its stopgap Marathon truck. By the time Leyland hit its stride again in 1980 with the T45, Volvo and Scania had a foothold – and retained the lead where trucks suitable for long hauls over Continental motorways were concerned. While BRS and its associates bought British and in bulk, the independents wanted the truck that suited them best; moreover, word got around that you could order your truck, go over to Sweden, be handed back part of the declared purchase price in cash, drive it home – and in the meantime be loaned a delightful young Scandinavian lady for the night.

The UK van market was a crowded one, with BL's Sherpa and EA; a wide range of Bedford light trucks and vans from GM; the Commer/Dodge Spacevan from a new (1965) Rootes plant at Dunstable; and, pre-eminently, the Ford Transit. First produced in 1965 in the former Hawker Hurricane factory at Langley, Berks, and later at Southampton, the Transit with its American-inspired styling was an immediate hit; *Top Gear* unearthed police statistics that by the mid-1970s 95 per cent of robbers used a Transit for their getaway. Ford began marketing and manufacturing the Transit across Europe, and in 1978 a facelifted 'Transit Mark 2' was launched. However British producers did not have the market to themselves, the Hiace Toyota light van in particular making heavy inroads from the late 1970s.

As long as car production held up, Britain's component makers – mostly in the Midlands but with Lucas having major plants in London and around the world – were buoyant, though questions were increasingly being asked about the apparent lack of quality control at some suppliers. Devaluation at the end of 1967 helped them and other British manufacturers develop an export business, but a 33 per cent slump in home demand for new cars little over a year later left them back where they started.

Of Britain's many – and usually tiny – speciality car makers, the most successful was Lotus, which in 1966 moved to a modern factory and test facility at the former Hethel RAF station in Norfolk. Jim Clark's death at Hockenheim in 1968 was a major blow, though Clark's teammate Graham Hill carried off that year's Formula 1 championship and Lotus would win again with Jochem Rindt and Emerson Fittipaldi. But the company continued to combine innovative features for the racetrack with sporty, lightweight cars for the road; notably the Esprit, which over 28 years to 2004 went through several upgrades to sell 10,675 examples. The turbulent 1970s were less kind to other small British car makers: Aston Martin, at the top of the range, struggled through a series of receiverships after its success with the DB5 famously driven by James Bond, and West Bromwich-based Jensen collapsed in 1976. At the other extreme Reliant, whose three-wheeled Robin attracted sales as well as ridicule, just limped into the 1980s.

Britain's motorcycle makers were also staring at disaster. The Mini killed the domestic sidecar market, the advent of the Rockers gave biking an ugly image and sponsors abandoned motorcycle racing for sexier competition on four wheels. Then in 1968 the launch of the Honda CB 750 – 'bigger, faster and better than anything the British could offer' according to the industry historian Ian Chadwick – put the American market at risk. The Japanese did not have things all their own way; the Norton Commando, also launched in 1968, was acknowledged as a quality machine, and BSA and Triumph developed acclaimed 3-cylinder models. But at a critical juncture the US government demanded that all imported bikes should have their gearshift and brake pedals in the Japanese configuration, handing the advantage to Honda and its stablemates as British manufacturers were forced to undertake an expensive retooling.

This constraint bit just as decades of underinvestment and mismanagement were coming home to roost. The industry was still dominated by craft-based production methods, with inflated workforces and the unions resisting new techniques that might have slimmed them. BSA – at its peak the largest motorcycle producer in the world – bucked the trend by installing a semi-automated assembly line considered the most advanced outside Japan; sadly the workers did not adapt, the new models produced did not perform and the company's problems intensified. Bert Hopwood, an engineer-turned-manager who had worked for every major British bike producer, placed the blame in his book *Whatever Happened to the British Motorcycle Industry?* firmly on management. Hopwood savaged Norton's owners for blocking a move to a modern plant, condemned BSA for bringing in trendy outside designers when it had a huge in-house design team, and fulminated that 'several of the top brass, in the last two decades of the BSA saga, disliked, if not openly hated, motorcycles.' Nor was Hopwood alone in ascribing the industry's collapse in the 1970s to its propensity for handing key management posts to executives who knew nothing about the industry and its products.

In 1971 BSA recorded a loss of £8.5 million, £3 million of that in respect of its motorcycle business. It concentrated production of the bikes themselves on the Triumph works at Meriden, with engines and components produced at Small Heath. But sales fell, the losses grew and in 1973 BSA went bankrupt. The Conservative government had contributed to the industry's problems by cutting off funding, but it now brokered a reorganisation under which the component makers Manganese Bronze took over BSA's non-motorcycle businesses (notably Carbodies) and a new company, Norton-Villiers-Triumph (NVT), was formed under Manganese's Dennis Poore, founder of *Autosport* and briefly a Formula 1 driver. NVT took on the motor-cycle businesses of both companies – BSA, Norton and Triumph – and Poore tried to halt the slide. His remedy was to increase effi-ciency by concentrating production on Small Heath and a plant at Wolverhampton, and in February 1974 he closed the Meriden plant, making 3,000 of its 4,500 workers redundant.

The Triumph workers objected not just to the redundancies but to production being switched to a rival plant, and staged a sit-in. Labour now returned to power with Tony Benn as Industry Secretary, and when shop stewards at Meriden proposed a co-operative to keep producing the 750cc Bonneville – popular in America – and the Tiger, Benn gave his backing. A deal was thrashed out under which the co-operative supplied Triumph machines to NVT – an arrangement that caused friction from the outset – and production resumed at a modest level. Before long NVT itself hit trouble, the production of Nortons ending when the government sought repay-ment of a loan; when the company collapsed in 1977 the co-operative, through another government loan, bought the rights to market its own products. The co-operative received further backing from Mrs Thatcher's incoming government, secured valuable African orders for police motorcycles, but finally gave up the ghost in 1983. By then, three-quarters of the world's motorcycles were made in Japan.

Workers at Meriden were not the only ones to seek a new direc-tion for their plant. As mentioned below, Fisher Bendix workers also launched a co-operative that would fail in the long term when their radiator plant was closed. Workers made redundant when the *Scottish Daily Express* closed its Glasgow plant in 1974 briefly produced a *Scottish Daily News* as a co-operative before funds ran out. When Lucas Aerospace ran low on orders in the mid-1970s and redundan-cies were announced, a group of activists in the workforce headed by Mike Cooley backed up industrial action by producing the 'Lucas

Plan', for a switch from armaments to socially useful products. The workers' militancy saved some jobs, but the plan was not adopted and Cooley, a senior design engineer, would be sacked in 1981.

The shopfloor activism that led to the Meriden sit-in, other less successful workers' co-operatives and waves of strikes that reverberated far beyond British Leyland had its roots, in part, in the Heath government's determination to reform industrial relations where Barbara Castle had failed. The 1971 Industrial Relations Act was intended to encourage responsible trade unionism and gave workers rights as well as new obligations, with the system policed by a National Industrial Relations Court. Union leaders and shop stewards saw it as a threat to their authority and to 'free collective bargaining'; the Trades Union Congress (TUC) organised mass protests and 1,500,000 members of the AEU staged a one-day strike. The TUC required its member unions to refuse to register under the Act and the T&G was twice fined for refusing to comply, though a number of smaller unions did so. As major unions ignored the Act and employers generally thought better of invoking it – most agreements arrived at in these years, including one I helped negotiate, specifically stated that they did not have any standing in law – it had little effect on manufacturing industry. The stand-off that finally discredited it concerned five dockers jailed for illegally picketing a freight terminal, who were freed at the urging of the Official Solicitor to prevent a national dock strike and get the government off the hook. But its effect was to radicalise workers in almost every factory.

Almost in parallel, trade unionists throughout Britain applauded the action of shop stewards at Upper Clyde Shipbuilders (UCS) in responding to the government-instigated closure of their yards with a 'work-in'. Instead of calling a strike, UCS's AEU convenors Jimmy Reid (a leading light in the Communist Party) and Jimmy Airlie, urged their members to carry on working in a disciplined fashion; Reid's insistence that there must be 'nae bevvy' reverberated across industrial Clydeside. Scotland rallied behind them, celebrities from Billy Connolly (who had worked at UCS) to John Lennon gave their support and early in 1972 Heath relented. UCS survived and, indeed, two of its yards remain in production today as part of BAE Systems, though after a chequered history.

The response of the men at UCS contrasted markedly with the usual public perception of British shipyard workers. Nor was the industry's reputation for indiscipline unfounded. The Boilermakers' leader Ted Hill told the respected industrial reporter Peter Paterson: 'It's the same as it always has been. On Monday morning the lads go into the back yard and chuck a stone up in the air. If it stays up, they go to work...' Yet the crisis that brought about the UCS work-in was symptomatic of the travails of the industry as a whole. Although Britain had ceded leadership in world shipbuilding to Japan in the 1950s as its yards failed to modernise to produce supertankers and bulk carriers, it remained a force: in 1965 out of 9.45 million tons of merchant vessels constructed worldwide, Britain produced 1.28 million tons, 13.62 per cent of the total; Japan's share was 4.86 million tons or 51.9 per cent.

Moreover there were encouraging signs. On Wearside Austin & Pickersgill was building its 'Liberty Ship replacement': the 14,000-ton 'shelter deck' SD14 general cargo ship. The first was launched in 1967, and between then and 1988 no fewer than 221 were produced against stiff global competition. Priced economically, the SD14 was an instant hit with Greek shipowners, repaying their faith by remaining a workhorse of merchant fleets into the next century. There were other innovations, too. Harland & Wolff in 1967 launched the *Myrna*, the first supertanker built in the UK and the largest vessel ever launched down a slipway, and the three-legged drilling rig *Sea Quest*, which uniquely had to be launched down three parallel slipways.

At the other end of the market, Britain took heart from the construction on the Clyde of the *QE2*, a 70,000-ton replacement for the Cunarders *Queen Mary* and *Queen Elizabeth*. Like its pre-war predecessors – furnishings intended for which adorned every shipyard worker's house in Clydebank – the *QE2* was built as much to maintain employment in a depressed area as to maintain Britain's prestige on the high seas, the government contributing to its £29 million cost. Cunard recognised that with the mass transatlantic market already lost to the airlines, its new flagship needed to combine style with economy; its steam turbines were far more efficient than conventional engines and it could be worked by a far smaller crew (still over 1,000) without the passengers noticing. But the *QE2* would be the last liner built in Britain; while she served with distinction for 39 years from her maiden voyage in 1969, her successors were built in France and Italy, John Brown's yard at Clydebank having stopped building ships on the collapse of UCS.

The inability of Britain's merchant shipbuilders to compete in the supertanker age led the Wilson government – at the request of both management and unions – to commission a study of the industry from Sir Reay Geddes, head of Dunlop. His report, published in 1966, recommended geographical groupings of yards that would achieve economies of scale and other synergies. A Shipbuilding Industry Board was set up in 1967 to provide financial support to yards that reorganised, but most companies wasted precious time jockeying for position. Harland and Wolff, isolated in Belfast, was the only yard to modernise on a heroic scale, running into serious financial difficulties as a result. Cammell Laird – which was building its only nuclear submarine, HMS *Conqueror* – fared the same and had to go to the government for help. Of the major companies, only Swan Hunter – which had already acquired Smiths Dock – organised a merger (with its neighbours Clelands and John Redhead), also acquiring yards on Tyneside from Vickers-Armstrong and Hawthorn Leslie. Two builders of smaller vessels on the Solent, Vospers and Thornycroft, merged in 1966 to form Vosper Thornycroft.

Once again, Tony Benn was the driving force in reorganising an industry. Early in 1968, at the same time as negotiating the merger of Leyland and BMH, Benn brokered several amalgamations of shipbuilders. UCS was the most significant of these, combining Fairfields at Govan, Stephens at Linthouse, Connell's and Yarrow's at Scotstoun and John Brown at Clydebank, where the *QE2* was nearing completion. The government took a 48.5 per cent holding in the consortium, and made it a £5.5 million interest-free loan.

On paper UCS's prospects were good: its yards had an order book worth £87 million. But some of its parts were struggling: Connell's had been trying to introduce basic production control for a decade; Yarrow – the only profitable yard – broke away in 1970; forecast economies did not materialise and the following year UCS went into receivership. Having just had to nationalise Rolls-Royce, Heath was more determined than ever not to support 'lame ducks', and despite a still healthy order book the government refused UCS a further £6 million in working capital. Then came the work-in, which for the moment saved all the UCS yards except Linthouse.

Geddes had had little to say about why Japan was winning new orders from Britain. The reorganisation he inspired led to three British yards – Harland and Woolf, Scott Lithgow and Swan Hunter – being large enough to build a supertanker, yet their combined production was only a fraction of Mitsubishi's. Matters were further complicated by a speculative boom from the late 1960s, with owners ordering ships in the confidence that as trade increased, they could sell them on immediately at a profit. A key player was the Israeli-owned Maritime Fruit Carriers (MFC), which ordered 11 supertankers from Swan Hunter, six from Harland and Wolff and two from Scott Lithgow through Panamanian shell companies. When the trade bubble burst with the oil crisis of 1973 and the secondhand price of supertankers collapsed, few of the ships had been completed; MFC declared itself bankrupt. It took a combination of diplomatic pressure, government loans and ruthless bargaining by shipowners like Stavros Niarchos for the yards to get the ships off their hands for even a fraction of the order price.

Nor had industrial relations in the yards greatly improved. In September 1972, 3,800 boilermakers at Swan Hunter's on the Tyne walked out in support of a 171 per cent pay claim at a time when the government was limiting increases to £2 a week; 2,400 other workers were laid off. The strikers' union told them to go back, but when they rejected £2.50 the strike was made official. The dispute was settled after eight weeks, but this combination of shopfloor militancy and weakness by union leaderships did little to inspire confidence in the industry.

The combination of Middle East war and soaring oil prices that triggered the sharp economic downturn came just as a record tonnage of tankers was on order around the world, and in 1975 and 1976 world merchant ship production peaked at over 33 million tons. British yards benefited from this, the 1.5 million tons produced in 1976 being their highest since the war – though their share of world production was now down to 4.5 per cent (Japan's share was slipping too, as South Korea became a serious competitor). But orders both for tankers and dry cargo vessels were drying up; in the three years to 1979 world production slumped by 57 per cent to 14 million tons, and Britain's production by 54 per cent to 691,000 tons. And the downward trend – for Britain at least – would continue.

It was against this background that the Wilson/Callaghan Labour government nationalised the shipbuilding industry in 1977. Cammell Laird, Harland & Wolff and UCS were already controlled from Whitehall, and they were joined in 1976 by Doxford & Sunderland, which had had to build ships in two halves then join them (up), but had modernised on a heroic scale to produce gas carriers after being taken over in 1972 by Court Line. When Court Line collapsed because of a crisis in another part of its business, the government took over the yard to save £133 million worth of orders and 9,000 jobs. Overall, rationalisation and modernisation had not taken place fast enough, and while the SD14 remained a success story, the creation of British Shipbuilders was a desperate throw to come through the crisis with the nucleus of a viable industry. Nineteen companies with yards from Cornwall to Dundee were taken into state ownership under the chairmanship of Admiral Sir Andrew Griffin; Harland & Wolff was kept separate because of the special case for supporting Northern Ireland's economy (and not alienating its largely Protestant workforce with extreme Loyalists itching to call a general strike).

Parliament took so long to create British Shipbuilders (BS) that its chief executive-designate, Cammell Laird's Graham Day, went home to Canada. With global demand still falling, within a year the company presented a gloomy corporate plan, involving a cut in capacity from 631,000 to 430,000 tons a year by 1981 and a reduction in the workforce from 33,300 to 21,200. It stayed unpublished, but rumours of redundancies began to spread in the yards just as Labour was securing the agreement of the Confederation of Shipbuilding and Engineering Unions to a national pay agreement replacing 168 local arrangements, which alienated shop stewards – and was conditional on no compulsory redundancies.

British Shipbuilders under Labour is best remembered for the fiasco of the ships ordered for Poland: a financially suicidal contract, concluded by BS and the Warsaw government which kept yards going by constructing a fleet of 3,000-ton mini bulk carriers at rock bottom prices for the state shipping line of a mercantile competitor. The demand created was artificial; at the former UCS Scotstoun yard, the seven freighters built under the deal between 1978 and 1980 were the last constructed there.

A more promising lifeline for Britain's shipyards – and indeed for a large slice of its precision engineering industry – was the advent of North Sea oil. Oil was first struck in 1969, and brought ashore in 1975. As the sheer scale of reserves became evident there was a demand first for drilling rigs and then for production platforms that dwarfed the North Sea's requirements in the 1960s when it was thought to offer only gas. As early as 1974 MPs were complaining that British industry was slow to invest in the North Sea, and while some UK companies became major players – notably the Aberdeen-based Wood Group – many orders went to the United States or to Norway. For platforms, new fabrication yards were opened at Ardersier and Nigg Bay in Scotland, but they did not survive long beyond the peak of demand, and workers and facilities were left high and dry. Scott Lithgow switched to platform production after the delivery of its last supertanker in 1982, and John Brown after the *QE2* was taken over by Marathon Oil, but their yards would close in 1987 and 2001 respectively.

Another sign of an industry in decline was the eclipse of C A Parsons, the Tyneside company that had manufactured turbines to power warships and liners, starting with HMS *Dreadnought* and the *Lusitania*. After the war Parsons provided propulsion systems for destroyers for Commonwealth countries as well as the Royal Navy, but after HMS *Glamorgan*, launched in 1964, the orders went elsewhere and Parsons became primarily dependent on power station orders. In

1968 Parsons merged with the switchgear manufacturer Reyrolle to form Reyrolle Parsons, and in 1977, as markets continued to contract, there was a further merger with the heavy engineering firm of Clarke Chapman to become Northern Engineering Industries (NEI).

Babcock & Wilcox was still prospering, but with the rundown of nuclear power station construction the company was seeking to diversify away from manufacturing into support services. Renaming itself Babcock International in 1979, it sold a 75 per cent stake in its original core businesses of boiler manufacturing and energy services to Mitsui.

The slump in Britain's motor and shipbuilding industries would have a serious impact on demand for steel, but all that was far in the future when Wilson's government was elected in 1964 on a commitment to nationalise steel in the hope that this would bring about a long-overdue rationalisation. Only then did Britain's steel makers begin to reorganise. Dorman Long, South Durham and Stewarts and Lloyds merged, and the British Iron and Steel Federation commissioned a report from Sir Henry Benson on ways of restructuring under private ownership. In 1966, just after Labour's re-election and with nationalisation now inevitable, Benson recommended concentrating steel making on five sites: Port Talbot, Llanwern, Scunthorpe, Lackenby (Teesside) and Ravenscraig, with special steels concentrated on South Yorkshire. Obsolete plants with 9 million tons' capacity would close, and the workforce would be cut back from 317,000 to 215,000.

The following year the British Steel Corporation (BSC) came into existence, taking over the 14 largest companies with 90 per cent of the capacity. The merchant banker Lord Melchett was chairman and Monty Finniston, a spiky Glaswegian metallurgist, his deputy; neither had run a major company before. Crucially, BSC had been weakened at the outset when the deputy chairman designate, Niall Macdiarmid of Stewarts & Lloyds, delivered a public attack on the way the undertaking was to be organised, and was sacked by the Minister of Power, Richard Marsh.

A sizeable private steel sector remained, consisting of mainly smaller plants linked to the heavy end of engineering or serving specialised markets. This sector ebbed and flowed with the economy, closures being offset by new arrivals such as Sheerness Steel; opened under Canadian ownership in 1972 to recycle scrap cars into steel coils and rods for the construction industry, with a capacity of 400,000 tons a year.

Finniston returned from a visit to Japan – which had just overtaken Britain and France to move second behind Germany in the global steel export table – convinced of the need for bigger plants, a view reflected in BSC's 1971 corporate plan. A giant new steelworks on a greenfield site producing 12 million tons a year was proposed, plus a smaller new plant at Redcar, with capacity to increase from 28 million tons in 1971 to 35 million in 1975 and 43 million in 1980. Edward Heath – who had decided that denationalising steel again would be more trouble than it was worth – was sceptical, and a compromise was thrashed out in 1973 which left out the greenfield plant and provided for a more gradual capacity increase to 36-38 million tons by the late 1980s. An early fruit of this was the £130 million Anchor project to extend Scunthorpe's Appleby Frodingham plant, increasing its capacity to 5 million tons. Even this strategy involved plant closures, and while the Iron and Steel Trades Confederation, representing the dominant production workers, was ready to consider them, local protest groups fired up by the success of the UCS work-in began to mobilise, with the backing of the T&G. The campaign to save the bar mill at Shelton works at Stoke-on-Trent was even commemorated on the stage; Shelton itself, which as recently as 1964 had been the world's first steelworks to introduce continuously cast production, would struggle on until 2000 with a tiny fraction of its original 10,000 employees.

The industry now hit a perfect storm. Melchett died in 1973, Finniston taking his place. The economic downturn triggered by that year's energy crisis demonstrated that demand for steel would, at best, not be accelerating at anything like the rate Melchett and Heath's Trade and Industry Secretary Peter Walker had expected. New capacity came on stream just as a surge in imports followed Britain's entry into the Common Market. And in March 1974

Labour returned to power with Tony Benn, radicalised by UCS and the shop stewards' new best friend, succeeding Walker. In 1975 Finniston proposed a 20,000 cut in a workforce already slimmed to 220,000 – which he followed with the claim that the 37 million tonnes of steel Britain was expected to need each year could actually be produced by just 50,000, triggering a row with Benn. Finniston's insistence on the need to cut manning was backed up by statistics showing that each worker at BSC was producing 122 tonnes a year, against 150 to 370 tonnes for Continental steel producers and 520 a worker at Nippon Steel. Most job cuts, however, came from plant and process closures rather than tighter manning. With demand for steel continuing to fall, Finniston's successor Sir Charles Villiers slashed production targets and Eric Varley allowed him to contemplate the end of steel making at Corby and Shotton, ruled out by Benn because the prospects of workers there finding another job were bleak.

Upheavals in the steel industry had only a limited effect on the West Midlands, where only a few smaller plants were based. But the collapse of the machine tool makers Alfred Herbert – a modern firm and in the early 1960s the largest in the world – had a severe impact on a Coventry already suffering from motor and motorcycle plant closures. The machine tool industry had got through the immediate post-war decades in reasonable shape, with many engineering firms without access to reparations retooling and orders from the Commonwealth buoyant. Most of the demand, however, was for conventional or general-purpose machinery, which left firms with little incentive to match the specialist machinery and more sophisticated products with numerical control, being developed by their German and Japanese counterparts. In the meantime Alfred Herbert consolidated its position with a string of takeovers (including parts of BSA), and a joint venture with America's Ingersoll.

When the industry's fortunes turned down, they did so rapidly. Herbert's expansion proved too much for the abilities of its management, who struggled to give direction to the sprawling organisation they had created. And from the late 1960s Herbert began losing its traditional markets – home and export – to competitors from Germany and Japan. The onset of metrication as Britain entered the Common Market increased the pressures on the industry. The company's acquisitions began to look like a costly mistake as it moved from profit into loss, and in 1975 it went to Labour's National Enterprise Board for £25 million to modernise and cut its borrowings. Then, in the late 1970s, a further surge of imports destroyed Herbert's customer base; it went into receivership in 1980 and closed the following year.

The near-collapse of Rolls-Royce came about for very different reasons. The company was then – as today – a leader in aircraft engine technology, and its problems stemmed from its success in convincing American plane makers of its expertise. As Britain's aircraft industry rationalised during the 1960s, Rolls-Royce took over Bristol Siddeley, whose range of engines produced at Filton included the Olympus which would power Concorde; Rolls was motivated in part by pique at its rival being selected as one of the engine makers for Airbus, and the takeover contributed to its later financial problems.

In 1967, Rolls-Royce offered Lockheed a new turbofan engine – the RB-211 – for the three-engined wide-bodied L-1011 TriStar airliner it was developing for American carriers. The engine combined features of two engines it had under development, and crucially saved weight by incorporating a fan stage built of carbon fibre. A year later, after negotiations in which the engine's power rating was raised and the price forced down, Lockheed placed an order with Rolls-Royce for 150 sets of RB-211s. Rolls-Royce was soon struggling to deliver an engine of the power specified, and the carbon-fibre fan stage had to be abandoned for titanium after – in its very final test – a chicken fired into it at high speed shattered the assembly. (This was a standard acceptance test in the industry; the failure of the VC10's Triplex windscreen to withstand a high-velocity chicken briefly imperilled that aircraft's certification, until it was discovered that a technician had mistakenly fired off a frozen one).

By September 1970, Rolls-Royce was staring at a loss on every engine, development costs for the RB-211 having almost doubled to £170 million. The government found cash to keep the project going, despite Heath's pledge not to assist 'lame ducks', but in February 1971 Rolls-Royce went into receivership. The collapse of Rolls-Royce would have killed the TriStar – which had hit technical problems of its own – and jeopardised trading relations with America; so Heath stepped in to nationalise the company, allowing development of the RB-211 to be completed. The Nixon administration, after some hesitation, guaranteed bank loans to Lockheed to get its airliner into production.

A new company, Rolls-Royce (1971) Ltd, chaired by the merchant banker Kenneth Keith, acquired the assets of Rolls-Royce, selling off the prestige motor car side of the business and for the first time organising its accounts so that it could see what it was spending on R&D. A new contract with Lockheed cancelled penalties for late delivery and increased the RB-211's price by £100,000 per engine (£49 million in total); the first Rolls-Royce-engined TriStar entered service with Eastern Air Lines in April 1972. The RB-211 went on to become a global success, being produced into the 1990s, on the strength of which Rolls-Royce reinforced its standing as a global competitor. But in the short term, Heath's 'U-turn' – which also involved the prices and incomes policy the Conservatives had pledged not to repeat when they came to power in 1970 – caused the prime minister trouble with the Right of his party, which included a then silent Margaret Thatcher.

Britain's aircraft industry in the mid-1960s had a spring in its step. The British Aircraft Corporation was marketing a number of new and successful products: the BAC One-Eleven (developed without government backing), the Lightning jet fighter and a range of guided weapons, plus the VC10 and such stalwarts as the Viscount. It was developing the TSR-2 strike and reconnaissance aircraft, and Hawker-Siddeley the revolutionary Harrier jump-jet, which made its first flight in 1964. Even more exciting was the Anglo-French supersonic airliner that would become Concorde; the treaty to develop the aircraft had been signed in 1962, and BAC and Aerospatiale were getting down to detail with high hopes that it would be a winner with airlines worldwide. The Treasury made a determined effort to extricate Britain from the project after Labour came to power; the deal being stuck with partly because of the damage a withdrawal would have done to relations with France, and partly because Tony Benn, the sponsoring minister from 1966, had hundreds of Concorde workers in his constituency.

In a review of the industry commissioned by Wilson on taking office, Lord Plowden, chairman of Tube Investments, concluded that it was 'exactly the sort of industry on which Britain should concentrate'. However, two decisions taken by the government in 1965 indicated that the scope for British plane makers to go it alone was limited, at least where developing military aircraft was concerned. The more controversial of the decisions was to scrap the TSR-2, which was already being flight tested as a successor to the Canberra, but the rejection of the highly innovative Hawker Siddeley HS 681 short take-off military transport was, in the long term, just as significant. Cancellation at so late a stage of the TSR-2, developed for the RAF in the late 1950s by English Electric as an alternative to the Royal Navy's Blackburn Buccaneer and taken forward by BAC, caused a political furore. Ostensibly it was axed because of rising costs; these had been inflated by Vickers billing to the Ministry of Defence the wages of TSR-2 workers who nipped across the runway to work on the civilian VC10. However, inter-service rivalry and doubts within the industry (even from Sir Barnes Wallis) about the final configuration of the aircraft contributed to its demise. The MoD went to extreme lengths to make sure the nine TSR-2s nearing completion were dismantled, to defuse pressure for the programme to be revived, but nearly half a century on resentment still lingers. In a repeat of the Skybolt fiasco, the government ordered the General Dynamics F-111 from the United States, only to cancel when costs and development times escalated; the eventual replacement for TSR-2 would be the Tornado.

The significance of cancelling the HS 681 was that it sent out, even more clearly than with the TSR-2, the message that, when push came to shove, the British government would choose a tried and tested American product over an adventurous one developed at home (the Harrier being a spectacular exception). The HS 681 was designed for moving small forces with their equipment into and out of war zones; there was even a plan to give it vertical take-off capacity that would have made it almost the transport equivalent of the Harrier. What the MoD ordered instead, and took delivery of in 1966, was the Lockheed C-130 Hercules, a propeller-driven workhorse that had entered service with the US Air Force in 1957 and was serving peerlessly in Vietnam. The decision to buy 66 Hercules (more of later variants would follow) has been vindicated by the aircraft's record in service with the RAF – and numerous other air forces – all over the world to this day. But the rejection of the HS 681 was painful for forward-looking thinkers in Britain's aircraft industry, who could see its chances of gaining even a home market for innovative planes it developed receding fast. It also convinced the government there was only room for one major British plane maker; months before forcing Leyland to merge with BMH, ministers tried unsuccessfully to persuade BAC and Hawker Siddeley to combine.

One determinedly independent company to fall by the wayside at this time was Handley-Page, producer of the wartime Halifax bomber; the ambitious airliners it developed in post-war years did not find a sponsor and by the time it found its niche with the 18-seat twin turboprop Jetstream, developed for the executive market and first flown in 1967, it was running out of funds. Handley-Page went into liquidation in 1970, Scottish Aviation (and later British Aerospace) taking over the Jetstream which became a commercial success with over 450 sold.

Another niche plane maker was Britten-Norman, the Isle of Wight-based company whose lightweight Islander regional aircraft, first flown in 1965, went on to sell 1,280 examples worldwide. The Islander did not, however, remain a success story for British manufacturing. High demand and lack of capacity led to most of the aircraft being built in Romania from 1969, and later also in Belgium. Britten-Norman went into receivership in 1970, was taken over by Fairey Aviation and when Fairey in turn hit turbulence was sold to Pilatus of Switzerland.

More stable was the larger Shorts of Belfast, who while moving increasingly into missiles produced the Skyvan, roughly twice the size of the Islander, of which 153 were produced between 1963 and 1986; two stretched regional airliner versions, the 330 and 360, sold nearly 300 examples over two decades from 1974.

Perhaps Britain's greatest export success in the field of aviation was achieved by the ejector seat manufacturers Martin-Baker. When the company's first seats – fired by an explosive charge – were developed just after the war, a relationship was built up with the US Navy. This paid off in the mid-1960s when first the Navy and then the US Air Force started fitting Martin-Baker 'sub-zero' ejectors as standard; more than 11,000 of the M7 model were installed in US military aircraft alone. Martin-Baker's global business grew rapidly, and by 1976 4,000 pilots' lives had been saved.

While the British military were ordering the F-111 and the Hercules from American plane makers rather than sponsoring home-grown aircraft, the government was developing a long-term strategy for BAC's participation in joint European projects over and above Concorde. In 1966 BAC and France's Breguet (later taken over by Dassault) agreed terms for developing the Jaguar supersonic strike and reconnaissance aircraft. Jaguar would be a commercial and operational success; first flown in 1968, 543 models were built, the RAF flying them until 2007 with the Indian and Omani air forces continuing to do so. While Jaguar was going ahead, however, France pulled out of a joint project with BAC for the Anglo-French Variable Geometry (AFVG) multi-combat aircraft, unwilling to let the British manufacturer take the lead. BAC found new partners in Germany's MBB and Aeritalia for what became the Tornado; entering service in 1974, almost 1,000 were built, and the Tornado is still in service with the RAF today, performing with distinction over Libya in 2011.

In 1967, the seeds of probably the most significant international aircraft project to date were sown with agreement between Britain, France and West Germany to develop the 300-seat A300 Airbus, with Sud Aviation as the lead company. Britain's participation once again involved killing a home-grown project: BAC'S Three-Eleven longer-haul variant of the One-Eleven, which several airlines, headed by Laker Airways, were ready to order and which was several years ahead of the Airbus in development. Having buried the Three-Eleven, the British government – when asked to contribute £60 million or one-third of the development costs – refused to join the Airbus consortium at the last minute in 1969. Tony Benn (a fan of Concorde) declared that the government was 'not satisfied that it was a good investment to go ahead with the project at this stage'. Hawker Siddeley, however, did remain involved, to build the wings as a sub-contractor. At that time Boeing had effectively cornered the long-haul market with the 747; Harold Wilson blamed bad trade figures on the eve of Labour's surprise defeat in 1970 on the arrival of a batch of jumbo jets. Ministers can hardly have appreciated the way the evolution of Airbus would not only create a global competitor to Boeing but – through Britain's refusal at that point to participate – move the industry's centre of gravity to France. It was ironic that France itself had come within a whisker of pulling out in 1968 because of the simultaneous cost of developing the Airbus 300, Concorde and the Dassault Mercure; had it done so the future of British, and indeed global, aircraft manufacture would have been very different.

The public's perception of Britain's aircraft industry became dominated by Concorde as the supersonic airliner moved from blueprint to reality, being rolled out in 1971. As in France, it was the subject of immense national pride, but there was also the prospect of its becoming the world-beater that would wrest the long-haul market back from Boeing. America saw Concorde as a threat, and the Soviet Union as a challenge; before long the US Congress was funding Boeing to design a competitor with longer range and seating more than Concorde's 110-odd; meanwhile the Tupolev TU-144 'Concordski' was in full development. These challenges encouraged BAC and the British government in the belief that there would be a sizeable market for Concorde, and indeed early on there were over 100 provisional orders from BOAC, Air France, Pan Am and 16 other airlines, five of them in the United States. But in truth Concorde, though graceful and charismatic, was a technological dead end. The economics of a plane carrying a relatively small number of passengers with heavy fuel consumption that offset the advantage of speed could only work on routes with a high concentration of premium-fare customers. The economics of manufacture also told against Concorde, with duplicated production lines on both sides of the Channel which would have kept costs needlessly high even had they produced far more than ten aircraft each. Moreover, although its test flights from 1969 were successful technically, reactions to the sonic boom it generated once the afterburners were switched on dictated that Concorde could never fly supersonically over land. Potential orders began to dry up, notably from US carriers, and while America's decision to drop its SST in 1971 after $1 billion had been expended removed a competitor, the total market for a supersonic airliner was visibly shrinking. The Soviet Union pressed ahead with the TU-144 for reasons of prestige, even after one crashed spectacularly at the 1973 Paris Air Show. But while it was refined to become technically competitive to Concorde – some of whose technologies dated from the 1950s – a further crash in 1978 led to only 102 commercial flights ever being made by Concordski, mostly for cargo.

Concorde made its first scheduled flights for British Airways and Air France in 1976, to Washington – after anti-British politicos in New York had prevented it landing there, ostensibly on grounds of noise; I was at the end of the runway when it took off on its return flight, and was deafened when the sound wave hit seconds later. New York was forced to give way the following year, and Concorde subsequently flew also to Dallas, the Gulf, Mexico City, Rio and Singapore – making diversions round Florida, India and Malaysia or flying subsonically over them because of local prohibitions. The plane was safe – it would be 2000 before one crashed – and more than covered its running costs on the transatlantic route (though not on others which were short-lived). But in the wake of the 1973 oil crisis the cost of operating Concorde, on top of the purchase price, led China and Iran to cancel their orders. No airline apart from BA and Air France took up its options (though Braniff and Singapore Airlines briefly took Concordes on lease) and production at Filton and Toulouse halted in 1979 with just 20 completed, at a heavy financial loss. What remained, however, was an industrial infrastructure in which, with the development of Airbus, France had become the leader.

With BAC struggling to find a market for Concorde, Hawker Siddeley was coming up with a world-beater which by 2012 would be the only aircraft its successor BAE Systems would be manufacturing outright: the Hawk trainer. More than 900 Hawks have been constructed for 18 air forces, the plane is manufactured under licence in India (after an initial export order in 2004) and the US Navy flies its own derivative, the T-45 Goshawk. The Hawk has been used as a fighter and for ground attack, and is the staple of the Red Arrows, the RAF's aerobatic display team. Adopted by the RAF in 1971, the Hawk entered service in 1976 and has provided continuous employment for the former Blackburn plant at Brough, near Hull, for over four decades, though an end to production is now in prospect.

Hawker Siddeley was also enjoying success with the Harrier, which entered service with the RAF in 1969 and the Royal Navy in 1980. Some were procured by the US Marines, whose pilots gave them an enthusiastic reception, and by the late 1970s McDonnell Douglas was manufacturing further batches under licence. The Labour government had high hopes of selling Harriers to China as it began to break with Maoism, but the deal was scuppered by China's invasion of Vietnam in 1979.

By then, Hawker Siddeley's aircraft construction activities (and Scottish Aviation) had been merged by the Labour government into the state-owned British Aerospace. (One company left high and dry by the formation of BAC, the nationalisation of its steel interests and, finally, the nationalisation of shipbuilding was Vickers, but it retained crucial heavy engineering capabilities – plus the Rolls-Royce luxury car plant at Crewe – and carried on.) The creation of British Shipbuilders under the same legislation may have been a counsel of desperation, but the aircraft industry was nationalised as a commanding height of the economy. It was perceived as having a prosperous future, but there was a need for careful rationalisation as the emphasis moved to collaborative projects; there was also a recognition that how the industry would develop depended on procurement decisions taken by state-owned British Airways and the Ministry of Defence. Moreover, BAe's export business was inextricably bound up with considerations of foreign policy; an agreement concluded by BAC in 1973 – after a smaller informal deal in 1965 – to supply jet fighters to Saudi Arabia to supply jet fighters to Saudi Arabia (America being unable to for fear of upsetting congressional supporters of Israel) would lead to a closer commercial relationship with sensitive diplomatic implications. Significantly, the creation of BAe was followed in 1979 by its rejoining the Airbus consortium, valuable ground having been lost to France and to Aerospatiale. BAe's enthusiasm for Airbus had led it to torpedo an initiative by Boeing the previous year for the British plane maker to make the wings for the 757, with Rolls-Royce supplying the engines; fortunately for Rolls, Boeing let them build the engines anyway.

Nationalisation of BAC and Hawker Siddeley was followed by a degree of rationalisation, but BAe continued to operate from most of the plants it had inherited from Britain's independent plane makers of the immediate post-war period – Brough, Broughton, Chadderton, Filton, Hatfield, Prestwick, Woodford, Weybridge (BAe's corporate headquarters) and numerous others. At no point even during the four brief years of state ownership was a strategic review conducted of what could be achieved by concentrating production in fewer locations; decisions were taken on an ad hoc basis as legacy projects expired. Consequently the British aircraft industry failed to centralise its activities at just the point when France was concentrating most of its efforts on developing Toulouse into what became, after Seattle, the world's largest centre for aircraft manufacture. A heavy price would be paid for this.

While successive British governments tried to promote a 'second force' in civil aviation to create competition for British Airways, no consideration was given to doing the same in aircraft manufacture. While the Wilson/Callaghan government, for both commercial and ideological reasons, opted to nationalise the industry as a whole, France, despite the concentration of strategic projects on Toulouse, continued to maintain Dassault alongside Aerospatiale as a separate and just about private-sector company, building everything from fighters to executive jets. Had an equivalent 'second force' company existed in Britain – or had any British manufacturer been ready to take on the role – it would have been possible, once BAe was privatised, for that company to take forward projects that were not of interest to BAe but nevertheless commercially viable. And when BAe eventually decided to concentrate on areas other than aircraft manufacture (apart from a few key co-operative projects), Britain would have retained a free-standing aircraft industry of its own. Instead, with BAe a virtual monopoly, its increasing loss of interest in more areas of its product range, notably in the field of executive jets, played into the hands of its mainly American counterparts.

When Tony Benn and his Left-wing colleagues drew up their shopping list for nationalisation, they baulked at interfering with the explosives-to-paint behemoth of ICI; it performed solidly in the national interest, did not need government assistance, appeared to have consolidated without outside encouragement and did not pose any kind of threat. But it had been manufacturing a wide range of products in too many plants, *Forbes* magazine observing much later that 'nothing short of a full-scale industrial revolution could have saved ICI', and under Sir Paul Chambers in the 1960s that revolution began. ICI improved productivity, invested in giant ethylene crackers at Wilton, set up a fibre spinning operation in Germany, but above all targeted the American market with a huge PVC plant in Bayonne, New Jersey. The course pursued by ICI had some inherent risks, and the greatest of these was overcapacity. Nonetheless, the expansion permitted ICI to produce chemicals at a more competitive price.

After the launch of the new strategy in 1967, ICI's sales in Europe surged by 33 per cent a year until the end of the decade. Its real preference, even after Britain had joined the European Economic Community (EEC) was for investing in the United States where in 1977 it took over a paraquat plant at Bayport, Texas. In the process it handed its German rivals a competitive advantage: Hoechst, Bayer and BASF all overtook

ICI in global sales over this period. After Chambers's departure in 1968 capital investment was maintained, but ICI was carried forward by its own momentum; its principal new investment at home was in plants to manufacture methanol and ammonia from North Sea gas. In 1979 it was still one of the world's five top chemical companies, but in contrast with its competitors with their global reach, was still heavily dependent on its home plants and markets.

Suffering from overcapacity in its fibres business, ICI disengaged from Courtaulds in 1964. It was irked when Courtaulds, after being barred by the Monopolies Commission from expanding its rayon interests, launched a bid in 1969 for English Calico. ICI responded by proposing a consortium of textile firms including English Calico, in which it would hold a 40 per cent stake; the Labour government set up a review which recommended no further mergers among the top five textile manufacturers. The weakest of these was Carrington & Dewhurst, which with ICI's backing had made some rash acquisitions and lost heavily trying to introduce crimplene to West Germany. When a boardroom coup forced Joe Hyman out of Viyella, ICI acquired the company and with government backing engineered a merger between Carrington and the core Viyella business; merging, as with British Leyland, a struggling concern with a forward-looking one.

Meanwhile British clothing manufacturers continued to lose out to imports. The government introduced import quotas in 1966, but these coupled with mergers in the industry did not halt the slide as was hoped, and in 1972 Conservative ministers unprecedentedly imposed tariffs on Commonwealth textile imports. Britain's entry into the Common Market produced a fresh challenge from Continental fabrics and Courtaulds, at the time the world's largest textile manufacturer, found itself on the defensive. Struggling to contain costs in the wake of the 1973 oil price shock, it also found itself faced with an excess of spinning and weaving capacity. Efforts were made to address this through restructuring and the closure of one major plant, but by the end of the decade Courtaulds was still producing nylon and polyester at a loss. Questions began to be asked about whether its financial backers had too readily facilitated its earlier dash for growth (a rare exception to bankers' perceived antipathy to investing in industry).

Britain's clothing manufacturers both benefited and suffered from having Marks & Spencer as the dominant retailer. Contracts to manufacture for the chain's conservative St Michael label were lucrative and, at this time, seldom abrogated. But they discouraged manufacturers from specialising as their counterparts in Germany and Italy were doing, and with few other retailers in a position to develop their own labels, competition was limited. The industry in the East Midlands, in particular, became very dependent on a single customer and range of products – the more so as the 1960s saw the collapse of demand for fully fashioned stockings with the advent of tights, dealing a fatal blow to Nottingham's hosiers.

The footwear industry in these years saw some retrenchment as imports began to squeeze British manufacturers – some small Northamptonshire shoemakers going to the wall – but it was also looking outward. Clarks took over two American shoe manufacturing and retailing chains in the late 1970s, and in 1979 Paul Fireman, an American sports goods distributor, saw a pair of Reeboks at a trade show and decided to sell them in North America.

The British pharmaceutical industry went through the 1970s without a single representative in the world's top ten, but was nevertheless increasing its influence to become the leading exporter after the United States. Particularly notable was the rise of ICI, from 67th to 23rd in the world league, as it developed pharmaceuticals from a fringe activity to a business essential to the balance sheet; yet as late as 1978, just 7 per cent of ICI's profits came from pharmaceuticals. There were three reasons for the rise of the sector: the development of new drugs, notably Glaxo's launch of ventolin for asthma in 1969; its expansion into overseas markets (Glaxo again opening plants in France and Germany); and attempts at rationalisation. Yet key players such as Beecham (soft drinks, toothpaste and pharmaceuticals) and Boots (pharmaceuticals, cosmetics and a national retail chain) had yet to decide where the strategic future of their businesses lay;

Wellcome – which continued its steady research-driven growth – and Glaxo were more tightly focused. In 1971 Beecham bid for an unwilling Glaxo – which argued that smaller research organisations had more and better ideas than large ones – and the following year Glaxo and Boots agreed to merge, but in each case the Monopolies Commission blocked the action. In 1978 Glaxo gained a foothold in the lucrative American market by acquiring the Florida-based Meyer Laboratories, which it built into Glaxo Inc with new headquarters and laboratories in North Carolina.

Meanwhile Arnold Weinstock was developing GEC into a global supplier of heavy electrical plant. Having completed a radical restructuring, Weinstock in 1967 launched the then largest takeover in Britain's industrial history; a successful £114.5 million bid for a reluctant AEI – which had many synergies with GEC – created Britain's largest electrical group (AEI had earlier sold its lighting interests to the fast-growing Thorn). The next year GEC – again with encouragement from the Labour government's Industrial Reorganisation Corporation – acquired English Electric, which had rejected a bid from Plessey. GEC was now a powerhouse of the economy; despite a further rationalisation as duplicate former AEI capacity was sold off, the company in 1974 employed 200,000 people.

Weinstock's great frustration was that even after Britain's entry to the Common Market, continental markets for power generation equipment stayed closed as France and Germany, in particular, continued to look after their own (as they do to this day despite efforts by the European Commission to force them to open their markets). To win export orders, GEC therefore had to compete against its German, American and Japanese counterparts in the developing world.

Possibly Weinstock's only blind spot was semiconductors. Just as the management of Ferranti never wanted to exploit its potential in computers, Weinstock hesitated to harness GEC's expertise in the field to take on the Americans and the Japanese. With Plessey and Ferranti also holding back, the government's National Enterprise Board put £50 million into a new Bristol-based semiconductor venture called Inmos, with factories at Newport and in Colorado. Weinstock belatedly agreed to a tie-up with Fairchild in the same field, but the American company was taken over, the venture fell through and semiconductor development was confined to GEC's Marconi plant at Lincoln, which would be expanded in 1981 and eventually taken over by Dynex of Canada.

Technical innovation and commercial success in Britain's electronics industry also continued unabated. Ferranti's navigation systems, range finders and target seekers were integral to the RAF's Harrier, Phantom and Tornado jets. Plessey in 1972 launched the first industrial capability-based security computer – the System 250 which the Army adopted (along with the Plessey-led Ptarmigan communications system) – and in the late 1970s worked up the digital System X telephone system with the Post Office (which had finally opened up to competitive tendering). Racal expanded steadily from its base of providing the Army with battlefield radio systems with Clansman entering service in 1976; in 1979 it bought Decca Radar. STC revolutionised telephony by pioneering fibre optic cables and installing a fully digital exchange at Moorgate as early as 1971. Heavier cables were the province of British Insulated Callender Cables, then at the top of its game with ten plants in production across Britain; in 1975 it renamed itself BICC. Smiths – relaunched in 1965 as Smiths Industries – sold its automotive instruments business to Lucas and built a strong aerospace market on both sides of the Atlantic with innovative high-tech products. The MoD's radar establishment at Malvern came up with the first liquid crystal display – finding no British firm interested in taking the concept forward, but Sony a ready taker. And, most dramatically, EMI produced a world-beater in the form of the CAT brain scanner.

Medical electronics was not one of EMI's core businesses; despite dropping the 'Musical' from its title in 1971, it was then best known as the record company that had launched the Beatles. The breakthrough was due to the genius of Godfrey Hounsfield, who had joined EMI's Hayes laboratories to work on guided weapons and in 1958 helped design Britain's first marketable all-transistor computer, the EMIDEC 1100. Hounsfield spent a decade developing a scanner, testing it first on a preserved human brain, then on a cow's brain from a butcher's shop and then on himself. In 1971 the brain scanner was tested on a cerebral cyst patient at Atkinson Morley Hospital, in 1973 the first brain scanner went on the market at £100,000 and in 1975 the whole body scanner was perfected.

EMI was swamped by orders from around the world, and within two years the market was worth £40 million; lasting commercial success seemed guaranteed. But while EMI had applied for a number of patents, competing machines appeared in the crucial American market and the orders began to tail off – more so when the US government began to ration new scanners because of the impact on hospital budgets. Other parts of EMI's business, notably music, began to experience problems and in 1979 – the year Hounsfield was awarded the Nobel Prize for Medicine – the company was taken over by Thorn Electric; the scanner business was rapidly sold to GE of America at a knockdown price.

In no field was Britain's abdication of global competitiveness greater at this time than in computing. The installation of the Atlas computer at Cambridge University in 1962 turned out to mark the end of Britain's claim to primacy as Ferranti's management lost interest in the sector and its computer interests were split: commercial computer development joined ICT with military computing continuing under the Ferranti banner. The merger that created ICT did not embrace capabilities in the defence field, so groundbreaking work by ICT, Ferranti, Plessey and the MoD's own research agencies continued without the co-ordination that might have kept Britain up with the pack, if not ahead of it.

The further merger that did take place in 1968 – engineered, once again, by Tony Benn – combined ICT with English Electric Computers (itself a merger of English Electric Leo Marconi and some computer interests of Elliott Automation), to create International Computers Limited (ICL). English Electric's dowry was a fuller order book, and a line of IBM-compatible mainframes which became the ICL System-4. The ICL board decided the System-4 was technically superior to ICT's 1900 series, and prepared to phase out the latter – only to reverse its decision under pressure from Benn and Clive Jenkins's managerial union ASTMS. Concerned that continuing with the 1900 when it lacked the System-4's compatibility with computers worldwide would limit ICL's ability to challenge, the former EELM directors resigned. Their apprehension was justified: although the 1900 achieved strong sales in the British public sector, its penetration of the private sector and export markets was limited. This was doubly frustrating as a ready market for the System-4 had been identified behind the Iron Curtain. ICL recognised that its computers had to have a wider compatibility, and in 1974 launched the 2900 series which incorporated elements of both the main-systems it inherited. It is still in operation as the Fujitsu Trimetra. One variant, the 2903 small business computer, achieved sales of 3,000 – ten times what the company had anticipated.

ICL broadened its range in 1976 by acquiring the non-US part of Singer Business Machines, and later its development and manufacturing plant in New York state. This brought the company a small business minicomputer which it developed into the ICL System-25, and wider geographical reach.

Over these years the great advances were in software, and almost exclusively they were made in the United States: the development of Basic (1964), the first floppy disk (1967), the formation of Intel (1968), the separate sale of software by IBM (1968), the formation of Arpanet and a network linking four US universities (1969), Bell Laboratories' introduction of Unix (1970), the foundation of Microsoft (1977) and the launch of the Internet (1979). Until the advent of computer gaming, Britain was left to play catch-up; significantly the first computer link-up to play Dungeons and Dragons was at the University of Essex in 1979. But there was the odd landmark; in 1976 the Queen sent her very first email, from the MoD's radar research establishment at Malvern. Again, though, a Chinese wall seemed to exist between Britain's commercial and defence computing development.

The arrival of large-scale computing and modern ranges of business machines caught some manufacturers on the hop, with devastating consequences for jobs. The arrival of the photocopier, pioneered by Xerox from 1959, wrong-footed makers of old-style duplicating machinery. One to suffer was the Tottenham-based Gestetner, which had built up a huge international business and employed thousands at its main plant. Gestetner only just survived the 1970s, belatedly moving into the new world of information technology with a greatly depleted workforce; since 1995 it has been owned by Ricoh.

Another field in which Britain momentarily secured world leadership was magnetically levitated transport (Maglev). This was the brainchild of Eric Laithwaite, professor of heavy electrical engineering at Imperial College, who had worked on Manchester University's first computer. Laithwaite discovered that the linear induction motor he invented was capable of lift as well as thrust. He saw its potential for powering an ultra high-speed train, and secured government funding for a short line for his 'tracked hovercraft' near Earith, Cambridgeshire. Though the prototype had just a mile on which to operate, it reached 104 mph on its first test run in February 1973, only for the government to cancel the project a week later. One factor in the cancellation was that British Rail saw Maglev as a threat to the tilting Advanced Passenger Train that it was developing.

In the shorter term, from 1975 BR introduced the 125mph diesel-powered High Speed Train, for which 195 power units were built. The HSTs – one of which reached 148mph – were probably Britain's most successful train since the war, and dozens remain in service today with millions of miles on the clock; but only Australia followed suit with its own 'XPT'. Meanwhile Maglev development continued around the world. The first commercial service was the Birmingham airport shuttle introduced in 1984 (with a vehicle built by BR). A mile-long driverless Maglev line opened in Berlin in 1991, and German's Transrapid company has taken the technology forward with lines in China and South Korea and many more planned. The economics of Maglev are widely questioned, but despite a crash on its test track in Germany in 2006 – killing 23 people – when a train travelling at speed hit an abandoned truck, the technology continues to win friends, but with Laithwaite's (and Britain's) pioneering role a footnote in its history. In 2007 Transrapid even proposed a high-speed Maglev network for Britain, but the government rejected the overture.

Throughout this period, Britain was losing its traditional export markets for locomotives and railway equipment. Derby's locomotive manufacturing works closed in 1966, and English Electric fulfilled its last major overseas order for locomotives, from Portugal, in 1968. Two years later the Chinese began constructing the TanZam railway, to link ports in Tanzania with Zambia's copperbelt without trains having to pass through Ian Smith's Rhodesia – two former British territories turning elsewhere for expertise, in part for political reasons. And in 1976 BR purchased thirty Class 56 diesel freight locomotives from Romania as part of a government initiative to woo President Ceaușescu, then mistakenly regarded as a liberal. The Romanian locos proved highly unreliable compared with later examples built by BR at Doncaster, and required heavy modifications to be fit for traffic.

Britain's nuclear industry parted company with its counterparts – losing its global edge – as it opted for the Advanced Gas-Cooled Reactor for its second generation of power stations. It rejected the Pressurised Water Reactor, used not only by other countries but – as developed by Rolls-Royce – in its own nuclear-powered submarines, the first of which was commissioned in 1963. While with computer development there had been a damaging divergence between Britain's commercial and military programmes, here the split was between nuclear power and weaponry on the one hand and nuclear propulsion on the other.

The last Magnox station – Sizewell A – came on stream in 1966, the first of seven AGRs in 1976; the last, at Dungeness, would only plug into the National Grid in 1983 after immense technical difficulties and probably the worst record of strikes in the history of Britain's construction industry.

The lead time in decision making in nuclear issues is such that within months of the first AGR entering service, a battle was being fought out in Whitehall over whether to continue with the programme, switch to the PWR or fudge the issue by ordering two more AGRs and one PWR. Tony Benn, Energy Secretary and not yet an opponent of nuclear power, was the minister in charge, and came under heavy pressure from the Central Electricity Generating Board to order two more AGRs followed by a PWR. However GEC and the Downing Street 'think tank' wanted an immediate switch to the PWR – a course of action Benn was less inclined to take after discovering that Arnold Weinstock had interceded with the Prime Minister, James Callaghan, before the decisive Cabinet meeting. The outcome was that no more AGRs were built after Dungeness; one PWR was ordered – Sizewell B – but the further programme that the generating and contracting industries looked forward to never materialised as the political climate changed against nuclear power.

New forms of nuclear power generation were explored at Dounreay throughout this period, but with ever-reducing chances of being adopted. The establishment's final prototype fast reactor achieved criticality in 1974 and began supplying the National Grid the following year, but two earlier experiments were wound up in 1969 and 1977 respectively; they had generated electricity safely and effectively, but there was no official appetite for taking the technology forward.

Meanwhile Sellafield was reprocessing spent fuel from Magnox stations – 35,000 tonnes between 1971 and 2001 – into just under half that quantity of new fuel, plus weapons-grade plutonium. During the 1972 miners' strike the reactors at Sellafield were pushed so hard that some of their waste was thrown straight into cooling ponds instead of being reprocessed, leaving an ongoing risk of contamination. After a protracted public inquiry in 1977/8, work began on the Thorp (thermal oxide reprocessing) plant, intended to bring a more sophisticated process to bear on spent fuel from foreign as well as British plants. It would have a chequered history, not entering service until 1994.

Throughout the 1970s, pit closures continued as the coal industry both contracted and modernised; the Clean Air Act of 1956 that followed a series of poisonous London smogs, the end of steam traction by British Rail in 1969 and the adoption of new processes by industry all took their toll on demand. While the Macmillan government had directed heavy industry to the coalfields, there was now little scope to do so and the emphasis switched to promoting light industry, with garment making initially at the forefront. Over the years companies making everything from televisions to potato snacks were encouraged to relocate or start up in the North-East, South Wales and central Scotland. While the aim was to find work for ex-miners, many of the jobs created went to women and male unemployment remained high.

An exception was the giant Ever Ready battery factory opened at Tanfield Lea, Co. Durham, in 1968; no woman was allowed on the shop floor there for 20 years. The plant appeared to have everything going for it, as Ever Ready held 90 per cent of the home battery market and had bought-out several potential competitors. The company spent heavily on R&D with a large laboratory in Tottenham, but through-out the 1970s stuck with traditional zinc-carbon batteries despite the success of longer-life alkaline batteries in the United States; Ever Ready salesmen were simply told to contradict the claims of alkaline. Up to 1977 Ever Ready had a stake in Mallory, the company devel-oping the Duracell alkaline battery; when it was forced to sell by the Monopolies and Mergers Commission, it dug in its heels even harder. With Ever Ready refusing to sell its batteries in blister packs, Duracell began to target Britain's supermarkets, a type of outlet Ever Ready ignored. Tanfield Lea – employing 1,500 at its peak – relied heavily on sales in Nigeria, which took almost half its output of 3 million batteries a day and won Every Ready a Queen's Award for exports; 500 workers had to be made redundant when a telex arrived from Lagos cancelling the import licence. Belatedly, Ever Ready opened an alkaline battery factory near Newcastle.

Britain's record in the manufacture of consumer goods in the late 1960s and 1970s was patchy. Producers of 'white goods' – even GEC with its Hotpoint range – found themselves too small to compete on the Continent after Britain joined the Common Market, while Zanussi and other European brands found the British market an easy one to penetrate. The Fisher-Bendix washing machine at Kirkby, near Liverpool, acquired by Thorn when it took over Parkinson Cowan as the industry desperately consolidated, was one of a number to close in the early 1970s. Shop stewards organised a sit-in which led to Tony Benn – over protests from his permanent secretary – to fund it as a workers' co-operative making radiators; it struggled on for a time, returned to the private sector, then closed.

The Dansette record player was an early casualty of Japanese imports, the last being sold in 1969. Britain's television manufacturers were next. They had things pretty much their own way until the early 1970s, when the Barber boom created a demand they could not satisfy and Japanese imports began to pour in; when boom turned to bust, they found the colour sets marketed at less than £200 by Sony and Toshiba hard to compete with. The government negotiated an agreement with Japan under which its manufacturers limited their exports to 10 per cent of the British market, but Japanese companies found a way round this: setting up plants in the United Kingdom, the sets produced could be marketed as British if half their components were British-made. Sony and Matshuishita were the first, but when Hitachi announced it was following suit in 1974 with a plant in the North-East making televisions largely for export, the home industry rallied its forces to protest.

The Japanese now wrong-footed their British competitors by moving their products upmarket, leaving UK manufacturers scrapping over the budget end of the market. Pye – in trouble from the mid-1960s when it closed its Ekco factory at Southend – sold its television manufacturing business to Philips in 1976. It had launched an early pocket calculator for the British market in 1974, but this was made in Japan and Malaysia. Other British television manufacturers were encouraged by the government to form partnerships with the Japanese: GEC teamed up with Hitachi in 1978, while Rank, having acquired Bush and Murphy, set up a joint venture with Toshiba. Neither consortium was harmonious, and within two years Rank had pulled out and Toshiba was making its own sets at the former Bush factory in Plymouth. Only Thorn went it alone, competing with the Japanese on quality and efficiency but, critically, not on volume.

The post-war housing boom came to an end in 1967, with an impact on manufacturers both of raw materials and furnishings. Blue

Circle was briefly the world's largest cement manufacturer, with 13 million tons annual capacity, until the downturn forced it to halve production. Brick sales fell back sharply, and between 1968 and 1971 London Brick bought out its three remaining competitors to give it a monopoly of the Fletton bricks used in housebuilding, and 43 per cent of Britain's total brick market. As brickworks in the south-east Midlands went out of production, the clay pits from which they had drawn their raw material became valuable landfill sites.

In 1969 the once-mighty Harris Lebus furniture works at Tottenham closed under pressure from imports – though Parker Knoll with its ergonomic and contemporary designs flourished, despite the burning down of its modernistic High Wycombe factory in 1970. Cutlery manufacturers struggled to compete as cheap blanks poured in from South Korea; shortly before Viners switched production there from Sheffield, the company's owning family denied responsibility for a planning application to redevelop its works for offices. Raleigh's crown began to slip as bicycles from Taiwan flooded onto the market – though the launch of its highly successful thick-wheeled boys' Chopper bikes in 1970 put off the reckoning for a time. Dawes of Birmingham captured the top end of the market through its upgraded Galaxy, launched in 1971.

Again one of the few bright spots was Wedgwood where from 1963 Sir Arthur Bryan, a former bank clerk with no qualifications in pottery but a passion for profit, embarked on a programme of expansion. As Wedgwood outperformed the targets Bryan had set for turnover and profits, it acquired competitors including William Adams, Royal Tuscan, Susie Cooper, Crown Staffordshire and Mason's Ironstone, to become a global player. Yet in the mid-1970s the House of Commons catering committee ordered £20,000 worth of crockery from a German manufacturer without inviting Wedgwood to bid; a decision that led to heads rolling but which, despite fury in the House and the media, could not be reversed. By 1975 Wedgwood had nearly 9,000 employees in 20 factories.

Britain's brewing industry underwent radical change in this period. The mergers that had marked the post-war decade continued: Bass made several major acquisitions, notably Charrington in 1967, and Whitbread – in a strategy designed to fend off unwelcome takeovers – continued the flurry of purchases which led to its raising production from 46 million gallons in 1961 to 163 million a decade later. After the Conservatives returned to power in 1970, the State brewery at Carlisle – nationalised by Lloyd George to keep drinking by munitions workers under control – was sold off to the Yorkshire 'real ale' brewer Theakstons. Yet more significantly the brewing combines were now starting to attract the attention of yet larger conglomerates. In 1972 Grand Metropolitan Hotels took over Watney Mann and Imperial Tobacco snapped up Courage, and in 1978 Allied Breweries merged with the bakers J. Lyons.

These takeovers coincided with, and were partly explained by, lifestyle changes which made the male-dominated boozer look to be an anachronism: more women customers, more food, a wider range of drinks which the brewery could distribute, imposing its mark-up. It was no coincidence that a hotel chain, a tobacco company and a food producer should see acquiring pubs and breweries as a natural extension of their business. But they also brought to the table a more ruthless interest in the bottom line.

The brewing industry of 1972 had changed little since before the war – or indeed since Victorian times. With the exception of a few modern mass production facilities – one of which brewed the popular but ultimately notorious Watney's Red Barrel – most beer was produced in town- and city-centre breweries; some of them like Courage's Anchor brewery continuously since the 17th century. These were not only unsuited for modern production methods but were a nightmare to get lorries in and out of. Courage opened a modern brewery on a greenfield site outside Reading in 1978, and the other majors concentrated production on the less ancient of the breweries they had acquired. There were two sequels: a revolt by drinkers against 'industrialised' beers such as Red Barrel which led to the formation of the Campaign for Real Ale (Camra) in 1971 – and a raft of brewery closures. A typical year, 1972, brought the closures of Benskin's brewery at Watford (taken over by Ind Coope in 1957), Bentley's at Woodlesford (Whitbread, 1968), Case's at Barrow (Bass, 1959), Groves & Whitnall, Salford (Greenalls, 1961) and the Star Brewery in Cambridge (Tolly Cobbold, 1939). In London, Charrington's Mile End brewery closed in 1975, Whitbread's Chiswell Street headquarters brewery – now the company's conference centre – in 1976 and Watney's Whitechapel brewery in 1979. Standardisation was bringing a more productive beer industry, with higher output, fewer breweries, less variety … and fewer jobs.

Food processing, too, came under a greater concentration of ownership: in 1971 Nestlé added Libby's canned foods to Crosse & Blackwell (acquired in 1950) and Findus (1963). Cadbury reached out beyond its base in chocolate in 1969 to merge with the soft drink maker Schweppes to form Cadbury Schweppes, a globally competitive company. Concentration of ownership in the confectionery industry was resuming as the untrammelled growth of the decade after the end of rationing slowed: Rowntree and Mackintosh's merged in 1969 (though remaining a private company), Bassett's acquired Clarnico and Murray Mints and itself merged with Trebor, who had taken over Sharp's. But apart from removing duplication in management and distribution, these mergers did not impact on productive capacity: under Trebor Bassett, Trebor mints were still made in Chesterfield, Bassett's jelly babies and liquorice allsorts in Sheffield and Sharp's toffee in Maidstone.

Despite two miners' strikes and a fuel crisis, unemployment remained fairly static at around 4 per cent until recession started to bite in the spring of 1975. It was still below 6 per cent – despite an increasing shakeout in heavy industry – when Margaret Thatcher came to power. Industrial relations in manufacturing – the traditional hotspots apart – had remained relatively good during the 1974-9 Labour government, provided employers did not take radical steps to put their house in order. By 1978, however, the unions were at loggerheads with Denis Healey over his attempt to reduce inflationary pressures by keeping annual pay rises down to 5 per cent after several years of restraint.

Some major employers – notably Ford – bought peace by agreeing a larger settlement with the unions, the government responding by threatening sanctions against the company which it then failed to get through Parliament because of its lack of a majority. But the public sector and service industries endeavoured to hold the line, prompting a wave of strikes – first by tanker drivers – which the *Sun*, in a rare allusion to Shakespeare, christened the 'Winter of Discontent'. Long and bitter disputes followed, especially involving council manual workers, with rubbish piling up in Leicester Square and gravediggers in Liverpool refusing to bury the dead. But the impact on manufacturing, though noticeable, was limited; at its worst production was down by 10 per cent with 235,000 workers laid off. But given the starkness of the images on television every night, it was remarkable that the Conservatives' majority in the June 1979 election was only 43. It is also worth remembering that the no-confidence vote which Callaghan lost by a single vote to force that election, was triggered not by industrial unrest, but by the deadlocked referendum result on devolution for Scotland – with a majority voting 'Yes', but not the 40 per cent of the electorate stipulated in an amendment forced through by mischievous Labour backbenchers. But despite the sacking of 'Red Robbo' later that year , the disruption would continue; the pain of British manufacturing industry was only beginning.

4

SCORCHED EARTH AND LAISSEZ-FAIRE: 1979-97

If continuity of government with an at times abrasively free-enterprise stance guaranteed success, Britain's manufacturers should have thrived during the 18 years of Conservative rule under Margaret Thatcher and John Major. Yet the reverse was the case with the manufacturing industry suffering painful reductions in markets, capacity and employment; not only in the strife-ridden period before the defeat of the miners' strike in 1985 but in the years after, when most trade unions belatedly realised that there were more of their members' jobs to be saved by working with the grain rather than against it. By 1997, just 4,238,000 Britons were employed in manufacturing – less than two-thirds the number in 1979 – but the incidence of strikes had plummeted; union membership had slumped from 13.2 million to under 8 million as large factories where the unions could organise most easily, closed their gates. Meanwhile standards of management markedly improved; there were few complaints from trade unions now of day-to-day incompetence at boardroom level – though more over catastrophic strategic decisions – and the growing incidence of management buyouts from the mid-1980s also testified to this.

While Mrs Thatcher did not rail against 'lame ducks' as Edward Heath had done, she regarded heavy industry with suspicion, and nationalised industries with outright contempt; 'If you were any good, you'd be working somewhere else,' she told the top management of British Rail. Her passion was small business, though as the impressionist Mike Yarwood observed, 'under Mrs Thatcher, you start off with a large one…' Her government's economic and exchange rate policies may have brought down inflation, but they took no prisoners as export orders dried up and imports flooded in. Furthermore, as she put it bluntly two years into her premiership with the pips squeaking hard, she was not going to follow Heath in easing the pain: 'U-turn if you want to – the lady's not for turning.' And while a decade later Michael Heseltine held out hopes of active government support, his promise to 'intervene before breakfast, before lunch, before tea and before dinner' was not followed through, the main focus under Major going to creating jobs in the regions by attracting companies from abroad – some of whom would pull out even before their subsidised plants had opened.

While privatisation, when it came, made formerly state-owned businesses more efficient, the way it was carried out by advocates of laissez-faire further weakened a number of strategic industries. Moreover, while the late 1980s and mid-1990s were periods of growth after severe recessions, unemployment climbed steadily to over 3 million and proved difficult to reduce as the creation of new jobs – often through investment by overseas companies who had driven their British competitors to the wall – could not make up for the loss of large-scale industrial employment. The eclipse of big British firms in turn brought casualties among their suppliers, and a serious loss of skills, some of which could still have been of value to the economy. There were also, toward the end of the Thatcher/Major era, worrying signs from the boardroom that a number of chief executives no longer had any enthusiasm for manufacturing, and wanted an easier and better-rewarded life – preferably in the United States.

During these 18 years, the shift in the economy from manufacturing to service industries accelerated – again with the composition of the FT 30 index reflecting a structural change. In 1982 the cable makers BICC and the rubber-to-engineering group BTR joined the index, at the expense of the shipbuilder John Brown and the asbestos maker Turner & Newall. The next year Associated Dairies (Asda) and Trusthouse Forte replaced United Drapery Stores and Dunlop, as it got out of manufacturing tyres. The year 1984 – when 'Industrial' was dropped from the name of the index – saw Hanson Trust come in on taking over London Brick, and National Westminster Bank and the privatised British Telecom ease out Tube Investments and the paper maker Bowater, later renamed Rexam. Guinness replaced Distillers in 1986 after a controversial takeover that would land several prominent City figures in jail, and Royal Insurance and British Gas took the place of Imperial Tobacco and Vickers. In 1989 British Airways supplanted Plessey when the company was dismembered, and two years later Reuter joined the index when Hawker Siddeley was taken over by BTR. Vodafone replaced Forte in 1996 on the latter's takeover by Granada, and the following year Lloyds TSB and Granada replaced BICC – which was steadily losing critical mass – and Hanson, on its breakup. At the end of 1997 Scottish Power entered the index after the merger of Guinness and Grand Metropolitan to form Diageo.

Overall, a quarter of the membership of the index shifted from manufacturing to services. The arrival of Reuter and the TSB (Trustee Savings Bank), part of Lloyds TSB, was a reminder that the 1980s was the decade when the City discovered that concerns which had never been thought to have a marketable value could be floated, at a considerable profit to somebody. The wheel in the casino started to spin after the 'Big Bang' of 1986, when at the government's instigation the London Stock Exchange switched from the traditional 'open outcry' trading to a screen-based system, and at the same time regulation was relaxed. One broking firm after another was taken over by American, Swiss, German or Japanese concerns, investment banks poured in from all over the world and while the City's position as a global financial centre was greatly reinforced, it soon became evident that almost every sector of the British economy was up for grabs.

Mrs Thatcher came to power with the economy weak, inflation edging up again, and the unions squaring up for confrontation over feared job cuts and the legislation promised to curb their power. During the 1979 election campaign she had promised to honour the findings of an inquiry under Professor Hugh Clegg (grandfather of Nick) into pay comparability between the public and private sectors, which had been set up by Jim Callaghan to end the 'Winter of Discontent'. When Clegg reported that summer, he recommended substantial pay increases which heightened inflationary pressures still further. Workers in the nationalised industries pressed for similar treatment, and the crunch came at loss-making British Steel. BSC was struggling to reduce capacity against resistance from the unions in the face of a demand from the incoming government to break even that very year; when the Iron and Steel Trades Federation and the National Union of Blastfurnacemen tabled a 20 per cent claim, management saw no way they could meet it. A 2 per cent offer was rejected, then 6 per cent with strings attached, and on the second day of 1980 the two unions – making up 103,000 of BSC's 150,000 workforce – walked out. The strike spread quickly to private sector steelworks and lasted 14 weeks before an inquiry under the former Labour minister Harold Lever recommended a 16 per cent increase in return for an agreement on working practices and local productivity deals. Mrs Thatcher had warned the strikers they were in danger of pricing British-produced steel out of the market; the dispute opened the door to a flood of exports, and the settlement was followed by a drastic programme of plant closures, 20,000 workers losing their jobs by the end of the year. Consett in Co. Durham went first, with the loss of 3,400 jobs; not far behind came Corby (11,000), the Normanby Park works at Scunthorpe (4,100), the Welsh steel-making plants of Shotton, Ebbw Vale and East Moors (Cardiff) and the Parkgate works near Rotherham. On the plus side, the government picked up the tab for both the closures and new investment; the £4.5 billion the Conservatives put into the industry between 1980 and 1985 comfortably exceeding Labour's contribution over the previous five years. Specialised but strategically important facilities were hived off; the River Don Works at Sheffield, with its unique heavy press dating back to 1897, was merged with Firth Brown in 1983 to form Sheffield Forgemasters.

To drive a slimmed-down BSC – sheared of restrictive practices and union demarcation lines and with its sights set firmly on improving quality and boosting exports – Mrs Thatcher's Industry Secretary

Sir Keith Joseph chose Ian MacGregor, a determined 67-year-old Scot who had spent most of his working life in America, first in mining then with the bankers Lazard Freres. MacGregor was aware of the challenges he faced, having been a director of BL since its nationalisation. His appointment to succeed Sir Charles Villiers was controversial not only because he was not a steel man, but because it entailed a hefty 'transfer fee' to Lazard which infuriated Labour and the unions. Under MacGregor BSC turned the corner, regaining the confidence of motor manufacturers who had switched to imported steel because of its superior quality, securing orders from the Continent and exploiting a growing market at home for construction steel. MacGregor used his influence with Mrs Thatcher to promote a scheme for a bridge across the Channel – as opposed to a tunnel – which would have greatly benefited BSC as a producer of construction steel; with support at Westminster and in Paris it was only narrowly edged out by the Eurotunnel project. By 1984, BSC was achieving better labour productivity than most Continental steel makers, with a workforce more than halved since nationalisation 17 years before. But by then, Mrs Thatcher had moved MacGregor to the National Coal Board (NCB), whose problems in coping with a declining market posed an even greater challenge.

A combination of pent-up wage demands, high interest rates which forced up sterling, increasing import penetration and an attitude from government which convinced Sir Keith's critics that he had the 'de-industrialisation' of Britain on his agenda, made the early years of Mrs Thatcher's government tough for manufacturers large and small, before inflation fell back and the economy began to revive. During that period, the closures came thick and fast. Embarrassingly for the government, a number were of factories Mrs Thatcher had visited in the run-up to her election, such as the award-winning Rank Xerox plant in the Forest of Dean. At Christmas 1979, Airfix closed the Meccano factory in Liverpool – the historic home of Dinky Toys –

without giving statutory notice to the workers. David Mitchell MP, chairman of the Conservatives' Small Business Bureau, accused the management of behaving like 'a caricature of a 19th century mill owner'. Soon after, another once great toy company, Dunbee-Combex-Marx, filed for bankruptcy, and in 1982 Lesney – whose Matchbox Toys had been a world leader in the 1960s – went into receivership. In each case, the inability of a manufacturer of die-cast metal toys to hold their market in competition with cheaper and usually less high-quality fare from the Far East was a major factor.

While the Thatcher government maintained support for the surviving workers' co-operatives first backed by Tony Benn, all of them collapsed over the next four years – though Triumph motor-cycles would continue as a niche product, thanks to the Derbyshire housebuilder John Bloor. In 1980 the Singer sewing machine factory in Glasgow, which had once employed 16,000 workers and boasted its own railway station, ceased production – women no longer having the time to make their own clothes as they went out to work, mainly buying cheap imports instead. The same year the Bradford MP Ben Ford told the Commons that woollen mills in Yorkshire were closing at the rate of one a week. And a year later the unthinkable happened: ICI, at the core of the economy, reported a pre-tax loss, and cut its dividend for the first time since 1938.

Smaller factories were being forced to close, too, as the manufac-turing sector shrank, with skills as well as jobs again being lost. The industrial estate at Elmers End, in south London, was typical. In the 1960s well over 1,000 people were employed there, but the recession hit it hard. In 1980 the Randak Tannery, with over 100 employees, gave up the struggle. Twinlock, a major manufacturer of loose leaf accounting stationery, hit problems, folding in 1987. And crucially the Muirhead radio electronics factory – from where the radio pioneer Alexander Muirhead had sent the first signals from apparatus he was designing for the Royal Navy in 1909 – closed its doors. Muirhead, then a publicly quoted company, continued some specialised work at other sites in the area, taking over Hunting Avionics in 1994 as it morphed into Muirhead Aerospace and being snapped up by an

American high-tech firm in 1999. The site of the industrial estate now hosts a Tesco superstore.

One further closure caused as much embarrassment to members of the previous government as to Mrs Thatcher's: the De Lorean car plant in Belfast. This was the fruit of the American motor industry executive John DeLorean's self-imposed mission to build the DMC-12 – a revolutionary stainless steel sports car with gull-wing doors – for the US market. It was also a desperate attempt on the part of the government to reduce violence and sectarian tensions in Belfast by creating meaningful jobs for Catholics as well as the Protestants who had traditionally dominated Northern Ireland's skilled engineering sector. The aim was laudable, and when the British government capped an offer to DeLorean from Puerto Rico to take his plant overseas (the Irish Republic having decided not to bid) the deal was done. The plant at Dunmurry, sited between Protestant and Catholic estates, was built in 16 months, but engineering delays and cost overruns made it a further two years before the first DMC-12 rolled off the assembly line early in 1981. Most of the workers had never held any kind of job before, and serious quality issues developed; the company set up three centres in the United States to put these right and offered an exceptionally generous warranty. By 1982 production and quality were settling down, but costs were higher than DeLorean had bargained for, the high rate of sterling was taking its toll and sales proved sluggish at 6,000 a year, half the break-even point. A stock issue on Wall Street fell through and when DeLorean lobbied the British government for further cash he was told he would need to come up with matching funds. The plant's survival was hanging in the balance when, that October, DeLorean was arrested following an FBI 'sting' operation and charged with conspiring to smuggle $24 million worth of cocaine into the United States. By the time he was acquitted, the Dunmurry plant had become another Linwood, this time with 2,500 jobs and over $100 million lost. The DMC-12 went on to become a cult car – partly though its starring role in the 1985 movie *Back To The Future* – but DeLorean died in bankruptcy; ministers' profligacy with taxpayers' money was savaged by the Commons' Public Accounts Committee.

The DMC-12 had only been made roadworthy through the intervention of Lotus, whose engineering consultancy was contributing to model development across the industry from Talbot to General Motors. Lotus's founder Colin Chapman was also caught up in the financial allegations when De Lorean collapsed, and was still under a cloud when he died in 1982. Lotus was acquired by GM in 1986, for whom it developed a range of engines, then in 1993 was sold on to the Italian businessman Romano Artioli, who also owned Bugatti. On Artioli's bankruptcy in 1996, a majority share in Lotus was acquired by Proton of Malaysia.

The early Thatcher years were difficult for Britain's own motor industry, which saw production dip in 1982 to a historic low of 887,679 and a slow recovery to follow. That recovery coincided with a marked reduction in disruption through strikes, from 4,183 days lost per 1,000 workers in the 1970s – ten times the level for the economy as a whole – to 1,397 in the 1980s.

Changing its name simply to BL in 1979, British Leyland as ever faced the greatest challenges, and under Sir Michael Edwardes made some progress in meeting them. Edwardes concentrated volume car production on Longbridge and Cowley, the latter in particular adopting some Japanese methods of working; MG at Abingdon was among the plants to close. He halted work on a successor to the Mini in favour of launching the slightly larger Metro in 1980; this was followed after Edwardes's departure in 1982 by the Montego. Production of both was interrupted far less by industrial disputes than their predecessors' had been, yet while the Metro in particular acquired a following, neither became the heavy seller BL needed to maintain its place in the volume car market.

In a radical departure reflecting the pressure BL was under from Japanese imports and quality, the company in 1979 entered into an alliance with Honda, whose first fruit was the Triumph Acclaim, launched in 1980. Effectively a rebadged Honda Ballade, the Acclaim replaced the Triumph Dolomite and was intended to challenge the Ford Escort, the world's bestselling car for three years from 1982. Although those who drove it (myself included) liked the Acclaim, it did not appeal to traditional Triumph buyers, nor attract a wider market, and was outsold more than five to one by the Escort. When the Acclaim ceased production in 1984, the Triumph marque expired. Mrs Thatcher used BL's co-operation with Honda to press the company to abandon a new generation of engine and buy Japanese instead, but management stood firm. However, Honda exerted a steadily greater influence over BL's model range, supplying more of the critical components.

BL's car exports to the Continent nosedived from 179,000 to 70,000 between 1977 and 1984, as the company's footprint almost visibly shrank; the company also closed its Belgian plant, which had turned out more than 600,000 cars – most recently the Mini and Allegro – to strong local protests. Land Rover and Jaguar were among its few bright spots, and in response to government pressure to move BL into the private sector, Jaguar was floated as a stand-alone company in 1984. Yet even Land Rover was struggling to retain vital export markets; Kenya's game parks at this time were switching from the traditional British-made transport for their tourists to Suzuki 4x4s with customised bodywork made in Nairobi.

Ford remained Britain's most successful car maker in the early 1980s, the 'jelly mould' Sierra joining its range in 1983. The opening of a new Ford engine plant at Bridgend in 1980, which the Labour government had worked hard to secure, improved the outlook in the medium term. What threat there was came from Vauxhall, which after the launch in 1983 of the Nova – a rebadged Opel Corsa – moved level with BL and then overtook it. Peugeot in fourth place sold steadily, depending on the Ryton plant after the closure of Linwood in 1981.

BL's struggle to stay in the volume car business lessened its interest in its truck and bus division just as traditional markets in the developing world were eroding and a new product range was needed. BL's truck assembly plant at Bathgate and former Bristol bus factory closed, and its tractor making business was sold; yet the company's remaining British competitors were also feeling the pinch with Seddon Atkinson selling to ENASA of Spain in 1983.

Contrary to the fears of the trade union movement (and the hopes of some within it) Mrs Thatcher's government moved more slowly to tame the unions than Heath had done. Though the TUC wasted little time in calling a 'Day of Action' in protest – a patchily observed one-day strike – the 'step by step' approach adopted by Jim Prior, her first Employment Secretary, made reform hard to oppose by tackling first the most indefensible excesses of union power, such as secondary strikes and picketing. It was 1984 before Norman Tebbit made strike ballots compulsory, and 1988 before Norman Fowler outlawed the closed shop. These were not easy measures for the Labour Party to oppose given the climate of public opinion; moreover Labour was weakened (suffering its worst election defeat for half a century in 1983) with many of its moderates having quit on the formation of the SDP two years before.

Labour's loss of the middle ground, coupled with job losses and the realisation that the power of trade unionists to disrupt the economy was steadily being rolled back, emboldened the Left in the party and the unions. It led to the adoption in 1983 of a manifesto memorably termed by Gerald Kaufman 'the longest suicide note in history', and to militant-led unions looking for an issue around which they could take on the government.

The critical dispute was not in manufacturing industry, but would have a profound effect on it. The National Coal Board, now with Ian MacGregor at the helm, was pushing through pit closures as demand for coal fell – not least from heavy industry. Strikes over closures and pay had been averted in 1981 and 1982 – the former by a tactical government retreat and the latter when members of the National Union of Mineworkers (NUM) accepted a 5.2 per cent offer against their leaders' recommendation to strike. In the meantime the NCB and the electricity industry, its largest customer, had built up stockpiles.

None of this fazed Arthur Scargill, the Bonaparte-like Marxist president of the NUM, whose deployment of flying pickets to close down other energy producers had wrong-footed Heath's government in 1972, and who had been the driving force behind the strike of 1974 that effectively brought Heath down. He saw this as the miners' final chance to coerce a government into guaranteeing their jobs, regardless of the demand for coal, and with the backing of the NUM's executive brought his members out on strike in March 1984; the trigger was the NCB's announcement of an accelerated pit closure plan.

Unfortunately for the Yorkshire-based Scargill, miners in less militant coalfields resented being told what to do by the union's hard-line executive, when its rulebook stipulated that a national strike could not be called without a ballot. Most miners in productive Nottinghamshire and some smaller fringe coalfields carried on working despite efforts by Scargill's pickets to intimidate them. Attempts to spread the strike to the docks, the electricity and steel industries failed as other unions thought better of putting their own members' jobs at risk, particularly as stockpiling and other preparations meant that the strike had far less impact on industrial output than had those of 1972 and 1974.

If the success of Scargill and his flying pickets in closing the coke depot at Saltley, Birmingham, in 1972 was a turning point in the miners' favour, the 'Battle of Orgreave' in July 1984, when police prevented violent pickets shutting down a BSC coking plant near Sheffield, was decisive in preventing the strike spreading. Industry muddled through, relying on coal from the working pits whose number gradually increased and on imports; and after a year that split communities and inflicted great suffering on the miners and their families, the NUM went back to work on MacGregor's terms. The irony was that had Scargill swallowed his arrogance and called a ballot, he would probably have won it and the government would have had little choice but to capitulate. As it was, the pit closures resumed, not only devastating coalfield communities but dealing a serious blow to Britain's sophisticated mining engineering and supply industries.

If the defeat of the miners' strike brutally returned the initiative from the unions to government, two confrontations in the printing industry effectively signalled the end of workers' ability to block change in manufacturing. By the mid-1980s the industry was operating in two distinct halves: a modern jobbing and periodical printing industry, and a Fleet Street where the printers of the National

Graphical Association (NGA) and their semi-skilled counterparts in the National Society of Operative Printers and Assistants (Natsopa) had blocked any advance on 19th-century printing methods. Vast armies of casuals, many with other jobs outside Fleet Street, were paid for doing little work or none at all, operating (until an Inland Revenue crackdown in the 1970s) under assumed names like Donald Duck to avoid paying tax and giving a cut to the local union bosses who decided who should take part in the racket. Management at the more profitable newspapers – notably the *Daily Express* – connived at these practices in the hope that the cost would put less well resourced competitors out of business – as happened with the *News Chronicle* in 1960. Any attempt to modernise was resisted, any new labour-saving equipment was 'blacked' unless an equal number of non-jobs was created and night after night, Fleet Street was brought to a halt by wildcat strikes. When pickets from Natsopa turned up outside the *Express* one evening in 1975, management gave them £15 a head to go next door and picket the *Telegraph* – which lost a night's production.

The process of producing newspapers, not just in Fleet Street but in those provincial centres where the NGA and Natsopa held sway, was archaic. Reporters typed their copy, which after subediting was retyped by NGA members into 'hot metal' on linotype machines – fitted with non-QWERTY keyboards as a deterrent to rule out non-members and women (the top line ran ETAOIN). Trays of type were fitted with tweezers into a metal frame constituting the page – and photographic plates added after an etching process dating from Victorian times – then a papier-mâché impression was made of the page, from which a semi-circular metal plate was cast. Multiples of four of these were bolted onto the rollers of the presses, which then started to roll.

Since the 1960s newspapers around the world had been adopting new techniques giving much better reproduction and employing far less labour. Automation had revolutionised the entire process; the *Baltimore Sun*'s newsprint warehouse needed three people to operate it, the *Daily Telegraph*'s 160. But while the rest of British manufacturing had at least begun to modernise, Fleet Street and many major provincial papers reached the 1980s with any kind of change blocked by the unions. By then, too, desktop computers were starting to render the typewriter obsolete, and systems had been devised in the United States enabling reporters to write their copy straight into the page, eliminating several tiers of production worker. This prospect made the Fleet Street unions even more intransigent.

The logjam was broken by the arrival of impatient new proprietors who shared Mrs Thatcher's view that management was entitled to manage. The first to take the print unions on was Eddy Shah, the owner of six local papers in the North-West. His ending of the National Graphical Association's closed shop on the *Stockport Messenger* in 1983, to produce it with the latest technology and far fewer workers, was met with a seven-month strike and violent picketing; but Shah emerged the winner. He went on to announce a cheaply produced all-colour daily, which duly appeared as *Today*. Shah's breakthrough led three senior *Daily Telegraph* journalists, led by the city editor Andreas Whittam Smith, to start *The Independent*, the first new quality daily for 131 years, printed – like *Today* – not on the premises but on the spare capacity of provincial evening papers. Crucial to this was electronic transmission of the page make-up – something the *Scottish Daily Express* had planned for an Inverness edition in the early 1970s only to be thwarted by the unions who insisted on every process being gone through again from scratch.

It was Rupert Murdoch who broke the unions in Fleet Street. He had built a power base with the hugely successful *Sun* and *News of the World*, produced by traditional methods, then in 1981 acquired *The Times*, weakened by a dispute that had closed it for months. He became incensed at the anarchy that disrupted the production of his titles, and cannily appointed Reg Brady, one of the most disruptive of his chapel officials, to a post in management. Meanwhile, under the guise of starting a new evening paper, he built a new printing plant at Wapping, just downstream from the Tower of London.

In January 1986 Murdoch transferred production of his papers to Wapping overnight, taking with him only the personnel he needed. Six thousand print workers and clerical staff, plus some 'refusenik' journalists, refused to move or were locked out, and the print unions declared an official strike. Day after day the staffs of the papers forced their way in through a phalanx of abusive and at times violent pickets, but the papers kept coming out and after a year in which more than 400 police officers were injured and 1,000 pickets arrested, the strike was called off. Britain's national newspapers were now free to modernise, and the message went out to unions throughout manufacturing that if they tried to block progress, they would be swept aside.

Crucial to Murdoch's success in breaking the print unions was a single-union agreement for Wapping which he negotiated with the electricians' union, the EEPTU. The electricians – distrusted by hardliners in the Trades Union Congress because they had humiliatingly booted out a corrupt Communist leadership – were the first union to break with the rule of 'one craft, one union'; in 1987 they were expelled from the TUC for concluding single-union deals with Thorn EMI and two newly-arrived Japanese electronics companies. But the worm was starting to turn as an increasing number of pragmatic, university-educated senior union officials realised that there were better ways of protecting their members' future than encouraging them to strike themselves out of a job.

Recession in the early 1980s, the plant closures that followed and the defeat of the miners had reduced industrial workers' appetite for militancy; it was no accident that in the mid-1980s the Socialist Workers' Party instead started infiltrating its troublemakers into public services like the NHS and London Underground, where they would wreak havoc for decades. The market for the skills of redundant industrial workers was shrinking; such skill shortages as existed were in the high-tech enclave of the Thames Valley. Norman Tebbit's recollection of how his father had 'got on his bike' to find a job, reminded redundant workers that they faced a stark choice between a lifetime on the dole while they waited for their old jobs to come back, or a search for a second career. As more and more chose the latter – not necessarily with enthusiasm – their unions realised that if they too did not change, their mass memberships would evaporate.

Between 1979 and 1997 trade union membership almost halved,

from 13.2 million to 7.8 million, a trend reflected in mergers between unions: 475 when Mrs Thatcher came to power, 252 when John Major departed. Not all of these mergers brought together workers in the same industry in a way that would end old rivalries; rather than form common cause with the engineers they were working alongside in the shipbuilding industry, the Boilermakers preferred to merge with the General & Municipal Workers. But as the unions' membership and influence declined (most rapidly in manufacturing), the less hidebound and militant – starting with the Amalgamated Engineering Union – followed the electricians' lead in wooing employers with single-union agreements guaranteeing discipline on the shop floor. One of the first concluded by the AEU was with Nissan, a key factor in securing its investment in the North-East. Next came Ford, who were ready to set up a high-tech component plant in Dundee creating 450 jobs, with a further 500 to follow if performance targets were met. One of the architects of the deal, concluded in 1987, was Jimmy Airlie, co-leader of the UCS work-in 15 years previously. Attracting the plant to Dundee was a coup for the government, who had worked hard to secure it, and offered hope in an area of industrial decline. But 11 other unions in Ford's negotiating machinery, led by the T&G, were incensed at being shut out of the process and protested with such vigour that Ford – fearing disruption at other plants – took the jobs abroad. It was also Dundee that witnessed the final twitch of suicidal confrontation by shop stewards – ironically from the AEU – when Timex closed its electronics plant in 1993 after 47 years following a six-month strike marred by serious picket-line violence. During the 1980s the plant, where the first Sinclair home computer was produced, had consistently broken production records despite almost continuous disruption.

The word 'privatisation' did not exist when Margaret Thatcher came to power, committed to a radical liberalisation of the economy. There were commitments to denationalise particular companies in state hands, such as the global telecoms provider Cable & Wireless, and more generally to roll back the boundaries of the State, but no strategy for privatisation as such. That only developed over her first and second terms in office; a desire to get loss-making state industries off the books and expose them to competition, the appeal of popular share ownership (in the wake of the success of 'right to buy' for council house tenants) and the need to generate income for the Treasury, made as strong a practical as an ideological case for a sell-off. Ironically, this coincided with a shift in share ownership generally away from individuals to institutions like insurance companies and pension funds, whose stake rose overall from 43 per cent in 1975 to 61 per cent by 1990; between 1979 and 2009 the proportion of shares held by private individuals slumped from 50 per cent to 8 per cent.

To start with, it was left to individual ministers to decide which, if any, of the concerns they were responsible for could and should be sold off. Only after the 1983 election was the process driven forward in a co-ordinated way, provoking Harold Macmillan (belatedly ennobled as the Earl of Stockton) to speak disparagingly of 'selling off the family silver'. A substantial part of the private sector was denationalised under Mrs Thatcher, but most of the concerns in question were public services or utilities: British Telecom, British Gas, the electricity supply and distribution industries, Britoil, British Airways, the British Airports Authority, the National Bus Company, the water industry and – under Major in the 1990s – British Coal and the railways. Yet even these privatisations not only deprived subsequent governments of control over energy supply but also had a direct impact on manufacturing industry, largely through the abandonment of centralised procurement or arrangements with a single supplier as the market opened up for everything from buses to telecoms equipment. Where this happened, established British manufacturers from Leyland to Plessey were the sufferers.

The public sector since the late 1970s had also included a portfolio of strategic manufacturing industries; as privatisation gathered pace, these too were disposed of, either through a stock market flotation or by a trade sale. As early as 1981 the government disposed of its 51 per cent stake in British Aerospace (the rest went in 1985, the government retaining a 'golden share' which would prove largely academic as the company's stock was increasingly held in the United States). In 1982 shares for the medical diagnostics company Amersham International were so heavily oversubscribed that ministers came under fire for letting it go on the cheap (it thrived in the private sector but eventually sold itself to America's GE Healthcare). British Shipbuilders was privatised in 1983, the surviving yards being sold off piecemeal in a race to get the merchant shipbuilding industry out of the public sector before its total collapse. The government's controlling interest in Inmos was sold to Thorn EMI in 1984 for £192 million, less than the taxpayer had invested; Rolls-Royce was floated in 1987, and the next year British Steel; Rover (as the car making side of BL had now become) was handed to BAe in 1988, who were paid a controversial 'sweetener' to take it on. In 1989, Short Brothers was sold to Bombardier of Canada, again with a substantial 'dowry' to cover future losses and capital investment, in preference to bids from GEC and Fokker. And that same year British Rail handed over its surviving major workshops at Crewe, Derby and York to a management buyout, Trafalgar House and the Swiss-Swedish multinational Asea Brown Boveri (ABB) respectively. (The giant Swindon works, which between the wars had employed 14,000 people, closed its doors in 1986). All these major contributors to British manufacturing were now exposed – in some cases not before time – to the chill forces of the market.

British Aerospace was in good shape when it was privatised, though it had done little to rationalise its sprawling empire. Britain had rejoined the Airbus consortium in 1979, which gave the company extra clout. (This was not always used: it was Germany, not Britain, that in 1989 secured an Airbus production line to offset the growing global influence of Toulouse's Blagnac airport and provide valuable jobs for Hamburg.) The A320 was well into development, and would make its first flight in 1987; the Thatcher government provided launch aid both for this airliner and the A330/340 – though Lord King, the autocratic chairman of British Airways as it was privatised, weakened Britain's position within Airbus by steadfastly ordering Boeings. Development work was under way with MBB and Dassault (who would pull out when not awarded design leadership) on the Eurofighter – consistently a project championed by BAe as benefiting the national economic interest rather than a 'must-have' for the RAF. The BAe 146 short-haul turbofan airliner, first promoted by Hawker Siddeley in 1973, had re-engaged management and was heading for its first flight in 1983 after the Thatcher government underwrote the project. By 2003 when production ceased, 387 models – latterly branded the Avro-RJ – would be sold, helping to confirm BAe's position as Britain's largest exporter. Put together at no fewer than five BAe sites, with other components bought in from the US and Sweden and with American engines, it was the last commercial airliner that could claim to be British-made.

BAe's commercial prospects were guaranteed in 1985 with the conclusion of the Al Yamamah ('The Dove') contract with Saudi Arabia, which over the next 20 years would earn the company £43 billion and remains by far its most lucrative income stream; the UK's largest ever export deal, it has provided jobs for over 4,000 Britons in Saudi Arabia and many more at home. The rationale behind it was Saudi Arabia's need for advanced jet aircraft and defence systems from a friendly power, and the inability of America to supply them consistently because of blocking tactics by pro-Israeli elements in Congress. British manufacturers had been supplying fighters to Saudi Arabia since 1965, and in 1973 an inter-governmental agreement worth £1 billion was concluded specifying BAC as the contractor for all parts of its defence system.

The full details of Al Yamamah have never been made public, and there were suspicions of murky dealings from the start. But the sheer scale of what BAe was to provide was on the record: under the 1985 agreement the Saudis were to purchase 72 Tornados, 30 Hawk trainers and 30 Pilatus trainers – all with full in-service support – plus a range of weapons, radar, spares and a pilot training programme. Under further agreements concluded in 1988 and since, more Tornados, Hawks and Pilatus plus specialised naval vessels have been supplied, and in 2006 the Saudis contracted to buy 72 Eurofighter Typhoons.

It was also in 1985 that the Eurofighter project began to gain critical mass. BAe and Germany's DASA were each given a 33 per cent share of production work, Aeritalia 21 per cent and CASA of Spain 13 per cent. The next year Eurofighter Jagdflugzeug GmbH was formed in Munich to manage development of the project, with a parallel alliance of engine manufacturers including Rolls-Royce. The main disagreement was over which radar system to adopt: Britain, Italy and Spain wanted one developed by Ferranti, but Germany had to be negotiated out of pressing for a system from Hughes, AEG and GEC-Marconi.

BAe's prototype EAP, on which the Eurofighter would be based, made its first flight in 1986. Two years later the House of Commons was told that the project would cost Britain about £7 billion; by 2011 the National Audit Office would estimate the actual cost at £37 billion. The German government saw this coming, and – just as the fall of the Berlin Wall raised doubts over the relevance of a fighter designed for Cold War dogfights over western Europe – voiced increasing misgivings; it took all the diplomacy of the British government to stop them pulling out in 1992. Germany continued to play hard ball, its defence minister Volker Rühe – the Eurofighter's most implacable critic – refusing in 1995 even to discuss with his counterpart Michael Portillo his refusal to contemplate a reduction in his company's share of the manufacturing to match the reduction in its order from 250 aircraft to 140.

Having successfully floated BAe into the private sector, there was a certain synergy about its taking on most of the Royal Ordnance factories that produced much of the weaponry and ammunition for Britain's armed forces. Archaically equipped, highly inefficient but in some cases essential to the national defence, the 12 factories still open, employing 19,000 staff, were in desperate need of reorganisation and a rethink of their future; but several of the sites – especially those at Enfield and Waltham Abbey which had already closed – were coveted by housebuilders. It made sense for BAe to take the factories over, incorporate those with a future into its own structure and close the rest. However, there was criticism that the terms on which BAe acquired the business in 1987 were a poor deal for the taxpayer; the company paid £190 million, then received £450 million from the developers. BAe did rationalise Royal Ordnance over the following 20 years, after which the title was dropped. The cutbacks involved Britain giving up the ability to manufacture some essential items itself; this would lead to embarrassment during the 1991 Gulf War when Belgium – despite being a member of both Nato and the UN, which were backing the operation – refused to supply ammunition needed by the British army.

One Royal Ordnance factory at Leeds was taken over by Vickers, which, with a second Vickers plant at Newcastle, would be awarded the contract to build the Challenger 2 tank in 1993. Vickers was rebuilding over this period, gaining then divesting itself of shipyards, and acquiring the automotive engineers Cosworth in 1990.

A second trade sale of a state-owned industry to BAe was harder to rationalise: that of Rover, the renamed car-making part of BL, to the aerospace company in 1988. The only logical explanation was that no other British company would take it on, but the government's payment to BAe of an undeclared £38 million 'dowry' raised more questions than it answered. In the event, Rover's need for capital for new models starved BAe of funds it needed to take forward its core business.

Against this background, stand-alone aircraft production by BAe was increasingly playing second fiddle to collaborative projects, or even outright transfer of the initiative. The Harrier might not be in its first flush of youth, but its role in recapturing the Falklands in 1982 won it many admirers. When, however, an improved and updated Harrier appeared in 1985, Boeing took the role of lead manufacturer. How this came about has never been fully explained; hitherto the US derivative of the Harrier had been produced by McDonnell-Douglas, which did not merge with Boeing for a further decade, and did so under licence from BAe. Another collaborative project involving BAe would have a very long lead time: at the 1990 Farnborough Air Show the Airbus consortium announced the development of what would become the A380 super-jumbo. It would be the last time so major an aerospace story was broken at Farnborough rather than the 'salon' at Le Bourget which was the showcase for France's, and increasingly Europe's, plane-making industry. Britain's, as embodied in BAe, was now effectively out of the business of developing its own new aircraft.

If the leadership of BAe imagined that by broadening the company from a plane maker into a conglomerate they were insulating it against shocks, they were mistaken. Recession at home had cut Rover's sales by a fifth – putting the car maker firmly into the red – and hit the market for new homes just as BAe's property wing Arlington Securities was expected to deliver profits. At the same time civil aircraft orders were hit by a global economic slowdown. In the summer of 1991 the company's share price fell below 100p for the first time, and days after BAe issued a profits warning a £432 rights issue came unstuck. That September directors led by the chief executive, Dick Evans, unceremoniously ousted BAe's chairman Professor Roland Smith, a marketing man whose ability to promote himself had attracted high offices ranging from the chair of Manchester United to the chancellorship of Manchester's technological university UMIST and a place on the court of the Bank of England.

Radical change was inevitable. With its weakened finances, even BAe was a potential takeover target, and GEC came close to acquiring the company; the fortunes of three entire sectors of British industry – aerospace, motor manufacture and heavy electrics – would have been very different had it done so. As it was, Evans kept BAe independent, wrote off £1 billion of assets (at the time the largest corporate write-off in British history), closed the historic former De Havilland plant at Hatfield that had produced the Comet, slashed its workforce of 127,000 by 47 per cent and began selling off 'non-core' businesses. [When London City Airport opened in 1987, the only aircraft able to serve it at first was the De Havilland Dash 7, produced by the Canadian subsidiary of the once-pioneering British company; with an even greater irony, DH Canada had just been sold by the Canadian government to Boeing, which halted production of the Dash 7]. De Havilland is now owned by Bombardier.

Some of the disposals – Rover (to BMW in 1994), Arlington

Securities and BAe's 30 per cent stake in Orange – made obvious sense, but out with the bathwater went a number of babies. BAe Corporate Jets was sold to Raytheon and British Aerospace Space Systems to Matra Marconi. With the heaviest job cuts – 40,000 – in BAe's regional aircraft division which had delivered the 146, the short-haul airliner market was forfeited to competitors in Canada and Brazil, and to the Franco-Italian ATR consortium (which BAe passed up the chance to join) which a decade later would be the only regional airliner builder exclusively producing turboprops. Yet with the Dutch plane maker Fokker going bankrupt in 1996, this market at the time did not seem strong.

BAe emerged from these changes with a business that derived three quarters of its revenue stream from military aircraft, and much of the rest from missiles. And while it was refocusing on its defence business (or losing critical mass, in the view of some) its American competitors were merging: Lockheed with Martin Marietta in 1995 – BAe signing up with the merged company in 1997 to develop the Joint Strike Fighter – and Boeing with McDonnell Douglas.

By contrast, Rolls-Royce prospered both prior to and after its return to the private sector in 1987. Its profitability and global reach had grown as it offered engines for a steadily wider range of civil aircraft, powering 17 different airliners against General Electric's 14 and Pratt & Whitney's ten. The company did betray a lack of confidence by briefly agreeing with GE in the mid-1980s that each should develop engines for certain types of aircraft, but after pulling out of that arrangement it proved an ever more successful global competitor; by 1998 it was supplying 35 per cent of military engine orders worldwide. Rolls-Royce did attempt to diversify when in 1988 it took over Northern Engineering Industries (NEI), a combine of heavy engineering companies in the power sector which had united to compete for a shrinking market. Here too, recession led to divestiture with NEI's surviving constituents sold off in the 1990s, most notably Reyrolle Parsons to Siemens. There was an abortive partnership with BMW to produce engines for regional and corporate jets (which Rolls-Royce carried forward as Rolls-Royce Deutschland) and the acquisition in 1994 of the Allison Engine Company, an American gas turbine maker which until not long before had been a subsidiary of GE. Allison had to be managed at arm's length because of the classified nature of its work for the Pentagon. However, during this period Rolls-Royce never lost sight of its core business, and in 1996 was rewarded with Airbus specifying its Trent 900 as engine of choice for the A380.

The state-owned sector of the steel industry, which in its entirety employed 154,000 people in the late 1980s, had gone through its upheavals in advance of privatisation. Productivity was edging ahead of Continental levels by the mid-1980s as demand for construction steel for the Humber Bridge, Canary Wharf and major North Sea developments – including, after the disaster of 1988, the rebuilding of the Piper Alpha platform – kept its plants busy. In 1989, the year after British Steel was floated on the Stock Exchange, the company – now run by a career steelman, Sir Robert 'Black Bob' Scholey – reported a pre-tax profit of £733 million. Then recession again reduced the demand for steel, Ravenscraig finally running out of road in 1992; its demise caused a chain reaction of other plant and business closures in Lanarkshire and beyond, and left the largest brownfield site in Europe which would stand vacant for two decades. Another casualty was the mile-long former Steel Peech & Tozer plant at Templeborough, Rotherham, which closed in 1993. Smaller and older specialist plants in both BSC and the private sector also went under in the bleak climate of the early 1990s – as memorably recorded in *The Full Monty*, the uncannily well observed 1997 movie about redundant Sheffield steelworkers who become male strippers, which would have swept the Oscars had it not been up against *Titanic*.

British Steel returned to profit in 1994, and continued to invest in greater efficiency and modern production methods in its major plants. Ministers' greatest concern became the continued subsidies paid by Continental governments to maintain excess capacity in their steel industries, enabling those producers to undercut the more efficient BSC on price. By 1997 BSC ranked second in Europe, its 17 million tonnes of output comparing with 17.5 million for Thyssen

Krupp, 16.1 million for France's Usinor, 14.8 for Italy's Riva and 12.5 from Luxembourg's Arbed.

By contrast, there was nothing orderly about the privatisation of British Shipbuilders. During the Thatcher government's first term BS's chairman Robert Atkinson, whose roots were in engineering, worked to achieve a leaner industry producing both naval and merchant ships, with break-even set for 1984 as orders picked up a little. Jobs were lost steadily, workers in the yards disappointing national union leaders with their acceptance of change – save for a six-month sit-in by Cammell Laird workers on a gas accommodation rig in 1984 that led to 37 men being sent to prison. After her re-election in 1983, however, Mrs Thatcher became impatient. She replaced Atkinson with Graham Day, the Labour government's original choice who had quit in disgust six years before as Conservative MPs fought nationalisation line by line, with the remit of getting shipbuilding out of the private sector.

Day began by selling the warship yards: Vickers (with Cammell Laird as a subsidiary) to a management buyout in 1986, followed swiftly by a stock market flotation as VSEL (Vickers Shipbuilding & Engineering Ltd) and eventual acquisition by GEC; Vosper Thornycroft and Yarrow to GEC in 1985/6; and Swan Hunter to a management buyout. Swan Hunter closed two of its three remaining yards, and in 1993 called in the receivers after Kvaerner at Govan beat it to the contract to build HMS *Ocean*; bought out of receivership by Jaap Kroese, a Dutch entrepreneur, Swan Hunter confined itself to repairs and conversions. Meanwhile the former Rosyth naval dockyard was sold by the MoD in 1996 to a resurgent Babcock, enabling it to service warships in the short term but also paving the way for it to build entire aircraft carriers. The warship yards acquired by GEC would start to adopt new techniques that might have saved their merchant counterparts; the advent of computerised design (CAD) which replaced the drawing office immediately made a small niche shipbuilder like VT more competitive. Day himself won global orders for BS with a new naval support ship.

The merchant yards were now in a desperate plight, despite the Confederation of Shipbuilding and Engineering Unions having finally agreed in 1983 to end the 'craft control' that had bedevilled efforts to modernise working practices. It took a political furore and a hefty government grant to persuade Trafalgar House, owners of Cunard, to have the replacement for their container ship *Atlantic Conveyor* (sunk in the Falklands War) built by Swan Hunter rather than in Japan. Global demand was also weak: by 1986 just 9 million tons of shipping was on order worldwide, 2 per cent from British yards. In this climate, privatisation yard by yard was a virtual death sentence. Scott Lithgow was sold to Trafalgar House in 1984; it closed nine years later. The Ailsa Yard at Troon was bought by Perth Corporation, producing small ferries until 2000, while Ferguson's Port Glasgow yard passed through various ownerships as it continued to build larger roll-on, roll-off vessels. Harland & Wolff was sold to Fred Olsen in 1989, continuing to construct offshore vessels and rigs. Brooke Marine of Lowestoft went to a management buyout, but ceased trading in 1992. Govan Shipbuilders was sold to Kvaerner – under whom it won new business, weathering a final strike over new working conditions in 1991 – then later on to GEC. Cammell Laird finished its final ship, HMS *Unicorn* (now HMS *Windsor*) in 1993 and closed, its main yard at Birkenhead reopening two years later for ship repairs. And North East Shipbuilders (including Austin & Pickersgill, which was still producing SD14s) closed when it ran out of orders in 1988; the final merchant vessel launched on Wearside was a ferry.

Then there was the privatisation of BL, at a point when Britain's volume car industry was at a very low ebb, with employment in the industry as a whole down to 264,000 in 1988. Total car production was back over the 1 million mark, but many – if not most – British drivers now preferred a foreign-built car and by 1990 Britain's trade deficit in cars and components would reach a staggering £4.18 billion.

Ford of England now had its strategy set in Cologne; Vauxhall's increasingly popular cars – it doubled its market share between 1980 and 1986 – had so little British content that the government lodged a formal complaint, and the former Rootes plant at Ryton was unashamedly building Peugeots. Motor industry R&D in Britain was by now largely confined to Land Rover, Ford (in ever closer partnership with Germany), Jaguar – which had doubled productivity after heavy losses and would be acquired by Ford in 1990 – some niche areas within BL and the small specialist manufacturers. Already under pressure from Japanese imports, Britain's home grown car makers now had to face the challenge on their home turf; in 1986 Nissan took the momentous step for the industry of opening its own plant near Sunderland, and before long Toyota (Derby) and Honda (Swindon) followed suit. The Nissan deal was a triumph for Mrs Thatcher; she could see the need for a progressive car manufacturer to keep Britain's own producers up to scratch, and out-lobbied Continental countries keen to accommodate the plant, securing it in the face of opposition not only from the Japanese trade unions but key figures in the company's own hierarchy. By the time Sunderland's last shipyard closed, the first of 4,500 local workers were proudly producing Japanese-designed cars, largely for export. Andreas Whittam Smith, the *Daily Telegraph*'s city editor who was soon to launch the *Independent,* castigated 'the nonsense of the British government simultaneously handing out £1,000 million to British Leyland in order to maintain it in business and giving a major rival in the shape of Nissan perhaps £100 million in grants because it puts its new plant in a development area'. But he conceded that the arrival of Nissan might teach British management the techniques to keep the likes of BL afloat.

How to get BL into the private sector without too much collateral damage was a puzzle for Conservative ministers and their Whitehall advisers. They were anxious to get the loss-making combine off the government's books, but faced the difficulty that while parts of it were profitable and a few even world-beating, the whole was weighted down financially by the demands of the volume car-making operation, despite its improving efficiency. There was a temptation to dispose of the most profitable parts of the business separately; when Paul Channon took over as Trade & Industry Secretary after Michael Heseltine's resignation over Westland, the first paper in his in-tray detailed a possible sale of Land Rover to Ford which he vetoed on political grounds. Weeks later, GM made an offer for Leyland Vehicles which one civil servant described as 'rape': it involved closing the Scammell plant at Watford, the Freight Rover van factory in Coventry, and GM's Bedford truck plant at Dunstable, reducing operations at the core Leyland plant and bringing in more components from Germany. Nevertheless there was encouragement in Whitehall for a deal – originally canvassed by Norman Tebbit in 1984 – that would have got the by now loss-making truck business off BL's hands, and also Land Rover which was suffering from Japanese competition. Slightly less draconian terms were negotiated with Detroit, but this deal too foundered on public hostility to the sale of Land Rover.

Later in 1986, BL itself took an important strategic decision: to rename the part of the business based on Longbridge and Cowley the Rover Group, with Graham Day as chairman, and find buyers for the rest. Rover's model range was by then essentially inspired by Honda, and its strategy was also in part controlled from Japan; it was barred from exporting the Rover 600 to the United States because it would undermine sales of the Honda Accord. Land Rover management proposed a buyout of its business; it was rejected with that part of the business being integrated with Rover, the launch of the Land Rover Discovery in 1989 being a rare success for the group.

By then British Aerospace had been persuaded to take on Rover, a move which guaranteed the car maker's survival in the short term at a cost to BAe's balance sheet that by 1991 was causing it to look for a buyer – having considered, then rejected, closing both Rover's plants at Cowley. Yet as late as 1993 Rover – with a model range essentially inspired by Honda, its reputation for poor quality behind it and workers rising to the management's challenge to meet the production standards of its Japanese competitors – was Britain's largest car producer, with 356,280 vehicles rolling off its production lines, comfortably ahead of Ford's 271,793 and Nissan's 246,281. However the competition from imports from an increasing range of Asian countries was intensifying all the time – reaching a peak in 1995 when Korea's Daewoo began the direct marketing of its cars, without establishing a chain of dealerships.

All the attention given to keeping Rover competitive led to ministers, civil servants and senior BL management taking their eyes off the ball as one of the great tragedies for British industry unfolded in the mid to late 1980s: the near collapse of the once mighty truck and bus building industry. One cannot imagine the Department of Trade and Industry (DTI) of the early 2000s, with its innovation and growth teams for key sectors, failing to notice what was going on and initiate some steps to prevent it. But in the 1980s intervention was a dirty word and the DTI's political head of the day, Lord Young, had set himself the overriding task of eliminating subsidies to nationalised industries and paying the money instead to advertising agencies to glorify the pro-enterprise stance of his department. If one had to select a figure for the 1980s to compare with Sir Bernard Docker and 'Red Robbo' in earlier decades, one would have a tough choice between Mrs Thatcher herself and Lord Young, the accountant of whom she memorably said: 'Other people bring me problems. David brings me solutions.' When BAe was persuaded to take on Rover, Young wrote that disposal of the company 'as a whole to a politically acceptable purchaser seems too good to be true.' And it was.

Bus manufacturing was undermined by a double whammy of government-inspired privatisation and deregulation (neither of them, in fairness, the work of Lord Young), on top of the phasing out, in the late 1970s, of the New Bus Grant from government. Privatisation of the constituent parts of the National Bus Company from 1986 cut off a guaranteed stream of orders for Leyland as companies were freed either to look elsewhere or – more often – cut costs by not placing new orders. Deregulation of all bus services outside London in 1985, while intended to free up the market for new entrants, also led to a boom in second-hand bus sales at the expense of new orders. Stagecoach, who would become one of the most successful of the private sector 'bus buccaneers', began its operations in Perth with old Routemasters from London. Other new entrants opted for smaller and cheaper 'midibuses' instead of the conventional single-decker

– creating a market for Optare, a combination of a Mercedes chassis and bodywork from the Leeds factory of C H Roe, ironically a discarded constituent of British Leyland.

The final straw for Britain's traditional bus makers was the franchising-out from 1988 of London Transport bus services, which ended the capital's policy of maintaining a standardised fleet designed specifically to operate in London conditions. In latter years London, in common with some other cities, had transferred its loyalty from Leyland (and its Daimler subsidiary) to the Metrobus, built in Birmingham by Metro-Cammell and Weymann. However, deregulation and franchising orders for the Metrobus dried up with privatisation and Metro-Cammell went out of business, some of its bus patents passing to Optare.

As privatisation and deregulation approached, orders for new buses collapsed and Leyland Bus – as it had been relaunched in 1981 – was left high and dry. By 1984 the Olympian was Leyland's only double-deck chassis left in production, with just 500 chassis produced; only 44 of the Leyland Nationals turned out at Workington that year were registered for the home market and sales of its up-market successor the Tiger stalled. In three years, Leyland Bus lost £80 million.

At the start of 1987, Leyland Bus management took over the company, but after an initial flurry of orders its fortunes declined; that year, just 177 new double-deckers were registered to British bus operators. Production at Workington was only kept going by an order from British Rail for lightweight 'Sprinter' trains based on the now-discontinued Leyland National; the plant closed in 1991 and part of it is now being used as a depot – ironically for MAN, Scania and Volvo trucks – by the Stobart haulage group. In 1988 Leyland Bus was sold on to Volvo, whose own chassis had been making an impact in the surviving British market. Leyland's model ranges were abandoned, and in 1991 the last bus chassis rolled out of the historic works near Preston.

By the time demand for conventional buses revived, only Dennis remained with the capacity to build a chassis and orders went abroad; Volvo gained a valuable market for bus chassis, as did Neoplan (Germany) and Irizar (Spain) for coaches. Some British body builders did survive, notably Alexander, Plaxton and, for a time, Duple; Wright of Ballymena grew to fill the vacuum. But continental chassis tended to gain continental bodies, Van Hool of Belgium faring well in the British coach market.

Ironically, one component part of Leyland Bus flourishes to this day: Ashok Leyland, its Indian arm sold off in 1987 to the London-based Hinduja Group. Ashok Leyland, which retains the old Leyland logo, is now India's second largest commercial vehicle manufacturer with an increasing footprint as a defence contractor, and operates a joint venture plant in Chennai with Renault Nissan.

If the collapse of Leyland Bus was an unintended consequence of government-ordained privatisation and deregulation, the eclipse of British commercial vehicle manufacturing was the result of simple lack of interest at boardroom level by one multinational motor manufacturer after another. The stampede to offload what was left of BL to the private sector led to Leyland's truck business – courted by GM the year before – being purchased by the Dutch firm DAF in 1987; Rover took a 40 per cent stake in the joint company. In a move that would have repercussions across British industry, one of its senior executives, George Simpson, a 25-year Leyland veteran, jumped ship to become chief executive of Rover and, through that appointment, deputy chief executive at BAe. One of DAF's first actions was to close the Scammell plant. The tie-up might have lasted, had not corporate excess by the company's Dutch directors led to DAF going bankrupt in 1993. A management buyout kept Leyland Trucks afloat, but in 1998 the operation was taken over by America's PACCAR, which had already acquired Foden and what was left of DAF. Leyland DAF Vans – then profitably produced in both Birmingham and Coventry – carried on after another management buyout. A further survivor was the Albion truck works in Glasgow, which had also made bus chassis until 1983; the subject in 1993 of yet another buyout, it would be sold on in 1998 to American Axle and Manufacturing.

Despite having recently shown interest in taking on Leyland Trucks, General Motors also lost enthusiasm for making lorries, buses and vans. Its exit from the heavy vehicle sector in Britain in the late 1980s was hastened by a perverse decision from the Ministry of Defence to procure a new generation of heavy military truck from Leyland, even though the available Bedford model had performed better in tests. Its interest in the lighter end of the market was based on hopes of merging Land Rover with Bedford to establish a real presence in the military and civilian 4x4 market. When the government insisted on packaging Land Rover with the former Austin Rover to make the latter more attractive to purchasers, management in Detroit could see little future for its light truck and van operation. The Bedford van factory at Luton was reorganised as a joint venture with Isuzu, making the Isuzu-based Frontera 4x4 and a range of Renault vans badged as Vauxhall or Opel. The Bedford truck plant at Dunstable was sold in 1987 to AWD, a company owned by David Brown which designed the DJB articulated dump truck built at Peterlee and was acquired in 1996 by Caterpillar. AWD continued to supply Bedford trucks to the military, and TL and TM trucks under its own badge, but tough foreign competition and the recession put the company into receivership in 1992.

Ford sold its British tractor-making business in 1991 to New Holland, a subsidiary of Fiat, which continued production at Basildon. It withdrew from the truck market because of overcapacity in Europe, and cut back its involvement in light commercial vehicles – again a decision in which its once independent British arm had apparently no say. While production of new generations of the Transit van continued at Southampton, Ford's truck operation at Langley was sold to Iveco of Italy in 1986, Ford taking a 48 per cent stake, and the Langley plant closed altogether in 1997. Iveco also acquired Seddon Atkinson from ENASA in 1990.

Britain between 1980 and 1997 saw its production of vans and HGVs tumble from 389,000 to 238,000. Yet in one related, specialised field it could boast a global success story: JCB. The company, started in a garden shed at Uttoxeter in 1946 by J. C. Bamford to make tipping trailers out of Army surplus parts, had by the 1980s become the world leader in making diggers and a wide range of related vehicles (so much so that JCB as a generic was included in the *Oxford English Dictionary*). JCB's success was proof to Mrs Thatcher that if its products were the best in the world and were sold with flair, there was no reason why a British manufacturer should not thrive. JCB was competing globally with the likes of Caterpillar (who closed their West Lothian plant in 1988) and Komatsu, but did so by offering a niche product and its variants rather than challenging across the board. The company's focus and self-belief contrasted markedly with the rudderlessness and strategic inconsistency of other automotive and equipment manufacturers, who could only envy JCB's steady growth to a company which today has a turnover of nearly 2 billion, 7,000 employees, plants in 18 countries and sales in over 150. Less fortunate was the fork-lift truck maker Lansing Bagnall, whose Basingstoke plant was taken over by Linde of Germany in 1990.

The yo-yo'ing fortunes of Britain's car makers during the 1980s and beyond posed challenges for component manufacturers, who responded in very different ways. Those in the strongest position owned the intellectual property in something the industry needed: Tube Investments with its Bundy tubes; Turner & Newall – which saw off all its Continental competitors – in pistons, bearings and friction materials; Lucas with diesel fuel injection systems; Hardy Spicer (taken over by GKN) with its constant velocity joint; BTR in seals and Pilkington in glass. Pilkington's float glass continued to dominate the global market, though in 1994 the US Department of Justice forced it to sign up to a 10-year waiver on its technology licensing agreements that applied to US manufacturers, arguing that they were a violation of anti-trust laws as the patent had expired. GKN dominated the world market for driveline products, but nearly came to grief in the 1980s through a disastrous attempt to diversify which took its eye off its core products; it came within a whisker of losing a crucial Ford contract to Japan's NTN Corporation, which had been producing GKN's own products under licence. GKN went on to reinvent itself from the descendant of a company making screws into a quality component maker for the worldwide motor and aerospace industries. The process was painful and ruthlessly executed, with 40,000 people losing their jobs as outdated plants and processes were sloughed off, but it ensured not just GKN's survival but its future. GKN got out of fasteners and steel making, built up its military vehicles and aerospace businesses and in 1994 acquired the Yeovil helicopter maker Westland, whose sale to America's Sikorsky eight years before had precipitated a Cabinet crisis that Mrs Thatcher at one point feared would force her out.

The arrival of Japanese car manufacturers did not initially lead, as in the United States, to an influx of Japanese component manufacturers who put local firms out of business; in their early years operating in Britain, two-thirds of Nissan's 198 suppliers, and half of Honda's and Toyota's, were British. There was some inward investment, notably Bosch's alternator plant in South Wales, but more significantly there was in the late 1980s a wave of takeovers of British component firms by foreign undertakings: in just three years the number of British-owned firms in the top 60 component manufacturers fell from 40 to 20. Nippondenso took over IMI's radiator operation, Magneti Marelli acquired Lucas's lighting, starters and alternator plants and Thyssen bought out Birmid Qualcast's foundry business.

The shape of Britain's car component companies – many of them wider engineering conglomerates – was changing. Dunlop never recovered from a disastrous merger with Pirelli which was undone after a decade in 1980; it was acquired by BTR in 1985 and the following year its tyre business was sold to Sumitomo – the descendant of Dunlop's original Japanese business. Michelin in 1985 made 2,500 employees redundant at Stoke-on-Trent, over a quarter of the workforce. Stirling Metals' foundry at Nuneaton closed in 1986 with the losss of 700 jobs because of cut-price engine blocks from Brazil. Tube Investments bought what was left of Alfred Herbert in 1982, America's Bundy Corporation (for its automotive tubes) in 1987 and Dowty Group in 1992; disposals included the Creda white goods brand to GEC. In 1982 TI franchised out Raleigh's American bicycle operation to Huffy, production for the US market being shifted to Japan; its Carlton factory at Worksop was closed in 1981 after repeated strikes. Smiths Industries gave up its clock, watch and vehicle instrumentation businesses in the early 1980s to specialise in aircraft components.

BTR under Sir Owen Green grew into a multinational; an attempt to take over Pilkington in 1985 as well as Dunlop was abandoned after meeting fierce resistance, but in 1992 it expanded further by acquiring what was left of Hawker Siddeley for £1.5 billion. Another fast-growing player was Siebe, which in Victorian times had pioneered diving helmets; under the leadership of Sir Barrie Stephens it acquired during the 1990s a raft of industrial automation businesses.

Lucas was probably the component manufacturer the motorist knew best; the company entered the Thatcher years with 18 factories producing a wide range of automotive products and business remained strong. There was some rationalisation: Lucas Aerospace's Park Royal plant which supplied torpedo components to BAe closed in the 1980s after a protracted strike by engineers in pursuit of a 35-hour week; the CAV magneto plant at East Finchley closed in 1991; and Lucas's heavy duty electrical business was sold to America's Prestolite in 1994.

George Simpson, who was in the process of selling Rover to BMW, took the helm at Lucas in 1993. By the time he moved on three years later to GEC, another dramatic change was imminent: the merger of Lucas, with a workforce of 46,000, with the Varity Corporation, a Buffalo-based component company with 9,000 employees formed out of the ruins of Massey-Ferguson. The stated intention of the merger, carried through by Simpson's successor Victor Rice, the son of an Essex chimney sweep, was to build the American side of the business. Rice launched a £65 million savings programme within the merged company, then in 1998 attempted to shift its head office to America and its primary stock market listing to Wall Street. Accusations were levelled from shareholders and the press that Rice and his associates had their eye on the far higher rewards that company executives were receiving across the Atlantic. The plan was abandoned, Lucas Varity was taken over by America's TRW Corporation in 1999 and within weeks Rice had quit with a reported £4 million payoff and £13 million in share options. The Lucas businesses were broken up, Perkins Engines being one of the few to survive under British ownership. By then Simpson was long gone, leaving one analyst to comment: 'He could fall through the roof of a department store and land up on the ground floor wearing a new suit.'

Nevertheless by 1997 Britain's motor industry appeared stronger than at any time for a quarter of a century, and with a highly optimistic outlook. UK car production for the year totalled 1,711,923 – almost twice the all-time low of 1982 – and analysts were confidently predicting 2,500,000 by 2010. Of the cars produced, 962,000 were exported: more than half the production of Rover, Vauxhall and all three Japanese car makers. These last, exporting to the European single market and with hopes of Britain adopting the single currency, had all reached break-even and were talking of expansion.

Ford, having overcome low productivity at Halewood and Dagenham which had threatened the future of both plants, was now achieving near-Japanese levels of efficiency; the decision to produce just one car – the Fiesta – at Dagenham and transfer the Sierra to Ford's Genk plant in Belgium had apparently transformed the economics of the sprawling complex. Alex Trotman, the British-born head of Ford worldwide, reckoned all the company's European capacity would be needed in the 'big upturn'. Yet it was becoming increasingly easy for Ford Europe to tell that despite improved productivity, its British plants were still less economic than their continental counterparts, particularly once it became UK government policy for the pound to 'shadow the Deutschmark'. As a result, most of Ford's investment in Europe in the 1990s went to Germany, Belgium – and Spain, which took over the lead from Dagenham in producing the Fiesta. Yet Ford saw potential in Britain at the high end of the market, investing in Jaguar and in 1994 also acquiring Aston Martin.

Vauxhall was making hefty profits with an updated model range, the Vectra having replaced the Cavalier in 1995. And Peugeot's Ryton operation was running at full capacity, gearing up to restart its second production line in 1998 as the Peugeot 206 joined the 306.

Yet the cornerstone of optimism about Britain's future as a quality volume car producer came from Rover – which in 1994 had been remarkably taken over by BMW. Though the Munich-based car maker had had its own difficulties in the early post-war years and took far longer than Mercedes to develop a reputation for quality and style, by the early 1990s it was the industry paragon. A decade before, the idea of BMW wanting even a stake in the walking disaster that was British Leyland would have seemed risible. Yet Rover, under the auspices of BAe, had been quietly turning the corner and now had much to offer – an impression that George Simpson was keen to encourage. BMW had been tracking Land Rover for over a decade as a means of boosting its 4x4 credentials, but like General Motors had been told it was not for sale separately. Outside Land Rover production, Rover was losing £100 million a year; it was essential to keep Land Rover as the bait for the sale of the whole. Moreover, under Simpson, Rover's workforce had been slimmed down to 33,000, 'just-in-time' delivery of parts and components was starting to work, and Japanese production methods – and components such as floor pans and engines – had made a real difference to quality. Indeed one of Rover's attractions to BMW's Bernd Pischetsrieder – a cousin of the Mini's creator Sir Alec Issigonis – was the scope it offered to help his company reform its own high-quality but conservative working methods and improve productivity. Furthermore, some of Rover's models were, in Stuttgart's opinion, starting to pose a threat to BMW's own product line; with the two companies under a single ownership, BMW quality could be injected into a Rover range that would complement its own products, not challenge them.

The deal struck between Simpson and Pischetsrieder at the start of 1994 for BMW not only to take on Rover but pay BAe £800 million for 80 per cent of it stunned the political and automotive worlds – and no one more than Honda. While Rover management stressed that its 15-year partner had had every opportunity to move toward a closer union and shut out BMW, Honda felt it had been scurvily treated, a view that won it considerable public sympathy. In due course, Honda sold its 20 per cent stake in Rover to BMW for a further £200 million. Meanwhile at Longbridge, BMW made its presence felt by terminating the Metro, and in 1995 by reviving the MG marque with the popular MGF. Longer-term work was soon under way on a new Rover range giving a British feel to BMW's technologies. Pischetsrieder was satisfied; a year after taking on

Rover he declared Britain 'the most attractive location in Europe for car production'. Exciting times lay ahead.

The same could not be said in the 1980s or 1990s for Britain's civil nuclear industry, which had not only abandoned dreams of world leadership but was struggling to complete the nuclear power stations it was committed to build and to reprocess the waste from them at Sellafield. The power station programme was overshadowed by the 20 years it took to get Dungeness B into commercial operation from the start of work in 1965, and by the interminable public inquiry that preceded construction of the last AGR, Sizewell B, which took a further seven years to build and was only connected to the National Grid in 1995. By then government appetite for further nuclear power stations had evaporated, and the main question about Labour, which looked set to return to power, was whether it would prematurely close those already generating. Nor, since the completion of the gigantic Drax B in 1986, had there been much enthusiasm for further coal-fired stations, with their high greenhouse emissions. All this was very bad news for Britain's turbine and nuclear contracting industries – which contracted.

Dounreay was now running down; its Prototype Fast Reactor was taken offline in 1994 and commercial reprocessing of nuclear waste at the site ended in 1998. But Sellafield continued to expand. Its vitrification plant, which seals high-level radioactive waste in glass, opened in 1991; it was joined by the MOX (mixed oxide) plant in 1997, intended to produce a blend of plutonium and natural uranium that behaves similarly to enriched uranium. The level of radioactivity in discharges into the Irish Sea was the subject of concern from the government of the Irish Republic throughout this period, though British Nuclear Fuels insisted the risk was greatly overstated. When as a *Daily Telegraph* leader writer I spent two days at Sellafield in 1988 to see the Thorp plant, which would not go operational until 1994, executives from BNFL who joined me for dinner made a point of nonchalantly munching shellfish collected close to the outfall pipe.

Meanwhile successive defence reviews and rounds of cuts had reduced Britain's nuclear deterrent from battlefield, air-launched and submarine-launched options to Trident, delivered from giant nuclear-powered submarines constructed by VSEL at Barrow. The missiles were serviced in Georgia, but the reactors powering the ships were made in Britain amid understandable secrecy, Rolls-Royce supplying the propulsion expertise.

Despite Mrs Thatcher's strictures against nationalisation, British Rail had retained, notwithstanding its straitened financial situation, a reputation for innovation. The diesel-powered High Speed Train had revived the fortunes of BRs Inter-City business, and by the early 1980s BR was ready with what it reckoned to be a real world-beater: the electrically-powered Advanced Passenger Train (APT), with tilting carriages enabling it to operate at higher speeds over conventional railway infrastructure rather than the almost-straight alignments needed by the Train de Grande Vitesse (TGV) in France.

The APT had been over a decade in preparation – in 1972 a series of national strikes had been triggered when an early prototype was moved by inspectors, after the drivers' union ASLEF 'blacked it' because not all of its members were to be paid a bonus for letting it be operated. Even so, political pressure for an under-fire industry to deliver results led to the first three APTs being rushed into service before all the technical wrinkles had been ironed out, the first carrying passengers from Euston to Glasgow in December 1981. The trip was a success, but the media – in a forerunner of the 'wobbly Millennium bridge' scare – picked up on the failure of the tilt mechanism on some carriages, and freezing brakes in the wintry weather. The APTs were withdrawn from passenger service after four days, and while they did resume in 1984 the project lost the support of management and the government and died. The tilting technology was taken forward by Fiat in its Pendolino trains, and in 2002 trains of this family – built largely in Italy and finished by Alstom in Birmingham – would successfully enter service on the Euston-Glasgow route. One is left wondering what opportunities Britain's train manufacturers could have exploited in this field, had BR and its political masters not lost their nerve.

Construction of the Channel Tunnel between 1987 and 1994 was Europe's largest post-war civil engineering project, and British industry benefited from it. Yet, sadly, many of the orders placed were the last of their kind. Six of the 11 giant tunnel boring machines that excavated the three bores were made by James Howden of Renfrew and Robbins-Markham, but the TBMs for tunnels on the high-speed Channel Tunnel Rail Link – the first section of which opened in 2003 – would all come from Japan, and those for Crossrail are being made in Germany. (Howden survives, though, under the ownership of Dublin-based Charter International, and Markham, whose Chesterfield factory was closed by Kvaerner in 1998, still manufactures TBM components as Davy Markham from the Davy site in Sheffield.) The Eurostar trains were constructed by GEC-Alsthom at La Rochelle, Belfort and Birmingham, with input from Belgium's La Brugeoise. The final batch of 'Tri-Bo' electric locomotives procured by Eurotunnel to haul vehicle shuttle trains through the tunnel were the last to be built by Brush at Loughborough; Brush and ABB also built BR's Class 92 dual-voltage electric locos for hauling freight trains through the tunnel – which, despite meeting the specifications of the French state railway were prevented from operating over its metals by the country's unions. For this sector of British industry, the opening of the Channel Tunnel was the end rather than the beginning of the story.

The Tunnel would, however, have an adverse and unforeseen effect on Britain's train manufacturers, who by now had lost large amounts of their export markets to Japanese competitors. Continental railways (and the Tunnel itself) have a higher loading gauge and larger 'envelope' for trains than Britain's; this meant that a continental manufacturer like Siemens or CAF could build a train to the tighter British loading gauge and deliver it to the customer through the tunnel, while if a British manufacturer won an order in France or Germany (which for reasons of State never happened) the train could not reach the tunnel over the British network because it was too big.

Privatisation of the railways produced two of the unintended effects that had marked the privatisation and deregulation of the bus industry a decade before: a drying-up of new orders and a consequent struggle by UK vehicle manufacturers to stay in business (demand for track, signalling equipment and the like was less elastic, but even here there were casualties). While most of the new private-sector train operators carried on with the trains they inherited from BR, many of these were elderly; yet it took time for the train companies, who had to acquire new trains through rolling-stock companies (ROSCOs) also carved out of BR, to decide what new trains they wanted and get them into service. From 1994 to 1997 not a single new passenger carriage was ordered, and during this time the former BR train building works at York which had been busy for years, ran out of orders and closed. There were redundancies at GEC-Alsthom – GEC had acquired Metro-Cammell's Birmingham works in 1989 – an order for trains for London Underground's Jubilee Line not fully compensating. Moreover, when new locomotives were eventually ordered in large numbers by Wisconsin Central, who had taken over most of BR's freight services, the contracts went to manufacturers in Canada and Spain. Locomotive manufacture at Crewe and Doncaster had ceased in the 1980s, and the closure in 1995 of Hunslet's Leeds works which had latterly made industrial shunters, left Brush as the last British manufacturer capable of building a loco.

Throughout the turbulent Thatcher/Major years, GEC under Lord Weinstock was a beacon of success, prudence and stability – Britain's largest private sector employer and its third largest company by market capitalisation after BP and Shell. Between 1960 and his retirement in 1996, Weinstock raised GEC's turnover from £100 million to £11 billion (with profits topping £1 billion), and its position appeared unassailable. GEC was seen as conservative; indeed from the mid-1980s it came under growing criticism from elements in the City for having expanded more slowly than Siemens (twice its size in 1972 and six times by 1997), and for sitting on a 'cash pile' of some £2 billion instead of making more acquisitions – for the facilitation of which those same elements hoped to be paid handsomely.

Yet during this period GEC continued to evolve, with an eye on the future. It made a number of acquisitions in Britain and America to establish a strong presence in military electronics; its crowning glory was the acquisition of Ferranti's defence electronics division in 1990 as part of the deal with Germany over the avionics for the Eurofighter. In 1985, GEC made a £1.2 billion takeover bid for Plessey, but it was blocked by the company and the Ministry of Defence; three years later it launched a joint bid with Siemens which fell foul of the Monopolies & Mergers Commission until the two bidders agreed to split the company. GEC took a 60 per cent stake in Plessey's telecoms business, which had been hard hit by the privatisation of British Telecom. In 1989 GEC sold a half share in its Hotpoint white goods business to America's General Electric having failed to compete internationally and then lost its lead to imports; GEC also baled out of the electric lighting business, selling its Osram subsidiary to Siemens. In 1989 GEC, significantly, merged its power generation and transport businesses based on Stafford, Preston and Washwood Heath, Birmingham with those of France's CGE to form a new joint venture: GEC-Alsthom; Weinstock negotiated this tie-up with Alcatel-AlstHom to give GEC access to French gas turbine technology in European export markets and create a competitor to ABB. And in 1995 GEC strengthened its position in naval shipbuilding by adding VSEL to the yards it had acquired as British Shipbuilders were privatised; the Monopolies and Mergers Commission had preferred a rival bid from BAe, but its advice was rejected.

When Weinstock moved up to become chairman emeritus of GEC in 1996, George Simpson was an apparently logical choice to succeed him as managing director. It was just two years since he had achieved the seemingly impossible feat of offloading Rover to BMW in return for a handsome sum, and Major's government was pressing defence contractors to consolidate. Simpson embarked on a major review of the business, and in July 1997 – weeks after the election of a Labour government which could have queried the strategy – announced that GEC would move away from joint ventures and concentrate on 'global leadership' in three fields: defence and aerospace, industrial electronics and communications. That year GEC was Britain's largest engineering exporter by miles, selling £2,052 million worth of goods abroad compared to £854 million for Lucas Varity, £798 million for Fiat-owned New Holland, £575 million for JCB, £512 million for Cummins UK, £476 million for the British arm of Caterpillar and £475 million for GKN.

Meanwhile the rest of Britain's electrical and electronics industry had been changing shape. Thorn's takeover of EMI had not been a success, and the companies demerged in 1996, both as shadows of their former selves. EMI's plant at Hayes, Middlesex which had employed 1,400 people in the 1960s was by then almost deserted; vinyl record production, in the years before it ceased altogether, had been transferred to a new plant at Southall whose glass roof caused records pressed on hot days to warp. The privatised Inmos microprocessor business did not prosper under Thorn, and was sold on in 1989 to France's SGS Thomson which two years earlier had acquired Thorn's television manufacturing business as it finally gave up the struggle to compete with larger-volume competitors of the Far East. Thorn concentrated its business on lighting, but despite having acquired companies in Europe, it could still not compete in scale with Philips and Siemens and in 1991 sold its lamps business to GE of America; GEC's parallel sale of Osram took British manufacturers right out of that market.

Sir Ernest Harrison had built Racal over three decades into Britain's third largest electronics company, and anyone buying £1,000 worth of its shares in 1961 would have been worth over £10 million by the 1990s. After Weinstock allowed Racal access to some of GEC's battlefield radio technology, the company bid for and won one of Britain's first two cellular telephone network licences in 1982, the other going to BT – and Racal Vodafone was launched at the start of 1985. Mobile telephony caught on in a way no one could have foreseen; 20 per cent of Racal Telecom, which owned Vodafone, was floated on the Stock Exchange in 1988, and before long this fraction of a subsidiary was valued at more than the entire parent company. It was indicative of the way British business was developing that even though Racal was a manufacturer, the country's commercial success in mobile telephony would be in establishing networks rather than in making the handsets – which became extremely lucrative for America's Motorola, Nokia of Finland and the Japanese/Swedish joint venture Sony-Ericsson.

Harrison demerged Vodafone from Racal in 1991, creating what would become the highest valued FTSE 100 company, but his action left what the City nicknamed the 'rump' of Racal – which had in the meantime acquired the security company Chubb – vulnerable to takeover. Racal demerged Chubb in 1992 to relieve the pressure and two years later shrewdly took a 22 per cent stake in Camelot, who would win the franchise to operate the National Lottery. It sold Decca Radar to America's Litton Industries in 1996, having built its communications business, winning a major government telecoms contract in 1988 and five years later acquiring the communications division of British Rail. Yet Racal's involvement in military communications – and the successor to its highly successful Clansman radio – would soon prove its Achilles heel.

For the once-great Ferranti, the end had already come. The company's management had spent two decades trying to get out of computers, in which Ferranti had once been a world leader, and while its laboratories produced much of the technology for early Sinclair, Acorn and BBC home computers, Ferranti sold its microelectronics business to Plessey in 1988, just as desktop computing was taking off as a global money-spinner. Next, Ferranti was the victim of power politics over the development of the Eurofighter. Britain, Italy and Spain all wanted the Ferranti-led ECR-90 as the aircraft's radar, but Germany preferred a rival system produced by Hughes, AEG and GEC. To keep a reluctant Bonn government in the consortium, Defence Secretary Tom King agreed with his German opposite number to go for the Hughes system, with GEC being given permission to take over what was left of Ferranti Defence Systems after it lost this vital contract.

The parent company – which had prestigiously gained a foothold in France's Ariane rocket programme – had seemed in good shape when in 1987 it took over the Pennsylvania-based defence contractor International Signal and Control (ISC). But not for the last time in that period did the grass look greener on the other side of the Atlantic, and the takeover of an American company proved a poisoned chalice. Ferranti restructured to take advantage of its newly acquired capabilities, unaware that an unexplained lucrative cash flow shown in International Signal's accounts – which its due diligence team had taken on trust – derived not from its stated activities, but from illegal arms sales for clandestine US organisations, which dried up the moment the company fell into British hands. In 1991 James Guerin, founder of ISC and co-chairman of the merged company, pleaded guilty in a Federal court to fraud committed both in the USA and in Britain. Late in 1993, Ferranti was forced into bankruptcy and a fire sale of its numerous businesses began, with GEC, Thorn, Thomson-CSF and Kvaerner all picking up bargains.

By then, Plessey too had gone, carved up between GEC and Siemens. In 1988 Plessey and GEC merged their telecoms units to form GEC-Plessey Telecommunications (GPT), at the time Britain's leading manufacturer in the field – though with just 6 per cent of global market share, well behind Alcatel, AT&T and Nortel. The merger was aimed at resolving deep-rooted tensions between Plessey and GEC in the telecoms field that had been all too apparent in the painful delivery of the System X telephone system. That December GEC (at the second attempt) and Siemens launched a bid for Plessey, valuing the company at £1.7 billion; it went through once GEC agreed to let Siemens take key elements of Plessey's defence business. In 1997 these businesses were acquired by BAe, and GEC under its Marconi badge took back Siemens's stake in GPT.

Another electronics company in decline was STC. It entered the 1980s under Sir Kenneth Corfield with no shortage of ambition, and its takeover of ICL in 1984 seemed to augur well. But this attempt to enter the mainframe computer business to achieve 'convergence' between computing and telecoms was widely seen in the industry as unrealistic, and imposed financial strains just as other difficulties were surfacing. The company had unwisely withdrawn, in 1982, from the consortium with Plessey and GEC that was starting to roll out the System X digital exchanges for British Telecom, and with privatisation, new business from BT dried up. With STC also paying the price for producing at a large number of sites, Corfield was forced out, and while ICL recovered under new management STC did not. In 1990 ICL was sold to Fujitsu for $1.29 billion, but STC's plight was terminal and in 1991 it gave up the ghost, being acquired by Nortel of Canada.

ICL's dream of becoming a world-leading mainframe producer had finally died in 1981 when a cash crisis brought a bid from Univac which was blocked by the British government in return for financial help. It decided to rein back on new model development – abandoning the development of hardware altogether during the 1990s – and acquire cheaper alternatives to some of its own technologies; in the process a relationship was formed with Fujitsu which became steadily more umbilical. The crisis within STC also brought new management at ICL, Peter Bonfield becoming chairman and managing director; before long ICL was contributing 60 per cent of STC's profits and Bonfield was rewarded with the top job at BT. In this period ICL acquired useful American and Danish subsidiaries, and absorbed several American businesses from STC's own portfolio. But the company's very success increased the temptation for STC to sell it, with Fujitsu the obvious candidate. In 2002, ICL would be renamed Fujitsu Services Ltd.

By the late 1980s, mainframe computer development – while essential to modern life – had been overtaken in the public eye by the rise of the microcomputer and the desktop. The British media's awareness of this was heightened by its own (belated) adoption of computerised production techniques, not just by Eddy Shah and at Wapping, but right across an industry that was now moving out of Fleet Street. The *Daily Telegraph*, probably the most technically backward of the nationals despite a circulation of 1.3 million, began computerising its newsroom in 1986. The following year it transferred its operations overnight – without losing a copy – to an office block at South Quay in the Isle of Dogs and a separate printing plant a few hundred yards away, which soon printed the also modernising *Daily Express*. (Lord Stevens of Ludgate, proprietor of the *Express*, forced a last-minute price reduction out of the *Telegraph*'s new owner Conrad Black as retribution for a juicily lubricious obituary of Stevens's recently deceased wife which the *Telegraph* had insouciantly printed on the morning the contract was to be signed).

By then, many readers of the national press already had their own computer. As early as 1979, Cambridge-based Acorn Computers (the name was chosen to come before Apple in the phone book) launched its first microcomputer, and throughout the 1980s its BBC Micro – made in Britain – performed strongly in the educational market. In 1980 Sir Clive Sinclair launched his ZX81, marketed at the appealing price of £99.95. And in 1984 Alan Sugar's Amstrad, a company established as early as 1968, launched its CPC 464 home computer in Britain, France, Australia, New Zealand, Germany, Spain and Italy – rapidly capturing a large slice of the market. While its early competitors were manufactured in Cambridge and Dundee, the Amstrad was unashamedly produced in Japan. In contrast with the Margolin family when they launched the Dansette and the founders of Racal who found manufacturing resources in Britain's thriving post-war electronics subculture, Alan Sugar had always commissioned his hi-fi products from Japan; when he decided to develop a home computer he simply went over to find the right firm to make what he wanted – for a decade reaping immense rewards.

Landmarks in the history of IT came faster and faster, with most of the advances in the United States and Japan – save for one spectacular exception. In 1980 Bill Gates developed MS-DOS, and the next year IBM – which had built up a strong manufacturing presence in Britain – launched a PC relying on this operating system. Sony launched the compact disc in 1982. In 1983 the first laptop and laserjet printer appeared and Michael Dell began building computers in his college room. 1984 brought the Apple Mac and the CD-Rom. In 1985 Microsoft launched Windows, and the .uk email address first appeared. The year 1986 saw Burroughs and Sperry merge to form Unisys, the second largest computer manufacturer and in 1989 Tim Berners-Lee proposed the basic concept of the Web.

A Londoner with a first in Physics from Oxford, Berners-Lee was a fellow of the Geneva-based European nuclear research institute CERN, which at the time had the largest internet mode in Europe. Berners-Lee married up Hypertext – a system for information sharing among researchers which he had devised in 1980 – with the Internet and (in his own words): 'Ta-da! The World Wide Web.' The first website, built at CERN, went online in 1991. Berners-Lee now lives in Massachusetts, but with a chair in computing at Southampton University; half a century before, he would have been researching at Manchester – with the likes of Alan Turing – or at Cambridge. His career path reflects not so much British failure (though a world-leading position in computing was not followed through) as the success of CERN in establishing itself as a research entity – stretching way beyond its original commitment to particle physics – that transcends national programmes and capabilities and is a true global competitor.

CERN formally launched the Web in 1992. In 1993 Intel announced its Pentium chip. Microsoft launched successive upgrades of Windows; 1994 brought Yahoo, 1995 Java and 1996 Internet Explorer. Many advances in technology spawned new products, with implications for Britain as companies from America and the Far East, which were now almost exclusively setting the pace, saw merit in manufacturing in this country.

A number of global high-tech companies already had a presence in Britain. IBM had long been manufacturing in the west of Scotland, NCR (who adapted more quickly and better than Gestetner to the computer age) had a successful operation in Dundee which in the early 1980s produced the world's most successful automated bank teller machines (ATMs). But during the 1990s they were joined by many others, welcomed with open arms by governments who saw them as an ideal way to rebuild Britain's manufacturing capacity when home-based firms and their backers had run out of steam. American, Japanese and Korean firms were not just after Britain's domestic market: they saw Britain – for reasons discussed in the chapter on Europe – as an ideal base for accessing the European Single Market established at the end of 1992, as the European Community steadily enlarged. It would be easier to list the big names that did not establish a British presence than those that did. By 1996, for example, production of television sets was almost entirely in the hands of Sony, Matsushita, Samsung, Toshiba, Mitsubishi, JVC, Hitachi and Tatung – six from Japan and one each from South Korea and Taiwan. And by the time inward investment peaked in 1997, new high-tech manufacturing plants making products for the information age had joined them across Britain – the bulk in those same regions where the Macmillan government had compelled British manufacturers to establish their new plants four decades before. Particularly welcome were three semiconductor plants: Fujitsu's at Newton Aycliffe, Siemens's on Tyneside, and LG's at Newport where 6,100 jobs were promised and John Major attended the groundbreaking ceremony. Again, in the short term, the strategy seemed a success.

It would be wrong to suggest that Britain had lost its capacity to innovate. The 1990s saw the advent of high-tech companies spun off from the universities that over time would take their place in high-value manufacturing; one of the first being the niche microchip manufacturer Wolfson Microelectronics, spun off from Edinburgh University in 1994. Moreover, a steady stream of potentially commercial innovations were generated not just in the universities and in small research-based businesses but, in the laboratories of the Ministry of Defence, brought together in 1995 as the Defence Evaluation and Research Agency (DERA). But a growing mis-match was becoming evident between that capacity to innovate and the readiness of the manufacturing sector to take actual products forward. Alan Sugar was not alone in taking the view that there was more chance of achieving a commercially successful product if he had it made in the Far East. Not all the flops can be blamed on Britain's increasing detachment from the world of manufacturing: Sir Clive Sinclair's C5 battery-electric car/bicycle launched in 1985 and made by Hoover at Merthyr Tydfil came unstuck because of uncertainty over its status on the road – a court eventually ruled it a tricycle – and because unlike Sinclair's successful microcomputer it was not taken seriously by the wider public.

One inventor did overcome the odds to create and manufacture (for a time) a revolutionary product in Britain: James Dyson with his bagless vacuum cleaner. But even he faced inertia that would have defeated someone less committed. Already the successful developer of a barrow whose wheel was replaced by a ball to give greater movement, Dyson – a graduate of the Royal College of Art – launched his 'G Force' cleaner in 1983. No British manufacturer would touch it because it would destroy the market for cleaner bags, so he launched it in Japan through catalogue sales from his factory at Chippenham (later Malmesbury). Dyson faced an immediate threat from Hoover who had pirated his design, and with great tenacity won $5 million damages in the American courts for breach of his patent. With his 'dual cyclone' concept secure, Dyson went on to sweep the world.

One victim of Dyson's success was the Electrolux plant at Luton, which, although production of most of its range had been moved overseas, continued to make vacuum cleaners. In 1993 the Swedish parent company ended the autonomy of its national manufacturing and sales organisations and made each product line subordinate to a management team in Stockholm. Local management in Luton introduced a 'step change' project – partly because of the threat Dyson was posing despite his cleaners costing twice as much – and Andersen Consulting was brought in to advise on how to change working methods and improve product quality. An early success was to reduce drastically the 6,000 'incomplete' machines the factory had been turning out every month. But several near-insurmountable barriers to change remained: the firm had long operated a 'last in, first out' redundancy policy, it was one of the last to pay workers on a piecework basis and the unionised part of the workforce was conservative in the extreme. Interference from Stockholm was a continuing problem, and it also became clear that the local management structure was ossified. After three years the initiative ran into the ground, and two years after that, in 1998, the factory closed. It would, however, gain a new lease of life in the next decade when Electrolux moved its British headquarters to the site, which after Electrolux's takeover of parts of the collapsed AEG, would also house from 2011 a state-of-the-art AEG Training Academy.

While Dyson thrived, Hoover was dealt a near-fatal and gratuitously self-inflicted blow in possibly the most bizarre chain of events in British corporate history. In 1992 the company launched a sales promotion under which anyone spending £100 on one of its products would be entitled to two round-trip air tickets to Europe – and before long America. The average ten-year-old could have pointed out that if you give away plane tickets worth £200 or more to anyone buying a £100 vacuum cleaner, you will lose money, but no one at Hoover seemed to appreciate this. Sales soared as the public bought appliances purely as a means of securing cheap air travel. One national newspaper columnist of my acquaintance got to know most of newly-accessible eastern Europe by purchasing Hoovers, taking them out to East Germany, Poland and the like, enjoying the free travel and selling them at the other end; when we bumped into each other at Berlin airport, he was carrying three Hoovers. Production had to be stepped up to meet the demand, but before long there were complaints from customers about the non-arrival of tickets; a protest group bought shares and staged a demonstration at the annual meeting of Hoover's American parent company Maytag. The promotion was halted, but court cases brought by non-recipients of tickets continued until 1998 – by which time Hoover was £50 million out of pocket. By then too, Hoover's British operation had been sold on to the Italian white goods maker Candy.

Throughout the 1980s and 1990s, Britain's pharmaceutical industry became less fragmented as it developed into a global competitor. In the early 1980s Glaxo, ranked 18th in the world, was largest with almost

£1 billion in sales, closely followed by ICI (still deriving less than 8 per cent of its income from pharmaceuticals), Wellcome, Beecham, then Boots and the fertiliser giant Fisons. Within years, Glaxo rocketed into second place in the world, just behind Merck, through its development of the anti-ulcerant drug Zantac, launched in 1981. Glaxo's chief executive Paul Girolami achieved this by pricing Zantac above its less sophisticated competitors and marketing it keenly in the United States in consort with Roche. In 1982 Fisons decided to concentrate on pharmaceuticals, selling its fertiliser business to Norsk Hyrdo. The decision turned out to be the wrong one; the patents on the drugs from which it hoped to build a lasting profits base expired, and in 1995 it sold its pharmaceuticals business to Rhone Poulenc (itself taken over four years later by Hoechst). Beecham finally decided to concentrate on pharmaceuticals, where its strength was in antibiotics; in 1986 it sold its soft drink brands – led by Tango and the UK franchise for Pepsi-Cola – to Britvic, and the following year took over Norcliff Thayer, an American producer of patent medicines such as Tums. Then in 1989 Beecham merged with the American pharmaceutical major SmithKline Beckman – which had become overdependent on one drug, Tagamet – to form SmithKline Beecham; the corporate headquarters stayed at Brentford. Wellcome removed its immunity from takeover in 1986 by floating itself on the stock market; up to then it had been entirely owned by the largely charitable Wellcome Trust, itself a major commissioner of medical and pharmaceutical research. In 1995 Glaxo, now under Sir Richard Sykes, made a successful £9 billion bid for Wellcome. Glaxo Wellcome marked its arrival on the scene with a new research centre at Stevenage, but by the end of the year 2,000 of its 11,500 R&D jobs had gone, Wellcome's complex at Beckenham being the main casualty.

During the 1980s ICI's pharmaceutical division not only experienced rapid growth but became a major contributor to the company's profits: 28 per cent by 1982, and rising. In that year a move to make pharmaceuticals a central pillar of ICI's future by launching a bid for Beecham was blocked by the company's board. That route for expansion closed off, ICI in 1993 took the equally radical step of demergingitsbiosciencebusiness—pharmaceuticals,agrochemicalsand biological products – into a new stand-alone company, Zeneca, under Tom McKillop, a career ICI scientist. This created another major player in the pharmaceutical industry not distracted by other product ranges, but was a critical part of another tectonic shift – at ICI itself.

ICI had seemed to grow in confidence from 1982 to 1987 under the leadership of the charismatic John Harvey Jones, who decided that the company had to lessen its reliance on its traditional base of bulk chemicals and heighten its involvement in the high-value end of the industry. He began by selling ICI's polythene business to BP in exchange for BP's PVC operations, with ICI's giant Wallerscote, Cheshire plant, where polythene was invented, closing in 1984. ICI's PVC interests were then added to BP's, and in 1985 merged with those of Italy's Enichem to create EVC, spun off and floated on the Dutch stock exchange in 1990. Harvey Jones also bought three American chemical and paint companies – one purchase (Beatrice) proved a mistake.

Harvey Jones retired to make a television series showing British firms how they could become more productive; one memorable episode showed him discovering that the Morgan Motor Company could make four of their iconic sports cars a week instead of three for no further outlay – and having his advice politely rejected. But he left ICI convinced that British industry had paid a 'very high price' for the international success of the City. He also observed: 'When I was chairman of ICI, all the advisers we had were paid more than I was. Now I ask you: who is likely to leave the biggest impact on the fate of the bloody country?' Since then, the gap has widened further, despite the best endeavours of some company chief executives to catch up with the prodigious remuneration of bankers and hedge fund managers.

Harvey Jones's less flamboyant successor Denys Henderson, who had successfully led ICI's paints division, sold off its stake in North Sea exploration. ICI also parted with some of its agricultural operations (to Norsk Hydro), and its soda ash business to Brunner Mond – from whom it had been acquired when ICI was founded in

1926. Henderson in 1991 decreed that the company's future lay in just seven sectors: pharmaceuticals, agrochemicals, specialities, explosives, paints, materials and industrial chemicals. But the impression was spreading that ICI was starting to run out of steam, with Hanson that year testing the water for a hostile takeover before succumbing to a defensive barrage from Henderson. Nevertheless Hanson's message that ICI was a rudderless conglomerate ripe for 'unbundling' struck home, and Zeneca was floated off, further reducing ICI's critical mass. Costs were cut dramatically, one third of ICI's 100,000-strong workforce being shed in just two years.

Under the team of Ronnie Hempel and Charles Miller Smith – brought in from Unilever – who took over from Henderson in 1995, ICI continued the move out of bulk chemicals. Several Unilever subsidiaries manufacturing speciality chemicals were acquired, culminating in National Starch and Chemical for $8 billion, and the Swiss Rutz & Huber paints business in 1997. ICI borrowed £4 billion to fund these acquisitions, putting itself under pressure to sell its remaining bulk chemicals businesses. ICI Australia – the country's largest paint manufacturer – went for £1 billion, and the polyester chemicals business to Du Pont for $3 billion. ICI ended the Thatcher/Major years in flux, minus some of its historical steady earners, with its future uncertain – but still profitable (profits peaked at almost £1 billion in 1995).

Hanson's near-bid for ICI marked the high point for one of the City's favourite businesses of the 1980s, and one of Mrs Thatcher's favourite businessman. James Hanson, with Gordon White, another feisty Yorkshireman, had founded Hanson Trust as far back as 1964, operating largely in the United States until Mrs Thatcher came to power with her gospel of enterprise. An early acquisition after a hostile bid, fiercely resisted, was Berec – the name Ever Ready had adopted in what its staff saw as a fatuous attempt to improve its image. Hanson sacked the top management, returned to the Ever Ready name, closed its costly R&D operation at Tottenham (after finding that rival sites had developed three competing batteries), moved key technical staff from there to the Tanfield Lea plant, cut the workforce of 2,900 by one third and – most controversially – sold off its German and Italian subsidiaries to Duracell.

Hanson speedily concluded that Ever Ready was no longer a global competitor and was destined to lose market share, but determined to go down fighting and make a profit for as long as possible. It relaunched Ever Ready's flagship alkaline battery as Gold Seal, promoted the brand hard and in 1991 made a £35 million profit. But it could see the writing on the wall and in 1992 sold Ever Ready for £132 million to America's Ralston Purina, a cat-food maker who had become the world's leading battery manufacturer. Ralston Purina quickly closed two of Ever Ready's four British factories; an early visitor from the company dismissed Tanfield Lea as 'a shit pit', and in 1996 that once-pioneering and dominant plant also closed.

Hanson, meanwhile, went from strength to strength, building a reputation as an asset-stripper, notably through its acquisition of United Drapery Stores in 1983 and subsequent sale of most of its parts. Hanson acquired London Brick in 1984, and two years later SCM, an American conglomerate stretching from chemicals and paper to typewriters; most of that company's businesses were likewise sold off. However, what really made the City sit up was Hanson's £2.5 billion takeover the same year of Imperial Tobacco; its fringe businesses were sold off for almost that amount, leaving Hanson with the lucrative tobacco manufacturing and marketing business for 'next to nothing'. By the time it bought Consolidated Gold Fields for £3.5 billion in 1988, Hanson was walking on water. Yet while setting its cap at ICI in 1991 highlighted that company's growing weaknesses, it also marked Hanson's high point – coincidentally just after Mrs Thatcher's replacement by the less rumbustious John Major.

The City came through the recession of the early 1990s less convinced that conglomerates had potential to deliver lasting growth and profits. Hanson and White were canny enough to realise this. In 1995 they spun off some of Hanson's manufacturing businesses as US Industries, and the following year divided their company into four – Hanson (largely extractive industries and the manufacture of building materials), Imperial Tobacco, The Energy Group and Millennium Chemicals; all were floated on the Stock Exchange. And at the end of 1997 James (now Lord) Hanson stood down as chairman.

Hanson's final major acquisition – of Beazer Homes in 1991 – brought to an end a transatlantic takeover story as bizarre, in its way, as Lucas's tie-up with Varity. From the 1960s Brian Beazer had built up the Bath-based company started by his father into Britain's fourth largest housebuilder; it acquired the French Kier construction group in 1986 after a hotly contested takeover, and diversified into building materials. In 1987 Beazer – now a quoted company – bought two small American housebuilders, a cement producer and a construction contractor; then, in 1988 caused a sensation in the financial pages by launching a hostile bid for Koppers, a Pittsburgh-based chemicals-to-aggregates conglomerate. Beazer's credentials as a born-again Christian counted for little against the campaign launched against the bid in Pennsylvania; its main target was American Express, majority owner of Beazer's merchant bankers Shearson Lehman, who had encouraged the bid. The governor of Pennsylvania cut up his Amex card and Shearson lost an estimated £7 billion worth of business in the state, but Beazer's bid for Koppers – increased to $1.7 billion – went through.

Now it had to be paid for. Koppers's corporate HQ and chemical division were sold off, but with recession hitting the housebuilding and materials industries on both sides of the Atlantic, Beazer Homes' borrowings were unsustainable and something had to give. In 1991 Brian Beazer agreed to a refinancing that would separate his company's British/European and American operations, leaving him in control of the latter but losing the original family business. Two days later, James Hanson rang Beazer and offered just £315 million for his entire troubled empire, with Beazer staying on as chief executive. The deal – the first in which shareholders in two different countries received a single offer at the same time – went through, and with Hanson's resources behind it the ship was stabilised. French Kier was soon sold off, Beazer Homes USA began to expand and in 1994 Hanson floated it off on Wall Street. Brian Beazer stepped down as chief executive almost at once; he remained in the United States, and at the time of writing was still Beazer USA's non-executive chairman. One can think of less complicated and costly ways to emigrate.

Not every ill-starred transatlantic takeover could be blamed on a British company. In 1995 the respected Milwaukee-based mining equipment maker Harnischfeger Industries took over Dobson Park, a comparable company best known for its Kango mechanical hammer whose home business had been devastated by pit closures. The Harnischfeger family had recently handed power to Jeffery T. Grade, a dashing CEO with a distinguished war record as a US Navy pilot who embarked on a heroic programme of acquisitions, paying $322 million for the Wigan-based Dobson Park. Grade upset Wall Street by consistently falling short of profit forecasts, running up heavy debts acquiring overvalued companies and – reporters from *Barron's* discovered – having invented his war record. After an agreement to sell paper-making machines to Indonesia backfired, Grade was ousted in 1999 and Harnischfeger filed for reorganisation. By then the rescuable parts of Dobson Park had been subsumed into Harnischfeger's Joy Mining Machinery division, which still has a presence in Wigan.

For the brewing industry, the Thatcher/Major years are best remembered for the 'Beer Orders' promulgated in 1989 by Lord Young. Designed to end the breweries' stranglehold over tied houses, increase competition and ensure a greater choice for the drinker, they had the effect of splitting the brewing and pub industries. This was not in itself undesirable, but the Beer Orders accelerated an internationalisation of the former which finished off many of Britain's great breweries. Much productive capacity – for lager at least – was lost to Belgium with beer prices forced through the roof to enable landlords to meet the rent demands and inflated wholesale prices of 'pubco' property companies, whose avarice and disinterest in the nation's pub 'regulars' would attract increasing censure in the House of Commons. These were long-term effects, anticipated by some but overshadowed by continuing mergers. Hanson, having acquired Imperial Tobacco, sold Courage to Australia's Elders IXL, who in 1990 rebranded it as Fosters, reflecting the shift in drinkers' taste toward lager. Allied

Breweries merged its brewing interests with Carlsberg in 1992 to form Carlsberg Tetley, its spirits business being merged with Domecq two years later to form Allied Domecq. And in 1994 Scottish & Newcastle acquired Courage, separating its pub estate and brewing arms, the latter being badged as Scottish Courage.

All the time brewery closures continued, driven now by a decline in demand for traditional beers as lager captured an ever larger market. The year 1986 saw the end of brewing at Darley's brewery, Thorne (acquired by Vaux in 1978), Wilson's at Newton Heath, Manchester, the Workington Brewery (taken over by Matthew Brown in the face of vigorous local protests) and Younger's Holyrood brewery in Edinburgh (Scottish & Newcastle). A decade later Home Ales' brewery at Daybrook , Notts (their 5 Star was my favourite), Greene King's at Biggleswade (ex Wells & Winch), Websters at Halifax (Watney Mann 1972), and Whitbread Flowers at Cheltenham (ex-West Country Breweries) all barrelled their final pint.

The 1980s and 1990s saw Britain's successful confectionery industry move from being largely insular and family-owned (in two cases by the Quaker families who had founded the business) into the mainstream of commercial life. The only global player was Cadbury Schweppes, a longtime public company but still with Cadbury family members on the board; Trebor Bassett was taken over in 1989, continuing with its non-chocolate product range to be run as a separate business. Terrys were taken over by Kraft in 1993, but the seismic merger in the sector concerned Rowntree Mackintosh. The company went public – as was the fashion of the day – in 1987, and immediately attracted unwelcome attention from Jacobs Suchard and Nestlé, who eventually won control with a $4.55 billion bid in 1988. In just a year Rowntree had lost its philanthropic family ownership and been taken over by an international company with – its workers in York feared – no commitment to its British workforce; under Swiss law as it stood, Nestlé itself was effectively immune from takeover. The Rowntree and Mackintosh brand names disappeared from all but their most popular product ranges, and – more worryingly for employees – the former Caley chocolate factory in Norwich was closed in 1994, Rolo, Yorkie and Easter egg production being moved to York.

For Britain's textile industry, the slide continued. Employment in the sector – over 850,000 in the 1950s – had plunged by 1988 to 164,500, a drop of over 80 per cent. Lancashire's cotton industry – save for a few high-end survivals – had all but disappeared, employing 32,500 people against 538,000 in 1954; in 1988 UK cotton spinning production fell below that of the Benelux countries. Yorkshire's woollen and worsted industry had fared fractionally better – 41,900 workers against a previous 197,200 – again relying mainly on the upper end of the market. Hosiery and knitwear output alone had stayed strong, employing 90,100 workers, mainly in the East Midlands and former coalfields, and with the sector relying very heavily on orders from Marks & Spencer and exporting little. The insularity of Britain's rag trade was not matched by its competitors: by 1995 the UK was a net importer of both textiles and clothing despite the valiant exporting efforts at the higher end of the market of Scotland's knitwear industry, which itself had shrunk in size. M&S was still making a virtue of selling clothes 'Made in England', but suppliers were told first that they could be cut abroad and finished in Britain, then that only the 'Made in England' label had to be sewn on in the UK. By the mid-1990s, those suppliers were transferring production wholesale to Morocco, and later to China.

Britain's textile machinery manufacturers were also losing ground, their share of global exports shrinking from 8.5 per cent in 1980 to 3.4 per cent in 1995; Germany held over 30 per cent of the market, and Japan was the main gainer. In 1982 the Lancashire-based Platt Bros, once the world's largest, went into receivership.

The fortunes of the industry were reflected in the experience of Courtaulds. A fall in demand and the transfer of production to cheaper locations in Asia brought a string of factory closures, notably its four Flintshire sites – which had at their peak employed 10,000 people between 1977 and 1989 – and its Preston plant in 1980;

stocking-making machinery from its Langley Mill factory, demolished in 1993, was bought by a niche manufacturer which now operates under the trade name Gio. By now the bulk of Courtaulds's profits were coming from the chemicals side of the business, with 23,000 employees, and in 1990 the company split itself in two. Courtaulds's chemical business was a global one, and when the global chemicals industry went into recession it embarked on a heavy cost-cutting programme starting with closure of its viscose plant in France; this left its other plants working close to capacity and the share price soared. In 1982 Carrington Viyella was swallowed up by a minnow one-seventh its size, Sir David Alliance's Vantona; ICI, which owned 49 per cent of Carrington Viyella, was happy to pocket the cash. A further merger in 1986 with the thread makers Coats created Coats Viyella. The Viyella fabric enjoyed a renaissance in the late 1980s as traditionalist designers like Laura Ashley took it up; Coats Viyella built a new mill at Barrowford, Lancashire, to produce the cloth, but demand subsided again and it closed within a decade.

The early 1980s also saw the end of Kagan Textiles, the group that pioneered Gannex and, after a series of mergers and takovers, had been for a time one of Yorkshire's most successful and efficient clothiers. The company was already in decline when Lord Kagan, who had fled abroad, was extradited from France in 1980 and jailed for tax fraud. The manufacture of Gannex ended soon after, and later in the decade Kagan's final mill closed.

Britain's shoe makers were also hard hit by imports, mostly from the Far East. Norvic of Norwich closed in 1981 and Etough's of Burton in 1989, and there were others. Even Clarks, who had tightened its grip on the children's market by taking over K Shoes the same year, felt the pressure, deciding in 1996 after heated debate within the owning family that the future lay in the brand rather than in manufacturing. Bata began running down production at East Tilbury as it shifted export production closer to the markets served. Yet Griggs continued to thrive as Doc Martens acquired one cult following after another. And Reebok, which had shifted most of its production from Bolton to Morecambe, also thrived as demand for its trainers soared at home and overseas; in 1984 it was taken over by a group of American investors who subsequently sold it on to Adidas.

The furniture industry took a hiding from the late 1970s from flatpack furniture – much of it imported from abroad – which proved immensely popular to do-it-yourselfers, despite the frequent absence of essential pieces and the failure of some that did arrive to fit. Parker Knoll morphed into Cornwell Parker in 1988 and embarked on a chain of acquisitions, closing its High Wycombe plant. Britain's furniture capital – which as recently as 1992 boasted 36 members of the British Furniture Manufacturers' Association – experienced not only that loss but the closure of G-Plan in 1992 with the loss of 700 jobs, the closure of Glenister's, the town's oldest surviving furniture maker, and the relocation of other companies to cheaper locations.

Wedgwood, a success story of the post-war decades, faltered in the recession of the early 1980s when it laid off nearly half its workforce. Its perceived weakness brought a hostile takeover bid from the London International Group, best known as the makers of Durex contraceptives. Sir Arthur Bryan fought this off, but realised Wedgwood needed a white knight and reckoned he had found one in the Waterford crystal company, who in 1986 bought Wedgwood for £254 million; the group was named Waterford Wedgwood. Wedgwood was the profitable part of the business, and under a new chief executive – Patrick Byrne, formerly of Ford – had its bottom line strengthened by the sale of non-core businesses and a reduction in the range of patterns from over 400 to around 240.

The Thatcher/Major years also brought a regrouping in Britain's paper industry, the main feature of which was a shift in control from British to foreign-owned companies. In 1967 the top ten paper and board producers were all British-owned; by 1997 only two were, and one of these – Arjo Wiggins Teape – was Anglo-French. At the same time the industry had modernised and its capacity had vastly increased: a far cry from the retrenchment that followed the Scandinavian challenge after Britain's joining of EFTA. The largest players were now David S Smith (British), UPM-Kymmene of Finland, SCA (Sweden), BPB (British) and Fletcher-Challenge of

New Zealand, who were about to sell their interests to Metsa-Serla of Finland. David S Smith had been a small packaging materials company until 1983, from when the entrepreneur Richard Brewster used it as a vehicle for acquiring and modernising seven British mills. Another British success story was Inveresk, which after management bought it back from Georgia Pacific in 1990 modernised to produce as much paper from four mills as it had from 17 in the 1950s.

Bowater separated its British and US interests in 1984, two years after selling its paper mills to a management buyout which became UK Paper and was bought in 1990 by Fletcher-Challenge, its packaging and building products business being repackaged in 1995 as Rexam. Reed hived off its paper and packaging business in 1988 to another management buyout; it was soon snapped up by SCA who took forward Reed's plans to modernise its newsprint mill at Aylesford, Kent. Unilever sold its Workington board mill to a Swedish company, and its Purfleet operation to BPB. Two new Finnish-owned mills creating jobs in areas where government direction of industry had failed – at Shotton and near Fort William – increased competitive capacity. Overall, the industry by 1997 had a success story to tell: although it was still meeting barely 40 per cent of home demand, exports at 1,438,000 tonnes were 840 per cent higher than in 1967, the markets having shifted from the Antipodes and South Africa to France, Germany and the Netherlands. Moreover, the proportion of imported wood pulp used in the production process had been halved, while recycling of waste paper had doubled to 59 per cent.

Nineteen eighty-nine brought seismic events in the wider world. That April the Chinese Communist authorities brutally suppressed a pro-democracy demonstration in Tienanmen Square, demonstrating their inflexible determination to remain in control. Seven months later the Berlin Wall fell, the critical proof that the Soviet Union had lost the political will to keep its ring of Communist satellite states isolated from the West. A crude reading of these developments would have been that Russia and neighbouring countries were now ripe for a transformation to capitalist prosperity, while China would remain in thrall to the disastrous economic performance that seemed an inevitable by-product of Marxism.

The reality would turn out to be very different. Over the decades that followed China, whose Communist Party had approved the opening up of the economy as far back as 1978, would embrace a rampant capitalism backed by subtle forms of protectionism and a distortedly favourable exchange rate policy, that would in turn generate an export-led boom giving it a near-stranglehold over the global economy, without relaxing central political control. This would come to fruition in the new century, but the groundwork was laid in the 1990s.

Meanwhile there was indeed a transition to capitalism in Russia and across central and eastern Europe. But as befits a country where the word *biznisman* meant 'criminal', the commanding heights of the Soviet economy – apart from those so bankrupt as to be unrescu-able – fell largely into the hands of well-connected opportunists and gangsters. British and other Western firms who rushed to invest in Russia in the belief that turning round a basket-case economy would be easy, were for the most part disappointed; while some of the most persistent did earn profits, many were defeated by the Russian way of doing things.

Russia's former satellite countries proved much more fruit-ful. Western firms during the 1990s found them ideal territory for investment, company after company harnessing cheap, well-qualified and motivated workforces and capitalising on a thirst for consumer goods denied them under the rigidity of communism. German firms took the lead, moving into a region of Europe the country had long regarded as its economic, and at times its actual, backyard. If the reunification of the two Germanies under Helmut Kohl, with the Communist Ostmark given an unmerited parity with the all-powerful Deutschmark, handicapped Germany's own economy for a decade, it proved a springboard for a surge of investment in Poland, Hungary and other highly receptive nations. Investment in new manufacturing plants by the likes of Volkswagen and Siemens paid off handsomely, strengthening their global competitiveness; moreover VW pulled off a coup in taking over and turning round Skoda, whose cars were previously a laughing-stock.

Britain's manufacturers did not follow suit. Conservative GEC was not looking to increase its manufacturing capacity, and had largely pulled out of making those consumer goods that could have been produced more cheaply behind the former Iron Curtain. Nor did it show interest in taking over existing plants there, most of which did not appear competitive. ICI, while attempting to refocus from bulk chemicals, was reluctant to add to its chain of domestic plants, though it did enter the paint business in Poland. The former British Leyland, having disposed of its plants in western Europe, lacked the resources to invest in the East; but before long it was part of BMW which had its own aspirations for *Mitteleuropa*. British Aerospace had more than enough capacity for building its shrinking range of products – coupled with a lack of will to stay in the lighter end of the civil aircraft market for which there might have been demand in the East. Nor were many smaller British manufacturers looking to the East as creating new opportunities; one of the very few exceptions was the train maker Hunslet, which briefly took over its Hungarian counterpart Ganz.

German firms' surge of manufacturing investment in these countries underlined the lack, by the 1990s, of sizeable British manufacturers with the confidence and ambition to compete on the European, let alone the global, stage. Such companies did exist in other sectors – notably Tesco, who identified the countries east of Germany as an opportunity at the very outset and built up success-ful chains of supermarkets in Poland, Hungary, the Czech Republic and Slovakia. But this merely emphasised the extent to which British business had given up on manufacturing – even before the wholesale transfer of work and jobs from Britain to eastern Europe that would follow in the new century.

5

SELLING UP AND
SELLING OUT: 1997-2012

The seismic general election of 1997 did not bring with a new government any discernible change in stance toward the economy, business and industry, as had occurred with every other such transition in probably a century. While New Labour under Tony Blair promised an energetic governing ethos after its landslide victory over an exhausted Tory administration weakened by internal divisions over Europe, there was to be no change in economic philosophy. Gordon Brown as Chancellor continued the fiscal policies which under Kenneth Clarke had brought steady recovery, initially keeping tight controls on public spending. Under his stewardship Britain enjoyed growth for a further decade, weathering global economic shocks and the collapse in 2000 of the dotcom boom. There were, at most, changes in mood: New Labour introduced a minimum wage and a right to trade union recognition, embraced the European Social Chapter and adopted a less confrontational stance to Europe generally. Brown also gave the Bank of England independence to set interest rates in return for stripping it of its responsibility for regulating the banks, the Old Lady of Threadneedle Street having been found wanting in the collapse of the Bank of Credit & Commerce International; its successor the Financial Services Authority would fare no better.

Unfortunately for British manufacturing, continuation of relatively benign economic policies was accompanied by the perpetuation – even intensification – of the 'hands off' approach pursued by Margaret Thatcher and John Major. Implicit in Blair's determination to persuade France and Germany, in particular, to give British business the same opportunities their firms enjoyed in Britain under the Single Market – which culminated in the Lisbon EU summit of 2000 adopting an ambitious, if abortive, programme of economic reform inspired from London – was a need to demonstrate that British companies were not in the government's pocket.

The manufacturing sector – despite continuing patches of excellence – was by now seriously weakened. And while the economy as a whole prospered in the decade up to 2007 as Brown's boast to have ended 'boom and bust' appeared justified by events, that base weakened further still, the number of people employed in manufacturing almost halving again from 4,278,000 in 1997 to 2,494,000 in 2010. Financial and business services were seen in government as the way forward for Britain, with manufacturing recognised as globally competitive only in aerospace and pharmaceuticals – a far cry from the 1950s. Strategies for innovation and growth were adopted for a handful of industries – starting with aerospace, the motor industry and electronics – but even these were cruelly exposed to the cold wind of market forces.

Economic growth created some 1.6 million new jobs between 2000 and 2010, most but not all in the service sector. Of these, more than 80 per cent were filled not by a new generation of British workers, but by immigrants. Labour proved as unable as the Conservatives to staunch a growing flow of legal and illegal economic migrants – many claiming political asylum – from countries around the globe, and eventually began to argue that immigration was beneficial to the economy. Even before the EU was enlarged in 2004 with the admission of the former Communist countries of eastern Europe, their inhabitants (starting with thousands of Poles) flooded in. With a readiness to work harder for less and frequently with better qualifications, they were snapped up by employers frustrated at the output of a British education system increasingly geared to getting 50 per cent of its charges to university – regardless of what they would study there and its relevance to their prospects for employment – rather than ensuring that the rest could read, write and add up. While most of the immigrants without high skills went into the service sector, they made an impact in some areas of manufacturing, notably food processing.

As workers flooded in to Britain, manufacturing jobs flooded out. Takeovers by multinationals in earlier decades that had not been followed up by investment, now brought plant closures as production was switched to cheaper or more corporately convenient locations in the EU, eastern Europe and the Far East. British-owned companies increasingly followed suit, though usually keeping R&D and design work at home; Hornby moved production of its model trains to China and Clarks its shoe production to Brazil and Asia. Raleigh ended volume cycle production at Nottingham in 1999 and four years later shifted its high-end manufacture to Vietnam; by now the frames for the iconic Dawes Galaxy were being manufactured in the Far East, though the cycles themselves were still assembled in Birmingham. Dyson moved vacuum cleaner production from Malmesbury to Malaysia after the local council rejected plans to extend the factory. Other entrepreneurs – like Alan Sugar before them – never even considered manufacturing in Britain: GHD, the Leeds-based manufacturer of hair straighteners, were clever enough to identify a potentially world-beating patent held by a South Korean inventor – they had the product manufactured in that country and marketed it with verve.

The luxury goods maker Mulberry warned that the level of National Insurance contributions might force it to start manufacturing in the Far East. A few companies – Boots after its merger with Allied and the building products supplier Woleseley – even moved their corporate headquarters to Zug in Switzerland to get round paying taxes in Britain. Meanwhile 'non-doms' – foreigners mainly in the financial services sector living in Britain – threatened to leave if the government stopped subsidising them for being rich. After the banking crash of 2007-8, their main argument appeared to be that if made to pay British taxes, they would go off and wreck someone else's economy instead. In this climate, it was no surprise that boardroom rewards in manufacturing far outstripped the pay of productive workers as directors tried to catch up with their counterparts in financial services. It was, however, somewhat easier to justify the £20 million paid in 2003 to Jean-Pierre Garnier, chief executive of the globally successful GlaxoSmithKline, than the 'rewards for failure' given to some of his most disastrous counterparts in other companies as they were shown the door – or the gargantuan pension pots awarded to themselves by the final owners of Rover when they took over the company. But these were the days in which Stephen Hinchcliffe, builder of the short-lived retail empire Facia, told his financial PR adviser that the first thing he did when he acquired a company was 'sit down and write myself a big fat cheque'. Hinchcliffe was sentenced in 2001 to five years for fraud, but generally corporate greed did not violate the law – and sometimes went almost unremarked. The days when the British economy was based on making things seemed a long way off.

The trade unions protested at each new round of offshoring, but could do little about it. Their membership in the private sector was falling in step with employment in manufacturing, reflected in a further round of mergers – most notably the AEU and the managerial and technical union MSF with the banking and paperworkers' unions to form Amicus in 2001, and then Amicus and the T&G in 2007 to form Unite. By 2011 the combined membership of Unite had fallen to 1.2 million, less than that of each of its main components in the 1980s and half that of the T&G alone in its prime. The unions' membership and muscle were now far stronger in the public sector, where by 2011 pay had overtaken that in the private sector. The Labour government's eventual generosity to the NHS in particular and its unwillingness to upset the unions by tackling increasingly unaffordable pensions, set the scene for a confrontation when the coalition government moved to make public sector workers retire later and contribute more to those pensions.

The 2000s were notable for the takeover of flagship British businesses by overseas firms – rather than the other way round. In 2001 Blue Circle sold out to the French cement maker Lafarge, making it the world's largest cement producer as Blue Circle itself had been around 1970; BOC (formerly British Oxygen) was taken over in 2006 by Linde of Germany; Boots the same year merged with the pan-European Alliance UniChem; Pilkington, also in 2006, sold out to the smaller Japanese company NSG; Hanson in 2007 to Germany's Heidelberg; the rump of ICI the same year to the Netherlands-based AkzoNobel and, most controversially, in 2010 Cadbury was taken over by the US multinational Kraft. Most of these takeovers, and many smaller ones, meant the shares of a smaller proportion of British industry being traded in London – and more decisions affecting it taken in boardrooms overseas. Moreover, takeovers by companies whose shares were quoted on Wall Street, in Tokyo or in Frankfurt, were increasingly overshadowed by acquisitions by private equity houses – most but not all of them American – which were accountable only to the individuals who had put up the money.

Britain's corporate landscape changed faster and faster as the money-go-round accelerated, and what a firm produced increasingly played second fiddle to what it could be bought and sold for. Once again the FT 30 index – relaunched in interactive form in 2011 – gives an indication of the broader picture. In 1998 the Prudential replaced faltering Courtaulds. The next year British Aerospace replaced the troubled Lucas Varity; GEC morphed into Marconi, and BTR, having taken over Siebe, into Invensys. The year 2000 brought the entry of the Royal Bank of Scotland after its takeover of NatWest, and of Logica on the merger of two of Britain's pharmaceutical giants into GlaxoSmithKline. In 2001 the caterers Compass joined the index after Blue Circle's takeover by Lafarge; British American Tobacco joined the index in 2002 on the collapse of Marconi; ITV replaced Granada in 2004 when the latter merged with Carlton, and in 2005 the Hilton group (soon to rename itself Ladbrokes after selling its hotels) supplanted Allied Domecq on that company's merger with Pernod Ricard. In 2006 Land Securities replaced P&O on the latter's takeover by Dubai's DP World, Alliance Boots took over the listing of Boots after its merger with Alliance UniChem, and Woleseley supplanted BOC, taken over by Linde. The year of 2007 was even busier: National Grid replaced Scottish Power after its takeover by Iberdola; the investment managers Man Group replaced Alliance Boots which had been snapped up by the private equity house KKR;

the advertising group WPP replaced EMI – by now purely a music and recording company – and 3i (the privatised Investors in Industry) supplanted ICI after its takeover by Akzo Nobel. Amid the global banking crisis, the pace slowed a little and 2008 brought only the renaming of Reuters as Thomson Reuters after a takeover, and of Cadbury Schweppes as Cadbury after the demerger of its soft drinks business. The year 2009 saw the arrival of Reckitt Benckizer after Thomson Reuters pulled its listing in London (still being traded in New York and Tokyo), and 2010 the arrival of Smiths Group after Cadbury's takeover by Kraft. The following year, British Airways was relisted as International Airlines Group after its merger with Iberia.

That bald timeline encompasses a host of remarkable and poignant stories, none more so then the fall of two of the giants of the 20th-century British economy – GEC and ICI – in circumstances the average coroner would record in the one case as suicide and in the other as wilful self-neglect. For while the demise of these two industrial behemoths, with government looking on as a mesmerised bystander, was not intended, it was most certainly self-administered.

The collapse of GEC almost the moment Lord Weinstock had relinquished control, follows the conventional pattern of Greek tragedy; overweening pride and loss of contact with reality leading to downfall, all played out before a horrified Weinstock who saw his once-mighty shareholding evaporate. Government, industry and Europe's industrial establishment all expected George Simpson to continue building on GEC's strengths; Weinstock acclaimed him as a 'man of vision' and Tony Blair gave him a peerage. He might have called an end to joint ventures in transport, power generation and some areas of defence, but the three areas he intended to build on – defence and aerospace (Marconi Electronic Systems), industrial electronics (GEC Industrial Electronics) and communications (GEC Communications) – all looked bankers for growth. To begin with, Simpson used the cash pile Weinstock had built up to expand;

$1.4 billion was paid for the American defence contractor Tracor, and Kvaerner's Govan shipyard was taken over. But his refocusing of the company also involved disposals.

Weinstock had formed the GEC-Alsthom joint venture with the French to boost GEC's export prospects in Europe for transport and power generation equipment. But the business did not fit into Simpson's plan. GEC's corporate withdrawal – both GEC and Alcatel sold off 23.6 per cent of the capital in 1998 – and the floating of the rebranded Alstom on the Paris stock exchange (delisting in London in 2003), left a sizeable and hitherto profitable chunk of British heavy industry in French hands with a minority of supine British directors unable or unwilling to protect it. When Alstom hit trouble in 2004 because of problems with its other activities in France, the restructuring (with the French government taking a 21 per cent stake), involved heavy job losses in Britain; notably at the former GEC Preston plant, one of Alstom's centres of excellence, and the end of train making at the Washwood Heath, Birmingham, facility GEC had acquired from Metro-Cammell.

Pressure was growing from the government, and indeed across Europe, for defence contractors to rationalise; BAe's managing director John Weston had been arguing for a while that 'Europe is supporting three times the number of the contractors on half the budget of the US.' That pressure became all the greater when Boeing took over McDonnell Douglas in 1997 to form a global giant in both civil and military aircraft manufacture. Weinstock had in the past considered GEC taking over BAe, and BAe was considering a merger with Germany's Daimler Chrysler Aerospace (DASA) when Simpson, at the start of 1999, negotiated the sale of GEC's Marconi Electronic Systems to BAe for £7.7 billion.

The sale strengthened BAe as a 'national champion' and created some sensible synergies: BAe was MES's largest customer, more of Britain's warship yards became singly managed and two contractors on avionics for the Eurofighter were now one. But it upset the French and the Germans – who promptly merged DASA, Aerospatiale and Spain's principal aircraft company CASA to form the giant EADS;

unlike BAe, a global competitor to Boeing. It also upset Blair, who had wanted BAe to merge with DASA. But Simpson still had two-thirds of GEC – and now a cash pile even bigger than Weinstock's: when the sale to BAe was completed GEC was worth £35 billion.

That situation did not last long. Simpson, determined to reposition GEC – renamed Marconi in November 1999 – as a leader in the high-tech communications industry, and with the company's new finance director John Mayo, embarked on a trail of acquisitions in the United States that made them regulars in the Concorde lounge at Kennedy Airport. In March 1999 they bought Reltec (a telecoms network products company) for £1.3 billion, Fore Systems (an internet switching equipment company) followed and a year later Bosch Public Networks and Mobile Systems International. Each of these acquisitions – which by their conclusion had used up the cash pile and forced Marconi to borrow – were expected to benefit the company by broadening its reach, especially the United States which accounted for 50 per cent of the global telecoms market.

In the second week of March, 2000 – just before the MSI acquisition – the dotcom bubble burst. Shares in companies with no actual value had soared to dizzying peaks, but from this point the high-tech stocks that made up New York's NASDAQ index lost 80 per cent of their value. It rapidly became clear that the companies Marconi had spent so lavishly to acquire were no longer worth anything like what had been paid for them, and that Marconi itself was now in trouble. A botched profits warning in July 2001 was followed by the departure of Mayo, by then deputy chief executive. A further profits warning that September left Marconi's shares classed as 'junk'; Simpson – months before his planned retirement – was sacked, and Marconi's chairman, Sir Roger Hurn, resigned.

A major restructuring enabled Marconi to limp on, concentrating on its now core business of developing and making telecoms equipment. It had high hopes of long-term business from British Telecom's 21CN project: the replacement of System X and other switching systems by an Internet Protocol system. Marconi was expected to be one of the contractors selected, and its exclusion from BT's list of successful bidders in April 2005 was too much for the company to survive. Ericsson purchased the bulk of the business, other elements in the telecoms and internet services field regrouping as Telent; now headquartered at Warwick and owned by the Pension Corporation, Telent has 2,000 employees in Britain and Germany – a far cry from the quarter-million who once worked proudly for GEC. Other fragments of GEC carried on under management buyouts, but by the end of the decade several of the gaps left by the shipwreck of the company were being quietly filled by Siemens, with 13 UK manufacturing sites employing 8,000 people, a renewables centre opening in Manchester in 2012 and a wind turbine factory in Hull creating 700 jobs. As for Lord Simpson, he prudently took leave of absence from the House of Lords in 2004.

The demise of ICI, like that of GEC, was the product of a flawed corporate vision; both companies were driven at high speed into a cul de sac, though ICI at least remained profitable to the end. However, the company had lost enthusiasm for the bulk chemicals business on which it was founded some time before; it sought to concentrate on the higher-value end of the market with a string of acquisitions, only to find that these did not integrate well and that important subsidiaries had to be sold off to clear the borrowings incurred. (Not all departures from bulk chemicals by companies in the sector involved abandoning commercially viable processes: the former Steetley Magnesite plant at Hartlepool, Britain's only producer of the material from which refractory bricks for the steel industry are made, closed in 2005 after a series of owners had failed to turn a profit.)

ICI's acquisitions dried up and the disposals continued: the company's petroleum business on Teesside and Tioxide, its titanium dioxide subsidiary, in 2000 went to the Huntsman Corporation – who also acquired assets originally sold to Du Pont when American regulators vetoed the deal, hitting ICI's share price at a critical moment. The loss-making remnants of its industrial chemicals business went to Ineos for £300,000. The acrylics business went too, but Charles Miller Smith's concept of a high-value chemicals business driven by innovation increasingly became a mirage. In 2006 Quest Fragrance,

ICI's flavours and fragrance business operating in 31 countries, was sold to Givaudan for £1.2 billion, and Uniqema, its Delaware-based skincare business created from five subsidiaries as recently as 1999, to the prudently-expanding British chemicals company Croda International for £410 million.

By then ICI comprised little more than the iconic Dulux paint business, and soon attracted a bid from the Dutch multinational AkzoNobel – the explosives division of which had been one of the original components of ICI. A first bid of £7.2 billion was rejected by ICI's shareholders, but an improved offer of £8 billion was accepted in August 2007. AkzoNobel already owned Berger Paints and the Darwen-based Crown Paints; the European Commission made it sell off the latter (to a management buyout) as had it retained both Dulux and Crown, AkzoNobel would have had 54 per cent of the UK market. ICI's adhesives business was sold to the German consumer chemicals company Henkel. ICI was dead, though such of its processes as had not been overtaken by technological advance lived on.

Another industrial giant of the 1930s and the post-war decades – Courtaulds – passed away at much the same time as its once deadly rival. Courtaulds plc, the non-textile side of the business, expired in 2000. Its aerospace sealants business – including a factory at Shildon, Co. Durham – was taken over by America's PPG Industries, and the chemical side of the company was acquired by AkzoNobel. The now-separate textile business moved largely offshore. In 2000 Sara Lee took it over, but the businesses did not fit and the American company became increasingly concerned at the size of Courtaulds's UK pension shortfall. In 2006, Courtaulds Textiles – still Britain's leading producer of underwear, employing 20,000 people in 16 countries – was taken over by the Hong Kong private company PD Enterprise, a major clothing manufacturer in its own right. The Courtaulds name survives.

There were further corporate deaths at the turn of the Millennium. BICC, which had been ailing for some time, sold its optical cables business to Corning in 1999, and its power cables businesses to the Kentucky-based General Cable Corporation; in earlier times GEC might well have been a bidder. General Cable sold parts of the business on to Pirelli, who in 2002 closed part of BICC's Erith works, transferring production to one of its other sites at Eastleigh. With the sale of its cable operations, BICC was left with the civil engineering company Balfour Beatty – taking its name in 2000.

Racal, too, reached the end of the line. It still had a future in 1998 when it reorganised its defence business into three sectors; as a member of the consortium chosen to deliver the Bowman radio for the Army, lucrative orders were in prospect. But Bowman got into greater and greater difficulties; Racal sold its telecoms business to America's fast-growing (and soon to be bankrupt) Global Crossing, and by the time the consortium delivering the bid collapsed, Racal had been taken over by Thomson-CSF, soon to be renamed Thales. The crash of Marconi, and of Ferranti some time before, effectively prevented Racal finding a home with a British bidder.

Equally ominous – and wholly unexpected – was a rash of closures affecting brand new high-tech facilities opened only recently under the Major government's drive for inward investment, on which so many hopes for jobs and growth had been pinned. Inward investment fell back after 1997, in part because of global economic troubles but also because of the Blair government's hesitation over whether to join the euro which made continental Europe a more attractive location for American and Far Eastern companies wanting a foothold in the EU. But the actual closures stemmed from a sudden deterioration in global prospects for the semiconductor industry, which left these new British plants highly vulnerable as the parent companies retrenched.

The first blow fell in August 1998, when Siemens announced the closure of its £1 billion semiconductor plant at Wallsend, with the loss of 1,100 jobs – just a year after it had been opened by the Queen. Siemens blamed overcapacity, a 95 per cent fall in microchip prices and dumping by Asian manufacturers. Critics blamed the high sterling exchange rate (around $1.67 against the dollar, not historically high, but rising against the Deutschmark to DM 3 as the advent of the euro neared). They noted that Siemens was just embarking on a joint chip venture in France with IBM. After the closure, Siemens was ordered to repay £18 million contributed by the taxpayer.

Weeks later, Motorola merged two plants in Glasgow because of plunging demand and prices for microchips. Then Fujitsu pulled the plug on its memory chip plant at Newton Aycliffe – chosen over Oregon with a fanfare just three years before – with the loss of a further 600 jobs. This closure was even more politically sensitive, as it was in Tony Blair's constituency; again the unions blamed the exchange rate. Fortunately that was not quite the end of the story, as the much smaller British telecoms equipment supplier Filtronic took over the gallium arsenide production facility at Newton Aycliffe for the production of compound semiconductors, selling it on to the North Carolina-based RF Micro Devices in 2007.

The global microchip crisis was not impacting solely on Britain: 1998 also brought a forced merger by Hyundai and LG of their chip businesses. Yet that in turn brought the most controversial closure of all: the LG plant at Newport which had been expected to transform the economy of South Wales by producing not only semiconductors, but a range of computer screens and television equipment such as cathode ray tubes. Hopes of 6,100 jobs being created had not long survived the start of construction; barely 2,000 people were taken on. Work on the semiconductor facility was never finished and the early years of the Welsh Assembly, which first convened in 1999, were taken up with recriminations over the £247 million paid to LG – in partnership with Philips – to attract it to Newport. Closure was in stages: all 870 jobs at the display production facility went in 2003, and three years later LG finally left Newport on the bankruptcy of its joint venture with Philips, production of LCD monitors being moved to Poland and China. LG returned £70 million of the subsidy, and Newport was left with a white elephant.

As with Newton Aycliffe, this was not quite the end of the story. The 750,000 sq ft LG building – described locally as 'an earthquake-proofed aircraft hangar' – was acquired in 2008 by Next Generation Data, who reopened part of it as a data hall for British Telecom, housing hundreds of server racks, and for Logica, managing the IT requirements of government clients. Just 120 people are employed at the facility in its new guise – but 500 more jobs were created when the Co. Fermanagh–based Quinn Group chose another former LG site in Newport as its new manufacturing base. It was acclaimed as 'the most modern radiator plant in the world', and for the taxpayer probably the most expensive.

The confidence that surrounded Britain's automotive industry *circa* 1997 was equally misplaced. Even before the world banking crisis brought a plunge in car and commercial vehicle production to mid-1980s levels, the industry was hit by one body-blow after another as decisions taken in Cologne, Detroit, Paris, Stuttgart and Zurich closed plants in Britain to refocus investment on continental Europe. One after another, the great automotive plants from the days when boardrooms in Britain took the decisions stopped producing cars or closed altogether. Only the Japanese-owned plants, which had been seen in the 1990s as an engine for driving up the productivity of British car makers, saved it from near-total collapse. Plants and companies changed hands to the point that, in the year of the Diamond Jubilee, not a single British-owned maker of more than a few dozen cars a year remained. Moreover Britain – in 1950 the world's second largest car producer – now accounted for just 1.8 per cent of global production; a performance barely comparable with its failed shipbuilding industry.

Between 1997 and 2008, UK car production fell from 1,711,923 to 1,446,619, and commercial vehicle production from 238,000 (already close to a historic low) to 203,000. A good two-thirds of each were for export, with the vast majority of cars, trucks, vans and buses on Britain's roads imported. The one bright spot was that Britain was producing far more engines – 2,396,717 – than vehicles, thanks to Ford.

Disaster did not strike immediately. Peugeot in 1998 started production of the 206 at Ryton, and the next year the former Rootes plant became the first in Europe to go on to a seven-day week to meet export orders. BMW poured investment into Longbridge and

Cowley, halting production of the Rover 100 (Metro) and in 2000, after 41 years, the traditional Mini. The Cowley-built executive Rover 75 was launched in 1998 – totally designed and engineered by BMW – and a new, updated Mini was eagerly awaited.

Rover's problem – and also BMW's – was that its mainstream models in the 200 and 400 series (rebadged the Rover 25 and 45) were not selling. Rover's global sales nosedived: from 364,350 in 1997 to 299,839 in 1998 and 203,755 in 1999, by which point its UK market share was below 5 per cent. Thousands of brand new Rovers were parked, unsold, at airfields across the Midlands, and the losses mounted – accentuated for BMW's German owners by the pound's high exchange rate against the mark and then the euro.

The German media began to refer to Rover as 'The English Patient', after the popular film of the day, and in February 1999 the Quandt family, who held a 48 per cent stake in BMW, decided they had had enough. Claiming that the Rover adventure had cost the company $500 million (a conservative estimate), they staged a coup to remove Berndt Pischetschrieder as BMW's chief executive; unrepentant about the purchase, he went on to become a successful CEO at Volkswagen. The BMW board nevertheless confirmed the investment in Longbridge, but in March 2000, a stormy supervisory board meeting ended in three members opposed to the Quandts resigning, and BMW pulling out of Rover. Cannily, BMW kept Cowley along with the rights to the new Mini which it was gearing up to produce, Rover's body panel plant at Swindon, and rights to the Triumph and Riley marques; Land Rover – which by 2000 was selling almost as many vehicles as Rover itself – they sold on to Ford.

The rump of Rover based on Longbridge – where the workforce was down to 9,000 – looked set to pass to the venture capitalists Alchemy Partners, headed by John Moulton. They aimed to let BMW continue producing the highly-regarded Rover 75 at Cowley, but halt production of the failing 25 and 45 and refocus a slimmed-down Longbridge on turning out 50,000 to 100,000 MGs a year. This proposal made sound business sense and with the benefit of hindsight could have worked, but aroused strong local opposition because of the thousands of jobs that would be lost at Rover and in its supply chain. There was relief when a counter-bid based on maintaining the volume car business came in from the Phoenix consortium, headed by John Towers, a former senior Rover executive.

BMW agreed to sell Longbridge for £10 to the 'Phoenix Four' – Towers, Peter Beale, Nick Stephenson and John Edwards. The sale went through in April 2000, together with Powertrain, Rover's engine plant, for £20 and Rover Capital, the company's car loans book, for £50. In the spirit of the age, the first thing the Phoenix Four did was organise themselves pay packages and pension pots totalling £42 million – 525,000 times what they had paid for the company.

The numbers went less well for MG Rover, as the company was rebranded. Producing the unsaleable Rover 25 and 45, and with Rover 75 production transferred to Longbridge, plus the MG TF, sales continued to decline: just over 170,000 in 2001, but barely 120,000 by 2004 – a quarter of the output in 1997 – despite the launch of a 'City Rover' hatchback developed in partnership with Tata of India, a car so suspect that Rover refused to let *Top Gear* test-drive it. A joint venture was agreed with Shanghai Automotive Industry Corporation (SAIC) to develop new models and technologies, with production of up to a million cars a year shared between Longbridge and locations in China. With SAIC putting in £1 billion for a 70 per cent stake, the deal would have been the salvation of MG Rover – at least in the short term – but it was vetoed by China's National Development and Reform Commission on the plausible ground that if BMW had not been able to turn Rover round, SAIC would be unlikely to.

By the end of 2004, with that verdict not yet in, MG Rover's accumulated losses had passed the £1 billion mark, and the company was in serious trouble; it had sold Longbridge to the property company St Modwen to raise cash, and the design rights for the Rover 25 and 75 to SAIC. Tony Blair intervened to back an alliance with SAIC, but the prospect of MG Rover 'going tits up', as one DTI official put it to me, increased to the point where the government withdrew its offer of a £120 million loan to keep the company afloat until a deal could be struck.

On 7 April 2005, MG Rover suspended production because it could not pay for more components, and shortly afterward the company placed itself in administration. With a general election imminent, Blair and Gordon Brown – spared adverse headlines by the death of the Pope – went to Birmingham to see what could be rescued. The government lent the company the money to pay the week's wages, but with SAIC refusing to buy the company – and threatening to sue anyone else who tried to produce the Rover 25 and 75 – Longbridge closed its gates. Six thousand Rover workers, and over 20,000 more in the supply chain, lost their jobs.

MG Rover's creditors were told there was little chance of their seeing any of their money, and the administrators prepared to sell its assets piecemeal. Despite renewed interest from SAIC, it was another Chinese state-owned firm – the country's oldest, Nanjing Automobile – that acquired most of the assets for £53 million, shipping out the Powertrain and Rover 25 production lines for reassembly in China. Despite Honda repossessing technology that had gone into MG Rover's model range, the first (MG-badged) cars rolled off those lines in Nanjing in 2007. That same year, Nanjing Automotive was taken over by SAIC, who had started to build the Rover 75-based Roewe 750. The rights to the Rover marque had by now been acquired by Ford, the owners of Land Rover. Throughout, the hope was held out by Nanjing and its successor that MG production would resume at Longbridge.

The National Audit Office cleared the government of blame for the collapse of MG Rover, but an accountants' report for the DTI was critical of the Phoenix Four, whom the Secretary of State, Peter Mandelson, said had not shown 'an ounce of humility'. The Four denied that they had enriched themselves while mismanaging the company and no charges were brought against them, but in 2011 they accepted disqualification as directors of any company from three to six years.

Britain's car making capacity had been greatly reduced even before MG Rover went 'tits up'. Ford had announced in 1999 that capacity at Dagenham would be increased from 272,000 to 450,000 vehicles a year, but just three years later car production at the plant – once Europe's largest – came traumatically to an end as the last of more than 10,000,000 Ford cars manufactured in Britain rolled off the production line. The decisive factor was a decision by Ford Europe not to tool the factory up for another generation of the Fiesta – by then the only model made at Dagenham, and secondary to its production in Spain; the sheer size and age of the plant made it harder to upgrade than comparable facilities in Germany and Spain in which there had been heavy investment. This left the only vehicles produced by Ford in Britain as the Transit and its derivatives in Southampton, only for that plant, too, to face closure in 2012. Ford retained Dagenham as a major producer of engines, around 1 million a year, with a tenth of its 1950s workforce of 40,000; a further 2,000 continued manufacturing EcoBoost engines at Bridgend. Part of the Dagenham site was earmarked by the Labour government for a giant prison.

The closure of Vauxhall's car plant at Luton in 2003 with the loss of 2,500 jobs was as big a shock. It had been considered one of Britain's most secure, but when the Vectra was discontinued GM Europe executives in Zurich decided it would be more economical to concentrate UK car manufacture on Ellesmere Port, whose future was secured for the time being with production from 2009 of the new model Astra. Luton's former Bedford van plant did stay in operation, GM buying out Isuzu's stake in 1998, and makes vehicles badged as Vauxhall, Opel, Renault and Nissan for the home and European markets, its star product being the Vivaro van.

Meanwhile, Peugeot's Ryton plant – despite its strong start to the millennium – had begun to struggle. It could not offer the economies of scale achievable at Peugeot's main plants in France and Spain, and also suffered by being at the end of a long line of supply which in tough times made its products uncompetitive. Ryton was effectively doomed when Peugeot decided not to assemble the new 207 there, and at the end of 2006 residual production of the 206 was moved to Slovakia. In January 2007 Ryton closed after nearly 60 years, 2,300 workers losing their jobs.

Britain's high-end car makers were faring better. Ford continued investing in Jaguar and Aston Martin, and from its acquisition from BMW in 2000, Land Rover. When Ford closed its production line at Halewood in 2000 after production of the final Escort, Jaguar took it over; it reopened the next year making the Jaguar X-Type, and later also the Land Rover Freelander. Jaguar's own Browns Lane, Coventry plant closed in 2006 as the company continued to lose money, with all production in the Midlands concentrated at Castle Bromwich. Jaguar Land Rover's R&D headquarters on the former V-bomber base at Gaydon, Warwickshire, also became the home of Aston Martin; production from the launch of the DB9 in 2004 was transferred there from the marque's traditional home at Newport Pagnell. In 2007 Ford sold Aston Martin – by then valued at almost $1 billion – to a Kuwaiti-backed consortium headed by David Richards.

Rolls-Royce and Bentley also passed from British hands to new, investing owners. Vickers put Rolls-Royce up for sale in 1998; BMW was tempted, but was outbid by Volkswagen who offered £430 million. However a clause in the ownership documents of Rolls-Royce inserted years before by its original parent stipulated if the automotive division was sold, Rolls-Royce plc would retain the Rolls-Royce name and logo. VW did not grasp this, and was infuriated when the aero engine maker licenced these to BMW, with whom it had recently been collaborating. A messy dispute culminated in BMW opening a new plant at Goodwood to manufacture Rolls-Royces in 2003, and VW retaining the traditional Rolls factory at Crewe – to manufacture a new generation of Bentleys. Emphasising its new commitment to performance, VW also in 1998 acquired Cosworth from Vickers.

Rolls-Royce, Bentley and Aston Martin all increased production, and were able to attract customers even when the global economy turned down. Demand for Rolls-Royces was high among the newly wealthy in Russia and – increasingly – China. Aston Martin fared well among bankers with bonuses and global admirers of James Bond chic, while the 'Baby Bentley' became the car of choice for lavishly rewarded Premier League footballers. Lotus, under Proton's ownership, developed a new model range, shared engineering development between its Norfolk factory, Malaysia, China and the United States and in 2010 re-entered Formula 1 after a 16-year gap.

Little by now was left of Britain's HGV industry, and capacity and production continued to decline. PACCAR, which had already acquired DAF Trucks and had owned Foden since 1980, took over Leyland Trucks in 1998. Foden production was switched to the Leyland plant, then discontinued in 2006 to allow more trucks to be produced there under other badges (including DAF but not Leyland); around 10,000 a year are now produced at Leyland, mainly for export. MAN closed the Sandbach factory of ERF, founded by one of the Foden family, in 2002, moving production to Salzburg. Iveco closed the Seddon Atkinson works at Oldham in 2004, transferring production to Spain. The dustcart maker Dennis Eagle was taken over in 2006 by the Spanish company Ras Roca. And when the Ministry of Defence sought bidders for the new generation of Army trucks, the choice was not Leyland v. Bedford as two decades previously but Germany's MAN v. America's Oshkosh.

Leyland's abdication from the bus market after swallowing up most of its British competitors had left the door open for Volvo – which now accounts for nearly half of all new registrations – DAF and MAN. But one British manufacturer thrived. Dennis moved on from the Dominator to the low-floor three-axle Trident 3 double-deck chassis, which sold heavily in export markets. In 2001 Dennis joined forces with two long-established bodybuilders – Alexander of Falkirk and Plaxton of Scarborough – to form a single company titled Alexander Dennis. Its range – with the capacity to provide body and chassis – has proved a match for Volvo: the Enviro400 is Britain's top-selling double-decker, and demand for the Enviro500 three-axle export version and the Enviro200 single-decker is also strong. Other survivors are Optare and the family-owned Wrightbus, who supply bodies for many Volvo double-deckers (Alexander bodying more DAFs) and is assembling the new generation Routemaster championed by London's mayor Boris Johnson.

Britain's high-end motorcycle industry had staged a minor revival as John Bloor rebuilt the fortunes of Triumph. The company overcame a fire that destroyed its Hinckley factory in 2002 on the eve of its centenary, and in 2008 expanded its companion plant in Thailand to produce 130,000 machines a year. Norton, too, flickered back to life after a series of false starts and a period of American ownership. Stuart Garner repatriated the company, opened a new factory at Donington Park and in 2011 secured a government loan to double production to 1,000 bikes a year. But Japan and Italy still firmly held the global market for racing and lightweight bikes, while in its own field Harley Davidson predominated.

The decline in automotive production had an inevitable impact on the wider engineering industry that was only partly offset by the slack created through the demise of Lucas. Turner & Newall – once an FT 30 index company – was bought out in 1998 by America's Federal-Mogul, before the extent of its liability for asbestosis claims had begun coming to light. It ceased its core operations in 2001, though subsidiaries like Ferodo continued to trade under the new owners. BTR and Siebe merged in 1999 to form Invensys; serious financial difficulties followed and it was 2004 before the company began to turn the corner after a number of disposals, going on to achieve critical mass. In the same year Rolls-Royce took over Vickers (minus the luxury car business hived off when Rolls was nationalised), selling its defence arm to Alvis; Alvis Vickers would be taken over by BAE Systems in 2004. GKN prospered to celebrate its 250th anniversary in 2009 as a solidly-founded global business, now producing components for Boeing in St Louis but reassuringly headquartered at Redditch. There were disposals (its armoured vehicles business in 1998 to Alvis, and Westland in 2004 to the Italian aerospace combine Finmeccanica), growth within the company (GKN Sinter Metals' powder metallurgy business), and acquisitions: several niche American companies and, in 2008, part of the Airbus UK plant at Filton.

Smiths Industries merged with TI in 2000, the combined Smiths Group selling off TI's automotive business. Smiths's successful US aerospace subsidiary was sold to GE in 2007 for $4.8 billion, and the next year Smiths reorganised itself into five divisions: detection, medical, John Crane (specialised industrial systems), Interconnect (critical electronic components) and Flex-Tek (fluid and gas moving components). In 2002 Michelin ended tyre production at Stoke – where it had once been the leading employer – with the loss of over 4,000 jobs, after its board in Clermont-Ferrand concluded that the plant, after decades of minimal investment, was no longer competitive. The process was sensitively handled, with the company going out of its way to help employees retrain and find other jobs and a Michelin Development Fund assisting local small businesses. However 1,000 workers were kept on retreading 250,000 mainly truck tyres a year, and in 2010 Michelin, sweetened by a £3.9 million government grant, announced a £20 million investment to modernise what was left of the plant.

Derby International, which owned Raleigh, parted with Sturmey-Archer (gears) to a Taiwanese company and Brooks (saddles) to Selle Royal of Italy in the 1990s. It sold off its equipment for volume cycle frame production in 1999, but financial problems persisted and in 2001 there was a management buyout of what was left of Raleigh, production in Britain finally ceasing soon after.

Pilkington retained its position as a global leader in glass manufacture, with 19 per cent of total production and a continuing record of innovation including self-cleaning float glass and energy-efficient glazing. But in 2006 the company fell to a takeover bid from Nippon Sheet Glass, which was half its size; the rationale being to create a competitor to match the even larger Asahi Glass. Private shareholders strongly opposed the takeover, but after NSG increased its offer the major institutions accepted. Pilkington has so far continued to be run from St Helen's, apparently accepted as the engine room for one of the world's big four glass companies.

Against this background of takeover and change, JCB – as a family firm less susceptible to a hostile bid – carried on undaunted, continuing to invest in its British factories as well as its 11 plants overseas, though forced into layoffs in the bleakest economic times. India (where JCB put £20 million into a new engine plant in 2010) was now the digger maker's biggest single market, with growth also surging in Brazil and Russia.

Of the three fields of high-tech industry in which Britain aspired to lead the world in 1952 – aircraft, computing and nuclear power – only in the first did it remain a global competitor by 1997. In the years that followed Britain gave up the capacity to manufacture a civil airliner, and effectively any large airframe, as BAe completed its transformation from a plane maker with strong European ties into a defence contractor with its cap set firmly at the United States where its shareholders were by now predominantly based. In the process, BAe through its acquisitions policy prevented Britain gaining a potentially dominant position in Airbus, then through sheer disinterest (though with a canny nose for timing) torpedoed the government's influence within the consortium.

As mentioned in the context of Marconi, it was the government's hope in the late 1990s that BAe would merge with Germany's DASA – the subsidiary of Daimler-Benz into which all the country's aircraft makers had been merged. This would not only have created a powerful plane maker in its own right, but a powerful counterweight to France's Aerospatiale within the Airbus consortium, where the crucial decisions were already being taken in Toulouse. BAe's Sir Dick Evans and DASA's Jurgen Schrempp agreed a merger at the end of 1998, but GEC then threw a spanner in the works by letting BAe know it was ready to part with its defence interests. The chemistry between BAe's Sir Dick Evans and GEC's Lord Simpson, the strategic view that the absorption of Marconi's defence interests would create a stronger competitor for American orders, and Evans's concern that an American competitor might snap up Marconi, overrode any sense of obligation to DASA.

The formation of BAE Systems in 1999 – the loss of 'aerospace' from the title was no coincidence – did indeed create a more powerful anglophone company, and one that over a decade would generate some £50 billion of exports, 80 per cent of them in defence sales. But its impact on Europe's aerospace landscape was seismic, as France, Germany and Spain responded by merging Aerospatiale, DASA and CASA to create EADS (the European Aeronautic, Defence and Space Company); with a workforce slightly larger than BAE Systems's 107,000, corporate headquarters in the Netherlands and a truly global reach. EADS not only held the lion's share in Airbus and a majority stake in the Eurofighter, it was the world's largest helicopter supplier and through Astrium – in which BAE Systems obligingly sold its 25 per cent stake – Europe's only serious player in space. It also had a 45.76 per cent stake in the supposedly independent French plane maker Dassault. Moreover, Daimler Chrysler in 2006 reduced its 30 per cent shareholding in EADS, putting France more firmly in the driving seat and in 2011 sold its stake to the German government.

Despite BAE Systems's choice of Marconi over DASA, the company was still looking for partners in Europe. In 2001 it joined EADS and Finmeccanica to set up MBDA, pulling together most of Europe's missile manufacturing capability into a single company with 10,000 employees and 13 plants in four countries, including Filton, Lostock, Stevenage and Henlow in Britain. Its products range from the anti-ship Exocet used so devastatingly by Argentina in the Falklands and the Milan anti-tank missile with which a Royal Marine holed an Argentine corvette, to more recently developed missiles like the Storm Shadow, fired from RAF Tornados against Colonel Gaddafi's bunkers in 2011. BAE Systems took a 37.5 per cent stake, its clout in this field increased by its acquisitions from GEC (Finmeccanica also bringing former GEC capabilities to the table).

Nor at this stage was BAE Systems lessening its commitment to Airbus, which provided a fruitful revenue stream. It participated fully in the restructuring of Airbus from a consortium into a single business, into which both EADS and BAE Systems transferred their Airbus factories in return for shares of 80 per cent and 20 per cent respectively in the new company, formed in 2001. However, for some time BAE Systems had little appetite for continuing to build civil airliners itself, and the sharp downturn in airline business after the terrorist attacks on America of 11 September 2001 gave it the pretext it needed to exit the sector. In 2003 it produced its last civil aircraft – the 6,033[rd] built in the UK since the end of the war – when the final Avro RJ (originally HS 146) came off the production line at Woodford, a further upgraded version having been cancelled. This left the Hawker 850 – a former BAE product – assembled by Hawker Beechcraft at Chester as the only civil aircraft being built in Britain, the Britten-Norman Islander being designed in Britain but fabricated in Romania.

As BAE Systems stepped up its engagement with the American market and Airbus went head-to-head with Boeing, overtaking it in new aircraft orders in 2003, the company grew steadily less comfortable with its involvement in the pan-European but now firmly French-based plane maker. Indeed Richard Olver, who took over as chairman in 2004, ruled out further European acquisitions or joint ventures and set a 'strategic bias' for expansion and investment in the United States. BAE Systems may also have picked up the first rumblings of the financial difficulties (stemming from development of the giant A380) that would afflict Airbus in 2007. By 2006 it had decided to sell its stake, conservatively estimated at £2.4 billion, but negotiations dragged on and eventually BAE decided to sell to EADS for the best price it could get, at a value to be set by Rothschilds. Days later, Airbus announced delays to the A380 and its share price fell. BAE could have stayed in and weathered the storm, but it pressed ahead – only to be told that the selling price would be £1.87 billion, way below even what EADS had expected to pay. The sale went through that October, Airbus changing its description from 'an EADS joint company with BAE Systems' to 'Airbus – an EADS company'.

If this looked to the outside world like a capitulation – and a pointless one at that – it went down even worse with the British government. Airbus had not only been a consortium of plane makers, but a partnership of governments, and BAE had taken its decision to pull out in minimal consultation with the Department of Trade and Industry, which managed the relationship. Labour's defence procurement minister Lord Drayson, a scientific entrepreneur in his own right, had been urging French and German politicians to stop interfering in EADS (Airbus's majority shareholder) to the point where he warned that Britain might withhold future contracts; now another potential weapon was denied him. Had the government been kept fully involved, it might have been able to negotiate some ongoing locus for itself in Airbus, as would the Germans; as it was, BAE Systems's desperation to get out, cut ministers' legs from under them. From now on the fate of Airbus, and the 14,000 British workers employed by it at Filton and Broughton, would depend on decisions taken in Toulouse, Berlin and Madrid. The only leverage the British government could still exert was through launch aid – if asked to provide it – and military procurement; this explained Whitehall's determination to keep the A400M military transport in development when by 2008 losses on it topped £1.5 billion.

Quite apart from the 1,600 redundancies announced in 2007 as the turbulence at Airbus reached its height, there were long-term concerns over Britiain's continued involvement. Unlike Germany, Britain had never stood out for an Airbus assembly line like the one at Hamburg, to which A320 production has been transferred, and most Airbus activity in Britain relates to the production of its wings. The increasing use of composites rather than conventional alloys in aircraft manufacture impacted heavily on Airbus, and there were fears for a time that adoption of these new materials might result in wing manufacture for new models being transferred from Britain to Spain, as BAE hesitated to embrace this technology. There were also logistical headaches in transporting the wings for the A380, which first flew in 2005, from North Wales to Toulouse: too large to be flown out in a Beluga transport like the wings for the rest of the range, they had to be taken down the river Dee by barge to the port of Mostyn for onward shipment to France. Nevertheless, Airbus UK has remained as fully engaged in the project as it can be given BAE's sacrifice of its political and boardroom clout. And in 2010 Airbus announced a £70 million investment at Filton to concentrate 2,500 of its employees onto a single Aerospace Park, this claiming to demonstrate its commitment to retaining a 'centre of excellence' in Bristol. Yet Filton, just like every car plant across Britain under overseas ownership, remains just one decision not to invest in a new model away from closure. Nor did Airbus's opening of an assembly line in Tianjin, China in 2008 bode well for Britain's long-term involvement. Moreover, British component suppliers generally find Airbus – unlike Boeing – barred to them.

BAE Systems's military aircraft portfolio was not without problems. A decade before the project's cancellation, the Nimrod MRA4 maritime reconnaissance aircraft was already running so far over budget that in 2000 the company wrote off £300 million, and two years later issued a profits warning. The Hawk trainer, in service for a quarter of a century, was the subject of fierce Cabinet debate before the MoD was cleared to order a further 20, with options for 24 more: the order was necessary to trigger a larger contract from India, in which later aircraft were manufactured under licence by Hindustan Aeronautics.

Production of the Tornado with Germany and Italy ended in 1998 with 992 aircraft delivered, and by then production contracts for the Eurofighter Typhoon were finally being signed by BAe, DASA, CASA and Aeritalia. Had BAe gone ahead with its merger with DASA, it would have had a 66.5 per cent stake in the project; as it was, it emerged with 37.42 per cent, outvoted by EADS with 43 per cent in a project that had originally been its brainchild.

Political wrangles over how many planes should be produced for each of the participating air forces and who should contribute the avionics had made the lead time for the aircraft an eternity. Lord Gilbert, returning to the MoD as a minister in 1997 after an absence of 18 years, recalled that what became the Eurofighter had taken up most of his time there in his previous incarnation, yet the plane had still to enter service. There were also continuing doubts over the soaring cost of the project (€120 million per aircraft on German estimates), whether the RAF actually needed the 232 planes it was committed to take, and indeed whether a highly sophisticated jet fighter planned in the Cold War for dogfights over the plains of Germany was what was most needed in a world where the threats now came from terrorists and rogue states in the Near East. However the contract concluded with BAE Systems who – not for the only time – made cancellation of the final tranche almost as costly an option as taking delivery of the planes.

It was 2008 – 54 months behind schedule – before the first Typhoons were delivered to the Luftwaffe and the RAF. In service the planes proved themselves technically sound, though they cost £90,000 an hour to operate, twice the cost of a Tornado. However the expense and over-supply of the successive tranches of Typhoon allocated to the RAF led the government to seek export markets, 72 being diverted to Saudi Arabia.

The Saudi order, concluded in 2005, fell within the continuing

Al Yamamah oil-for-planes agreement, then entering its third decade. By then, despite its commercial benefits, Al Yamamah was attracting attention from the media and the legal authorities which was even more unwelcome to the secretive Saudi royal family than to BAE Systems. A former BAE Systems employee had notified the Serious Fraud Office (SFO) in 2001 that he had evidence of the company operating a 'slush fund', and two years later the SFO's follow-up letter to the MoD was leaked to *The Guardian*. In 2004 a BBC documentary alleged that the 'slush fund' was connected to Al Yamamah and totalled £60 million, and that bribes had been paid to Prince Turki Bin Nasser, a son-in-law of the Saudi defence minister and the man handling the Saudi end of Al Yamamah. A later programme accused BAE Systems of having paid 'hundreds of millions of pounds to the ex-Saudi ambassador to the US, Prince Bandar bin Sultan.'

The National Audit Office had been investigating the finances of Al Yahamah since 1992, when it gave the project a clean bill of health but unprecedentedly did not publish its report. But it was the SFO who took the issue forward, making two arrests in 2004. BAE Systems officially welcomed the investigation, but by 2006 the ongoing inquiry was threatening to compromise the sale to Saudi Arabia of the 72 Typhoons. Stories were planted with the press that the Saudis might order Rafales from Dassault instead, and the Saudi government threatened to withdraw anti-terrorism co-operation (crucial in view of Al Qaeda's origins in Saudi Arabia and in the wake of the July 2005 London bombings) if its royal family's dirty washing was aired in a British court. With the Attorney-General Lord Goldsmith negotiating a plea bargain for BAE Systems and Tony Blair pressing for the prosecution to be dropped, Prince Bandar pointedly called on President Chirac to add credibility to the Rafale alternative. In December 2006 Lord Goldsmith halted the SFO investigation on grounds of public interest, Blair saying that Britain's 'strategic interest' in its relationship with Saudi Arabia came first. A High Court judge refused to accept the termination, but was overruled by superior courts. The first Typhoons were delivered to the Saudi Air Force in 2009.

BAE Systems's embarrassment gave heart to its competitors in the

United States, not because they were in a position to bid for Saudi orders but because BAE Systems's growing clout in US markets – which traditionally had been closed to foreign companies – could be neutralised if it were found to have engaged in bribery. The Department of Justice launched its own investigation in 2007, concentrating on claims that a US bank had been used to channel payments to Prince Bandar. In May 2008 BAE Systems's chief executive Mike Turner and Nigel Rudd, a non-executive director, were briefly and embarrassingly detained at American airports, and a number of subpoenas were issued against BAE Systems's US subsidiary and some of its employees. A plea bargain was reached in 2010, under which BAE Systems paid a $400 million fine for what Judge John Bates called 'deception, duplicity and knowing violations of the law on an enormous scale' – but escaped a formal conviction which would have led to its being blacklisted internationally from future contracts.

Conscious of the need to disown such practices if it were to continue to win contracts worldwide, BAE Systems set up a review of its own conduct under the distinguished former judge Lord Woolf; this concluded that 'in the past BAE [Systems] did not pay sufficient attention to ethical standards in the way it conducted business' and made 23 recommendations for guaranteeing business standards, which were implemented. However the company was by then embroiled in what the SFO described as potentially the biggest corporate corruption investigation in British legal history – over payments of £7.7 million made to a Tanzanian businessman in connection with a £28 million contract for an air traffic control system concluded in 2001, and deals with three other countries where it suspected bribes had been paid. The system supplied to Tanzania had been condemned by the International Civil Aviation Organisation as 'not adequate and too expensive'. This time BAE Systems did strike a deal with the SFO: it offered the people of Tanzania £30 million, and agreed to pay a fine of £500,000 for failing to keep proper records. When the case reached Southwark Crown Court in December 2010, the judge made plain his irritation that the fine was to be deducted from the £30 million – putting him under pressure not to impose a stiffer penalty.

As BAE Systems went for the American market, it not only made acquisitions across the Atlantic but broadened its range to offer as much to armies as it could already provide for navies and air forces. BAE Systems broke precedent in 2000 by acquiring Lockheed Martin Aerospace Electronic Systems, the first of a series of American companies engaged on advanced and classified work that required the company to leave (or put) US citizens in charge. In 2002 the company lost out to Northrop Grumman in a bidding war for the American aerospace, automotive and defence business TRW. But two years later it outbid General Dynamics to take control of Alvis Vickers, and the next year snapped up United Defense Industries, one of GD's main competitors and make of the US Army's iconic Bradley Fighting Vehicle. In 2007 BAE Systems increased its transatlantic presence by acquiring Armor Holdings, a maker of tactical wheeled vehicles. The following year it became Australia's largest defence contractor with its purchase of Tenix Defence, and purchased the British intelligence and security technology group Detica. Then, in September 2012, BAE Systems effectively conceded the failure of its strategy by announcing that it had in principle agreed a merger with EADS. The implications of a deal that seemed likely to augur a further contraction in Britain's aerospace industry were still being debated when Germany's Chancellor Angela Markel blocked it, refusing to countenance any dilution of her government's stake in EADS – and leaving BAE with a crisis of identity and confidence. Over time BAE Systems sold off its German naval systems business to ThyssenKrupp and EADS, and its 35 per cent holding in Saab, whose Gripen fighter aircraft had been dogged by allegations of bribery to secure exports.

BAE Systems by now was gaining more business from the Pentagon than from the MoD, but there were no guarantees of success in a highly competitive American market. The company won a lucrative contract in 2007 to remanufacture the US Army's Bradleys, but suffered a major setback two years later when its former Armor Holdings business was beaten by Oshkosh for the $3.7 billion Family of Medium Tactical Vehicles contract. BAE Systems and another bidder, Navistar, protested, but the award stood and the company made a £592 million writedown in its accounts. Though it continued to compete energetically for US military contracts, there were hints that BAE Systems might be trying to restore the balance of its business.

As BAE Systems took shape, Labour ministers realised that a monolith – in some respects a monopoly, and the MoD's largest contractor by a factor of four – was being created, and they were not entirely happy with what they saw. Delays and cost overruns had long been endemic, but those for the Nimrod MRA4 and the Astute class nuclear submarines were heroic even by the MoD's standards. BAE Systems did itself no favours upstaging the government's announcement in 2002 that its Glasgow shipyards had been given an order to build Type 45 frigates, by announcing a raft of redundancies. Ministerial tempers were raised further when Admiral Sir Raymond Lygo, the company's chief executive in the 1980s, told the BBC that BAE Systems routinely quoted unrealistic prices to make sure it won contracts from the MoD.

Deteriorating relations with government contributed to a boardroom coup in 2002 that saw John Weston replaced as chief executive by Mike Turner. But things did not improve, and BAE Systems paid the price. Woundingly, the MoD built up Vosper Thronycroft as an alternative builder of warships to BAE Systems; it then announced that France's Thales, not BAE, would take charge of the programme to build two giant aircraft carriers. And at the start of 2004, Airbus and Thales were chosen ahead of BAE Systems and Boeing to deliver the £13 billion PFI contract for a new fleet of air tankers for the RAF, just as the National Audit Office coruscated BAE over £3.1 billion in cost overruns on the Typhoon, Nimrod and Astute. The *Evening Standard* quoted a senior MoD source as saying: 'You don't employ a plumber who continually floods your house.'

BAE Systems took the initiative by bringing in Richard Olver from BP as its chairman, and relations immediately began to mend – Turner leaving early in 2008. BAE Systems was given pride of place in the Defence Industrial Strategy published by the MoD in 2005 (though Thales remained involved), control over the aircraft carrier project was wrested back, and while strains continued over overruns, a degree of confidence between government and BAE Systems was restored, just as Al Yamamah was coming to the boil.

The lead times now expected for any new aircraft mandated that when production of the Typhoon was at its height, the government and BAE Systems were already looking to the next generation of fast jet. This was a collaborative project mainly with the United States: the Joint Strike Fighter (JSF) or F-35 Lightning II, a single-seater fighter required by the Pentagon to replace a range of fast jets from the F-16 to the Harrier, and by the MoD to supersede the Harrier and probably the Tornado. The development contract was signed in 1996, and five years later the project was awarded to Lockheed Martin, with Northrop Grumman and BAE Systems its 'Level 1' partners. Not only would BAE Systems be involved in manufacture, but Rolls-Royce was supplying the VSTOL (Vertical and Short Take-Off and Landing) technology it had developed from the Harrier for the fighters that were to replace that aircraft. Astonishingly, the technology was transferred to Lockheed Martin so comprehensively that Britain, under the agreement carelessly concluded by the MoD, would have lost the ability to operate and maintain its JSFs independently. It took a visit to the Pentagon in 2006 from Lord Drayson, threatening to pull Britain out of the project, for the RAF and its contractors to be allowed access to their own technology.

The JSF – named the Lightning in homage to earlier fighters produced by Lockheed and BAE Systems's constituent English Electric – is being assembled in the United States, Britain, Italy and Turkey. In Britain, most of the work will be done at BAE Systems's Warton and Samlesbury plants, though Rolls-Royce (in partnership with GE) are providing some of the engines, and GKN and Martin-Baker (who opened a factory in Pennsylvania in 2000 to make sure of continuing orders from the Pentagon) are among other UK companies with a total 15 per cent stake. The Pentagon has ordered 2,443 F-35s for its various forces; the MoD originally contemplated 150 for the RAF and Royal Navy, but will take fewer. The first test flight was made in 2006, and the first F-35s should enter service with the RAF in 2013. In the meantime, there has been a familiar political debate in the United States about delays (with an order from Australia at risk) and soaring costs, as the $65 million originally quoted for a basic

F-35 – excluding the engines – has gone out of the window. The Royal Navy has already decided, partly on cost ground but also because of fears of cancellation of one variant by the Pentagon – to switch from the VSTOL to the carrier-launched version of the J35.

By 2010 BAE Systems was producing just two conventional aircraft itself: the Hawk, and the Nimrod MRA4 – an upgrade of the original Comet-based Nimrod with more powerful engines, more advanced avionics and surveillance equipment and – critically – fewer crew, and the means for them to escape if the plane got into difficulties, which earlier Nimrods lacked. The MRA4 had made its first flight in 2004 and flown at the Farnborough Air Show in 2006, but ongoing problems meant that none had been released into service when in October 2010 the MRA4 was unilaterally cancelled as part of the coalition government's emergency package of cuts; nine years late and £789 million over budget. The squadrons that had been due to fly them were disbanded, and the aircraft themselves cut up. A year later, with production of both the Eurofighter and (finally) the Hawk running down, BAE Systems announced almost 3,000 redundancies at Brough, Samlesbury and Warton – with a consultation on the end of manufacturing at Brough.

There is a growing belief in the military community that manned fighters are obsolescent – not least because of the enormous cost of training pilots – and that the future lies with pilotless UAVs (Unmanned Aerial Vehicles) or drones. They came into their own in Afghanistan both as reconnaissance aircraft and as weapons – notably General Atomics' Predator. To date the MoD's largest UAV contract, worth almost £1 billion, has gone on Watchkeeper, a development by Thales of the Israeli Hermes 450; next in line is the Fire Shadow loitering munition from MBDA. BAE Systems is one of several British companies to be working on new-generation UAVs. Much of its most interesting work in this field is of necessity classified, but BAE Systems's Taranis, developed with Rolls-Royce, GE and QinetiQ, is in the public domain; its futuristic design has already sparked a host of reports of UFO sightings. Further down the road, BAE Systems and Dassault are collaborating on a UAV known as Telemos.

Rolls-Royce throughout this period continued to go from strength to strength, both as a constructor of aircraft engines and in its wider activities. Its engines were chosen to power new airliners by both Airbus and Boeing – though a mid-air explosion in a Trent 900 on a Qantas A380 in 2010 briefly raised questions. Its expertise with nuclear submarines made it a major participant when in 2008 the Labour government ordered the construction of a new generation of nuclear power stations – bringing together civil and military nuclear expertise a mere half-century late.

Rolls-Royce acquired Vickers in 1999 for its marine business – selling on the rest of the company including the Rolls-Royce luxury car operation – and in 2011 bid jointly with Daimler AG for Tognum AG, manufacturer of MTU diesel engines, greatly strengthening its capability in this field. While Rolls-Royce's headquarters remain firmly in Derby where it employs 11,000 workers, it began building an aerospace manufacturing plant in Virginia in 2009 and has also transferred some of its R&D to eastern Germany, benefiting from the generous grants the EU has permitted Berlin to make to attract business to the region post-reunification.

The decline in volume terms of Britain's aircraft industry was reflected in a thinning-out of component and avionics manufacturers. Some British firms stood their ground, like GKN, or expanded: Cobham, which since 1997 has built up a £2 billion annual business in communications and electronic warfare systems, and continues to acquire niche companies on both sides of the Atlantic, is a prime example. Surrey Satellites, a spin-off from the University of Surrey, became a global leader in the production of small satellites – and was duly snapped up by EADS Astrium. Chemring, a Fareham-based firm (that for almost a century had made electric light filaments), expanded its toehold in defence markets from the early 2000s with a string of acquisitions to make it a leading manufacturer in Britain and overseas of countermeasures equipment for vehicles, ships and aircraft, pyrotechnics and detection systems.

QinetiQ, the former research arm of the MoD privatised from 2003, has created technologies for aerospace firms and defence contractors the world over. Though barred from becoming a manufacturer as such, QinetiQ has originated some important niche items such as the Tarsier radar for detecting debris on airfield runways, which could prevent a repetition of the Concorde crash of 2000 and save the RAF tens of millions in repairs to jet fighters damaged by 'Fod'.

One niche manufacturer emerged in the late 2000s in a field that had begun to look like a dead end: hovercraft construction. Griffon Hoverwork was put together by the Gibraltar-based Baird Group in 2009 from two smaller companies in Southampton and the Isle of Wight; one with roots in the pioneering work of the 1950s. Offering a range of civil, military and rescue hovercraft seating from 5 to 180 – one of them capable of carrying two battle tanks – Griffon has picked up a range of orders from customers as varied as the Royal Marines, the RNLI, the Indian Coastguard, the Lithuanian Border Police and Avon Fire and Rescue. Its associate company, Universal, has developed the versatile Ranger 6x6 armoured car, powered by MAN engines, in which it is trying to interest the Army – despite the MoD's preference for buying American-originated vehicles 'off the peg' – and to win export orders.

As defence industries have become internationalised, foreign-based multinationals have manufactured more in Britain. Thales, partly owned by the French government, built on its acquisition of Racal Electronics by taking over the Glasgow optical engineering firm of Barr and Stroud from Pilkington. In 2001 it bought out BAE Systems's stake in Thomson Marconi Sonar to become the second largest participant in the UK defence industry after BAE Systems. Thales has been selected to deliver Watchkeeper for the Army and is part of the EADS-led Future Strategic Tanker consortium for the RAF; its acquisition of Alcatel's railway signalling business has also brought it work in Britain. Moreover, while Thales's selection to build the Royal Navy's two new aircraft carriers in 2003 did not survive the improvement in BAE Systems's relations with government, it remains a vital part of the 'carrier alliance' with BAE.

Raytheon UK added new capabilities, notably through its acquisition of Hughes and Texas Instruments in 1997. Sharing the Broughton plant with Airbus UK, it has fitted out the Shadow RMk1 reconnaissance aircraft – based on the Beechcraft King Air turboprop, first flown in 1964 – operated by 5 Squadron from RAF Waddington. General Dynamics is another American contractor to have won substantial business with the MoD, and heads a research consortium engaged with several British universities; its manufacturing effort in Britain relates mainly to armoured vehicles. And while the European contribution to Boeing's aircraft like the 787 Dreamliner is being led from Spain, some work is contracted out to British companies; the Rickmansworth-based Senior Group makes engine structures and mountings and other components on both sides of the Atlantic, for aircraft including both the 787 and the Airbus range. Boeing is also investing in R&D at Cambridge, Cranfield and especially Sheffield universities, and Ipeco, a family firm in Southend that makes pilots' seats.

Shipbuilding throughout this period was dominated by naval issues: overcapacity in the yards, a requirement for fewer new warships, and efforts by the MoD to retain a choice of prime contractors. In 1997 the MoD could choose from BAE Systems, GEC, Kvaerner and VT; before long three of these would disappear, but roles would be found for Thales and Babcock as the troubled order for two giant aircraft carriers got under way. At the same time, merchant shipbuilding in Britain, while still in decline, refused to lay down and die.

Kvaerner got out of shipbuilding in 1999, selling its struggling Govan yard to GEC-Marconi, who already owned nearby Yarrow and the former Vickers yard at Barrow, which in 1997 had been awarded the contract to build three Astute class nuclear submarines. Almost immediately, Marconi Marine was absorbed into BAE Systems, making it the dominant force in naval shipbuilding. Not quite a monopoly, though; with ministers keen to maintain competition, a contract for three Type 45 destroyers was awarded to VT, which had built up a lucrative business building smaller naval vessels for export and the odd luxury yacht.

VT moved its main construction facility from Woolton to Portsmouth dockyard to fulfil the order, the final stages of which would be carried out by BAE Systems on the Clyde. The MoD involved VT in plans for the construction of the aircraft carriers, but before the contract was signed VT – seeing a brighter future in the services and training side of its business – first transferred its Portsmouth yard to a joint venture with BAE Systems, then in 2009 sold it to BAE outright, acquiring BAE's training subsidiary in return.

The MoD also tried to increase competition in 2000 by awarding contracts for two Auxiliary Landing Ship Dock ships to BAE Systems and two to Swan Hunter, its first order for a ship for seven years. Swan Hunter's vessels were to cost £210 million and be in service by 2004; by 2006, the cost had risen to £309 million and only one of the ships had been delivered. The MoD cancelled the contract, barred Swan Hunter from future naval work and, humiliatingly, had the second ship – RFA *Lyme Bay* – towed to BAE Systems Govan for completion. Swan Hunter's owner, who had bought a second yard on Teesside from Kvaerner with an eye on expansion, closed the Wallsend yard and sold all its equipment to India, where it was reassembled at Bharati Shipyards. Swan Hunter is now a ship design and support business with some 200 employees.

BAE Systems's performance, meanwhile was arousing considerable criticism, not all of it justified. Quite apart from friction with the government over its perceived arrogance, BAE Systems repeatedly fell foul of MPs for delays and cost overruns on the Astute class submarines. A series of cutbacks to the Royal Navy kept its yards busy refitting destroyers, frigates and submarines that had been sold to friendly powers – but also led the MoD to discover that the cost of the refit would come close to the sale price, the taxpayer gaining almost nothing from the transaction. BAE Systems also upset Britain's wealthy ally, the Sultan of Brunei, by completing on the Clyde three corvettes which his navy refused to accept, claiming they were not up to specification. An arbitrator sided with BAE Systems, but Brunei still refused to accept the ships and in 2007, after three years of stalemate with the corvettes still in the yards, the Sultanate put them up for sale. BAE Systems also came under attack in the Canadian parliament when in 2004 a diesel-powered Upholder class submarine, refurbished at Barrow after sale to the Royal Canadian Navy, shipped water off Northern Ireland, triggering an electrical fault with one sailor dying and three being injured. Critics blamed poor workmanship by BAE Systems until it was found that someone on board had failed to secure the hatch cover before submerging.

The order for what became the 72,300-ton aircraft carriers *Queen Elizabeth* and *Prince of Wales* finally bore home to BAE Systems how unpopular it had become with the government; Thales initially being selected as prime contractor despite its lack of a UK shipyard (its naval shipbuilding in France would be merged with the state-owned DCN in 2007). To Gordon Brown as Chancellor, this was not a problem but an opportunity: it opened the way to involve Babcock, the operator of the naval dockyard at Rosyth which he had fought hard to save and whose shop stewards formed his local powerbase. Heavy lobbying and a raising of its game by BAE Systems reduced Thales's stake in the 'carrier alliance' to 16 per cent shared with Babcock, but the French company continued to lead on design. The contract as formally signed in 2008 split the work between seven yards: BAE Systems's at Govan, Scotstoun and Portsmouth; Babcock Marine's at Rosyth – where final assembly would take place – and Appledore; A&P's Hebburn yard (ex-Hawthorn Leslie and Swan Hunter); and Cammell Laird, back from the dead, which won a £44 million order to build the flight decks. With Brown as prime minister from 2007, work on the carriers raced ahead with contracts let at high speed – 80,000 tonnes of steel being ordered from Corus with the aim of cutting as much as possible before the impending general election to forestall cancellation by an incoming Conservative government. Costs spiralled from the £3.9 billion originally estimated; when the coalition took office in 2010 it found the project in its entirety unaffordable, but the contracts (as also with BAE Systems for the final tranche of Typhoon) too tightly drawn to cancel. With public finances in a desperate state, it took the decision to continue building both carriers, but to mothball one and leave the one that did enter service without any aircraft to begin with. The rapidly-conducted defence review that accompanied the cuts announced that October posited an even smaller navy, and very limited orders for new ships once the carriers had been finished. Even before then, concern was growing within BVT that once the carrier order was fulfilled, two of its three yards would be surplus to requirements.

Babcock's involvement in the carrier programme was one of several indicators of its revival after a couple of decades on the sidelines. Chaired after his departure from BAE Systems by Mike Turner, Babcock embarked on a series of acquisitions that took it back into the engineering sector it had exited (where its classification by the London Stock Exchange was concerned) as recently as 2002; with maritime and nuclear work its priority. In 2007 Babcock acquired DML, operators of the Devonport naval dockyard and owners of Appledore Shipbuilders. It went on to take over International Nuclear Solutions and the Bristol-based nuclear engineering company Strachan & Henshaw, then in 2009 the state-owned UKAEA Ltd, experts in nuclear waste and decommissioning; this last acquisition guaranteed Babcock a role in the atomic power station programme. The company also developed the services side of its business, in 2010 taking over what was left of VT for £1.32 billion.

Babcock and Rolls-Royce (and in niche areas Davy Markham) were the only major British contractors left from the civil nuclear power programme of the 1950s or with a serious capability in the field. So when the Labour government in 2008 made a commitment to a new generation of nuclear power stations, the field was clear for Britain's erstwhile competitors to reap the rewards of continuous engagement with this form of energy. British Nuclear Fuels had struggled to develop a commercially viable business, the Thorp plant finally closing in 2010 after a history of delays in opening, under-use and heavy losses. Britain's reputation in the field of nuclear power had taken a heavy knock in 2000 when Japan turned back a shipment of nuclear waste, reprocessed at Sellafield, after it turned out that workers at the MOX plant which handled it had been falsifying technical readings. The shipments only resumed in 2010, the year before the tsunami that caused near-disaster at the Fukushima nuclear power station and put question marks over Japan's nuclear industry, prompting the closure of the MOX plant with the loss of 800 jobs.

The most ambitious of Britain's surviving merchant shipyards was Harland & Wolff, which in 1998 – 37 years after completing the *Canberra* – broke away from its increasing heavy construction business to bid against four Continental competitors to build the Cunarder *Queen Mary 2*. The order went to the Alstom subsidiary Chantiers de l'Atlantique at St Nazaire, who delivered the 151,400-ton liner, then the largest passenger vessel ever built, at the end of 2003. In that same year Harland & Wolff completed its final ship to date: the sealift ship *Anvil Point* for the MoD. Later in the decade its ship repair and refitting business revived, with its Goliath crane being recommissioned in 2007. Harland & Wolff also became a pioneer in offshore energy generation systems: in 2008 the yard completed the world's first commercial tidal steam turbine, and offshore wind turbines became a major part of its workload.

Cammell Laird, too, refused to give up the ghost, but equally had its share of misfortune. The company won a £50 million contract with an Italian cruise line to construct an extra section for one of its ships, but with the work nearly complete the customer refused payment and in 2001 the company went into receivership. After several changes of ownership, the Birkenhead yard was relaunched in 2008 as Cammell Laird Shiprepairers and Builders, having picked up a £28 million MoD contract for a Royal Fleet Auxiliary overhaul. Its medium-term future was assured in 2010 with the order for the flight decks for the aircraft carriers, but the cancellation of a hard-won commercial contract around the same time forced the company to make 180 of its 700 workers redundant – sparking what was now a rarity in the industry: an unofficial strike. Nor were the old ways entirely dead elsewhere: an owner having a ship converted in a Tyneside repair yard had to fly in workers from Poland to finish the job because not enough locals with shipyard experience were ready to come off benefits.

One British shipyard still builds merchant ships, though of modest size: Ferguson, the sole surviving yard on the Lower Clyde, which under a series of owners has continued to build roll-on, roll-off ferries. But Ailsa finally closed as a shipbuilder in 2000, though its yard has been used since for ship repair and fabrication work.

Another heavy industry that had become increasingly technological – train manufacture – continued its decline even though heavy traffic growth after privatisation produced a glut of orders for new rolling stock. Both the main British manufacturers were long-established, but under foreign ownership: Alstom, based in Birmingham and Preston, and Bombardier, at Derby. When the new private-sector operators began ordering trains after a damaging hiatus of nearly three years, Alstom offered a range branded Juniper – in addition to the Fiat-engineered Pendolino tilting inter-city trains it produced for Virgin – and Bombardier the Turbostar diesel multiple unit and its Electrostar electric counterpart. Bombardier secured the lion's share of the orders, and the Juniper range – ordered by only four operators – suffered through a lack of in-service support aggravated by mechanical teething troubles. When Alstom hit financial trouble in 2004, a strategic decision was taken to end train making in Britain, with the Birmingham works concentrating on maintenance and refurbishment and the role of the former GEC 'centre of excellence' at Preston being reduced. The following year, Bombardier closed the former Charles Roberts carriage works at Horbury after the completion of the final Voyager diesel train for Virgin.

Meanwhile trains were starting to be ordered from overseas manufacturers. This was nothing new: Britain's railways had over the decades ordered quite a few steam locomotives from the United States and Germany, and some of its first electric trains were made in Switzerland by Oerlikon. Moreover, the new generation of diesel freight locomotives for the privatised railway was coming from GM Canada and from Spain. But now Siemens – ironically testing its German-made trains on a track at the former RAF base at Wildenrath made specially bumpy to accord with conditions on the Southern Region – broke into the British market on a grand scale. Small orders from Heathrow Express and commuter lines in West Yorkshire were followed from 2003 by contracts for over 1,400 mainly electric carriages, the largest from South West Trains. The Siemens Desiro trains proved highly reliable in service, though their demands for electric power forced Network Rail into a hurried £2 billion upgrade of the supply. From then on Siemens, along with Bombardier and (from its Continental plants) Alstom, were certain to prequalify for any British rolling stock contract they wanted.

In 2006 the Department for Transport (DfT) took charge of rolling stock strategy, and its first project was a replacement for the ageing diesel-powered High Speed Train. With half the inter-city network electrified and half not, much of the industry expected that the DfT would propose an electric unit that could be hauled over non-electrified systems by a diesel loco. But the civil servants had a better idea: a single 'bi-mode' train equipped with both types of motors, which in order to avoid a change of locomotive claimed to take nine minutes, would carry around a substantial weight of unused diesel engines and fuel over the electrified system. The diesel motors could also be used to supplement the train's electric power, raising the question of why electric traction was specified at all. Persisting with the idea in the face of ridicule from the technical press, the DfT solicited interest not only from the usual suppliers but from Hitachi, and eventually awarded the Japanese conglomerate the contract in preference to a joint bid from Bombardier and Siemens. Key to Hitachi's bid was that a small plant would be set up to assemble the Super Express trains at Newton Aycliffe, Co. Durham. When first the Labour government and then its coalition successor queried the technical sense and the economics of the train, Japan put up a formidable lobbying campaign headed by its prime minister to make sure the deal stuck.

The next major contract was for around 1,200 carriages for the Thameslink route crossing London from south to north. This time Siemens and Bombardier went head to head, and in June 2011 Siemens was named as preferred bidder. A political row erupted as Bombardier announced 1,400 redundancies at Derby, with the plant's future in doubt once an order for Tube trains was completed. Ministers insisted that the way the Labour government had interpreted European directives had left them no option, but two uncomfortable facts emerged: that Siemens had undertaken in large orders for other countries, to have them assembled in the customer state, but had not been required to with the Thameslink order; and that the decisive factor was Siemens's alliance with heavyweight banks that made the cost of financing the PFI package to build and maintain the trains cheaper. Ironically, Bombardier's German plants build more trains than Siemens.

Meanwhile what was left of the rest of the industry was contracting and regrouping. Brush, which built its final locomotive for Eurotunnel in 2002, acquired five years later the Hunslet-Barclay works at Kilmarnock; which had survived the crash of Hunslet. In 2011 Brush itself, with a healthy order book for upgrading locos and rolling stock, was taken over by Wabtec, a subsidiary of America's Westinghouse.

The trend in the European aerospace industry at the turn of the millennium toward larger and less nation-based players was paralleled in steel. In 1998 France's Usinor took over Belgium's Cockerill Sambre to create Europe's largest steel producer by output: 22.9 million tonnes per year. British Steel the following year capped that by merging with Hoogovens of the Netherlands to offer a combined output of 23.7 million tonnes; Thyssen Krupp – itself the product of a merger – with 17.5 million tonnes was now third. In global terms the new company – named Corus – was third, behind POSCO of South Korea and Nippon Steel.

The euphoria surrounding the formation of Corus did not last long, as another global downturn impacted on orders. Within a year, the company – with a capacity already down to half of what the Heath government, three decades before, had thought British Steel would need – had lowered its production targets by 1 million tonnes per annum, amid accusations from the unions that it was shifting work and jobs to the Netherlands. By 2003 the merged company was losing almost £400 million a year, and sought to buy time and clear some of its debt by selling its non-core aluminium division to Pechiney of France. Despite the merger, the Dutch half of Corus had retained its own supervisory board, which vetoed the sale; while insisting that it was not trying to benefit Corus's Dutch operations at the expense of those in Britain, the board said it would only approve the sale if the company invested €200 million in its Netherlands plants over the next five years. Three years later, parts of the aluminium business were sold without objection to Aleris of the United States.

Still under pressure, Corus was taken over in January 2007 by Tata Steel of India, which had increased an earlier bid to £6.7 billion to cap a rival offer from Brazil's CSN. In the spirit of the times – the Glazer family would acquire Manchester United in the same fashion – Tata secured a loan to cover half the cost of the takeover against Corus itself.

Under Tata – whose name Corus took in 2010 – its British steel-making operations underwent reorganisation and retrenchment. The rail-making mill at Workington had already closed in 2006, production being transferred to Scunthorpe, and at the start of 2009 3,500 redundancies were announced worldwide, 2,500 of them in Britain and 900 at Rotherham. Worse was to come: later that year the moth-balling of the giant Teesside Cast Products plant and blast furnace at Redcar, where the company had just invested £40 million, was announced. The closure stemmed from the unilateral cancellation of a contract to take 78 per cent of Redcar's steel slab output until 2014 by four international companies – Alvoy, Dongkuk Steel Mill, Duferco and Marcegaglia – who had realised at the height of the global financial crisis that they could obtain it more cheaply elsewhere. Redcar's MP Vera Baird flew to Italy to try to persuade Antonio Marcegaglia to honour his agreement, Tata headed for the courts and the unions threatened strike action over the loss of 1,600 jobs. Fortunately for the devastated local community, the company – which had kept on some 500 workers – managed to find a buyer, and in March 2011 Teesside Cast Products was acquired by Sahaviriya, Thailand's largest steel maker, for $469 million. Months later, as production resumed, the consortium agreed to pay Tata £80 million in compensation.

Tata Steel Europe now employs 50,000 (including workers at plants in the Netherlands, France and Norway), a far cry from the 317,000 in one country when British Steel was formed. With capacity also down, the industry is some five times as productive as when it was nationalised in 1967. The 18.2 million tonnes of capacity Tata inherited from Corus pales beside the 120 million tonnes Tata aims to have worldwide by 2015. Yet Tata, now Britain's largest industrial employer, still operates integrated steel plants at Port Talbot and Scunthorpe, and manufacturing sites at Shotton, Llanelli, Llanwern, Rotherham (2), Stocksbridge, Motherwell and Cambuslang.

Britain's steel industry today extends well beyond Tata. There is a strong and resilient independent sector, far smaller than half a century ago but producing high-value output, much of it for export, with greatly reduced workforces. Some companies have had a bumpy ride: Sheerness Steel went into receivership in 2002 – hit by a surge in the price of scrap as shiploads were exported to feed the hungry steel mills of China – before being taken over by the Saudi Al Tuwairqi Group. It closed in January 2012 but that June the parent company announced plans to reopen it. Sheffield Forgemasters has, throughout a chequered career, retained key capabilities for military and civil nuclear projects and can pour the largest ingots – 570 tonnes – in Europe. With the nuclear power programme reviving, Forgemasters in 2010 commissioned a new 4,000-ton forging press and Lord Mandelson announced a £80 million government loan to enable it to supply forgings that would otherwise have to be imported from Japan. The incoming coalition cancelled the loan, causing a local outcry and leaving Forgemasters to seek alternative means of finance. Months later, the coalition found Forgemasters the cash for other projects.

Britain's pharmaceutical industry consolidated further with the mergers in 1998 of Zeneca with the Swedish-based Astra to create AstraZeneca, and the following year of GlaxoWellcome with SmithKline Beecham to form GlaxoSmithKline (GSK); both companies being headquartered in London with their primary listing on the London Stock Exchange. GSK today is the world's fifth largest pharmaceutical company – behind Pfizer (US), Novartis (Switzerland), Merck (US) and Bayer (Germany) – with 99,000 employees worldwide, an annual turnover of £28 billion and an annual R&D spend of £4.5 billion. AstraZeneca – after a series of acquisitions worldwide – ranks ninth, with over 50,000 employees, around £20 billion in sales and an R&D spend of £2 billion.

Both rankings, however, are lower than when the companies came together, for despite those apparently strong figures, Britain's pharmaceutical giants have been on the back foot. The drugs from whose development their constituent companies made billions over the years have been coming to the end of their patents, and they face growing competition in the marketplace from firms concentrating on generics. There is a constant race for their research teams to come up with new drugs of equal value; the challenge made greater by the increasing concentration of pharmaceutical R&D into larger and larger units in defiance of the 'small and diversified brings better results' doctrine championed by Glaxo in the post-war years. Pharmaceutical R&D in Britain has been helped by opposition in the United States to stem cell research, but hindered by the violent action of animal rights extremists against any research involving animals, highlighted in the quasi-terrorist campaign against Huntingdon Life Sciences. Nor have the high-quality employment they bring in research and manufacturing always been welcome: witness the rejection by the local council and John Prescott in 1998 of the Wellcome Trust's plan for a 'biotech cluster' science park alongside its genomics campus at Hinxton Hall, near Cambridge. (Incensed, Wellcome considered moving its R&D abroad before a smaller development was approved.) They have also come under heavy pressure – to which they have responded – to make cheap treatments available for diseases rampant in the developing world. And like other pioneering pharmaceutical companies the world over, they are at permanent risk of litigation – especially in the United States – from patients who have either suffered side effects from a drug, or have been persuaded by lawyers that they have.

By the end of the 2000s, both companies were battening down the hatches. GSK in 2007 acquired a new chief executive Andrew Witty, with a lower profile and less stratospheric pay package than Jean-Pierre Garnier (AstraZeneca's David Brennan receiving an almost frugal $1.5 million). Both companies – and especially AstraZeneca – entered into partnerships with other companies to develop and market specific new treatments. GSK cut 7,000 jobs in 2008–9 alone, while AstraZeneca in 2010 opted out of several fields of research, closing research establishments at Charnwood, Leicestershire and in Bristol, plus laboratories in Sweden and Delaware. Both companies began switching clinical trials from the NHS to China, GSK also transferring its neurological research there from Harlow.

Another major British player in pharmaceuticals, Boots, was taken over in 2006 by Alliance Unichem (86 years earlier, it had been acquired by America's United Drug Company amid a storm of protest, then sold back to the Boot family). The merger took the company's headquarters to Switzerland for tax reasons, but its deputy chairman Stefano Pessina, had further plans: within a year it became the first FTSE 100 company to be snapped up by an American private equity firm – Kohlberg Kravis & Roberts – with Pessina himself also taking a stake. A further structural change in the industry had come in 1999 with Rhone-Poulenc's decision to split May & Baker into two. Its Norwich site became part of Bayer Agrochemicals while its Dagenham facility lost its R&D function as Rhone-Poulenc merged with Hoechst to become Aventis.

One new entrant to the UK market was the Hyderabad-based Dr Reddy's Laboratories, India's second largest pharmaceutical company, which had prospered producing out-of-patent generic drugs to the world's less tightly regulated markets. During the 2000s it raised its quality thresholds and began to conduct its own research, and in 2002 Dr Reddy's arrived in Britain with the purchase of BMS Laboratories of Beverley and its subsidiary, Meridian Healthcare. This gave it a base to manufacture generic drugs for countries throughout the EU, and by 2005 Dr Reddy's was conducting clinical trials in Belfast of a cardiovascular drug of its own.

The greatest global coup in pharmaceutical R&D during this period was the development of Viagra by Pfizer at its Sandwich research base in 1998, coupled with the subsequent realisation that it was not only of benefit to heart patients but an explosively successful treatment for erectile dysfunction. Yet Pfizer, too, began to retrench on its R&D and from 2007 closed laboratories in Michigan, France and Japan. In February 2011 it announced that it was pulling out of Sandwich with a very heavy loss of jobs; months later the Open golf championship was held there, leaving the town's largest employer with an awkward corporate message to put across.

The travails of the British textile industry over this period were inexorably caught up with upheavals at Marks & Spencer. Under Sir Richard Greenbury the company posted higher and higher profits, peaking at £1.15 billion in 1997/8, but these fell sharply as a perception that M&S had become arrogant and detached from its public struck home. The company's reputedly stuffy product range, its belief that it did not need to advertise and, until 2001, its refusal to accept any credit card other than its own brought a sudden loss of business; and its first reaction was to cut costs by ordering its clothing from overseas. Most of M&S's clothing had been supplied by four manufacturers – William Baird, Coats Viyella, Courtaulds and Dewhirst – and all were confronted with a sudden loss of business. Dewhirst had to close its Stoke-on-Trent factory at the end of 1998 and sack 400 workers in Middlesbrough. Coats Viyella underwent a management buyout as it responded by downsizing, losing 1,200 out of 2,000 British jobs with the closure of factories at Alfreton and Sutton-in-Ashfield. Coats – still a British-based if largely overseas-manufacturing leader in the thread business – stopped producing the Viyella fabric, and in 2003 sold off the Viyella and Jaeger retail businesses for £1, the former passing to Austin Reed in 2009. Since 2003, Coats has been owned by the financial services company Guinness Peat. William Baird, losing 40 per cent of its business overnight, sued

M&S for £54 million for breach of contract, but lost; the Court of Appeal ruling that despite M&S having done business with Baird for 30 years, no express contract existed. Baird tried to reinvent itself as 'Britain's largest concession retailer', but again hundreds of jobs were lost. And Courtaulds, which lost less of its M&S business, reacted by moving more of its underwear production to the East, notably Sri Lanka. It closed its Bairnswear factory at Worksop in 2000, and in following years its factories at Limavady – kept going until then with help from the Northern Ireland government – and Middlesbrough. Courtaulds's Grimsby site producing Tencel fibre was sold to Austria's Lenzing group.

Sir Richard left M&S in 1999, one bad year eclipsing the memory of the company's growth and success under his leadership. Customer dissatisfaction with the poor sizing of its cheaper, Asian-sourced clothing range helped drive profits down to £145.5 million in 2001 before it began to recover with a new policy of engaging the public. But Britain's textile industry continued to suffer.

Much has been made in the new century of the popularity of high-end British textile brands. They are unquestionably a retail success, with stores opening apace in the Far East, but again the manufacturing has shifted away from Britain. Burberry does still employ 2,000 workers here – one third of its workforce – but now only at Castleford, where its famous trenchcoats are made, and at Keighley. In 2006 a campaign by celebrities failed to prevent its factory in the Rhondda closing, with work being shifted to China, and three years later its sewing facility at Rotherham also shut. Burberry has been consistently profitable, but some of its competitors have struggled, both Pringle of Scotland and Aquascutum – each under Far Eastern ownership – continued to lose money despite innovative products and marketing. Aquascutum, taken over by Jaeger in 2009, sold on its small factory at Corby to Swaine Adeney Brigg, but Pringle, which in the 1960s employed 2,000 people in Hawick, closed its mill there in 2008, while maintaining its headquarters in the town. The luxury clothing and handbag maker Mulberry still produces its wares at a factory in Somerset, but in 2011 threatened to set up its second abroad unless given a 'holiday' from

National Insurance contributions; this was embarrassing for the coalition government, as David Cameron's wife Samantha had just opened London Fashion Week wearing a Mulberry dress.

Britain's footwear industry went much the same way, with prestige shoemakers like Church's and Loake continuing to manufacture in Northamptonshire, but the rest of production transferred to the Far East. For ladies, most Jimmy Choo fashion shoes for the designer's Bond Street flagship store are made in Italy. The shift in public taste from conventional shoes to trainers – produced almost exclusively in the Far East – hit the industry very hard. While Reebok trainers are still made in Manchester, the company's Morecambe factory closed in 2009, the year it closed its headquarters at Bolton's Reebok stadium. Clarks – still a family company – finally stopped making shoes in Somerset in 2005, now manufacturing their entire range in India, Brazil, Cambodia, China and Vietnam. Bata closed its once ground-breaking East Tilbury plant the same year. Doc Martens transferred production to China and Thailand in 2003 – though production of a 'Vintage' line to the original specifications returned to Northamptonshire in 2007.

One company's fight to survive attracted wider attention, through the 2005 movie *Kinky Boots*. The brogue makers W. J. Brooks of Earls Barton – then one of six shoe factories in the town – hit problems as low-priced imports took the market, and had to cut its workforce from 80 to 30. Then its fourth-generation managing director Steve Pateman took a phone call from a woman who ran a fetish and transvestite shop in Folkestone, asking if Brooks made fetish footwear. Pateman got an initially disbelieving staff to run up a range of samples, and shaved his legs before posing for the catalogue in stiletto-heeled thigh boots. The business took off again, only to be torpedoed by a bad debt from an American customer that forced its closure in 2000, leaving Barkers the only surviving shoemaker in Earls Barton.

Cheap pirated copies from the Far East have become a permanent challenge for luxury and consumer goods makers throughout the West, as governments from China to Thailand prove unable or unwilling to crack down on counterfeiting. 'Knock-off' replicas of

Burberry, Jimmy Choo and more can be found in markets across the Far East – and increasingly closer to home as rogue exporters fuel demand in a cash-strapped West. Plagiarism has had an impact right across British industry; James Dyson had to sue to stop Hoover pirating his revolutionary vacuum cleaner design, and smaller manufacturers lack the resources – or a credible legal path – when ripped off in the Far East. Severn Lamb, a small Stratford-upon-Avon company exporting theme park rides like monorails and miniature trains to 40 countries, tendered for an order in South Korea only to find that a local firm had pirated its design and submitted a half-price bid. At a trade fair in Singapore its managing director Patrick Lamb found a stall three away from his own that had 'borrowed' his company's literature; to his surprise, a courteous approach brought an offer of partnership because the would-be plagiarist had realised he could not match Western quality.

Not that British manufacturers alone have suffered from piracy: in 2011 a chain of five 'Apple' shops in the Chinese city of Kunming selling fake Ipads was discovered by a tourist.

Wedgwood's merger with Waterford Crystal began to look a poisoned chalice in the early 2000s as the company struggled; the millions of euros put in by its major shareholder Tony O'Reilly being offset by heavy losses despite the transfer of much of its ceramics production to Indonesia. A fall-off in demand for traditional dinner services was blamed. An attempt to raise capital on the stock market was torpedoed by the banking crisis of 2008; 370 workers at British porcelain subsidiaries lost their jobs, and with workers at Waterford's Kilbany factory staging a sit-in against redundancies, the company went into administration. In February 2009 Waterford Wedgwood was acquired by the American private equity fund KPS Capital Partners, who outbid members of the Wedgwood family. KPS merged Waterford with one of its American competitors, but retained Wedgwood's Barlaston plant with a reduced workforce. The apparent rescue of Wedgwood was soured by legal efforts by the Pension Protection Fund – set up to secure savings lost when companies collapse – to have the Wedgwood Museum's historic collection of porcelain auctioned off to cover a £134 million company pension fund liability, triggering furious local protests.

By 2011 the number of people in the Potteries employed in its traditional industry had fallen from 70,000 in the 1920s and 30,000 in the 1970s, to 8,500. But despite ever-increasing competition from the Far East, the industry refused to collapse. Burleigh Pottery, its workforce cut from 500 to 50, arranged for its factory to be bought by the Prince's Trust, renting back the space it needed to continue producing its most sophisticated pieces. And with an upsurge in interest in ceramics, a number of new designer-inspired companies were also setting up in the Potteries.

Britain came out of the 2000s with 8,360 furniture manufacturers – most of them very small, with 112,000 people employed and an annual output worth £8.3 billion. The High Wycombe area could still boast seven companies just making chairs, and at Princes Risborough nearby Hypnos manufactured beds. But most British furniture makers faced an uphill task as the volume of imports continued to rise, and closures increased. Undermined by a series of department store collapses, Parker Knoll closed its factories at Chipping Norton, Andover and Bridgend; it is now based in Derbyshire with its manufacturing in Lithuania.

White goods manufacture in Britain continued to decline. Hotpoint, the market leader, lost its connection with GEC when Marconi sold its remaining half share to Indesit of Italy in 2001; General Electric (USA) transferred its 50 per cent to Indesit seven years later. In 2001 Hotpoint still employed 7,000 workers in Britain, but as production moved to Italy and Turkey, factory closures followed. The Creda plant at Blythe Bridge, Stoke, went in 2007, Hotpoint's flagship Peterborough fridge factory in 2008 and its plant at Bodelwyddan, North Wales, which had been turning out 800,000 washing machines a year produced its last in 2009. However, its tumble drier factory at Yate, near Bristol, survives. Electrolux, having stopped making vacuum cleaners at Luton in 1998, closed its cooker factory at Spennymoor, Co. Durham a decade later, production being shifted to Poland. Nor was the recording industry immune: in 2000

EMI closed its last domestic CD pressing plant in Swindon and concentrated production on Haarlem in the Netherlands.

The collapse of television manufacture in Britain under pressure from imports from China, Turkey and eastern Europe was terminal. The industry had become concentrated in South Wales, and either side of the Millennium 2,000 jobs were lost as Hitachi, Panasonic and Sony plants were run down; LG's closure at Newport in 2003, with jobs also lost at Southport, continued the trend. With the exception of a few high-end models, the end of television manufacture in Britain, which had pioneered the medium, came in 2009 when Sanyo closed the former Pye factory at Lowestoft.

The brewing industry, already in retreat, was hit hard by the combined effect of changes in public taste – away from beer toward lager and, later, chilled cider – a wave of pub closures as publicans found themselves squeezed between 'Pubco' landlords more interested in maximising the rent or the development value of the property than in selling beer at a price drinkers were prepared to pay, and a sharp fall in demand not fully compensated for by a surge in take-home alcohol sales as supermarkets slashed their prices.

Against this background, the flood of brewery closures continued: 1999 saw the loss of Ward's and the Cannon breweries in Sheffield, the former Hancock's brewery in Cardiff, Mitchell's in Leicester, the Lion Brewery in Blackburn and, most significantly, the Vaux brewery in Sunderland, the icon of a region. The next year Carlsberg Tetley finally closed the Wrexham lager brewery.

The major brewing firms continued to reorganise, with British ownership (and consequently production) weakening. Bass followed Scottish & Newcastle in splitting its brewing and property arms, selling the former to Belgium's Inbev – which sold on Carling and Worthington to Canadian/US brewers Molson Coors. The licence to brew draught Bass was taken up by Wolverhampton and Dudley Breweries at its Marstons brewery in Burton upon Trent. Production of bottled and keg Bass in Burton was discontinued, these beers being imported by Anheuser Busch. In 2008 Heineken and Carlsberg took over Scottish & Newcastle for £7.8 billion, Heineken taking the brewer's UK business – to which it applied its brand name – and the two companies splitting its export markets. Scottish Courage's brewing business had been in sharp decline, demand for Courage Best bitter plummeting 31 per cent between 2001 and 2010. The brand was sold on in 2008 to Wells & Youngs of Bedford – which had already closed Young's Ram brewery at Wandsworth, dating back to the 1550s – and in 2010 the modern Courage brewery outside Reading also shipped out its last barrel.

Guinness merged in 1997 with Grand Metropolitan to form the London-based multinational Diageo. In 2005 it closed its Park Royal brewery in west London, one of the great industrial sites of the 1930s; all the Guinness now consumed in Britain is imported from Dublin.

Carlsberg Tetley, now known as Carlsberg UK, closed Tetley's Leeds Brewery in 2011 after 186 years, to the accompaniment of a critical motion in the House of Commons; Tetley's Bitter is now brewed at Hartlepool, Tadcaster and Wolverhampton.

Burton remains Britain's brewing capital, its position strengthened by the closure of so many breweries in London (Fuller's is a rare survival). Six Burton breweries remain in production, two of them majors. Coors Brewers produces Carling and Worthington bitter at the former Ind Coope brewery. Marston's produces its own bitter, and draught Bass under licence from InBev. The independent Burton Bridge Brewery has survived, and the town also boasts three of the increasingly popular microbreweries.

Even before Kraft's controversial takeover of Cadbury, much of the ownership and manufacture of Britain's confectionery was slipping out of the country. Kraft closed the Terry's chocolate factory in York in 2005, moving production to Poland, Sweden, Belgium and Slovakia. Nestlé moved the production of Smarties – now in a hexagonal packet for easier storage instead of the traditional tube – offshore from the former Rowntree factory in York in 2006. And Cadbury, late in 2007, announced that it would close the former Fry's factory at Somerdale, Keynsham, some lines going to its other British factories and the remainder to Poland.

HP Sauce – that most British of products with the Houses of

Parliament on the label – was on the move too, after Heinz purchased its parent company from Danone for £440 million in 2005. HP's Birmingham factory – with its unique pipeline carrying vinegar over the Aston Expressway – was closed in 2007 amid bitter protests both locally and in Parliament and calls for a boycott; production of HP and Daddie's sauces transferred to the Heinz plant at Elst in the Netherlands. Only sachets of HP sauce continue to be produced in Britain, at Heinz's Telford factory. Patriots were relieved that Lea & Perrin's sauce did not follow suit; requiring a different set of ingredients, it continues to be produced in Worcester, bottling having returned there from Birmingham.

The slippage of Britain's major industries from public share ownership to private investors affected one heavy hitter in the food sector: United Biscuits, acquired in 2000 by the Finalrealm consortium and sold on in 2006 to a consortium of the private equity houses Blackstone (based in New York) and PAI Partners (Paris).

No company, though, seemed more embedded in Britain, its heritage and its way of doing things than Cadbury; founded by Quakers in Birmingham in 1824 and until 2000 with a Cadbury (Sir Dominic) as chairman. Even after the demerger of Schweppes, the company, with a turnover of £5.3 billion and 71,000 employees, looked too large to be taken over, and indeed was breaking out of its traditional markets in the Commonwealth and the developing world. Ironically, Cadbury became a target for Kraft by acquiring a chewing-gum business in the United States that was on the global cheese-to-chocolate conglomerate's radar screen.

When in 2005 the French dairy giant Danone was rumoured to be the target of a bid from Pepsico, President Chirac ordered the passage of a law, nicknamed the 'Loi Danone', to protect companies in 'strategic industries' from takeover. The British government saw no reason to follow suit, believing in the freedom of the marketplace and eager as ever not to fall foul of the European Court or to give an excuse to other EU member states to be protectionist. Kraft began buying shares in Cadbury, and in September 2009 launched a £9.8 billion bid for the company. Public opinion, Cadbury workers and the government were horrified; Lord Mandelson warning Kraft not to try to 'make a quick buck' out of Cadbury, and the trade union Unite claiming that 30,000 jobs were at risk. Kraft's chairman Irene Rosenfeld saw the acquisition as 'the logical next step in our transformation toward a high-growth, higher-margin company', building 'a global powerhouse in snacks, confectionery and quick meals.' Kraft assured workers at Somerdale that if the takeover went through their plant would be reprieved, a higher price of £11.5 billion was negotiated and in February 2010 Kraft took control of Cadbury, whose chairman, Roger Carr, declared: 'We believe the offer represents good value for Cadbury shareholders and are pleased with the commitment that Kraft Foods has made to our heritage, values and people throughout the world.'

A week later, Kraft announced that the Somerdale factory would be closing after all, leaving workers there claiming they had been 'sacked twice'. The House of Commons' Business Select Committee, infuriated by Ms Rosenfeld's 'dismissive' refusal to appear before it, declared: 'A company of Kraft's size and experience ought to have acted with better judgment' in promising to save Somerdale, and urged a tightening of the Takeover Code to prevent such behaviour. There was also anger when it was discovered that Kraft had been enabled to take over Cadbury through a £7 billion loan from RBS, a bank 84 per cent owned by the UK government. However, ministers had already come to realise that owning a bank does not equate to having control over it: RBS and Lloyds – in which the government had also taken a stake as it tottered – proved no readier than other banks to respond to government pressure to keep lending to small businesses, and returned to paying eye-watering bonuses to their investment bankers as soon as they were able. So RBS's financing of a hostile takeover of a major British firm should have come as little surprise.

Kraft emerged from the takeover with 14.8 per cent of the global confectionery market; Mars, with a long-established and benign presence in Britain, is its nearest competitor. After the closure of Somerdale, it was left with seven UK factories employing 2,500 workers, with much of the Cadbury chocolate and biscuit range produced under licence by Premier Foods and other suppliers. Kraft dispelled some of the pessimism with an early investment at Cadbury's iconic Bournville plant. But it was also noticeable that Kraft products that had never sold well in Britain – such as the Oreo biscuit and some of its Continental chocolate brands – were suddenly at least as heavily promoted as traditional Cadbury lines. Meanwhile, Britain still lacks a 'Loi Danone', though the original remains unchallenged by Brussels. And as the future of yet another major contributor to the UK economy became determined from abroad (in Cadbury's case St Louis) the unspoken question in the City, at Westminster and among the trade unions was: 'Who's next?'

The answer soon came, as four major British manufacturers were taken over by foreign companies in the apparent absence of any British conglomerate with either the ambition or the resources to do so. Chloride, the power equipment maker, fell to ABB for £860 million. The metals group Tomkins went to a Canadian private equity firm for £2.9 million. In 2011 the toolmakers Charter International – who had already moved their tax domicile to Dublin – went to the American pump and valve maker Colfax, and the offshore engineers Hamworthy were taken over by Wartsila of Finland for £383 million. Only Charter attracted interest from a British bidder: the turnround specialist Melrose.

The global banking crisis of 2008 and the recession that it triggered in almost every developed country except Australia had dire effects for commerce and manufacturing around the world. It also had many causes. Chief among these was reckless 'sub-prime' mortgage lending in the United States, with the risks laid off to banks around the world, but there were many contributory factors to the sheer scale of the collapse when it came. In Britain, government spending and the public deficit soared as Gordon Brown loosened the purse strings after his early stringency as Chancellor, straining to the limit and beyond his 'golden rule' that governments should break even over the lifetime of an economic cycle. Major British banks – and 'demutualised' former building societies who rushed into areas of financial services which they did not understand – lent unwisely, recklessly underwrote American lenders' liabilities without considering the risk, developed a hubristic arrogance and embarked on takeovers which generated huge bonuses but spelt grief for the balance sheet if there were a downturn – notably Royal Bank of Scotland's outbidding of Barclays to capture the Netherlands' ABN Amro at the very top of the market. The Financial Services Authority, hailed by Brown as a 'world class' regulator, failed ignominiously to do its job while nitpicking over details in the share prospectus of any serious business trying to raise capital. Worse still, it remained in complete denial after the roof fell in about its lack of application, ability and competence. Yet whoever was most at fault, the outcome was an evaporation of liquidity in the banking system which caused banks to collapse, threw economies into recession, reduced demand for manufactured goods and made it harder for businesses to borrow.

Globally, but centred on Wall Street, the investment banks had generated ever larger deals, takeovers – and bonuses for their staff. As the market neared its peak, a Barclays executive told me of the banker visiting Monte Carlo who enquires as to the ownership of the largest yachts he sees in the harbour. 'That's the Goldman Sachs yacht, that's the Bear Stearns yacht and the one over there is the Lehman Brothers yacht,' he is told. 'What about their clients?' the innocent banker asks. 'They can't afford yachts', comes back the reply. It is easy to speculate why clients should have enabled investment bankers to enrich themselves at their expense; the one time I asked a successful bond trader friend why they seemed to be getting away with behaviour which in any other walk of life would have been regarded as theft, he told me: 'The clients expect it.' Had the investment bankers' casino operations been kept separate from commercial banking – as they had in the United States under the Glass-Steagall Act of 1932, passed to prevent a recurrence of the Great Crash of three years before – the conventional banks and their depositors would have had some protection. But in 1999 the banks had persuaded Congress and President Clinton to repeal Glass-Steagall, so when the investment bankers' chickens came home to roost, mainstream banks connected to them paid the price.

Nor on Wall Street were the investment banks solely to blame. The ratings agencies who determine the creditworthiness of companies and nations, failed spectacularly not just to pick up on time bombs ticking under the American economy, but merrily continued to rate as 'Triple-A' the banking systems and economies of countries heading for the precipice, such as Ireland and Iceland. After the crash, of course, the ratings agencies became ultra-cautious, even downgrading America's creditworthiness in the summer of 2011.

The testosterone-charged boardrooms of financial institutions from the City to Wall Street and right round the globe, ignored Christ's parable of the house built upon sand, the bankruptcies of Enron and Global Crossing in 2001/2, and the prophecies of lone voices like the Lib Dem economic spokesman Vince Cable – everything was just fine as the money-go-round whirled faster and faster. Mortgages of 125 per cent were loaned on both sides of the Atlantic to homebuyers who either had little chance of ever being able to repay them, or who would be instantly vulnerable should the economy turn down. And with every further advance, more toxic debt was laid off to banks who failed to probe the risks they were taking.

The first hint of trouble came on 7 February 2007, when HSBC – the UK clearing bank that would suffer least in the collapse despite having the heaviest exposure – announced losses linked to US sub-prime mortgages. In March, Countrywide – America's largest lender, which had pushed sub-primes to the limit – hit serious trouble, eventually being rescued by Bank of America. As house prices plunged, more and more borrowers defaulted on their loans; the lenders', and banks', chances of getting their money back evaporated. Weeks later New Century Financial, another specialist in sub-prime mortgages, filed for bankruptcy. That May, Bear Stearns disclosed that two of its hedge funds with large holdings of sub-prime mortgages had incurred heavy losses, and in August, BNP Paribas warned that two of its funds were in trouble. Later that month came the first banking casualty: Germany's Sachsen Landesbank, rescued by the Baden-Wurttemberg Landesbank. British banks began to worry if their rivals would survive, pushing up the Libor rate at which money is lent between them to way above base rate. And on 14 September depositors withdrew £1 billion from Northern Rock – a former building society that had offered exceptionally generous mortgages – in the first run on a British bank for 150 years; the government had to step in to guarantee their savings.

During the autumn of 2007 major banks the world over, starting with Switzerland's UBS, reported losses from sub-prime related investments. The US Federal Reserve launched a co-ordinated effort by central banks to shore up the banking sector, and the Bank of England began cutting interest rates to an eventual 0.5 per cent. On 21 January 2008, global stock markets suffered their largest fall since the terrorist attacks of 11 September 2001 as the likelihood of the 'credit crunch' leading to a global recession struck home. In February the government nationalised Northern Rock; March saw JPMorgan Chase rescue Bear Stearns with the involvement of the US government; and April brought a Bank of England scheme for banks to swap potentially risky mortgage debts for government bonds.

That August Alistair Darling, Brown's successor as Chancellor, infuriated the new prime minister by saying the downturn would be more 'profound and long-lasting' than most had feared. If anything, his warning proved an understatement, with Brown eventually grasping the need for action at home and on a global scale and putting in place what would prove to be textbook measures for dealing with the emergency. Early September saw the Bush administration take over the two semi-public mortgage lenders Fannie Mae and Freddie Mac, with their $5 trillion of loans. Then on 15 September the Bank of America agreed to a $50 billion rescue package for Merrill Lynch – and the American investment bank Lehman Brothers, with a large presence in London, collapsed. Days after, on our way into the *Daily Telegraph*, the distinguished – but that morning harassed-looking – City journalist Jeff Randall, told me: 'I never dreamed I would arrive at work wondering if Citigroup would still be there.'

In the days that followed, the FTSE index dropped below the 4,000 mark for the first time in five years; Barclays took over Lehman's

North American banking divisions and Nomura some of its operations in London; the FSA woke up and banned the short selling of bank shares; the government took a majority stake in RBS (which had lost £34.6 billion in a single year) and in Lloyds, after forcing it to take over the toxic Halifax-Bank of Scotland; and Santander of Spain bought the 'good' part of Bradford & Bingley (the government nationalising the rest). The Icelandic government took over the first of its failed banks, but Icesave then crashed; Morgan Stanley and Goldman Sachs gave up their status as investment banks to qualify for help from the US government; the US Congress agreed to a $700 billion banking bailout; and the Irish government rashly guaranteed all deposits in the country's main banks for the next two years. Then, in October 2008, Brown and Darling pushed through a bailout of Britain's banks whose eventual cost has been estimated at up to £850 billion. In return, the banks were supposed to ease lending to manufacturers and other key businesses, at a time when they were otherwise hoarding assets to rebuild their shattered balance sheets.

By the end of October 2008, Britain was in recession. Business had been feeling the impact of the credit crunch for some time, but the repercussions became steadily worse despite an emergency cut in VAT. The retail sector was hit first, the collapse of Woolworth at the start of 2009 with the loss of 30,000 jobs being followed by a series of closures of High Street chains; fashion, music and bookshops fared especially badly. Building firms also failed by the score. Gulf State governments, through their sovereign funds, snapped up valuable assets at bargain prices, notably with DP World taking over P&O. They showed little interest, however, in manufacturers.

As the banks tightened credit, Britain's manufacturers tightened their belts. With hindsight, the remarkable feature of the banking crisis is not how many firms in the sector went out of business, but how few. The most prominent casualty was LDV Group, the former Leyland DAF Vans operation which had gone on producing commercial vehicles at the former Wolseley plant in Birmingham despite increasing financial difficulties. LDV had gone into administration in

2005, and been bought by the Russian GAZ group. Though the new owners had big ideas, the plant remained starved of investment and the product line shrank to one model: the Maxus van, planned as a joint venture with Daewoo before that company hit the rocks. LDV's line of credit ran out, and the last Maxus was produced in December 2008. Attempts to sell the company as a going concern failed, and eventually the production equipment was shipped off to China.

Other closures followed, but as before the crisis, mainly as a result of multinationals moving to lower-wage locations. As the crisis gathered pace, Lexmark had closed its printer factory at Rosyth, transferring production to an unnamed cheaper country. In 2009 Hoover – which had closed its vacuum cleaner plant at Cambuslang four years before – stopped making washing machines at Merthyr Tydfil after 61 years. Dundee suffered a serious blow when NCR closed its once-innovative ATM factory. Panasonic slashed jobs at its Newport and Cardiff plants – but closed 27 facilities in other countries.

Orders for new cars – and consequently production – fell off a cliff as the recession bit across Europe (by 2007, 77 per cent of cars produced in Britain – more even than in 1950 – were for export). Honda shut its Swindon factory for four months as it struggled to clear the backlog of unsold cars, and workers across the industry experienced layoffs, accepting shorter hours and even pay cuts. UK car production of 1,446,619 in 2008 (plus 203,000 commercial vehicles) may have been almost the lowest since 1993, but it slumped further in 2009 to 999,460, before recovering in 2010 to 1,270,444 (plus just 123,018 trucks and vans). In 2005, before the closures of Longbridge and Ryton, the industry in its widest form had employed 869,000 people; by 2009, 140,000 of these jobs had been lost. Falling production also hit the component makers: Linamar's former Ford factory in Swansea closed in 2010, and Bosch's in Cardiff in 2011.

One British car manufacturer – Vauxhall – survived after the narrowest of squeaks. All America's Big Three car makers – Chrysler,

Ford and General Motors – were in trouble; their chief executives asking Congress late in 2008 for a $34 billion bailout and staggering the lawmakers by each arriving in their own corporate jet. Ford posted a $14.6 billon loss – the worst results in its 105-year history – and Chrysler survived only through Fiat taking a 35 per cent stake. But GM's plight was the worst – burdened by $6 billion in losses for the first quarter with similar liabilities from its car finance subsidiary and massive employee pension and health benefit costs. President Obama effectively fired GM's chief executive Rick Wagoner at the end of March 2009, and that June GM filed for bankruptcy to reorganise.

GM executives in Detroit had already warned that the company's businesses in Europe might survive for only a few weeks. With the future of GM's operations around the globe in the balance, Opel sought a cash injection from the German government – at this point it finally became plain to all that while Vauxhall sold more cars in Britain than Opel did in Germany, GM Europe's British factories, with 4,300 employees, were expendable. Its manufacturing operation in Germany had greater critical mass, the German government and banking system were more attuned to supporting industry, and Germany was where the decisions were taken. Lord Mandelson worked hard to press Germany not to accept a deal involving the closure of Vauxhall and lobbied the bidders: Fiat; a consortium led by Sberbank of Russia and Magna International of Canada; the Belgian-based investor RHJ International; and Beijing Automotive Industries who were disqualified over 'intellectual property issues'. Fiat withdrew as GM agreed a separate deal to find a buyer for the Saab motor business (eventually to Spyker, only to file for bankruptcy in 2011). A sale to Magna was close to agreement when GM decided that its European arm was, after all, crucial to its long-term strategy. GM's British plants at Luton and Ellesmere Port survived, but Opel's at Antwerp closed; GM Europe's corporate headquarters was moved from Switzerland to Germany.

Meanwhile, Ford raised much-needed cash in 2008 by selling Jaguar and Land Rover to Tata Motors of India for $2.3 billion. The takeover went through as 1,400 jobs were cut, but manufacture of the marques in Britain was said to be secure; the great attraction for Tata was their highly-rated design centres. Tata did propose closing Jaguar's historic Castle Bromwich plant and concentrating production at its other sites, but an upsurge in orders (mainly from the Far East) and profitability led to the plan being dropped. In 2011, the company then announced that it would build a £355 million engine plant in Wolverhampton, creating 750 jobs with the prospect of 1,250 more; behind it was a decision that Jaguar Land Rover should once again produce its own engines, instead of taking them from Ford.

By 2010 the top five car makers in Britain were Nissan (423,000), Mini (216,000), Land Rover (179,000), Honda (139,000) and Toyota (137,000). Rover, Ford (save for commercial vehicles) and Peugeot had gone, and none of the majors were under British ownership. With Europe's car industry having, on Ford's estimate, an overcapacity of 35 per cent, question marks remained over every plant, as only continuing decisions to invest in new models – as made by BMW and Nissan in 2011 when they put £500 million and £192 million respectively into the Mini and the Qashqai – would keep them open.

The industry could still boast a broad infrastructure; BMW's decision safeguarded jobs at Swindon, Hams Hall near Birmingham as well as Oxford; Nissan's its drawing office facilities in London, and at Cranfield as well as at Sunderland. But the UK car component industry had been steadily weakening (though 2,000 manufacturers remained), partly through closures forcing car makers to buy from abroad and partly because companies like Nissan had taken conscious decisions to bring in more parts from the parent company. In April 2011 Nick Reilly, GM Europe's chief executive, warned that Britain would have to reinvent its component industry if it were to retain car manufacture. Companies like Nissan and Toyota, as well as his own, were finding it hard to compete with those whose plants on the Continent were surrounded by component makers, because they had to import so many parts, with shipping costs and currency risks to factor in.

Almost as he spoke, the terms of the game changed. The Japanese tsunami halted car production not only in that country but in many of its companies' plants around the world (like Toyota's in Derbyshire) that had become dependent on parts from home – and also those of other manufacturers like Fiat, whose cars were dependent on Japanese semiconductors. Encouraging a wider production of automotive components became an imperative, and when that June David Cameron hosted a summit for vehicle makers at Downing Street – including Carlos Ghosn of Renault-Nissan, Sergio Marchionne of Fiat and Dieter Zetsche of Daimler – the need for Britain to grow its supply base was near the top of the agenda.

One flicker of hope came in April 2011, when the first MG6 rolled off the production line at Longbridge after a gap of six years; one of the world's largest factories having been reduced to a 69-acre site leased by Shanghai Automotive. The MG6 (a distant relative of the Rover 45 and 75) was designed in Birmingham, with the parts manufactured in China – where the car had been launched the previous year – and assembled at Longbridge. The workforce was small and production only a fraction of Longbridge's in its heyday, but a scathing reaction to the MG6's launch from Jeremy Clarkson on *Top Gear* was offset by a congratulatory visit from China's prime minister Wen Jiabao.

Another Chinese car maker – Geely – also took a stake in the British motor industry. Manganese Bronze had remained the premier maker of black cabs, and after disposing of its components division in 2003, looked around for partners. In 2007 – a year after its main competitor, Metrocab of Tamworth, had gone out of business – Manganese launched its TX4 model for London in partnership with Geely; four years later Geely concluded an agreement for Manganese to launch its vehicles in the UK. The deal came at a time when Manganese was under pressure: the Peugeot E7 people carrier was proving popular with cab companies outside London, and the Mercedes Benz Vito had made an impact in the capital since being cleared to operate there in 2008 – despite its lack of the black cab's traditional tight turning circle. When that May Boris Johnson announced incentives for the introduction of electric cabs, Volkswagen immediately launched its Milano electric taxi. Then, in October 2012, after a costly product recall Manganese went into administration.

In one field, Britain's automotive expertise has remained a world leader: in producing high performance cars, especially for Formula 1. No fewer than eight of the F1 teams are based in Britain, and five of them (Force India, Mercedes, Red Bull, Renault and Williams) within 40 miles of Silverstone. Their technologies are highly developed; Woking-based McLaren is a car manufacturer in its own right. Around the F1 teams in Britain has grown up a cluster of firms developing components and precision equipment, such as Mercedes-Benz High Performance Engines at Brixworth and Prodrive in Banbury. Though not a mass employer by motor industry standards, F1 and the companies supporting it employ tens of thousands of people, and in towns like Brackley, dominate the local economy. Moreover, there is a read-across between F1 and the wider automotive industry; Ricardo, based at Shoreham, Sussex, works on new engine technologies with car makers in Germany and Detroit, and in 2011 created a new 'green' engine-building facility for McLaren. Provided F1 does not, for commercial or political reasons, break its strong historic ties with Britain, the future of this end of the motor industry looks extremely promising.

The end of the recession caused by the banking crisis cooled the panic that had struck British manufacturing and the economy as a whole, but did not presage a return to expansion as concerns over the indebtedness of Greece and other Eurozone countries spooked the markets. UK growth remained extremely sluggish through 2011, with great uncertainty of the impact on employment, demand and industrial capacity of the spending cuts imposed by the coalition, after Labour's defeat the previous year – and indeed, for firms who had set their eyes on the American market, by the US government. Some companies – notably Smiths – warned that a slowdown in government procurement (in its case for air travel security systems)

was starting to affect their order books. Others, notably in the field of 'green' energy, protested that the refocusing of government grants toward smaller schemes was cutting demand for products they were just gearing up to produce in response to previous incentives. One of the few companies in this field to continue investing was Siemens, the dominant force in wind-generated electricity, who in 2011 opened a renewables centre in Manchester employing 340 people.

The coalition took a more positive approach towards manufacturing than its predecessor, the Liberal Democrat Business Secretary Vince Cable declaring that it had to be at the core of any economic revival. One encouraging sign was a revival of inward investment in 2010 to the highest level since 1997: 728 projects, compared with 562 for France and 560 for Germany. But Germany was catching up; many Chinese firms choosing to set up their European bases there with Britain still heavily reliant on investment by US corporations. It was also a sign of the times that government grants to encourage development in those same regions where Harold Macmillan had tried to redirect industry half a century before, were now going mainly to foreign or foreign-owned businesses. Of 50 totalling £450 million awarded in 2010 with the aim of creating 100,000 jobs, the largest went to Nissan, Haribo (the German sweet maker which had transformed a liquorice allsort factory it had acquired at Pontefract), Bentley (Volkswagen) and Pilkington (NSG). Moreover, 2012 closed with a weakened BAE Systems licking its wounds after being denied its merger with EADS, and vehicle manufacture by Ford in Britain coming to an end with the closure of the Transit plant at Southampton, production having been moved to Turkey.

6

THE CULPABILITY
OF GOVERNMENT

Successive British governments over the past 60 years – with the possible exception of Margaret Thatcher's – have trumpeted that a strong manufacturing sector is essential to the economy – and, furthermore, that they are doing all they can to support it. Yet the overall trend throughout that period has been one of retreat and failure. From years of conversations with ministers, and from having worked in the then Department of Trade and Industry, I know that Westminster and Whitehall are full of able people who sincerely believe they are doing all they can to enable British industry to function better and seize its opportunities; yet the outcome is very different. Strangely, the only person I have met with the humility to be aware of this mismatch and of their own part in it, is Norman Tebbit, who confided at the height of his influence in government: 'I know that 50 per cent of the decisions I take are wrong. What worries me is that I don't know which 50 per cent they are.' So how is it that good intentions over six decades have produced such a disastrous outcome?

There are many areas in which British governments, their policies and day-to-day decisions have had a direct impact on manufacturing: economic policy; industrial policy; regional policy; research policy; procurement; transport policy; energy policy; education policy; not to mention multifarious forms of regulation. There is also the European dimension, which I deal with in the next chapter. The word 'policy' as applied here reflects the stance taken by government on a particular issue. Unfortunately the culture of Whitehall has traditionally regarded policy as an achievement in itself, and policy making as the ultimate purpose of government and the province of the brightest civil servants; the implementation and delivery of those policies is all too often viewed as a grubby if regrettably necessary exercise not worthy of men and women with Firsts in Classics.

✦

The central aim of British economic policy since the 1950s – as indeed that of all major industrialised countries – has been to maximise non-inflationary growth with low unemployment and a stable and competitive exchange rate; until the early 1970s, also, a balance of payments deficit was to be avoided. But the structural problems facing the economy, political and industrial pressures and the impact of global events have left governments, for much of that time, firefighting to generate any growth at all against a background of uncomfortably high unemployment, inflation or both; not to mention a balance of payments deficit which seems to have become less of a threat the larger it has grown. And it is an unpalatable truth that whatever medicine has been applied and how great or limited its efficacy, the competitiveness of manufacturing and exporting industry has steadily reduced. When the economy has been doing badly, investment has stalled, factories have closed and jobs and skills have been lost; when it has been ostensibly doing well, imports have been sucked in and the strength of sterling has made it harder for British products to compete in global markets.

Moreover, every period of apparent economic wellbeing – the 'never had it so good' years of the late 1950s and beyond, the 'Barber boom' of the early 1970s, the 'Lawson boom' of the late 1980s, the sustained prosperity from 1994 to 2007 engineered by Kenneth Clarke and Gordon Brown – has ultimately come to a juddering halt. The 'July measures' of 1966, the energy crisis of 1973 and the three-day week, the recession culminating in 'Black Wednesday' and the global banking crisis of 2008–9, all had their particular causes; but each can be seen in the light of history as correctives to cavalier handling of the economy. Brown seemed for a time to have ended 'boom and bust', but like so many of his predecessors he overconfidently took the brakes off and the economy – and industry – eventually paid the price.

Britain's economic growth has consistently lagged behind that of its competitors, in Europe and beyond. From 1955 to 2010 annual growth was 2.36 per cent – ranging from a historic quarterly high of 5.3 per cent in early 1973 as confidence peaked, to a low of -2.5 per cent just a year later as the three-day week kicked in. By contrast the OECD puts average annual global GDP growth between 1971 and 2009 at 3.1 per cent, one quarter higher than for the UK. Tellingly, the OECD has also calculated that over the same period Britain went from being one of the world's leading exporters to a performance that is merely average: in 1971 exports made up 22.5 per cent of Britain's GDP against 13.7 per cent for all the world's economies; in 2004 Britain fell behind the world average for the first time, with its exports comprising 25.3 per cent of GDP against a global 25.8 per cent.

Britain's relative economic decline – and the even steeper erosion of its manufacturing base – cannot be blamed entirely on government, any more than on the fuddy-duddy management and bloody-minded unions who were for so long (and where the unions were concerned, with greater reason) the scapegoats. Moreover, there are bound to be times when rectifying excessive inflation, unemployment or the like will require measures that make it harder for industry to do its job. But there have been times – notably the early 1980s – when a determination in government to tackle a particular economic ill once and for all, has had an equally terminal effect on parts of British industry. Nor, over the years, has the manufacturing sector been exempt from the Treasury's ultimate question about any strand of economic policy: 'Yes, we know it will work in practice. But will it work in theory?'

Most British governments over the last 60 years have been pragmatic rather than ideological in the economic policies they have pursued; indeed for much of that time they have been prisoners of events. Whatever their overall policy stance – free-market or socialist

– only Margaret Thatcher's government has attempted consistently to impose its own economic theories on the nation – with success on the narrow measure of defeating inflation, but at the price of lasting damage to industry and, arguably, society. The Labour government of 1974–9 came to power committed to almost as ideological a programme, but a combination of encountering reality and the loss of its majority led to the abandonment of most its doctrinaire pledges, apart from the nationalisation of aircraft and shipbuilding. Yet none of the more pragmatic policies employed by other governments over the decades could prevent growth falling behind as Britain became steadily less competitive.

The Churchill–Eden–Macmillan–Douglas-Home government which ran the country from 1951 to 1964, consisted of men haunted by the memory of the mass unemployment of the 1930s and its effect on the fortunes of the Conservative Party; Churchill may have won the war, but his landslide defeat in 1945 was largely the result of a public determination not to go back to those bad old days. Their response was to keep unemployment artificially low, creating extra costs and uncertainties for business. One of the least ideological of 20th-century governments, the Tory administration of the 1950s, pursued near-consensus economic and social policies which became known as 'Butskellism' – after Labour's last Chancellor Hugh Gaitskell and his Conservative successor Rab Butler. Direct taxes were high (a legacy of wartime) and indirect taxes low (during the war and just after there had been few 'luxury' goods on sale to tax); the principal economic regulator used was restricting demand for and access to hire purchase, which blossomed in the 1950s as consumer goods came within the reach of the population at large. This was achieved through curbs on lending, higher interest rates (Bank Rate of 7 per cent was considered the 'crisis' level) and increases in Purchase Tax, the precursor of VAT levied on a far narrower range of goods. Successive Tory chancellors tried to use this regulator to fine-tune the economy, but instead produced surges in growth followed by slumps in demand, making it hard for manufacturers to cope and reducing the attractions of investing in new or expanded plant. Harold Macmillan's 'Never had it so good' of 1958–9 was followed by an application of the brakes that left 'stop-go' discredited. His Chancellor Selwyn Lloyd called a 'pay pause' in 1961 to keep wage increases in line with growth in productivity, which briefly weakened West Germany's competitive edge but could not politically be prolonged without a hostile response from the unions. With wages unrestrained again and the economy bouncing back from the appalling winter months of 1963 which saw unemployment briefly rocket to almost 1 million, Reginald Maudling in the run-up to the 1964 election went for unrestrained growth. This briefly gave confidence to British industry but simultaneously sucked in imports just as Japan, in particular, had manufacturers ready with enticing products to meet the demand; the effect was to create what Harold Wilson was able to characterise as an imminent balance of payments crisis.

Wilson inherited an overvalued currency and sluggish growth in productivity. He believed Britain could achieve sustained annual growth of 3.8 per cent – fractionally less than his Conservative predecessors had aimed for – through incentives to industry and pay and price restraint, a doctrine spelt out in George Brown's National Plan of 1965, but sadly a pipedream. On coming to power, Wilson and his Chancellor James Callaghan blocked an attempt from young Turks led by Anthony Crosland to consider devaluation of the pound from the $2.80 set in 1949 (prior to which it had been $4.03). Sterling was then still a reserve currency – indeed at the time of Suez the oil price for Iran, Iraq and Libya was still set in pounds – and with the UK economy performing weakly, the result of Wilson's refusal to devalue at the outset was a series of sterling crises over three years and an uncompetitive exchange rate that left British exporters struggling. By the time Callaghan was forced into devaluation to $2.40 at the end of 1967, considerable damage had been done both to the currency (through pressure on the sterling area reserves) and to British industry.

Wilson's refusal to take the most obvious club from his caddy, forced him to try other measures which did far more damage. Soon after taking office, he imposed a surcharge on imports, upsetting Britain's trading partners while sending out the message that our export industries were uncompetitive.

In the Budget after Labour's re-election in 1966, Callaghan announced a radical new tax aimed at shaking labour out of the service sector and diverting it into manufacturing: the Selective Employment Tax (SET). Levied on employers in service industries – after bitter argument over borderline cases – it did not have either of the effects intended. Restaurants, hairdressers and others laid off staff to reduce their exposure to SET, while manufacturing, through its exemption, was handed a perverse disincentive to improving productivity.

Weeks after that Budget, a fresh balance of payments crisis exacerbated by a merchant seamen's strike (one of whose leaders was John Prescott) led Wilson, claiming Labour had been 'blown off course', to slam on the brakes. As well as a deflationary package (the 'July measures'), he declared a wage and price freeze, with the pre-existing Prices and Incomes Board now given teeth. The T&G leader Frank Cousins quit the Cabinet – in which he had not been a success – in protest, but the unions broadly went along with the freeze. Problems began a year down the road when the policy was relaxed to allow small increases; immediately individual groups of workers started pressing to be treated as exceptions, usually to catch up with another group whom they were convinced had jumped ahead of them. The number of strikes began to edge up, prompting Barbara Castle to introduce her *In Place of Strife* reform package which the unions – aided within the Cabinet by Callaghan and Richard Marsh – rallied to kill.

If Roy Jenkins, the reforming Home Secretary who swapped places with Callaghan after devaluation, thought a more competitive rate for sterling would bring economic peace, he was mistaken. A gold crisis in March 1968 and rumours that autumn about a devaluation of the franc and possible revaluation of the Deutschmark led to a further sterling crisis at the end of the year, with heavy cost to the reserves. During 1968 Jenkins twice raised taxes, paving the way for a steady but cautious export-led recovery which, by the spring of 1970, gave Wilson confidence of winning re-election – until an adverse opinion poll as the votes were actually being cast.

Edward Heath came to power promising free-market solutions to Britain's problems, and a shift from direct to indirect taxation as entry to the Common Market led to the adoption of VAT (replacing Purchase Tax and the unlamented SET). The Chancellor with whom he had planned this strategy, Iain Macleod, died within weeks of taking office, and Macleod's successor Anthony Barber lacked his combativeness and intellectual firepower. One early change effecting the economy – the shift to decimal currency in February 1971 – was mandated by government, Labour having prepared a reform which was intended to benefit business. Another was dictated by events: the floating of sterling from August of that year as the post-war Bretton Woods system of fixed currency parities collapsed. This effectively meant the end of the Sterling Area, most countries choosing to float their currencies against both the pound and the dollar. At first the pound appreciated to $2.65 – creating pain for exporters – but soon it slipped into a steady decline.

The twin spectres of unemployment and inflation now raised their heads. Just 582,000 people were out of work when Heath came to power in 1970, but within two years the psychological 1 million mark was passed. At the same time inflation – until then considered a phenomenon confined to Germany in the 1920s – began creeping up, not helped by businesses 'rounding-up' prices at decimalisation. In 1971 inflation leapt to 9 per cent, a rate not seen since the Korean War, and wage demands rose. Having alienated the unions with his Industrial Relations Bill, Heath was in no position to bargain, so in November 1972, after a damaging and costly miners' strike, he introduced a 90-day price and wage freeze backed up by a Counter-Inflation (Temporary Provisions) Act. This was followed by a Price and Pay Code, with increases strictly limited, and a Pay Board. Barber had already set the scene for a 'dash for growth' in his 1972 Budget, with a stimulus package he estimated would add 10 per cent to GDP growth over two years, with special incentives for industry. Growth now surged, and at its peak, in the summer of 1973, Enoch Powell warned on *The World At One* that the economy was heading for disaster because Barber had lost control of the money supply; few took any notice.

The twelve months that followed were a perfect storm. Egypt

invaded Israeli-occupied Sinai and was crushingly defeated, global oil supplies were disrupted just as the OPEC cartel sent prices soaring, and the miners – claiming they had slipped from first to 18th in the wages league – cashed in with a gargantuan pay claim. A work-to-rule was followed by an all-out strike, a three-day week was ordained to conserve power supplies with unemployment soaring briefly to 3 million – though, tellingly, with industrial production little affected as firms improvised – and Heath, after hesitating, called a general election to decide 'Who governs Britain?' At the height of the campaign it became clear that the miners – regardless of the impact of their claim on the economy – did have a case, and after a minority Labour government took power they accepted 30 per cent and went back to work; leaving 1974 the worst year for strikes since the general strike of 1926.

Few governments can have taken office to a worse economic backdrop than Harold Wilson's in March 1974. The oil price increase had sent inflation soaring, and a string of 'catch-up' pay demands, particularly in the public sector, increased that pressure further. To alleviate it, Labour subsidised the prices of key foodstuffs. Michael Foot as Employment Secretary pushed through the repeal of Heath's trade union legislation, and as the rate of inflation neared 30 per cent, Wilson and Chancellor Denis Healey – after a round of pay settlements well in excess of 20 per cent that triggered further price increases – persuaded the unions to enter into a 'Social Contract' to moderate pay demands, with the lowest-paid guaranteed £6 a week. Inflation peaked at 23.2 per cent in 1975 before falling back to 8.3 per cent by 1978, and unemployment fell back to around 5 per cent – though rising steadily thereafter.

For its first seven months until a further election, Wilson's government lacked a parliamentary majority – but its acquisition of one that October spooked the markets. Labour had alarmed the business community with the promise of a 'wealth tax', and Healey's (apocryphal) promise to 'soak the rich until the pips squeak'. Tony Benn's threats of nationalisation added to the panic. With turnover and profits plunging, stock prices fell until in January 1975 the FT all-share index reached a low of 62.16, from a high of 228 in May 1972. Then the worm turned, the market remembering the dictum that 'even socialists eat', and prices doubled in eight weeks.

These upheavals had a disastrous effect on sterling, which by mid-1976 was down to $1.60; the last remaining (Commonwealth) countries who had kept their sterling reserves in London were seeking redress, and Britain's own reserves were again being eroded in the battle to prevent sterling going through the floor. Labour now secured a loan of $5.3 billion from the International Monetary Fund, then applied for a further $2.9 billion 'standby credit'; the Fund's insistence on £2 billion of spending cuts in return split the Cabinet just after Callaghan succeeded Wilson as prime minister. The cutters won – but the economies made turned out to have been greater than was necessary to steady the ship.

Healey's stewardship of the economy kept the lid on most of the continuing problems until the autumn of 1978, when the unions rebelled against being tied down to a 5 per cent pay norm. An increasingly desperate government – by now again without a majority – tried to impose sanctions on employers who paid more, spectacularly failing to get an Order through penalising Ford. Public sector workers and key groups like tanker drivers now jumped on the bandwagon, resulting in the 'winter of discontent' of early 1979.

Margaret Thatcher came to power with inflation rising again, public sector and nationalised industry workers queueing up with sky-high pay demands and industry tired and uncompetitive. Her recipe – once she had reluctantly honoured her pledge to fund a further round of inflationary public sector pay rises in the name of 'comparability' – was to squeeze inflation out of the system by curbing the money supply, just as Powell had suggested six turbulent years before. The weapons Sir Geoffrey Howe adopted as Chancellor were high interest rates (up to 17 per cent), an increase in VAT (to 15 per cent), economies including the linking of pension increases to price rather than wage rises, and two severely deflationary Budgets. The resulting slowdown in the economy brought inflation down from 18 per cent in 1980 to 4.6 per cent in 1983; apart from a blip to 10.9

per cent in 1990 in the wake of the Lawson boom it has never been appreciably over 6 per cent since. Manufacturing industry benefited from a lower rate of wage increases once it became evident, even to the unions, that the steelworkers' 16 per cent pay settlement had led directly to the loss of thousands of jobs. But before that point was reached, it had to weather a period of low domestic demand, high borrowing costs and an exchange rate that priced British goods out of export markets. In the space of two years, unemployment more than doubled to break through the 10 per cent barrier as factory after factory closed.

Having slain the dragon of inflation – and some distressed maidens as well – Sir Geoffrey moved to the Foreign Office and Nigel Lawson took his place. As a prime mover of privatisation, Lawson planned to fund some public spending with proceeds from selling nationalised industries and a reduction, he hoped, in the 'External Financing Limit' as perennial loss-makers like British Leyland were moved off the books.

Lawson was also keen to stimulate the economy by cutting taxes; he began slowly, then in his 1988 Budget threw caution to the winds. Believing – on the basis of Treasury statistics – that the economy was slowing, he cut the standard rate of income tax for the second year running (to 25p) and slashed the top rate to 40p. His reliance on tax cuts to the exclusion of other methods led critics to brand Lawson a 'one-club golfer'. The statistics were wrong and the economy was in fact starting to overheat. With this added stimulus the housing market boomed, lending rocketed and imports soared, the runaway boom fuelled also by the abandonment of tight controls on the money supply and Lawson's policy of 'shadowing the Deutschmark'. Only three months after his Budget, Lawson began raising interest rates, doubling them between June and October 1988 as he sought to curb the headlong rush. With great skill Lawson managed to resign in October 1989 over an issue that had nothing to do with his stewardship of the economy: sniping at his policies from Professor Alan Walters, Mrs Thatcher's personal economic adviser.

It fell to John Major to tighten the screw, hoping to slow the economy rather than bring it to another grinding halt. There was much debate over whether there would be a 'soft landing' or a 'hard landing'; at the height of it Major told me he was far from convinced there would be a landing at all. The issue was unresolved when in November 1990 he succeeded Mrs Thatcher as Prime Minister and Norman Lamont became Chancellor.

Lamont was the unluckiest of Chancellors, though he underlined this lack of good fortune with an uncertain touch. He took office with Major just having taken Britain into the European Exchange Rate Mechanism (ERM); a policy Lamont was sceptical about but which he justified as dispensing with the uncertainty of floating exchange rates. The landing was very hard indeed. By the end of 1990 the economy was in recession, which bit steadily harder as Lamont prematurely detected 'green shoots' of recovery and argued that rising unemployment was 'a price worth paying' in the fight against inflation. Major, in support of his Chancellor, observed: 'If it isn't hurting, it isn't working.' Lamont had to raise VAT to 17.5 per cent to keep the budget deficit down, weakening demand further, and it was the third quarter of 1992 before growth returned, by which time another batch of manufacturers had gone out of business. Throughout this period Lawson was constrained in cutting interest rates by sterling's position within the ERM; though Britain's rate of inflation fell back, Germany's unexpectedly increased, leading the Bundesbank to raise its interest rates and leaving sterling exposed.

Britain's withdrawal from the ERM on 'Black Wednesday', 16 September 1992, was a political disaster from which Lamont – and arguably Major – never recovered. Those closest to the process were convinced that the discipline already imposed by the ERM laid the groundwork for an economic recovery that would last for a decade and a half – which indeed took place. But in the shorter term Lamont used the freedom he had gained to target lower inflation and cut the deficit in the public finances, which was running at its highest since 1975/6. This was due both to higher spending on benefits as unemployment rose again towards 3 million, and the reduction in the tax take as the manufacturing sector contracted still further. Interest rates – raised to 15 per cent on Black Wednesday in a forlorn bid to keep sterling within its ERM band as £27 billion in reserves were poured away – were cut back to 10 per cent, and further reduced to 6 per cent early in 1993. But confidence in Lamont was ebbing even before he rashly declared during a by-election the Conservatives lost that 'Je ne regrette rien', and in May 1993 Major sacked him.

Kenneth Clarke arrived at the Treasury just as the recovery began to strengthen. He was able over four years to cut income tax further to 23p, reduce the government's share of GDP and halve the budget deficit (though controversially imposing VAT at 8 per cent on fuel bills). Interest rates, inflation and unemployment all fell, but with the Conservative Party in disarray over Europe, sound economic performance could not rescue Major's government and in May 1997 it went down to a shattering defeat.

Gordon Brown picked up where Clarke left off, inheriting a budget in balance and – to frustration within the Labour Party – kept to the Conservatives' spending targets to demonstrate Labour's 'prudence' to the markets. His strategy worked: the economy stayed strong, side-stepping the mild recession that embroiled Britain's competitors in 2001, with Brown accumulating a 'war chest' to be spent on improving public services once they had been reformed. Yet, once again, the resulting high exchange rate inflicted pain on industry, and having given up control over the setting of interest rates to the Bank of England on taking office, there was little Brown could do about this. Brown kept the City broadly on side, apart from exempting pension funds from tax relief, and also contrived to sell a large slice of Britain's gold reserves at the bottom of the market – driving the price down further by announcing that he would do so.

Confidence grew as Brown began to take his foot off the brake, but with GEC, ICI and Rover all going under, manufacturing remained weak while the financial services sector boomed. From 2005, when unemployment bottomed out at 1.36 million, Brown let spending rip, especially on the NHS where GPs were unaccountably given a contract by the Department of Health paying them substantially more for giving up weekend work and house calls.

Ever more of Brown's energies went into forcing Tony Blair to honour his promise to stand down in his favour, and after ten years as prime minister Blair reluctantly handed over in June 2007. The economy seemed in good shape, and in his final Budget Brown cut income tax to 20p. In the process, however, he left a time bomb ticking for his successor (and, at the time, friend) Alistair Darling: the abolition from 2008 of the 10p tax rate for the lowest paid, which struck at the heart of Labour's natural support.

By the time Darling delivered his first Budget in March 2008, the credit crunch had hit and Northern Rock had crashed. Darling was readier than Brown to admit that the global economy was heading for crisis, just as in the run-up to the 2010 election he was more prepared than his prime minister to concede that spending cuts could not be avoided by re-electing a Labour government. As the banking crisis unfolded, Brown – once it registered on him that it would not be over in months – took the lead on the world stage in devising packages to prevent the collapse of both the banking system and the global economy. Darling introduced palliatives to offset the abolition of the 10 per cent tax rate, and in his 2009 Budget, with demand for new cars plummeting, brought in a £2,000 'scrappage' payment to motorists who gave up cars over 10 years old to encourage them to buy new. The scheme was a success, bolstering demand during a critical year until the economy began to plateau – though its benefits for British manufacturing were limited as it applied to imported as well as home-produced vehicles, and most of the latter were exported to markets that were still flat. With demand still weak, Darling later cut VAT from 17.5 per cent to 15 per cent for 13 months. Unemployment rose to 2.5 million in the summer of 2009, then plateaued, with most workers receiving no wage increase because there was nothing in the kitty. In his third and final Budget, on the eve of the election, Darling introduced a 50 per cent top rate of income tax on the 300,000 Britons earning over £150,000 a year, in the face of threats from hedge fund managers and others to follow Boots and Woleseley and relocate to Switzerland – the attractions of Ireland as a corporate tax haven having lessened with the collapse of its economy.

The election of 2010 was fought under the shadow of a budget deficit of £154 billion for the year just concluded (10.4 per cent of GDP), with a further increase in prospect as increasing interest payments were added to an expected rise in the annual shortfall between expenditure and income. Labour tried to play down the need for cuts, but the Conservatives hammered home their inevitability. The Liberal Democrats also predicted cuts, but nevertheless proposed abolishing student tuition fees.

Labour lost the election, but David Cameron's Conservatives failed to win it as they had expected to. The gravity of the continuing economic crisis, with Britain only just out of recession, told against any party trying to govern alone as in 1974, and after a week Cameron formed a coalition with Nick Clegg's Liberal Democrats, to secure a working majority. To remove any grounds for uncertainty in the markets, the two parties agreed to govern for a complete five-year parliament.

Cameron's close associate George Osborn became Chancellor, and immediately moved to cut the deficit, aiming to balance the books by 2015. In his first Budget in June 2010, he increased VAT to 20 per cent, imposed a pay freeze for public servants and ordered a 25 per cent spending cut by all departments apart from Health and International Development: 77 per cent of the reduction was to come from spending cuts, 23 per cent from higher taxes. Spending on some areas of government activity dried up at once, a cull of quangos followed, tuition fees were increased and that October, after a hurried and acrimonious defence review, massive defence cuts were announced. The Nimrod MRA4 reconnaissance aircraft was cancelled – a serious blow to BAE Systems, who critics felt had regarded the aircraft as a permanent milch cow. The order for the F-35 Lightning Joint Strike Fighter was substantially reduced. Brown's two aircraft carriers survived, but with one to be mothballed on completion and with no aircraft available to fly from the other for several years.

Despite warnings from Labour, the trade unions and left-leaning economists of a 'double-dip recession', Osborne stuck to his guns. Growth remained sluggish throughout 2011, by the end of which he hoped to reduce the annual deficit to £122 billion, and recession did indeed return for a time in 2012.. Pressure increased for him to have a 'Plan B' ready in involving less severe cuts, and from the wealthy, to abolish the 50 per cent highest tax rate which they claimed was counterproductive; in the meantime even a fall-back in the level of sterling could not compensate manufacturers for continuing weak demand at home and even more fragile export markets – Germany apart. Convulsions in the Eurozone with the risk of Greece and possibly other countries defaulting, and the downgrading of the United States' debt from AAA to AA+ that August for the first time in the country's history, merely confirmed that unstable and taxing economic times would continue.

It is impossible for government to create competitiveness; the most it can do is try to create the climate for it. All governments have provided incentives, especially for businesses to invest, but there have been times – particularly in the 1950s and 1960s – when it seemed to politicians that some industrialists would rather have faced a firing squad than invest in the modern plant and machinery needed to keep up with their foreign competitors.

Equally, Britain has never attempted to create the close partnership between government, the banking system and industry that exists in Germany, which relies heavily on government and finance at *Länder* level – a regional tier for which there is no UK equivalent. Nor has there ever been the umbilical connection between government and business that exists in France, which with its democratic system of government and virtually Stalinist economy, is the diametric opposite of post-Maoist China. The idea of government collaborating with industry to help ensure its success – apart from isolated deals like Al Yamamah – was anathema during the early Heath years and the 'hands off' era from 1979 until the early years of the Blair government. Yet the strategies existing during the rest of the post-war period to help industry compete, tended to be limited in scale, and consequently in effect.

Nor has export-led growth been the driver of the policies of any government over the last 60 years, whatever ministers may have claimed. While this has undeniably been an aim of most post-war governments, it has never been an all-consuming priority as it was for several decades with Japan and is now with China. Whitehall has never possessed the equivalent of Japan's all-powerful MITI, let alone the attitudes that made it so successful. The Department of Trade and Industry, even when its ministers have wanted it to be proactive, has consistently been outgunned not only by the Treasury but even by some of the departments responsible for sectors of activity impinging on manufacturing, public procurement and exports. Nor, even, have manufacturing and exports always been under one governmental roof. Under Churchill and Eden there were the traditional Board of Trade, the various departments such as the Ministry of Power which spon-sored nationalised industries, and the Ministry of Supply; this was a legacy from wartime which largely dealt with defence procurement but also oversaw aircraft production and until 1954, sponsored both the development of the nuclear deterrent and the civil atomic energy programme. In that year the two were separated, with the creation of the UK Atomic Energy Authority (a fag end of which, UKAEA Ltd, was acquired in 2009 by Babcock). The Ministry of Supply did a certain amount to foster key industries, for example insisting in the early 1950s that London's surplus wartime 'utility' buses were sold abroad so that UK operators had to keep Leyland, AEC and other manufacturers busy by buying new; the only second-hand vehicles permitted to stay in Britain were those the Ministry itself needed to transport workers to nuclear sites like Dounreay. The MoS was abolished in 1959, with most of its functions rolled into the MoD. The split between the Board of Trade and Tony Benn's Ministry of Technology – which adopted an aggressively interventionist role but lacked suzerainty over exports – continued in the 1960s with the DTI only being created under Edward Heath's Whitehall reforms of 1970. The two functions were separated again by Harold Wilson in 1974 and were not reunited until 1983, by Margaret Thatcher.

During the 1950s and into the 1960s most British manufacturers were prospering; government initiatives were concentrated on diverting new factories away from London to the New Towns, and from the overheating West Midlands to areas of high unemployment – with ultimately disappointing results. In any Budget where a further stimulus was needed, provision was made to build 'advance factories' at public expense in such areas, for new and expanding businesses to move into. A degree of competition was guaranteed by the Restrictive Trade Practices Act of 1956, which prevented the cosy monopolistic arrangements some companies and groupings had enjoyed since before the war. Relations between Conservative ministers and the Federation of British Industry (renamed the Confederation of British Industry or CBI in 1965 to avoid confusion with the detective agency) were generally cordial, though there was frustration over the impact on demand of hire purchase restrictions. In 1962 relations with 'both sides of industry' were formalised through Selwyn Lloyd's creation of the National Economic Development Council (Neddy), to find ways of arresting Britain's relative economic decline; its initial target was a highly optimistic annual 4 per cent growth rate until 1966. Neddy in turn spawned 'Little Neddies' which concentrated on individual sectors of industry, businessmen, trade unionists and civil servants working together. The one major change Churchill's government was elected in 1951 to implement was denationalisation of steel; this was carried out slowly and piecemeal, and had yet to be completed when the Conservatives lost power 13 years later.

Labour returned to power in 1964 committed to renationalising steel, but otherwise to intervene with industry in a supportive fashion. Soon after taking office, it set up the Geddes Committee to consider the future of shipbuilding, the one sector in serious trouble. But ministers soon concluded that British industry was suffering from fragmentation and outdated structures, and in 1966 Wilson launched the Industrial Reorganisation Corporation (IRC), to broker mergers and create more competitive units. Driven forward in government by Michael Stewart and Tony Benn, the IRC, led by Charles Villiers, attracted bright young bankers like Alastair Morton, who would bring the Channel Tunnel to fruition, managers of the calibre of Geoffrey Robinson, who would head Jaguar and briefly serve under Gordon Brown at the Treasury, and Geoffrey Owen, future editor of the *Financial Times*. The period is remembered for the catastrophic government-engineered merger of Leyland Motors with BMC and the creation of the short-lived Upper Clyde Shipbuilders, but the IRC itself performed valuable work in bringing together companies in fields like engineering, between which there was a natural synergy. It was also ministers, and not the IRC, who took the counter-productive decision in 1969 to pull Britain out of the embryonic Airbus consortium.

Edward Heath came to power committed to letting successful businesses thrive free of government interference, with 'lame ducks' going to the wall. Such an approach was far more in tune with the philosophy of Iain Macleod and of the right of his party than with his own instincts; as a *dirigiste* Heath would have been thoroughly at home as president of France. However events forced a 'U-turn' on Heath after barely a year, when the collapse of Rolls-Royce compelled him to step in and nationalise the company until its finances could be stabilised. The collapse of UCS and the subsequent work-in with its strong political support again compelled the government to inter-vene, the 1972 Industry Act giving it powers to do so across the board.

The increase in union militancy during the early 1970s prompted by Heath's Industrial Relations Act and fuelled by events at UCS radi-calised much of the Labour Party and, crucially, Tony Benn. The party returned to power in March 1974 – much to its surprise – committed to a major programme of nationalisation and to the creation of a National Enterprise Board (NEB), investing in economically strate-gic firms and concluding 'planning agreements' with them. Aircraft and shipbuilding were renationalised as promised, and the NEB was established. However, in the 15 months before Harold Wilson moved him from Industry to Energy, Benn was preoccupied by the rash of workers' co-operatives that had grown up, backing them as far as – and in one case beyond – the point his civil servants would permit. After Eric Varley replaced Benn, the Department of Industry took far more interest in keeping whole companies afloat in concert with their owners, notably Chrysler UK.

The most celebrated product of the NEB was the Ryder Report on the future of British Leyland; however the ink on this was barely dry when the company went bust and the government took it over. The NEB also suffered from being the child of a period of extreme difficulty for British manufacturing, which meant that it was called on to rescue firms like the machine tool maker Alfred Herbert, instead of 'backing winners' as Wilson and Benn had hoped. Indeed the overriding priority set itself by Whitehall's civil service mandarins during the late 1970s – and not just where industry was concerned – was the 'management of decline'. Yet there was one forward-looking achievement: the creation of Inmos in 1978 to give Britain a stake in the production of computer chips. The company never made money, costing the taxpayer £211 million until it was taken over in 1989 by SGS Thomson, but it did capture 60 per cent of the global market in static RAM devices, and originated the innovative transputer.

It was under the Labour governments of 1974 to 1979 that 'industrial democracy' came closest to being introduced in Britain. Michael Foot saw giving workers a stake in how their companies were run as a way of reducing industrial unrest, and appointed a commission under the academic Alan Bullock to recommend whether, and how, this could be done. The business community was largely against the idea, seeing worker participation as undermining the rights of shareholders, directors and management, and the three industrialists on the committee produced a minority report raising objections. But in 1977 the Bullock Report was published, proposing that workers' representatives should sit on boards of directors, and they should be chosen by the trade unions. This delighted the unions, who hoped for early legislation, but did not go down so well on the shop floor which had a mind of its own, and still worse with groups like the Institute for Workers' Control which saw the interests of the unions and of the workers they claimed to represent as far from identical. With industry still in a fragile state, the government, which had lost its majority and was relying on a deal with the Liberals, let the matter slide.

Margaret Thatcher came to power saying much the same about British industry as Heath had done; the difference was that she meant it. The pain manufacturers suffered over the first three or four years of her government was not just a result of Sir Geoffrey Howe's economic policies; it stemmed also from the view of her first Industry Secretary, Sir Keith Joseph, that manufacturing should fend for itself. It appeared to all too many, that Sir Keith's policies would lead, intentionally or otherwise, to deindustrialisation. Mrs Thatcher set the tone by studiously ignoring 'Neddy' – which withered on the vine, finally being abolished in 1992 – and denouncing 'interventionism' with the barely concealed message that many of Britain's ills stemmed from interference with industry, not just by her Labour predecessors but also by Heath, who was still glowering at her from the Tory benches.

There were pluses for industry in some of her government's early policies, notably James Prior's 'step by step' approach to trade union reform (which she privately opposed) under which ground was won a little at a time instead of all the unions' sacred cows being slaughtered at once; eventually strike ballots were introduced and the closed shop outlawed with none of the unrest that had accompanied Heath's Industrial Relations Act. The defeat of the miners in 1984–5 took place over the partly related issue of closures and Arthur Scargill's refusal to ballot all his members, but its impact was to knock the stuffing out of the unions as a whole – with all but their most ideologically-blinkered leaders forced to blame one of their own. Yet overall, the early 1980s were grim for British manufacturers, Mrs Thatcher making plain her preference for slightly flashy or ruggedly egotistical businessmen who made money rather than things, or – better still – accountants. It took individual deals or projects to capture her imagination, her legacies including not just Al Yamamah but the capture of the Nissan plant for Sunderland.

It is hard now to appreciate that when Mrs Thatcher led the Conservatives to power in 1979, privatisation had yet to emerge as a 'big idea'. There were commitments to denationalise some state businesses, and it did not take long for the likes of Cable & Wireless to be floated on the stock market. But the emergence of privatisation as a doctrine took some five or six years, as ministers lost their timidity and began to realise that great swathes of the public sector – including key manufacturing industries – could be sold off.

While privatisation became a key ideological tenet of Thatcherism, it was driven by two very different imperatives, under the banner of giving 'Sid' – the target potential small shareholder in the British Gas flotation – a personal stake in the fruits of the economy. On the one hand ministers and the City wanted to see successful flotations of companies that would prosper in the private sector. On the other, however, many nationalised industries were making a thumping loss, and while there was a powerful argument for getting them out of state ownership it was far from clear who would want to take shares in them with little prospect of any financial return. Fortunately for ministers, one reason why many nationalised industries – manufacturing as well as utilities – appeared to lose money was that whatever they spent on investment showed up on the red side of the ledger; these undertakings were not allowed to borrow on the markets. As late as 1981, the Post Office's lobbying efforts were directed not at getting its telephone business privatised, but freeing it to borrow. The prospect of nationalised industries running up debts which did not appear on the books horrified the Treasury; asked to find a way of achieving this, a committee under its senior mandarin Sir William Ryrie produced a set of rules so tightly drawn that the idea was dropped for a decade. However, Mrs Thatcher was convinced that some nationalised industries lost money precisely because they were not subjected to private sector disciplines; over time, and with the imposition of tough management, ways were found to transfer not just British Steel but the remnants of British Leyland (as Rover) to the private sector. Some former state industries sank, but rather more swam.

With privatisation came deregulation. In the City, the 'Big Bang' galvanised trading. In the bus industry, services began to run where and when buccaneering operators thought they could fill their buses – not as the Traffic Commissioners and the T&G thought desirable. The Sunday observance laws which made it legal to buy a newspaper but not a Bible on the Sabbath were eventually repealed, as was the Shops Act of 1950 which limited weekday opening. Overall, these changes and others stimulated economic activity, but there were unintended consequences. August British merchant banks and stock-broking houses were swallowed up by American, Swiss, German and Japanese banks. Orders for new buses collapsed as new entrants to the industry made do with secondhand vehicles, inflicting severe damage on Britain's bus manufacturers. And Sunday trading not only sucked in more imports but contributed to the decline of the High Street as out-of-town shopping centres mushroomed. Many of these including Bluewater, Meadowhall, Merry Hill and MetroCentre (the largest centre in Europe) were developed on industrial sites left derelict during the 1980s: respectively a former Blue Circle quarry near Gravesend, Hadfield's steelworks site between Sheffield and Rotherham, the former Round Oak steelworks near Brierley Hill in the Black Country, and a brownfield site outside Gateshead.

The biggest political row over an individual company during the Thatcher years concerned the future of the Yeovil-based helicopter company Westland. The company got into trouble and accepted a bid from America's Sikorsky, but the Defence Secretary Michael Heseltine became convinced a 'European solution' involving British Aerospace and Agusta of Italy was preferable; he conducted an almost Messianic campaign in Whitehall to this end, openly briefing against Cabinet colleagues in a breach of protocol last seen from James Callaghan when he rallied support against *In Place of Strife*. Failing to get his way, Heseltine dramatically resigned in the first week of 1986, halfway through a Cabinet meeting. It then transpired that Leon Brittan, the Trade and Industry Secretary, had authorised the leaking of a communication from the Solicitor-General to Heseltine accus-ing him of 'material inaccuracies' in a letter claiming that Westland stood to lose European orders if it merged with Sikorsky. The ensuing furore resulted in Brittan's resignation, though there were many who detected the hand of Number 10 in the leak. Ironically, Westland is now a subsidiary of Agusta's successor company, Finmeccanica.

Although Mrs Thatcher's government generally adopted a 'hands off' approach toward manufacturing industry, it was as assiduous as others before and since in promoting exports. Whitehall has always encouraged British exporters – most recently through UK Trade & Industry – and official support has been valuable to many in landing contracts, particularly with friendly governments. Consequently executives at Matrix-Churchill, a hard-pressed Coventry machine tool firm, were delighted when, after the company's takeover by Iraqi interests in 1987, it was encouraged by ministers to supply to Saddam Hussein's regime not only tools capable of producing sophisticated weapons, but materials that could be used for making munitions; applying for export licenses in a way that would not attract attention. After Saddam's invasion of Kuwait in 1990 and the first Gulf War, it was discovered that Matrix-Churchill had been supplying Saddam with sensitive equipment in apparent breach of a prohibition on such exports. Three directors of the company were prosecuted, and only when the case came to court did it emerge that Alan Clark, then a defence minister, had encouraged the exports and that a couple of colleagues had come within a whisker of lying to the Commons over whether the ban had been relaxed. The case was hurriedly dropped, leaving several politicians (though not Clark, who had been disarmingly frank) fighting for their careers, and businessmen thinking twice about accepting help from government in exporting sensitive goods.

John Major's replacement of Mrs Thatcher brought a much less astringent tone, but no substantive change in government's approach to industry. Michael Heseltine followed his appointment as President of the Board of Trade in 1992 with the declaration that he would 'intervene before breakfast, before lunch, before tea and before dinner' in support of British industry; but rhetoric was about as far as the break with Thatcherism extended. Even as he spoke, Heseltine was planning a fresh wave of pit closures. Nor had the Thatcherite dragon yet been slain: when Heseltine in 1994 planned to provide £22.5 million in launch aid for Shorts' Learjet 45 – as has been given on a larger scale for successive generations of Airbus – Michael Portillo at the Treasury singled it out as a cut the DTI could make, minuting that it was a 'remnant of the interventionism of the 1960s and 1970s.'

As the recession of the early 1990s gave way to steady growth, one positive for manufacturing employment was the increasing effort put into attracting inward investment. Ministers came to accept that British business had become less interested in promoting manufacturing – even in the promising field of high-tech – and over the decade following the arrival of Nissan, ministers spent more and more time in Japan, South Korea, Germany and the United States encouraging firms to set up in Britain. Their efforts met with considerable success, though as with the enforced moves of heavy industry to the regions in the 1950s and early 1960s, not all the firms attracted stayed long.

The return of a New Labour government under Tony Blair in 1997 did not bring any great change in Whitehall's attitude towards industry. Most of the early policy changes affecting manufacturing were essentially social measures: the minimum wage, the right to trade union recognition, adoption of the European Social Chapter to which Major had refused to sign up. And as industry felt the strain when Gordon Brown's initially tight financial policies forced the pound up, it became evident that 'Hands off!' remained the watchword, to the increasing frustration of the trade unions.

During New Labour's second term, the worm began to turn. From 2002 the Department of Trade and Industry set up a series of Innovation and Growth Teams, starting with one for aerospace, to work with industry to set priorities for R&D and beyond. For months before the collapse of Rover on the eve of the 2005 general election, officials in the DTI did everything they could to keep the last British-owned volume car maker in business, short of putting in money. In 2006 Brown from the Treasury created the Technology Strategy Board, based in Swindon with the research councils. This has done valuable work identifying areas of innovation that could bring results, coaxing businesses into undertaking R&D in areas of need and matching promising graduates with those businesses; in its first five years it created 6,000 graduate jobs and contributed £4 billion to the economy. Yet the most potent subliminal messages coming out of government as Blair's decade in power ended and Brown's began, were that financial services were as important to Britain – if not more so – than manufacturing, and that where Britain's remaining industries were concerned, it did not greatly matter who owned them.

The global banking crisis discredited the first of these two arguments, and Kraft's takeover of Cadbury was a wake-up call in respect of the second. In the closing months of the Labour government Lord Mandelson, back in the Cabinet as Business Secretary after a spell as a European Commissioner, began looking at ways of stopping the rot.

His successor when the coalition took office was Vince Cable; the former chief economist at Shell who, as the Liberal Democrats' Treasury spokesman, had publicly warned Brown that the position of the banks was unsustainable. Industry was not immune from the coalition's early and deep spending cuts: defence industries were hit particularly hard, and Sheffield Forgemasters was one of several strategic businesses to have a government loan (temporarily) cancelled. But against this background, and with unemployment rising again from a high base, Cable stepped up the efforts begun by Mandelson to generate a revival of manufacturing, though with the caveat that growth in the sector could be no more than modest.

Industrial policy and regional policy are closely interlinked, but that does not mean that over the past 60 years they have always gone hand in hand; a number of regional initiatives have been good for the region concerned but less so for the long-term welfare of the industry in question, while efforts to devolve aid to industry to regional bodies have dissipated its impact.

The fear of a return to pre-war levels of unemployment in the 'Assisted Areas' dominated not only economic policy but industrial and regional policy during the 1950s and beyond, and grants were paid to firms ready to move or set up within them. These incentives and outright direction by ministers resulted in new motor, steel and other plants being diverted to Scotland, Wales and Merseyside instead of existing facilities being allowed to expand. In the short term jobs were created, but poor economics of scale, long supply chains and – in some cases – poorly motivated workforces led to the likes of Bathgate, Linwood, Ravenscraig, Shotton and Speke surviving for no more than a generation. One particular decision was both nakedly political and disastrous: Macmillan's 'judgment of Solomon' in 1957, that instead of building a large strip mill beside the existing plant at Ravenscraig, there should be two smaller ones – the other at Llanwern at the opposite end of Britain – to appease as many voters as possible.

In tandem with the diversion of new industry to the regions, successive governments from the 1940s to the 1970s developed New Towns on largely greenfield sites, to which not only the populations of the first bombed-out and later decaying inner cities were 'decanted', but also higher-tech industries. When a company like Cossor or STC needed new premises, it made sense all round to relocate manufacturing capacity from London to a new town like Harlow or Basildon. What was not considered was that moving skilled labour out of the capital would alter the social mix of the population who remained – or that those left behind would have a more limited range of employment to strive for. Moreover, not all the new towns achieved critical mass where industry and employment were concerned; the tendency of manufacturing firms moved from Liverpool to collapse once they relocated to Skelmersdale led the town's MP, Michael McGuire, to brand it a 'disaster area' in 1977. And when the booming electronics firms of the 1950s faltered or merged, the skilled workforces that had moved with them to other new towns were left high and dry. The Ford (now New Holland) tractor works established at Basildon in 1964 is one of the relatively few original New Town employers to survive.

In the 1950s most decisions on industry and the regions were taken centrally, conforming with the post-war dictum of the Labour Treasury minister Douglas Jay that 'the man in Whitehall knows best'. Only in Northern Ireland – which had its own civil service and until 1973 its own legislature – and in Scotland (though the political decisions had to be taken at Westminster) was government operating on the spot. The first change to this arrangement came in 1963 when Lord Hailsham (Quintin Hogg) was appointed Minister for the North-East, in response to a blip in unemployment as pit closures and shipyard redundancies took their toll. Hailsham was little more than a cheerleader, but a principle had been established. In the years that followed, firms making everything from batteries to clothing and potato crisps were attracted to Co. Durham, in particular.

Harold Wilson took a step further in 1964 by appointing a Secretary of State for Wales, the Principality previously having been run out of the Home Office. The priority for the first incumbent, James Griffiths, was similarly the creation of more jobs to offset those lost through pit closures; white goods and television plants were attracted mainly to South Wales – though within 40 years they would, again, almost all be gone. While Labour had come to power committed to wider regional planning, few concrete steps were taken in that direction.

The Heath government's main concern with the regions was in redrawing boundaries as it reorganised local government, creating six metropolitan counties covering the conurbations around Birmingham, Leeds, Liverpool, Manchester, Newcastle and Sheffield and new counties such as Avon and Humberside. These new authorities proved quite effective in campaigning to attract industry, but were killed off by Mrs Thatcher after only a dozen years along with her main target, the Greater London Council. The Assisted Areas remained, despite a Royal Commission concluding that the grants system was 'empiricism run mad; a game of hit and miss played with more enthusiasm than success.' In 1973 Northern Ireland came under direct rule from Westminster, with ministers offering ever more generous incentives to manufacturers to invest in the province in the hope that creating jobs would reduce the level of violence – culminating in the De Lorean affair.

It was during the Heath years that the argument began over whether concentrating Britain's international transport connections in the south-east of England was leading that region to overheat and slowing development in the rest of the country. The point was first made by opponents of the plans – pushed forward under Heath – for a new third airport for London on the Maplin Sands in the Thames Estuary, and for a railway tunnel under the Channel at its narrowest point. It would resurface in the early 1980s – after Labour's cancellation of both those projects – in the debates at Westminster over whether Manchester Airport should be expanded as an alternative to siting the third London airport at Stansted and, later, over the revived private-sector plan for the Tunnel. The argument over the siting of airports had greater validity, as there had long been complaints from businessmen in Scotland and the regions that they had to travel to Heathrow to catch a long-haul flight. In the event Manchester was expanded alongside Stansted, but while it has thrived it has not attracted the volume of business travel, especially to the United States, that had been hoped. The argument over the Tunnel was overshadowed by the impossibility of building it anywhere other than between east Kent and northern France. However Parliament recognised that its existence could be a magnet to industry by insisting that passenger and freight services be operated through the tunnel from as far afield as Scotland. The 'north of London' Eurostar and sleeper services were stillborn because of the disastrous economics of running them and severe time disadvantages, even before competition from low-cost airlines kicked in. While freight trains do run through the tunnel from the Mossend terminal in central Scotland, the vast majority of the freight carried to the Continent continues to travel on HGVs, either on shuttle trains through the tunnel or on ferries. It is also the case that industrial estates and business parks in the Ashford area, close to the English portal, have boomed since the tunnel opened.

The snap election of February 1974 not only brought Heath's defeat but a breakthrough by the Scottish National Party that scared Labour, in particular, out of its wits. Largely the product of the discovery of North Sea oil and the Upper Clyde Shipbuilders work-in, the election of seven Nationalist MPs in February and eleven that October led Labour hastily to drop its opposition to any form of Home Rule and bring forward plans for a devolved Scottish Assembly with limited powers – including the attraction of industry. The abortive outcome of the Scottish devolution referendum in March 1979 (a parallel proposal for Wales was defeated) led directly to the defeat of James Callaghan's government by one vote on a motion of no-confidence and the general election that brought Margaret Thatcher to power.

Though attraction of inward investment had long been an aim of government, it was Mrs Thatcher's that made a success of it. While she eschewed 'interventionism' to keep existing industries going as steel, shipbuilding and the motor sites closed and reduced the size of the Assisted Areas, she secured the groundbreaking Nissan factory for Britain. Her Northern Ireland, Scottish and Welsh secretaries lobbied energetically to attract investment, offering substantial regional development grants sometimes in competition with each other. Nicholas Edwards, her first Welsh Secretary, tried to entice Nissan to Wales rather than Wearside, and after losing that battle set his sights on attracting other Japanese firms, declaring: 'The first thing to do to attract modern industry is to build a golf course.' Under Edwards and his successor Peter Walker, jobs flooded into South Wales at almost the rate they were lost as the pits closed, and inward investment across the UK continued to increase under John Major, peaking in 1997.

New Labour came to power with regional policy commitments to the fore: devolution for Scotland and Wales, a settlement in Northern Ireland, and Regional Development Agencies for each of the English regions. A degree of autonomy for the English regions to make them comparable with Germany's *Länder* was pressed for by Tony Blair's deputy John Prescott, as a response to concerns that the North-East of England, in particular, would miss out on new inward investment once devolved Scotland and Wales were able to offer greater inducements, backed up by political muscle. The devolved administrations were duly set up, as were the RDAs, but the regional tier of government was stillborn after proposals for the North-East were heavily defeated in a referendum in 2004. Blair instead gave responsibility for each of the regions of England to a member of his government, but in practice this was essentially a political move.

The political imperative to devolve real power to the RDAs under New Labour led to strategic R&D programmes, run hitherto by the DTI – such as for aerospace – being fragmented among the RDAs. This proved a retrograde step: some of the agencies had no interest in the projects they were expected to part-fund, and the process of fragmenting a programme and then having it delivered jointly by several RDAs pushed up administrative costs. By the mid-2000s, a specific RDA was being put in the lead for each such programme (the North-West leading on aerospace given BAE Systems' activities in the region) and some of the damage was undone. With the abolition of the RDAs, these programmes are again centrally funded from Whitehall.

The RDAs did some valuable work in setting priorities for improving training and the infrastructure, and attracting industry, but their administrative costs were high for the benefits delivered and they were among the first victims of coalition spending cuts.

Regional policy involves much more than the activities of central government and bodies created by or answerable to it. Local authorities and consortia have long taken a proactive role in attracting investment, but equally the decisions of local planners and council planning committees have done much to hamper the growth – and even the continuance – of manufacturing. As early as 1980 the Conservative Cabinet minister John Biffen warned that Britain's surviving village blacksmiths were struggling to continue in the face of complaints from newly-arrived commuters about the noise, smell and non-rustic ambiance that they created. In the early 1990s Hampshire County Council rejected plans to site what became Disneyland Paris in the county because its planners did not consider the local level of unemployment high enough to support it. In 1998, South Cambridgeshire council rejected plans to extend the Wellcome Trust's Genome Campus because of fears that the village of Hinxton would become part of Cambridge's urban sprawl. And four years later South Wiltshire council blocked an application by James Dyson to extend his vacuum cleaner and washing machine factory at Malmesbury, prompting him to switch production to

Malaysia (though R&D stayed put). Nor were 'Nimby' councillors or hidebound planning officers always the obstacle: government plans for a major new medical research institute next door to St Pancras Station and the British Library were fought every inch of the way by a vocal community group which insisted the site had to be used for social housing. When Dame Fiona Reynolds, director-general of the National Trust, withdrew in 2011 from talks with coalition ministers over reform of the planning system, her insistence that they must reject any suggestion that the changes were designed to assist economic growth drew attention to the belief of many – in local government as well as the world of conservation – that the actual purpose of planning controls is actively to impede it.

Research policy over the past sixty years has been overshadowed by two fundamental concerns: is Britain striking the right balance between civilian and defence R&D, and should research and innovation policy be handled by the government department responsible for industry or the one sponsoring the universities? Behind these concerns lie further arguments for debate: have civilian and defence R&D been kept so far apart that relevant industries are handicapped by there being two completely separate paths of development, and how can innovations originating in universities and research establishments be converted into a commercially marketable product that a British manufacturer will take up?

The argument over the correct balance between civilian and military research was strongest during the Cold War, when defence spending was at its height. Some of the criticism, naturally, came from Left-wing scientists who questioned the ethics of defence-orientated research, but the argument had a practical side as well. In Britain there was a heavy imbalance between R&D spending on new generations of principally military aircraft, and on other strategically important areas of manufacture such as chemicals or more general electronics, on which the French, German and Japanese governments were concentrating with considerable success.

British industry also suffered from the artificial barriers erected by government in the 1950s between the development of computer and nuclear technology for commercial use and for military applications. The effect was to handicap efforts by British companies to keep up with their American competitors in both these fields. Research into computing largely remained in the universities and when a second generation of Trident submarines was canvassed, the lack of facilities in Britain had by 2011 led to an agreement that the new nuclear hydrodynamics test centre would be in France.

The balance between civilian and military research shifted over the years as businesses from pharmaceutical companies to Rolls-Royce financed their own R&D – though appreciating help from government where it was given. The ultimate stage was reached in 2003 with the privatisation of the bulk of the Ministry of Defence's research and evaluation operations as QinetiQ, with a brief that included rolling out as many as possible of its scientists' inventions into the market place. (Around 30 per cent of the former DERA remained in the MoD's hands as the Defence Science and Technology Laboratory, ironically because the Pentagon refused to discuss sensitive issues of nuclear, chemical and biological warfare with a private company).

Government-supported civilian research has traditionally been administered through the research councils, now seven in number: strictly independent bodies with around 9,000 staff in their own establishments, and which support around 50,000 researchers – mainly in the universities – at any one time, and the award of 8,000 PhDs a year. Much of what the councils sponsor is 'pure' research, but there are obviously those that read across the industry from the Medical Research Council to the Biotechnology and Biological Sciences Research Council (founded in 1994) and the Engineering and Physical Sciences and Research Council. In the 1960s, an Industrial Research and Development Authority (IRDA) was created specifically to encourage research leading toward innovation, but it withered on the vine. Only in 1981 did a research council officially acknowledge the existence of engineering in its title, though until 1994 it was lumped together with purist particle physics. The academic establishment's belief that pure science is inherently superior to the applied version dies hard.

The tug-of-war between business and the universities over where innovation policy should have its centre of gravity has generally been won by the academics. The creation of the Department of Education and Science, prior to the 1964 general election, under Quintin Hogg set the pattern with Hogg declaring: 'Ever since 1915 it has been considered axiomatic that responsibility for industrial research and development is better exercised in conjunction with research in the medical, agricultural and other fields.'

The Wilson government brought science closer to industry in 1967 when Sir Solly Zuckerman, chief government scientific adviser, took charge of a Cabinet level committee involving the Ministry of Technology as well as the DES. But it was 1992, under John Major, before the research councils began reporting to the Office of Science and Technology (OST) in the Cabinet Office. In 2006 the OST was renamed the Office of Science and Innovation, one fruit of an intensive consultation by Gordon Brown before launching a 'Ten Year Science Strategy' from the Treasury. The academics reclaimed innovation policy in 2007 when the Department of Universities, Innovation and Skills was created, but two years later industry gained equal access when the super-Department of Business, Innovation and Skills was created for the returning Lord Mandelson, for the first time bringing research, industry and the universities under one, rather large, roof.

In recent decades, Britain's universities have come to appreciate the benefits to themselves of parlaying the fruits of their research into commercial products and services through 'spin-off' companies, and of taking high-tech businesses under their wings. The first such venture, Cambridge Science Park, was opened by Trinity College in 1970, and since then the growth of high-tech firms around the city has transformed its economy from low-wage to a high-wage

– and put such a strain on the electricity supply that the National Grid is struggling to keep up. Other universities have followed suit, finding spin-offs not only a valuable testimony to the quality of their research but a vital source of income as funding from government has tightened.

Arguments over the relevance of Britain's research and innovation set-up to manufacturing industry and its competitiveness continue unabated. Many in the field of innovation look wistfully at DARPA, the Pentagon's agency for 'blue skies' thinking; some of its ideas like a 'futures market' in terrorism have stretched credibility, but it has played an invaluable role in challenging America's boffins and innovators to come up with revolutionary new technologies, many with civilian applications. Others wish that Britain could replicate Germany's Fraunhofer Institutes – a chain of 57 research units across the Federal Republic employing over 10,000 scientists and engineers with an annual research budget of €1.4 billion, much of which comes from industry. Fraunhofer prides itself on the role its research units play in increasing the competitiveness of the German economy at regional as well as at national level.

R&D is alive and well in key sectors of British industry, from BAE Systems and Rolls-Royce, through Jaguar, Land Rover and companies connected to Formula 1, AstraZeneca and GlaxoSmithKline. QinetiQ continues to originate new technologies that are snapped up by manufacturers – not always in Britain. The Society of Motor Manufacturers and Traders launched an annual award for innovation in the industry in 2010, and has met an enthusiastic response. At a niche level Roke Manor Research – in turn a part of Plessey, Siemens and now Chemring – comes up with innovations like Hawk-Eye, the ultimate arbiter of LBW decisions in cricket and line calls at Wimbledon. But despite the increasing commercialisation of university research, questions persist over whether the correct balance between 'pure' and 'applied' research has yet been achieved – not to mention whether wider British industry possesses the flair and the financial backing to turn great innovations into world-beating products.

The way government buys things – from aircraft to paper clips – can have a critical effect on the fortunes of most sectors of British manufacturing; if intelligently handled, it can also be a spur to innovation. But all too often over the decades, government procurement has been amateurish, wasteful of taxpayers' money, dogged by delays and at times downright damaging to the industries it claims to be supporting. Some of these problems are endemic to governments worldwide: a quick flick through any American, Australian or Indian newspaper will produce some story of overpayment for basic items, delays in getting military equipment into service and more. But Britain seems to have elevated inept public procurement to a fine art.

The most spectacular examples of mismanagement have consistently involved the MoD and its suppliers, but the problems exist right across the public sector, and it is only since the early 2000s that serious attempts have been made from the Cabinet Office to raise the government's game, securing better value, eliminating waste and making suppliers know where they stand. Under the coalition, Francis Maude persuaded Whitehall departments to start placing joint orders for the first time, after discovering that some were spending far more than others on basic items of stationery: £73 for a box of paper that cost another department £8, or £2,000 for a laptop another was able to buy for £350.

The Public Finance Initiative (PFI), introduced under John Major in 1992 and greatly expanded by Gordon Brown as Chancellor, has not helped. The purpose of PFI was to entrust the provision of items from new hospitals and schools to new trains, to private sector suppliers under build-and-maintain contracts, removing the capital cost from the public accounts but at the price of heavy payments over 30 years or so. Built into many PFI contracts has been a tariff of charges for services the contractor will provide; the euphoria over saving money in the short term led to rather too many prices like £300 for changing a light bulb or £900 for supplying a Christmas tree creeping through, and an early priority for the coalition was to renegotiate the most profligate of these contracts. The most notorious PFI product – the Public-Private Partnership (PPP) to modernise the Underground forced on London by Brown – collapsed under the weight of its financial unwieldiness while Labour was still in power; Transport for London saving millions after the Metronet consortium hit the financial buffers by taking both its operations and those of the smaller Tube Lines in-house. The one company to emerge with credit from the PPP fiasco was Bombardier, whose provision of new trains on time and to budget led to further contracts for Tube trains which kept its Derby factory going when the Department for Transport routinely began steering orders for new main-line trains to its German and Japanese competitors.

One of the most notorious examples of a thoughtless procurement was the ordering of Rosenthal crockery from Germany for the House of Commons' dining rooms in the 1970s without Wedgwood or any other British firm being invited to tender. The impression that our MPs did not regard British china as worth considering sent out an immensely damaging message for the industry, not least in export markets, and the discovery that Wedgwood could almost have matched Rosenthal on price led to the chairman of the Refreshment Committee being ousted.

It has proved immensely difficult over the years to persuade different public sector organisations to co-ordinate their purchasing to secure the best deal and operational uniformity. Britain's police forces, particularly in the field of IT, are notorious for refusing to order any piece of equipment if another force is using it. Each of Britain's new-generation light rail systems has seemingly been designed to make sure the trams ordered for it from continental manufacturers must be different from those running elsewhere; pushing up costs by removing the scope for placing larger combined orders which might have made it worthwhile for a British firm to tool up to supply them – it was 2011 before ministers friendly to light rail stepped in and demanded co-ordination. And the insistence of many individual NHS Trusts on ordering their own IT systems from different suppliers despite the existence of a national programme for unified record-keeping was one reason why the coalition in 2011 abandoned the national programme with the best part of £11 billion spent on it.

Much waste in procurement – and resistance to the purchasing of innovative products – stems from inflexible procedures within departments. A British company devised a new form of incontinence pad for use in hospitals and care homes which stood to save the NHS millions of pounds in laundry costs. It could not be introduced – to the frustration of the DTI which was backing the company – because there was no mechanism within the bureaucracy of the NHS to transfer money from the laundry budget to the budget for appliances. As a result, patients had to go on sleeping in urine-soaked sheets, and British manufacturing lost a product with potential.

Yet the greatest failure in government procurement over the years has involved defence hardware, from jeeps to jet fighters. By 2011, the Public Accounts Committee was reporting that the MoD's 15 major procurements were £8.8 billion over budget and 32 years behind schedule. The sole consolation is that contracts placed since 2002 have fared rather better. Moreover, those schedules run from when a contract is actually signed; there had at that time been a 28-year delay in bringing to fruition the department's Future Rapid Effects System project for 3,000 new armoured fighting vehicles.

Two of the most notorious examples of a failed procurement both concern the Nimrod derivative of the De Havilland Comet – first flown commercially in 1952 – for which its makers and the RAF found a continuing use as an early warning and reconnaissance aircraft. When in the 1980s the military saw a need for an airborne early warning system to detect approaching hostile aircraft or missiles, the United States was already using a variant of the Boeing 747 codenamed AWACS, topped by a gigantic intelligence-gathering and communications mushroom. The MoD, commendably, decided to buy British, and British Aerospace and GEC got together to offer the AEW3, an update of the Nimrod fitted with British avionics and radar. The MoD opted for Nimrod in 1977, with the planes – steadily reduced in number – to be in service by 1982. The Falklands War came and went with other aircraft having to fill the breach, and by 1986 the Nimrod's radar was still under test, with

£1 billion spent on the project against a projected £200-£300 million. When ministers in the Thatcher government began to lose patience and to revisit the AWACS option, their former colleague James Prior called in a group of Lobby correspondents, including myself, and assured us that the problems were close to being resolved. When my story appeared in the *Daily Telegraph,* I had a call from a technician on the project to say that on the AEW3's most recent test flight, two targets had been identified: a ship crossing the North Sea at 13,000 mph and the bowl of the aircraft's own lavatory. Weeks later, the Cabinet agreed to buy AWACS and write off the cost of the Nimrod project.

Just six years after the AEW3 was cancelled, the MoD decided a replacement was needed for the RAF's Nimrod MR2 marine reconnaissance aircraft, which had been in service since the early 1970s. After considering bids from Lockheed and Dassault, it opted for BAe's proposal to put new-generation surveillance equipment in yet another set of upgraded Comet airframes, with new wings and Airbus glass cockpits; the contract was signed in 1996.

The project was fraught with problems. No two of the airframes were of precisely the same dimensions (leading BAe to take over the work when Flight Refuelling Ltd struggled with it), there were problems with corrosion and the new wings turned out to be flawed, causing a delay while a new design was produced. As the in-service date moved forward from the 2003 first envisaged, the number of aircraft required was cut from 21 to nine, but the cost escalated, forcing BAE Systems to issue a profits warning in 2004. The cost per aircraft rose from £142 million to £433 million, and by the time the MRA4 was cancelled in 2010 without a single aircraft having been released into service, the project was £789 million over budget and almost nine years behind schedule. Nearly 400 workers at BAE Systems immediately lost their jobs.

Contrary to the claims of protesting former senior airmen, the MRA4 even then was nowhere near being ready for service. The *Financial Times* reported that when the decision was taken to scrap the aircraft, it 'was still riddled with flaws.... Safety tests conducted [in 2010] found there were still "several hundred design non-compliances" with the aircraft. It was unclear, for example, whether its bomb bay doors functioned properly, whether its landing gear worked and, most worryingly, whether its fuel pipe was safe.' Moreover, concerns over the MRA4's aerodynamics meant that it was effectively grounded at the time of cancellation.

Defence Secretary Liam Fox described the MRA4 project as an example of the worst of MoD procurement performance: 'The idea that we ever allow ourselves into a position where something that was originally Nimrod 2000 – where we ordered 21 reduced to nine, spent £3.8bn and we still weren't close to getting the capability – is not to happen again.' Yet the Nimrod was far from being the only horror story. The Astute class nuclear submarines entered service years late and billions over budget, as did the Eurofighter, likewise a number of major procurements – such as the first attempt at FRES – were cancelled before contracts were signed.

Nor have procurement blunders by the MoD only affected British suppliers. In 1995 an order worth £259 million was placed with Boeing for eight Chinook helicopters for special operations, but someone forgot to specify that they would need night vision equipment and other refinements. When delivered, they turned out to be only capable of being flown on a bright, sunny day in Wiltshire. The Chinooks were parked in air-conditioned hangars during lengthy recriminations (not involving Boeing), and were unavailable for service either in Iraq or during the worst of the conflict in Afghanistan. An upgrade was cancelled on grounds of cost, then approved at a much higher figure. The National Audit Office concluded in 2008 that the blunder had cost £500 million and compromised vital military operations; blame was placed squarely on the MoD. The first of the Chinooks ordered in 1995 was finally released into service 14 years later.

How do fiascos like this happen? They should not be in the interests of the MoD, whose clear objective was getting new military hardware into service, within budget, as expeditiously as possible. Nor in the long term do they benefit contractors like BAE Systems; they may have been paid billions, but the eventual failure of a procurement does considerable damage to their reputation. Moreover, as in the case of PFI, the abandonment of other bidding processes before signature of a contract not only angers the winners, but upsets losing bidders who have spent millions gearing up for a project that would never happen even if they won.

Some of the problems clearly do lie within the MoD. Each procurement is run through an Integrated Project Team of brass-hats and civil servants, which assesses the bids, recommends a preferred bidder, crawls over the small print of the contract and then works with the contractor to bring the project to fruition. In principle, this is an admirable arrangement, and the process is crawling with procedures to ensure that strict ethics are observed between the MoD and competing bidders. The problem is that with many procurements, signature of the contract is merely the prelude for a deluge of instructions from the MoD for details to be altered, and new features to be added as they become available or desirable; indeed without some upgrading a platform or its weaponry will be obsolete when it enters service. There are many reasons why costs soar and delays stretch out, but this is one of the principal ones.

One of the worst examples was the procurement of the Bowman radio system for the Army in the 1990s. The cost of bidding for the contract nearly brought down both Racal and Plessey as the specifications were repeatedly changed by the MoD's procurement team, and then the winning consortium including BAE Systems, Racal and ITT had the plug pulled on it in 2000 with the project eight years behind schedule. The MoD then rebid the contract, awarding it the second time to a consortium including CDC Systems (now General Dynamics), ITT, BAE Systems and Thales. Racal never recovered from the cost of developing a system seen in the military as flawed because of repeated MoD alterations, and to this day Bowman is known in the Army as 'Better Off With Map And Nokia'.

There have also been efforts to obtain 'value-for-money' that have ended by achieving the opposite; awarding a contract for an inferior product or inflicting such damage on a valued British contractor that it finds it hard to stay in business. There was a fashion in the 1990s and a little beyond for the MoD to ensure a fully competitive process by putting together rival partnerships to bid for a contract: say an aircraft and a radar manufacturer on each side, plus niche players. To make matters even more competitive, it could happen that a poor aircraft and the better radar were put into one bid, and the more suitable aircraft and a less satisfactory radar into the other. The inevitable consequence of this was that if the partnership offering the better radar failed to be named as preferred bidder because of the merits of the aircraft in the other – or vice versa – valuable industry capacity and skilled jobs were lost.

Another reason why costs of major procurements soar above the original estimate was candidly admitted to soon after the Millennium by Admiral Sir Raymond Lygo, BAe's chief executive in the 1980s. He said: 'It's a well-known fact, whether anyone admits it or not, that you'll never get any programme through the government if you revealed the true cost. You say: "Right, we can do this and we'll do it for the price" and then the programme goes ahead. But you know automatically that it's going to cost more than that because it will. So after a year you say: "I'm terribly sorry, but the costs have now risen." The Treasury has long assumed this for infrastructure projects, generally putting a buffer of 30 per cent over estimate for what the eventual outcome will be, but in the eyes of cynics this has stemmed from a desire to prove projects unaffordable rather than any realism over costs – and it has not been applied to defence procurements.

Cost overruns and delays in delivery are nothing new: committees of MPs and the National Audit Office have been fulminating over them at least since the 1980s. But the MoD has appeared constitutionally incapable of raising its game. Moreover a new issue arose which it twice spectacularly failed to come to grips with: negotiation of a contract under which it would cost almost as much to cancel a programme as to run it through to completion. Despite having belatedly discovered that the contract it signed up to in the early 1990s for the Eurofighter effectively made it impossible to save money by cancelling the RAF's final tranche of aircraft, the MoD insouciantly signed one with BAE Systems in 2008 for the two *Queen Elizabeth* class aircraft carriers, which again made it almost as costly to cancel the ships as to complete them. The belated discovery of this tied the coalition's hands and obliged it to finish both ships then mothball one of them, having as a result to make unpopular and damaging cuts across the rest of the Royal Navy. There were suspicions in government that Gordon Brown, in whose political backyard the final assembly was to take place, had agreed to this 'poison pill' to make sure the project was not cancelled – just as Kenneth Clarke had left a hole in the transport budget prior to 1997, in order to force Brown to privatise National Air Traffic Services.

John Hutton, Brown's Defence Secretary, became so concerned at the state of major procurements that he commissioned a review from Bernard Gray, a former MoD policy maker. Gray's findings were damning: the department's insistence on running a 'substantially overheated equipment programme, with too many types of equipment being ordered for too large a range of tasks at too high a specification' was hampering operations in Afghanistan by leaving troops without the equipment they actually needed. The failure of FRES to deliver a single vehicle to theatre ten years into the programme was another sore point. After the coalition took office, Liam Fox brought Gray back to the MoD as chief of defence materiel with instructions to 'think the unthinkable'; revolutionary changes were forecast and there were early signs that a combination of the need for cuts and Gray's recommendations would lead to a drastic reduction in the number of senior service personnel inside the ministry.

A recent concern of UK defence contractors has been the MoD's insistence that to obtain value-for-money it must buy hardware 'off the peg' instead of collaborating in the process of development. In almost every case the only product available 'off the peg' is American (or French), precisely because the MoD will not give its seal of approval to hardware developed by British manufacturers short of a full-blooded procurement. Moreover, even if a product exists that would attract export orders if the MoD even took one on loan, the department will not give any indication of support short, again, of an outright procurement – which is just what ordering 'off the peg' is designed to avoid. Without the backing of the MoD, UK Trade &

Industry (an agency of the Department of Business) is unable to give its full support for the drive for export orders. This is not a problem French or German defence contractors have; their countries' defence ministries are quite happy to endorse equipment that might be exported to friendly countries, not least because at some stage in the future its own forces might wish to purchase them 'off the peg'. There again, defence procurement in France, especially, is not designed as an ordeal for the bidder: the French MoD actually operates a website on which anyone wishing to sell, say, boots to the Army can engage directly on-line.

A further difficulty is that caution in Whitehall about letting even our friends share some sensitive technologies has handicapped British firms in key export markets. It is, surely, one thing not to declare our hand to North Korea, but quite another to jeopardise defence co-operation with the United States. Matters came to a head in 2011 over difficulties faced by contractors in obtaining export licences for sophisticated equipment for dealing with IEDs (improvised explosive devices) which had taken a high toll of British troops in Afghanistan. Executives from Thales UK, Finmeccanica, TRL (a subsidiary of America's L-3) and Chemring told ministers that departments' insistence on considering each order on a 'case-by-case' basis – nominally to guard against sales to abusers of human rights – was jeopardising orders worth millions of pounds even to the United States. The heart of the problem, they said, was that where decisions were taken on a case-by-case basis, officials were 'playing safe by saying "No"'.

While the MoD is sometimes accused of too cosy a relationship with major defence contractors like BAE Systems, it equally attracts criticism for preferring not to buy British. QinetiQ found that the only way it could get the MoD to adopt some of its more advanced technologies was to sell them to the Pentagon, after which interest would suddenly develop in Whitehall. Moreover, the MoD does its best to infer that American equipment bought 'off the peg' is in fact British. The Mastiff and Wolfhound armoured fighting vehicles purchased for the Army to use in Afghanistan are in fact derivatives of the Cougar manufactured by Force Protection in South Carolina, then fitted by NP Aerospace of Coventry with British weapons and armour – not much more, industry insiders say, than sewing the 'Made in England' label into Marks & Spencer clothing manufactured abroad. The Foxhound, ordered to replace the vulnerable and much-criticised 'snatch Land Rover', is likewise a derivative of Force Protection's Ocelot, which undergoes 'final assembly' by Riccardo at Shoreham.

Not all the MoD's most controversial procurement decisions, however, are taken on its side of Whitehall. In 1990 Downing Street went along with Germany's choice of a Hughes-based radar system for the Eurofighter over the MoD's preference for Ferranti's offering in order to keep the Bonn government in the programme – doing irreparable damage to Ferranti which had to be taken over by GEC. And more recently it has been claimed that MAN of Germany was awarded a contract for Army supply vehicles ahead of the original choice of America's Oshkosh in order to keep the same government, now relocated to Berlin, sweet over the increasing expense of the aircraft.

Transport and infrastructure policy in Britain since the 1950s has been dominated first by the need to complete post-war modernisation, then to accommodate the surge in traffic on the roads, the growing demand for air travel, the drive for privatisation and deregulation and most recently by the need to increase capacity without damaging the environment. Each of these has had a considerable impact on industry, with even the construction materials and equipment industries that have benefited from the motorway building programme wrong-footed by the inability of government to plan in a way that provides a steady volume of work – partly because of financial constraints and partly because of delays imposed by the planning system.

During the 1950s the emphasis moved on from replacing buses, trains and infrastructure worn out during the war, to modernising the railways and building the first motorways. All the main transport providers – road, rail and air – were owned by and answerable to the government, with decisions taken centrally. Enormous sums were invested in the railways as diesel trains replaced steam and new goods yards and flyovers were constructed – some rendered redundant soon after by service cuts. A start was made on electrifying the main lines north from London, bringing valuable work to the electrical and cable industries, but the stop-start nature of electrification over the decades prevented industry from deriving the full benefit – and forced up costs. As a general rule, though, Conservative governments have invested more in the railways than Labour.

From the 1960s, with the railways fighting a loss of passengers and – even more so – freight to the roads, the emphasis was firmly on road building. Roads of all categories have been steadily upgraded over the past 60 years, but for most of that time the emphasis has been on getting in place a system of inter-urban motorways that can cope with demand. The first to open, in 1958, was the section of the M6 bypassing Preston; the M1 followed in stages and Britain can now boast 2,173 miles of motorway, probably close to the maximum we have room for – increasingly now the emphasis is on widening existing motorways rather than building new ones.

The arrival of the motorways not only gave manufacturers a speedy new means of bringing in components and distributing their products – it transformed the road haulage industry. Road haulage in Britain had grown out of the fairgrounds, where the heaviest traction was in use, and its drivers remained rugged individualists. They fought against the 'spy-in-the-cab' tachograph until it was imposed from Brussels in 1986, since when it has proved invaluable in recording the dangerously long hours worked in Britain by Continental truckers.

When the industry was nationalised after the war, long-distance lorries – all limited to 20 mph – took days to transport goods between, say, the ferry ports, the North and Scotland. By the 1950s, roads like the A5 and A6 carried almost continuous convoys of lorries, and the motorways came not a day too soon. The 1950s and 1960s also saw the rise of the independent road haulier, as private enterprise was allowed to compete with the state-owned British Road Services. Haulage firms and, even more importantly, the drivers themselves, wanted faster, more efficient, more comfortable lorries that were easier to drive. After a period when they automatically bought British from Leyland, Foden, Bedford and others, they began to see the attractions of the more advanced vehicles developed by Volvo, Scania and other European manufacturers. Britain's truck-building industry conspicuously failed to rise to this challenge, not least because much of it had gravitated to British Leyland which was preoccupied by the battle – ultimately lost – to save its volume car operation. Most of Britain's truck builders closed or were taken over by foreign companies, with the bulk of production eventually moving abroad. Nowadays the lorries two abreast on the motorway in front of you will most likely be MANs, DAFs or Scanias.

Development of civil aviation was firmly in the hands of government, both BOAC and British European Airways – merged as British Airways in 1974 – being owned by the State. The development of civil airliners by the then widespread British aircraft industry hinged on what those airlines would accept, and the failure of the Hawker Siddeley Trident, in particular, to gain export markets was a result of the plane having been produced to BEA's rigid specifications. Britain's coolness toward the Airbus consortium at the outset, and its lack of clout after rejoining it in 1979, had much to do with British Airways' insistence on ordering all its long-haul jets from Boeing, even before it was privatised in 1987. Nor did efforts by successive governments to encourage competitors to BA benefit Airbus much, let alone Britain's fast-shrinking civil aircraft industry: successive challengers including Laker Airways, British Caledonian, DanAir, bmi and Virgin all tried to compete having ordered at least some Airbuses, but only Virgin survives, having in the 1990s exposed a 'dirty tricks' campaign against it by BA. Laker went bust, BCal and DanAir were both swallowed up by BA, and bmi is going the same way. BA belatedly abandoned its disdain for Airbus; at the time of writing it operates 99 Airbuses, and 136 Boeings.

The damage done to Britain's bus manufacturers by the privatisation and deregulation of bus services has been detailed elsewhere, so too the impact of railway privatisation on its train builders. But the bad news for Bombardier, by the mid-2000s Britain's only surviving train builder, did not end there. As passengers flocked back to the railways after privatisation, the train operators ordered thousands of new trains: most electric, some diesel. Alstom captured some of the first wave of orders before ceasing to manufacture in Britain in 2005 – though it continued to bid. Hitachi, encouraged by the Labour government, eventually won the order for commuter trains on High Speed 1 into Kent, Prince Philip observing as he boarded one at St Pancras: 'Don't we make trains any more?' But the vast bulk of orders went to Bombardier and Siemens.

Then, in 2006, Transport Secretary Alistair Darling, under pressure from the Treasury, abolished the stand-alone Strategic Rail Authority and handed control of the railways to his civil servants; one of the officials placed in the lead was described to me by a railway insider as 'looking throughout as if he would rather be translating Homer'. The consequences were bizarre: micro-management of the timetable, a short-lived technical policy which held that further electrification was impossible without a revolutionary new form of signalling, and the evolution of the 'bi-mode' Inter-City Express (IEP) project, the classic example of a horse designed by a committee turning into a camel. Labour's final Transport Secretary Lord Adonis overruled his officials to order a new wave of electrification, set the stage for High Speed 2 to Birmingham and the North, and ordered a review of the IEP, for which Hitachi had been named the preferred bidder. His Conservative successor Philip Hammond pressed ahead with the IEP, but only after the Japanese prime minister had lobbied David Cameron.

The Department for Transport also took responsibility from 2006 for procurement of new rolling stock, despite the fact that privatised rolling stock companies (ROSCOs) leased trains to the operators. A tendering process costing millions was imposed on Virgin's acquisition of extra Pendolino carriages from Alstom – at the end of which the DfT refused to allow them to enter service for a year until Virgin's franchise expired (a decision partly reversed as its absurdity registered).

It might have been expected that having taken responsibility for what new rolling stock was ordered, the DfT would develop a strategy involving a reasonable continuity of orders for Derby, subject to quality and price. What in fact happened was that the Department did its best to stimulate competition between Hitachi and Siemens, while cutting off orders for Bombardier. When the train operators chose the manufacturer, 70 per cent of orders went to Bombardier, but after the DfT took over the IEP contract was awarded to Hitachi and the crucial order for 1,200 carriages for the Thameslink route went to Siemens. No-one doubted the quality of Siemens's product (Bombardier indeed had recently been through a poor patch on delivery times) but there was no indication at any point that the DfT regarded the continuance of Britain's train building industry as desirable.

Neither British industry nor society as a whole has been well served by an education system that since the 1960s has essentially been concerned – whatever its proponents have claimed – with 'dumbing-down'. The aim of successive governments has been to give more education to more of the population in the belief that this will raise standards and increase opportunities, when in reality it has achieved precisely the opposite. Undoubtedly some children have benefited from the raising of the school leaving age to 16 in 1972, and from the aim of governments since the 1990s of sending 50 per cent of school leavers to university. But it is hard to escape the conclusion that almost every educational reform over the past 60 years has contributed to a decline in standards – despite the insistence each year by examination boards that more children than ever have secured top GCSE and A-Level results (Highers in Scotland) and the awarding of ever more First-class degrees by indifferent universities anxious to trumpet their own excellence.

Part of the blame for this must lie within the Department for Education. Edward Short, Labour Education Secretary in the late

1960s and ex-headmaster of one of the toughest boys' schools on Tyneside, reckoned that too many of his officials were low-calibre and ultra-trendy; he predicted that even his successor Margaret Thatcher would be unable to get the better of them. Over the decades Education gained a reputation in Whitehall as one of its least impressive departments, and the low point was reached in 2010 when the incoming coalition Education Secretary, Michael Gove, publicly blamed his officials for botching the announcement of which schools were affected by cuts to Labour's school rebuilding programme.

The relationship between Britain's schools and the world of industry has never been strong. Traditionally the schools aimed at academic excellence, in the belief that this would ensure pupils a good job when they left. Such links as there were have tended to involve further education colleges, where many school-leavers acquired vocational qualifications. Engineers, in particular, have complained for decades that the educational system does nothing to encourage young people into the discipline – a campaign conducted at times with a shrillness that suggested that engineers felt they were put, by society, into the same pigeonhole as paedophiles, estate agents, journalists and MPs. The educational system has succeeded in producing a steady supply of well-trained engineering graduates, but with worrying gaps in specialised fields. A decade ago, I heard the chief executive of Shell lament that the limited supply of graduates in petroleum engineering meant that his engineers working in Nigeria could no longer retire at 45. Yet whenever the subject comes up in a radio phone-in, the conversation is dominated by complaints from young engineering graduates that they cannot find a job.

For decades, the great debate in British education was over the merits of comprehensive schools compared with grammar schools. The strongest advocates of comprehensives were Labour politicians who had moved up the ladder after receiving a grammar school education and appeared unwilling to let subsequent generations enjoy the same social mobility. The defenders of the grammar schools, for the most part, seemed to be middle-class parents who were hoping their neighbours' children would fail the 11-plus. The debate was not edifying, but it was resolved firmly in favour of the comprehensives on the back of outstanding performance by a few 'flagship' schools like Eltham Green and Holland Park, and since the end of the 1980s few grammar schools have been left.

This debate, however, ignored almost entirely the secondary modern schools to which the 50 to 80 per cent of children who failed the 11-plus were sent – and the small number of technical schools intended to prepare pupils for skilled jobs in industry, which disappeared when the system was reorganised. There was an assumption that by sending former secondary modern pupils to comprehensives, the stigma of educational failure would be removed and that exposing them to teaching intended for brighter pupils would enable them to advance. Again, some children have benefited, but many more have not and some who would have been high-flyers have been held back.

Sadly for pupils and for society as a whole, the shift to comprehensives coincided with the adoption of radical new ideas by the educationalists of the 1960s. The aim of their 'child-centred approach' was to let the child absorb knowledge, instead of the teacher delivering it. The teaching of pupils of different levels of ability in separate classes to maximise the potential of each was widely replaced with 'mixed-ability teaching', ensuring that the brightest did not develop and the least gifted did not understand. Formal classrooms and lessons were replaced in many schools by cosier environments in which it was harder to teach or maintain discipline. There were even schools where children were not encouraged to learn 'until they are ready'.

By the mid-1970s these dogmas were starting to have a disastrous effect on educational standards. Matters came to a head with a public dispute over teaching methods at William Tyndale junior school in Islington, where left-wing teachers were 'offering working-class children real choices and a broad educational experience' – in other words, in the view of many parents, not teaching them anything. A two-year power struggle over who ran the school culminated in a public inquiry that castigated almost everyone involved, but especially the teachers.

James Callaghan – along with Churchill and John Major the only recent prime minister not to have gone to university – sensed the mood, and launched a 'great debate' about educational standards. It has continued ever since. Some of the absurdities of progressive education have been put back in their box, but the concern about low standards has persisted, with increasing evidence that many pupils fail to advance after leaving primary school and even fall back. By 2011 the point had been reached where one third of 11-year-olds in London schools could not read, write or add up properly. Employers have increasingly complained that many school-leavers were incapable of performing basic tasks; traders at the Westfield shopping complex next door to the 2012 Olympic site had to lay on tuition for almost 800 of the 2,000 long-term employed they took on, almost equally for literacy and numeracy – and that was after choosing the brightest applicants. Universities have expressed concern that students with apparently glittering A-levels are unable to spell, punctuate or complete elementary sums. And university tutors voice alarm that most of their brightest students these days have not been educated in British state schools – or in Britain at all.

There is considerable evidence that many of the pupils who would formerly have attended secondary modern schools are faring worse under the comprehensive system, despite smaller classes and staying on an extra year – with boys performing noticeably worse than girls. Not all the blame can be placed on the schools or the educational establishment: the breakdown of discipline in the home, the increasing number of children reared by single parents and rising levels of truancy have certainly not helped. There is some validity to the complaint of the Lib Dem deputy premier Nick Clegg that teachers are prevented from doing their job by the need to act as surrogate parents. Many teachers will argue that the regime of testing and school league tables introduced in the late 1980s by the Conservative Education Secretary Kenneth Baker, has encouraged schools to concentrate on their brightest pupils, with the less academic being, in some cases, actively discouraged from entering public examinations in case their grades pull the school's average down.

The charge to refocus the educational establishment on delivery rather than self-congratulation was led, until his premature death in 2011, by Richard Pike, chief executive of the Royal Society of Chemistry. He cited exam papers kept 'meaninglessly easy' to ensure schools' places in the league tables, 'Mickey Mouse' degrees funded by government, a GCSE higher mathematics paper which was easier than an 11-plus practice paper from 1960, and the need for universities to run remedial maths courses for chemistry students as 'many had not opened a textbook in the subject in two years'. The criticism was taken up by Eric Schmidt, chairman of Google, who told the 2011 Edinburgh Television Festival that he was 'flabbergasted to learn that computer science isn't even taught as standard' in Britain's schools, and that a 'drift to the humanities', with scientists and engineers denigrated rather than encouraged to be polymaths, had contributed to the UK 'throwing away its computer heritage'.

Nor are the universities without blame. The head of Birmingham University's school of philosophy emailed colleagues in 2011 urging them to be 'very generous' when assessing applications from prospective PhD students, saying that if the department was 'too choosy' about taking those who were up to the demands of the course it might be fined by the university for under-recruiting. And colleagues of mine have had wives working in academia who have been under orders to pass students who had failed.

One priority since Harold Wilson's 'technological revolution' of the 1960s has been the creation of more universities, the production of more graduates in science and engineering and, more recently, the bloating of the university system to accommodate half the population between 18 and 21. The first of these aims has been accomplished; many of the new universities of the 1960s and 1970s have built an excellent record in undergraduate study and in research. The second was on track for a time as the number of science graduates soared, but in recent times as universities have struggled to economise, a number have found physics and chemistry more costly to teach than hospitality management and media studies, and have closed scientific departments. In addition, some of the brightest mathematicians and scientists have, since the late 1980s, been snapped up by the invest-ment banks with salaries no productive industry could match.

The third has produced a growing proportion of graduates regarded by employers as not prepared for the world of work, or for whom no employment that can make use of their qualifications exists. This is not solely a British phenomenon; the existence of a growing core of graduates with no hope of work has fuelled unrest in countries around the globe. Most damaging of all, though, the expansion of the universities has sucked into that sector large numbers of academic staff who would previously have gone into the secondary schools. This has created a shortage of secondary school teachers in maths, languages and the pure sciences, with many classes in these subjects having to be taught by staff not qualified to teach them. By 2011 Stephen Odell, chief executive of Ford Europe, was warning that for its industry to survive in an increasingly competitive world, the UK had to improve its educational infrastructure to increase the take-up of science, tech-nology, engineering and mathematics in universities. However, he added that creating the right skills base had to be matched by 'the right pro-industry policies in place to make investing in Britain of benefit to all stakeholders concerned.' Weeks later Sir James Dyson warned that he might have to move his R&D operations abroad if British universities could not turn out more engineering graduates.

Dissatisfaction with the results secured from an ever more costly educational system has spread beyond employers and academics to parents. The political parties have remained largely unengaged, in part because so many of their members come from one or other of the vested interests with a stake in making the system larger and less attuned to the needs of society and the economy. The Liberal Democrats – and Nick Clegg personally – suffered a major loss of face when they abandoned their commitment to abolish student tuition fees after joining the coalition and acquiesced in an increase to a maximum £9,000. Yet had they opened up the long-overdue argument over whether the university sector is now too large, they could have made some progress toward their objective. Why they did not may be explained by the Lib Dem MP who told me: 'We can't say anything sensible about education. Too many of our party members are teachers.'Yet even in the Labour Party, for whom comprehensives were long the Holy Grail, a debate is opening up below the radar. My local MP's re-election party in 2010 suddenly polarised into a discussion between party members wanting a return to selection (parents) and those determined to keep an open education system (teachers).

Richard Pike's concern was not just for universities or the study of chemistry; they were ultimately for the economy. He noted that all high school students in China, India and Japan study maths up to the age of 18, giving those countries' industries a better educated workforce. One reason cited for immigrant workers, especially from eastern Europe, taking so many of the new jobs created in the UK economy during the 2000s was that despite English not being their first language, they were better educated.

There have been cautious moves toward introducing vocational courses in schools for pupils who will not be staying on beyond GCSE or going to university, but progress has been slow. Under Gordon Brown's 'New Deal' to eradicate youth unemployment, over-18s not in work or full-time education were offered training to prepare them for employment. This initiative had considerable success until firstly the economy turned down and secondly, reluctant trainees realised they could skip the New Deal by obtaining a doctor's certificate saying they were suffering from 'stress'.

The post-war years brought a reduction in the number of apprentices being set on, creating the risk of skill shortages or of employers 'poaching' trained staff by offering to pay them more, rather than go to the time and expense of offering training themselves. The Douglas-Home government in 1964 established Industrial Training Boards (ITBs) to improve the quality of training and share the cost among employers. The ITBs substantially improved the quality and relevance of training, and there was a modest revival in the numbers of apprentices recruited to 110,000 a year, most of them boys. Then the collapse of traditional industries – some of the ITBs almost being left without an industry to train entrants for – reduced the demand for apprentices, and a gap opened up between young people still entering those industries who were steadily less well trained, and those in high-tech industries where highly structured apprenticeships offered a road to technical qualifications. Reporting in 1986 on a shortage of skilled labour in the West Midlands, Roger Eglin wrote in the Sunday Times: 'In many firms it goes beyond the issue of not carrying out training, to a positive antipathy.' National Vocational Qualifications (NVQs) were introduced that year in an attempt to revitalise vocational training, but the apprenticeship system only revived when John Major's government in 1994 introduced 'modern apprenticeships' administered by Sector Skills Councils. Extended for the first time to the service as well as the manufacturing and construction sectors, these have proved a considerable success with numbers of apprentices back up to, or even slightly higher than, the level of the 1970s.

The Attlee government emphasised the need to raise the calibre of management by collaborating in the creation of the British Institute of Management, which, as the Chartered Institute of Management since 2002, continues to play an important role in developing managerial techniques. The long-running argument over the status of engineers reflects a frustration in the profession that it is far easier for an accountant to rise to the top in industry than an engineer. The continuing scope for self-made entrepreneurs to prosper is shown in the success not only of the likes of Lord Hanson but of Sir James Dyson, a design student before he became an engineer. And the perception of managers – reflected in the 1950s film *I'm All Right, Jack* – as chinless ex-public schoolboys (or indeed as 'trouble at t'mill' egotists) has undergone a fundamental change. Long gone are the pre-war days when Courtaulds deliberately packed its board with public school men in the belief that they had all the answers. Today, one would like to think, boards are recruited on merit – though a pattern has grown up of remuneration committees mutually inflating boardroom salaries, and of the main qualification for a non-executive director being that he or she already holds a dozen similar appointments. In these areas, however, government can do no more than encourage or warn.

Few areas of government involvement with economic activity give rise to as much controversy as regulation. Business groups claim that the cost of complying with regulations imposed from Whitehall and Brussels amounts to many billions a year; an extrapolation from estimates from the Department of Business's Better Regulation Task Force of the impact of regulation on GDP puts the total annual cost at between £145 and £175 billion. The balance between the enforcement of necessary standards – particularly where safety in factories is concerned – and the tendency of government to demand ever more form-filling from struggling businesses, has been hard to strike to the satisfaction of all. Ever since Harold Wilson's 'bonfire of controls' in the late 1940s, governments have committed themselves to reduce regulatory burdens on business and industry, yet the amount of regulation has steadily increased. New Labour in 1997 set up a 'better regulation task force' under Lord Haskins, but despite its best efforts the Whitehall culture of 'if it moves, regulate it' continued to thrive; indeed on some estimates the cost of regulation to business increased by £80 billion over the lifetime of the Brown/Blair government, though that does include the cost of paying the minimum wage. When 13 years later Vince Cable announced an intensified drive to abolish superfluous 'red tape', it was instructive that his department, instead of involving what was now the Better Regulation Executive, set up a brand new working party.

Some regulation is necessary. The poor safety record of manufacturing industry and the danger inherent in many processes led to the creation of the Factory Inspectorate as far back as 1833, and the establishment of the Health and Safety Executive in 1974 was a logical step to extend safety standards across the wider economy. Manufacturing industry has largely escaped the crazier excesses of the health and safety culture in more recent times, most of which stem from misunderstandings of sensible regulations by low-level officials in the public sector, or to demonstrate at a time of cuts that their job is essential.

Regulations that have impacted most on manufacturing industry have involved safety, working hours and conditions and wages.

Landmarks have included the Equal Pay Act of 1970, successive pieces of legislation passed under the Thatcher government setting a framework for unions to call strikes, the Employment Rights Act of 1996, the National Minimum Wage Act of 1998 and the Equality Act of 2010. Across business as a whole, compliance with the Data Protection Act is estimated to be costing £8 billion a year. Further regulation by the European Union, some of it subsuming actions a UK government would have taken – is discussed in the next chapter.

Two pieces of recent legislation have had considerable repercussions for corporate Britain. The Export Control Act of 2002, a cornerstone of Robin Cook's 'ethical foreign policy', imposed restrictions on the sale or marketing of sensitive equipment with a potential military use or the transfer of the equivalent technologies to foreign powers. Pushed through hastily by Cook when Leader of the House, it had unintended consequences: the Ministry of Defence and DTI briefly feared the 2004 Farnborough Air Show might have to be cancelled, and while it went ahead, the display of unmanned UAVs had to be scaled back because under the Act they were technically classed as guided missiles. Further legislation had to be passed in 2008 to put matters right.

The second is the Bribery Act of 2010, which filled a vacuum in the law whose existence was recognised at least as far back as the Poulson affair of 1972, when a Yorkshire architect was found to have corrupted public officials up and down the country in pursuit of contracts. The United States Congress legislated in 1977 to make corporate bribery of foreign officials a criminal offence, after a series of abuses by big business came to light – including the Lockheed scandal which led to Prince Bernhard of the Netherlands being forced from public life. While the UK signed up to the OECD Anti-Bribery Convention of 1997, there was still a gap in British law, left open partly because of the business community's insistence that if it were filled, France would make a clean-sweep of export orders to the Middle East and much of the developing world.

Matters were brought to a head by the exposure of the massive sums paid to Saudi princes and others by BAE Systems front companies to secure repeat orders under the Al Yamamah project, and of the payments made to facilitate the purchase by Tazania of a supposedly unsuitable air traffic control system. The decision not to prosecute BAE Systems and certain individuals was taken on national security grounds, not through any lack of laws under which charges could be brought. But the episode did highlight the absence of any specific offence of bribing a foreign official, and with BAE Systems's American rivals lobbying to have it barred from bidding for vital contracts from the Pentagon, work already in progress on creating such an offence was accelerated. The Act, as passed, not only outlaws the bribery; it also makes it an offence for a company to fail to prevent bribery. This provision has aroused some concern in Britain's boardrooms, with directors fearing they will need eyes in the back of their heads when their salesmen set out to win exports.

Manufacturing has also been affected by controls over what the public may purchase. The old-established firm Britain's offshored production of its toy soldiers to Hong Kong in 1966 because of safety regulations preventing the manufacture of toys from lead; this was the result of a laudable initiative to prevent lead poisoning in the workplace. The company soon found it cheaper to make the soldiers from plastic; had it not done so, their sale in Britain would have been banned anyway because of the risk of children putting them in their mouths and swallowing fragments of lead. Environmental regulation also impacted severely on the phosphorus manufacturer Albright & Wilson after the damage caused to Britain's inland waterways by phosphorus-based detergent was identified in the late 1970s, and Turner & Newall was only saved from financial disaster as the full extent of asbestos poisoning in the workplace became evident in the 1990s by the fact that it was already on the ropes.

Britain's firework industry was dealt a near-mortal blow even before the arrival of cheaper, less reliable and arguably less safe fireworks from China in the 1990s. In the 1950s, a wide range of manu-facturers – Brock's of Hemel Hempstead, Pain's of Salisbury, Standard of Huddersfield (floated on the stock market in 1959) and Waeco/ Wessex enjoyed huge sales as the majority of families let off fireworks on Guy Fawkes Night. Concerns over safety and animal welfare, pursued obsessively by a handful of MPs, led to penny bangers and jumping crackers being outlawed. Children were barred from buying fireworks, the minimum age starting at 13 and being raised to 18. The banned range of fireworks was extended in 1997 – when a parliamentary report put the number of injuries at 1,000 a year, 400 of them to the eyes, though with fatalities extremely rare – and in 2004 single-shot air bombs and the once ubiquitous rocket you could fire from a milk bottle were banned. By now Britain's firework industry had all but disappeared, with demand met by imports from China. Pain's Wessex survives as a subsidiary of Chemring; Standard was bought out by Black Cat of China in 1998, ceasing production in the UK.

The problem for most manufacturers with environmental and safety regulations, though, has not been that their product range or essential processes have been affected, but that despite being only peripherally affected they have had to invest heavily to meet the new requirements. Debate continues over whether Whitehall is needlessly over-zealous in regulating, all the more forcefully because in a fragile economic climate the cost of compliance can sometimes make the difference between staying in business or giving up.

7

EUROPE: OPPORTUNITY OR HANDICAP?

The development of the British economy since the early 1950s has been inextricably tied up with Europe – though sections of the business community would profoundly wish otherwise. Britain's refusal to join the Common Market when it was founded, its eventual membership once the founder-members had put the needs of agriculture ahead of those of industry, the refocusing of UK exports toward Europe rather than the Commonwealth and the impact on industry of regulation from Europe and its state aids policy have all contributed to the radical changes that have come over the nation.

British governments over this period, pulled one-way by the pro-Europeans and the other by the Eurosceptics, have ended up zig-zagging between the two. Overall the effect has been that Britain never fully engaged with the Common Market as it developed into the European Union, and in consequence has reaped only some of the benefits available, but all of the disadvantages.

At the heart of the ongoing debate lies the question that has been there from the start: is involvement with Europe an opportunity for British industry, or a handicap? The answer depends on the kind of businessman you ask, for over the decades two very different person-alities – almost caricatures – have emerged. On the one side you have the pro-European: a consensus man, used to team working, with a degree (perhaps an MBA), able to speak a foreign language and maybe involved with the Confederation of British Industry. On the other, the

Eurosceptic: self-made, ruggedly individualistic, better at telling other people what to do than working with them, a member of the Institute of Directors, distrustful of foreigners but prepared at a push to take over a company in the United States. The differences crystallised during the premiership of Margaret Thatcher, who greatly admired businessmen in the second camp like Lord Hanson and Lord King.

The first of these schools of thought is convinced that membership of what is now the European Union has been beneficial to British industry, but would have been more so had the right decisions been taken: entry when Britain could have influenced the Common Market not to put so many eggs in the agricultural basket, greater engagement in decision-making in Brussels instead of hostile semi-detachment, adoption of the euro to remove one final barrier. To many of these, the survival of the single currency despite the crisis now afflicting Ireland, Greece, Italy and possibly other members is proof that the euro can work.

The second has a very different reading of events: we should never have had anything to do with the Common Market, the voters were deceived into thinking it was a purely economic organisation, and regulation from Brussels reinforced unhelpfully by Whitehall has prevented British business showing true enterprise while its Continental competitors have blithely ignored the rules. To them, the plight of the weaker Eurozone countries is proof that the euro has failed – as it was always going to – and indeed that the EU as a concept is doomed in the end to failure.

The argument between these two schools has been under way with varying degrees of intensity for six decades, peaking when Britain voted to stay in the European Community in 1975, when Margaret Thatcher made her Bruges speech of 1988, in the aftermath of the Maastricht Treaty of 1991, as John Major and then Tony Blair dithered over whether to take Britain into the euro, and after David Cameron in 2011 vetoed a new European Treaty to tackle the crisis in the Eurozone because of its possible adverse impact on the City. No doubt it will continue as long as the English Channel exists.

❖

In the aftermath of the Second World War, politicians across Europe resolved that their continent must never again be left in ruins by war, and began to propose political structures to ensure this. They had the support of the United States and of Winston Churchill, then in opposition, who in Zurich in 1946 advocated a 'kind of United States of Europe' and at Strasbourg in 1949 insisted that Germany had to play its full part.

The first such structure, established by the Treaty of London in 1949, was the Council of Europe. Its ten founder-members, including Britain, France, Italy and the Benelux countries (Belgium, the Netherlands and Luxembourg) – but not initially West Germany – saw the Council as a motor for European unity, but principally in the field of the law, cultural co-operation and shared human rights. It was through the Council of Europe that the European Convention and Court on Human Rights were established in 1953 – paving the way for the Human Rights Act of 1998 and consequent decisions by British courts and tribunals giving the criminal rights over society, for which the separate European Union has wrongly been blamed.

Next came the organisation from which the Common Market – and ultimately the EU – would develop: the European Coal and Steel Community (ECSC). Promoted by two Frenchmen, Jean Monnet – the civil servant regarded as the 'father of Europe' – and foreign minister Robert Schuman, the ECSC was created by the Treaty of Paris and concluded in 1951. Attlee's Labour government declined to join; it had just nationalised the steel industry, and could see little to be gained from joining an organisation largely preoccupied with linking France's steel mills in Lorraine to the coal mines of Germany when most of Britain's steel exports went to the Commonwealth. The ECSC, with Monnet at the helm, went ahead with France, West Germany, Italy and the Benelux countries as members, setting a pattern for the Common Market and its successors with France taking the political leadership and a resurgent Germany increasingly supplying the economic muscle. Crucially the ECSC, which Churchill's government again refused to join in 1954 – preferring a formal associate membership – enabled the main steel industries on the Continent to modernise by relocating new plants on the coast to receive coal from the likes of Australia, and their deep-mined coalfields to contract at a faster rate than Britain's. The idea of a Common Market was first proposed in 1953 by the Dutch foreign minister Johan Willem Beyen, and struck an immediate chord with the six members of the ECSC. Churchill told his Cabinet: 'We help, we dedicate, we play a part, but we are not merged and do not forfeit our insular and Commonwealth-wide character.' He need not have worried: an argument between the leaders of West Germany's ruling Christian Democrats over whether Britain should be invited to join was won by the Chancellor, Konrad Adenauer, who wanted Germany and France to lead the Common Market together. Agreement was reached between the Six to set up a European Political Community, with a common defence force replacing national armies, but was vetoed by the French National Assembly. Yet France was reluctant to stand completely alone after its shattering defeat at Dien Bien Phu, and an intergovernmental conference at Messina in 1955 laid the groundwork for a Common Market. Britain sent, then withdrew, an observer, and Harold Macmillan, then Foreign Secretary, came to believe that in not encouraging Churchill, and subsequently Churchill's successor Anthony Eden, to participate he had contributed to a historic opportunity being lost. Under the Treaty of Rome of 1957 the European Economic Community and Euratom (the latter to plan for the replacement of coal and oil by nuclear power) came into being at the start of 1958, with headquarters in Brussels.

Creation of the Common Market, with internal tariff barriers removed, gave a stimulus to German industry in particular, as it gained access to hitherto protected markets in France and Italy. It also encouraged French business – over a period when France lost Algeria and declared many of its colonies independent – to find new markets in Europe: between 1958 and 1973 the share of its exports going to the EEC rose from 22.2 per cent to 48.6 per cent. Italy's industries also thrived, despite an incidence of strikes even greater than in Britain. The result was an acceleration of economic growth throughout the EEC, to a level consistently ahead of that achieved by the United Kingdom.

Car production in France and Germany doubled during the 1960s, but Britain's car makers were handicapped in tapping soaring demand within the EEC by the high tariffs that remained in place; while UK car exports to the rest of Europe did more than double over the decade, its German, and even more its French, competitors fared better. On the back of their success – though BMW and later Volkswagen did go through crises – the German and French governments saw no need to force through defensive mergers of the kind that created British Leyland, leaving several car makers in each country with clear identities rather than one blundering conglomerate.

The EEC from the outset developed policies and a budget skewed in favour of protecting its farmers: not just France's peasant *cultivateurs* but the many German smallholders who also had jobs in their country's booming factories, and Italians in the *Mezzogiorno* who developed a flair for claiming subsides for non-existent olive groves. The emergence of the Common Agricultural Policy (CAP) as so dominant a feature of the Common Market could well have been avoided had Britain, with at the time a very different system of agricultural support, been at the negotiating table. It has often been asked why the EEC did not develop a corresponding Common Industrial Policy; by its own lights it did, through the Coal and Steel Community, but responsibility for industries beyond steel remained with member governments and the industries themselves, limiting the scope for creating a truly world-beating European manufacturing sector.

The launch of the EEC, coupled with the Suez fiasco of 1956 – which had lost us friends in the Middle East and alienated the United States – and the achievement of independence by its first African colonies forced Britain (under Macmillan), as France had, to reconsider its position in the world. The realisation grew that a powerful trading bloc was being created on the Continent, and that Britain's non-participation was playing into German hands. A proposal from London that the Six put the Common Market on hold in favour of a wider and looser customs union was brushed aside, and as the

EEC became reality Britain promoted a grouping of the nations left outside the Six: the European Free Trade Association (EFTA).

In 1960 the 'Outer Seven' – Austria, Denmark, Norway, Portugal, Sweden, Switzerland and the United Kingdom – signed the treaty creating EFTA in Stockholm. Customs duties on industrial – though not agricultural – products were to be phased out, but unlike the EEC this grouping did not establish a common tariff on goods from outside. Though trade between the EFTA partners expanded, the effect on British industry was negative: tariff reductions opened British markets to Scandinavian newsprint – causing serious damage to the paper industry – and Swedish HGVs, catching the previously-dominant Leyland at a vulnerable point.

Macmillan now came to the conclusion that Britain's economic future lay in Europe, rather than in its ties with the Commonwealth, and in 1961 applied for membership of the EEC. Negotiations began despite a bitter reaction from, in particular, New Zealand, whose agriculture depended heavily on access to Britain, and the assertion by the Labour leader Hugh Gaitskell that a federal Europe would mean 'the end of Britain as an independent European state, the end of a thousand years of history'. The talks had progressed beyond Britain's acceptance of the CAP to the detail of how far New Zealand and other Commonwealth economies should be protected when, at the start of 1963, President de Gaulle unilaterally vetoed Britain's membership, declaring: 'The entry of Britain would completely change the Common Market, which would become a colossal Atlantic grouping under American domination and control.' When Harold Wilson made a fresh approach in 1967, de Gaulle stymied it with the threat of a further veto.

Left on the margin of Europe though still the prime mover of EFTA, Britain did what it could to align itself more closely with its Continental neighbours. The Labour government in 1965 announced a switch from imperial measure to the metric system – a decision of immense significance to British industry because it paved the way for their products to be interoperable with those produced in Europe, at the price of widespread retooling. This in turn created a major opportunity for the British machine tool industry, but equally opened the way for imports of precision metricated tools, especially from Germany.

Next came the announcement in James Callaghan's 1966 Budget that Britain would abandon pounds, shillings and pence and go decimal – a change that took effect in 1971. Many Commonwealth countries were already taking such a step as their currencies broke the link with sterling, and the change was seen as marginally beneficial both to business and to children's education – not that numeracy has improved since then.

Individual businesses were also considering whether to expand into Europe despite – or in consequence of – Britain's exclusion from the EEC, seeing the rising prosperity within the Common Market as an opportunity. ICI created a new subsidiary, ICI Europa, to open plants in Europe – mainly in the Netherlands – and promote exports. GEC decided that the strength of Siemens in Germany and Alcatel in France left it with few opportunities. Lucas, concluding that the domestic market was too small and too plagued by 'stop-go' to be relied on, built a brake plant in Germany, and in France entered a joint venture with Ducellier to make lighting equipment. Dunlop took the bolder step of negotiating a full-blooded merger in 1970 with the Italian tyre and cable maker Pirelli in a bid to achieve economies of scale; however the two companies proved totally incompatible and the merger was unwound after ten years. There was also interest in corporate tie-ups within EFTA: the ball bearing makers Ransome & Parkes negotiated an alliance with SKF of Sweden, world leader in the field, only to be blocked by the Industrial Reorganisation Corporation which forced a merger with two smaller British firms that left the company that emerged – Ransome Hoffman Pollard (RHP) – over-dependant on the home market. RHP would eventually be sold, in 1990, to NSK of Japan.

When Edward Heath won the 1970 election on a pledge to take Britain into the EEC – de Gaulle having recently died – Wilson abandoned his earlier enthusiasm, scorning 'the marginal advantage of selling washing machines in Dusseldorf.' For Heath – a European at heart and French president *manqué* despite his atrocious French accent – joining the Community was not just an economic but a political commitment. A fierce parliamentary battle that split the Labour Party led to a comfortable majority in favour of going in; Heath signed the Treaty of Accession and at the start of 1973 Britain joined the EEC along with Denmark and Ireland, taking its membership to nine. British civil servants took up posts in the Commission, two British Commissioners (Christopher Soames and George Thomson) installed themselves in Brussels and British MPs took their seats in the then-nominated European Parliament (Labour initially staging a boycott).

British industry was well prepared for EEC membership in the sense that it knew it was coming; however not every firm or sector did much to capitalise on it. There was a good deal of resistance as a series of directives on 'harmonisation' emanated from Brussels setting common technical standards. While adopting these enabled British manufacturers to compete in European markets, there was a belief that in too many cases the new standards differed little from those already observed by their Continental competitors, leaving only the British with the need to retool and at a stroke opening what had previously been a closed market to Continental rivals. Nevertheless the EEC began to account for a growing proportion of Britain's trade – imports and exports – as tariff barriers came down; between 1952 and 1972 it had increased from 12 per cent to 21 per cent of the total, but the shift now accelerated, to 30 per cent by 1977 and 40 per cent by 1990. Textile and clothing exports to EEC countries, in particular, surged – increasing by 150 per cent during the 1970s. Glaxo – which had targeted both Europe and the United States from the late 1960s – saw Europe overtake the Commonwealth as its main export market by the end of the 1970s. By contrast, Britain's car exports to the rest of the EC plunged by two-thirds as the industry reached its nadir, while German motor exports to Britain rose by 60 per cent (as Ford and Vauxhall covered the gaps in production at their strike-hit British subsidiaries) and France's by a quarter. British exporters' refocusing on Europe was hastened by Australia increasingly seeing Japan rather than Britain as its obvious trading partner; global disapproval of apartheid also led some British businesses that had traded heavily with South Africa to divert their export efforts to Europe, with varying degrees of success.

An element of uncertainty was created by Labour's pledge to renegotiate the terms of membership and then hold a referendum. A Labour government did not seem very likely at the height of the Barber boom, but when, months later, Heath rashly called a snap election over the miners' strike, Labour found itself returned to office. Wilson and Callaghan carried out a perfunctory renegotiation, some minor concessions were made, and in June 1975 the voters of the United Kingdom – in their first ever referendum – voted by two to one to stay in.

Eurosceptics have since claimed that the EEC Wilson recommended Britons to vote for – though not several of his Cabinet, who campaigned against –was purely a trading bloc, with no political functions or ambitions, and that the public was tricked into backing an inexorable process towards a politically united but unaccountable Europe. My own recollection, having covered the referendum for the *Daily Telegraph*, is that the political dimension was not stressed as much by the 'Yes' campaign as it had been by Heath when Britain went in; for him, the reasons for joining were manifestly political. But if concerns over the impact of membership on Britain as a sovereign state were not adequately raised during the campaign, this was not through subterfuge but because of the dire state of the British economy in the months between inflation peaking just short of 30 per cent, and the government having to seek an emergency standby credit from the International Monetary Fund. In those circumstances membership of a Europe that might grow politically stronger seemed, if anything, a reassurance. Moreover the 1975 referendum, like others since, was also fought on personalities, the decisive argument for many at the height of the controversy over Tony Benn's radical policies as Industry Secretary being: 'Tony Benn wants to come out. Tony Benn is a loony. So vote to stay in.'

The period of ambivalence toward the EEC in Whitehall and at Westminster prior to the referendum put Britain at a disadvantage in staking out a position for itself in Brussels. The Irish Republic, by contrast, used the 30 months during which contradictory messages were coming from London to seize the initiative in Europe, and before long was reaping the rewards of its enthusiasm in generous regional and other grants – the basis of over three decades of prosperity.

Britain thus had even more ground to make up when full engagement with the EEC was resumed in mid-1975. Struggling with a shaky home economy, frequent strikes and in some sectors a corporate loss of confidence, British industry was not as well equipped to compete in Europe as it would have been in 1958. British Steel also found itself competing in a market suffering acutely from overcapacity; BSC's rapid contraction following the strike of 1980 was matched by organised cutbacks on the Continent brokered by the EC under the Davignon Plan, which penalised Germany's more efficient steel industry at the expense of its heavily subsidised competitors, notably in Italy and France.

Margaret Thatcher came to power in 1979 determined to end what she saw as a situation in which British taxpayers were forced at gunpoint to hand over their hard-earned money to subsidise peasant farmers, wine lakes and the sale of cheap butter to a Soviet Union which was about to invade Afghanistan. Her main target was the French; it may have been no accident that President Giscard insisted on entering a conference room before her, observing that she might be a lady but he was president of France. But after her repeated statement 'Give me my money back!' eventually secured a rebate on Britain's budgetary contribution at Fontainebleau in 1984, Britain began to be seen as more of a team player. However the signals from Downing Street remained confusing: in 1986 Mrs Thatcher signed up to the Single European Act providing for the creation of the Single Market six years later, and in 1990, just before her overthrow, her government joined the Exchange Rate Mechanism (ERM). But the diatribe against 'federalism' which she launched at Bruges in 1988 showed her deeply antipathetic to closer union, and it was her 'No, No, No!' in the Commons on this very point that promoted Sir

Geoffrey Howe to deliver the resignation speech that persuaded a majority of Conservative MPs that she had to go.

Crucially, Mrs Thatcher argued within the EC for a wider, rather than deeper, community. She championed the enlargement of the EC, starting with the admission of Greece, Portugal and Spain, partly on economic grounds but also because she hoped that the wider the membership, the harder it would be for the small nucleus of lawyers, civil servants and politicians in Brussels who were working for the elimination of the nation state to achieve their objective. The advocates of a much tighter union, political as well as economic, realised this all too clearly and France, in particular, tried to foil enlargement both before and after the collapse of communism in central and eastern Europe produced a crop of new candidates. (Only Austria and Finland joined during the 1990s).

As 1992 approached, British business, and the CBI, worked hard to capitalise on the arrival of a single market – in goods but not yet in services – as non-tariff as well as tariff barriers came down. Mrs Thatcher spoke up strongly for the opportunity the Single Market presented, but it was notable that most of the businessmen around her shared her instinct that closer trading links with the United States were preferable. And as negotiations leading to the Maastricht Treaty got under way, there was increasing pressure from Eurosceptics and the political Right of the business community for a North Atlantic Free Trade Area (NAFTA), which would throw a spanner in the works of European political integration and hamper Britain's economic integration in Europe. While this received little overt support from government, it raised just enough questions in European capitals about Britain's good faith to weaken John Major's position in the Maastricht negotiations.

The Maastricht Treaty, signed in February 1992, paved the way for the introduction of the euro, and advanced political co-operation under three 'pillars': justice and home affairs, police and judicial co-operation; common security and foreign policy. Britain reserved its position on joining the single currency, and vetoed the inclusion in the Treaty of a 'social chapter' which was endorsed separately by all the other members. This last committed the signatories to 'promotion of employment, improving living and working conditions, proper social protection, dialogue between management and labour, the development of human resources with a view to lasting high employment and the combating of exclusion'. The Social Chapter was widely seen by British business as an attempt to subject companies to additional expenses deriving from the 'European social model': the provision for workers of generous social protection and benefits that imposed heavy extra costs on employers and reduced their competitiveness.

It became a recurrent theme of Continental criticism of Thatcherism that Britain was gaining an unfair competitive advantage – particularly in securing inward investment – by driving down employment costs and safeguards for workers so that, for example, it was easier for an employer in Britain to dismiss staff or make them redundant. By the early 1990s France, in particular, was complaining that Britain was indulging in 'social dumping', the criticism reaching its height when Hoover was persuaded to create new jobs at its Cambuslang plant instead of at a rival location in France. However, the contrasting degrees of social protection were not always good news for job creation in Britain; when the global economy turned down at the end of the 1990s and multinationals retrenched, finding it difficult to make workers in France, Germany and the Netherlands redundant they closed plants and sacked workers in Britain instead.

The signature of the Maastricht Treaty did not in itself spark great controversy in Britain; Major was widely felt to have fought his corner well. But after his unexpected re-election months later, the Right of the Conservative Party – some of whom had been hoping for defeat so that they could stage a pitched battle over Europe – began depicting Maastricht as having crucially weakened British sovereignty, campaigning first for a referendum and then for the treaty's defeat in Parliament. Britain's withdrawal from the ERM in September 1992 intensified the debate over Europe, with Lady Thatcher stirring the Eurosceptic pot. Ratification of Maastricht only scraped through the Commons in July 1993 after Major had been forced to seek a vote of confidence. Unrepentant, the Tory Eurosceptics continued their guerrilla war against Major, provoking him in the summer of 1995 to resign the Conservative leadership and challenge his critics to 'put up or shut up'. John Redwood resigned as Welsh Secretary to stand against him; Major defeated him, but not by a crushing majority. The rebels carried on, pressing the pro-European Chancellor Kenneth Clarke not to sign up to the euro.

Major became increasingly isolated in Europe as he was forced by his party to take a harder line, and his difficulties intensified with the advent in the United Kingdom of BSE ('Mad Cow Disease') as a result of sloppy farming practices. When Germany banned the import of British beef and the EU's agriculture ministers followed suit, Major launched a policy of 'non-co-operation' with Brussels which increased the strains – and weakened Britain's influence – further.

By now, Britain was physically connected to the Continent for the first time in tens of thousands of years. The opening of the Channel Tunnel in 1994 probably had a greater psychological than economic impact, but it unquestionably anchored Britain to the Continent at a point close to the border between France and Belgium. While it did not, as widely predicted, kill off the cross-Channel ferries which many hauliers continued to use out of choice, it did make trade more reliable by reducing the impact of French shipping and dock strikes; it also – through the discontinuance of a number of economically marginal ferry routes – concentrated most cross-channel traffic on the Folkestone/Dover area. (An expected modal switch in freight traffic from road to rail did not happen, rail freight through the tunnel being little more than had been previously transhipped on train ferries; the tunnel would prove useful, however, to train operators importing new rolling stock from Germany).

Parliament had only approved the Tunnel after securing assurances that it would benefit the regions of Britain: Scotland, Wales, the South-West, the North and the Midlands. Though passenger train services were promised, then cancelled on economic grounds (£130 million worth of sleeping car trains from GEC-Alsthom were sold to Canada at a knockdown price without ever carrying a passenger). Rail freight terminals for Tunnel traffic were opened as far afield as Mossend in Lanarkshire, but have never been used to capacity, and while Northern firms did see an increase in exports by road, most of the increase in economic activity the Tunnel stimulated was in the south-east of England.

After the Tunnel was opened, a series of academic papers were published by Dr Henry Overman of the London School of Economics, and others, demonstrating that ever since Britain had joined the EEC in 1973, the prosperity of manufacturing industry had increased in inverse proportion to its distance from Dover. They also identified a steady shift of manufacturing toward the South-East, despite the regional grants and incentives that had continued to be offered (though now under the auspices of Brussels). Indeed the studies found that 'the average distance from Dover of an average £1 of exports fell by around 35 per cent' over the 20 years from 1973 to 1993 – and the Tunnel exacerbated the trend. Moreover, the Tunnel proved an even greater stimulant to imports than to exports: it was estimated early on that half the wagons arriving laden at British freight terminals were returning to the Continent empty, and British hauliers were quick to complain that Continental competitors like Norbert Dentressangle, Willi Betz and, later, Waberer's of Hungary were putting them under pressure. Certainly, for European distributors and, by inference, manufacturers, the existence of the Tunnel led to them treating Britain far more as part of their home market. The same studies that showed British manufacturing being pulled toward the Channel also found that in 17 out of 80 sectors of manufacturing, increased import competition had cost jobs even before the Tunnel stimulated it further.

The election of a Labour government under Tony Blair committed to 'put Britain at the heart of Europe' after 18 years of Tory ambivalence was widely welcomed across the EU, as was Britain's immediate acceptance of the Social Chapter with none of the dire consequences for business that had been predicted. However, it did not take long for Blair – or his European partners – to realise that Britain's interests, and the determination of elements within the EU to thwart them, remained unchanged. Matters would come to a head in 2002 with a bruising set of negotiations over the continuance of the budget rebate secured by Mrs Thatcher, in which Blair lost some ground.

Early in Blair's premiership, Britain secured a surprisingly easy victory for its policies of greater competition and deregulation in Europe. At the Lisbon EU summit in March 2000, Blair persuaded all his counterparts to sign up to a radical agenda for improving the EU's competitiveness in global markets through greater investment and job creation in knowledge-based industries, extension of the Single Market to services and a drive to get rid of unnecessary regulation. Caught on the hop, France and Germany had little alternative but to agree, but over time they regrouped to fight back – especially to protect their state-owned energy monopolies. Blair pointed out to President Chirac the unfairness of a situation in which no British electricity company could trade in France, while Électricité de France was able to supply 10 Downing Street (it actually provides the backup supply) after taking over London Electricity. While some progress was made on broadening the Single Market, the Lisbon Agenda eventually ran into the sand.

By then the adoption of the euro across continental Europe (and in Ireland) was imminent, but when euro banknotes and coins became legal tender at the start of 2002 Britain, Denmark and Sweden did not participate. Blair was keen to go in, though eventually promising a referendum, but Gordon Brown was very reluctant and set conditions whose fulfilment looked unlikely. The battle lines over the euro, within the business community and across the country at large, were much the same as those over membership of the EU as such. Campaigning groups for and against were launched: Britain in Europe in 2000, with tacit government support, and a variety of 'antis' campaigns, notably Business for Sterling; the membership of both was fairly predictable, though the list of 'anti's included some surprises. The argument against joining the euro was threefold: that abolishing Britain's historic currency would erode both its political and its economic sovereignty by handing control to a European Central Bank; that the euro would prove unworkable; and that changing to the euro would be irrelevant to businesses that traded with the rest of the world. Arguments in favour revolved around the benefits for British business trading in Europe of eliminating currency transactions, and of ending exchange rate fluctuations that affected the pricing of British goods in key European markets. It was also claimed that staying outside the euro would be a disincentive to further investment in Britain in particular by Far Eastern companies. There was some evidence to support this point. Several major Japanese companies had, in the 1990s, located plants in Britain exporting to the Continent in the expectation that it would become part of the Eurozone, and when in their view Blair began to dither they began turning up the heat.

By the time Blair handed over to Brown in 2007, it was evident that while the euro had defied the scare stories and functioned adequately as a currency, early British membership was not in prospect. And while the euro itself survived, the debt crisis that struck Ireland, Greece, Portugal and Italy in 2010-11, and the subsequent cost to Eurozone members of bailing out those countries, made membership look even less attractive. Moreover, inward investment rose during this period despite Britain's non-adoption of the euro.

The 'big bang' of EU enlargement championed by Britain since the fall of the Berlin Wall 15 years before, finally took place in 2004 when ten new member states joined: the Czech Republic, Estonia, Hungary, Latvia, Lithuania, Poland, Slovakia and Slovenia from the former Communist bloc, plus two former British possessions, Cyprus and Malta. (Five of those countries have since adopted the euro).

Economic ties had already been developed, and Germany, in particular, had taken advantage of them to open new high-tech, low-wage factories; British firms, as we have seen, were more concerned with transferring production to these countries from the UK. However, the main effect of this round of enlargement was to trigger a surge of immigration from the new member states – and especially Poland – most of it to Britain (though there was an upsurge of resentment in France about the advent of the 'Polish plumber'). The scale and impact on the UK economy of this influx of mainly young jobseekers has already been covered; suffice it to say that it was the direct result of an enlargement pressed for by Britain, but whose consequences had not been fully thought through in Whitehall. The further acceptance into EU membership of Bulgaria and Romania in 2005, was qualified by some member states with continuing curbs on immigration from those countries; Britain gave their citizens an absolute right of entry, but insisted that any wishing to work applied for an 'accession worker card'.

The continuing arguments over closer political union which brought the Amsterdam and Nice Treaties of 1999 and 2003 respectively, the abortive European constitution and the subsequent and slightly less radical Lisbon Treaty of 2009 (which Gordon Brown insisted on signing after the official ceremony), impacted much less on British industry. In fact the international agreement that caused most concern at that time was the post-9/11 deal struck with the United States for the speedy extradition of terrorist suspects, which the American authorities used with enthusiasm to secure the detention and transfer across the Atlantic of a number of British businessmen they claimed were guilty of fraud.

Although the EU does not have a strategy for industry, it does claim to have at least the framework of an industrial policy; indeed the Maastricht Treaty included a provision creating the legal basis for one. When push comes to shove, however, that policy comes down to no more than improvement of the internal market, trade agreements and anti-dumping measures, social and regional policy where industrial change is having damaging effects, competition policy (including state aids), R&D, 'strengthening of co-operation between enterprises' and remedial measures for sectors under pressure.

Most British businesses would prefer the EU not to have an industrial policy on the lines of the CAP, and leave oversight and encouragement of industry to be exercised by member governments, or not exercised at all. But some policy stance – and action – by the European Commission in this field has proved essential to maintain fair competition. The Commission certainly has an important role to play in identifying and prosecuting pan-European and multinational cartels, imposing fines for price-fixing in sectors ranging from washing powder and plastics to shipping rates. The reasons for its vigour in this respect are historical: a desire to prevent the re-emergence of the industrial cartels that dominated pre-war Germany.

The EU could also have an important role in R&D, but while its research budget for 2012 is a staggering €7.6 billion, little of this is likely to feed through to the production of innovative and improved manufactured goods. Only one of the Commission's four prestige research programmes – BRITE-EURAM, which covers work on basic industrial technologies and advanced materials – has a direct relevance to industry, and the thrust of its much-hyped Framework programme over the years has been the partnering of universities in different member countries with each other, rather than connecting them to industry.

In some respects, Brussels' interest in industry has actually lessened. Despite the EU having developed from the European Coal and Steel Community, it has not taken a major initiative on steel since the Davignon Plan of 1980. Its visibility was low during the crisis over the survival of General Motors' European operations, and it has kept out of the restructuring of aerospace – apart from waving through launch aid for successive generations of Airbus on a scale that eventually led Boeing (which in turn received heavy disguised subsidies from the US government) to protest to the World Trade Organisation. Nor has it exercised a strategic role in ensuring that Europe has the capacity to produce components essential to industries across the board – for the last decade there has been no mass producer of semiconductors in Europe, a deficiency shown up by the disruption to the supply chain caused by the Japanese tsunami of 2011 and the subsequent floods in Thailand. It may be no coincidence that in that year Ford Europe's chief executive Stephen Odell described the mindset within the European Commission as 'industry-sceptical'.

Where direct aid to industry is concerned, the EU is engaged on two levels: through the direct provision of grants under its regional aid policy to buoy up the economies of the weaker regions of the community, and by policing the assistance that member states give. The aim of EU state aids policy is laudable, and a keystone of the Single Market: to prevent member states pouring money into uncompetitive industries to keep them in being, at the expense of more efficient companies in other countries – carefully targeted support to encourage growth and innovation is welcomed. It took time to tighten the constraints: in 1997 Germany was still subsidising industry to the tune of €11.7 billion, Italy €9.4 billion, France €5.7 million, the UK €2 billion and Spain €1.9 billion. But now Italy can no longer prop up its steel industry with annual subsidies of €2 billion, and the days when many continental countries routinely subsidised their bloated flag carrier airlines have finally gone.

Where Britain is concerned, there has been persistent criticism from industry that the Department of Business and its predecessors have used the fear of falling foul of Brussels to avoid making grants that, in some cases, could have made the difference between the survival and collapse of strategically valuable companies. There is a reason for this caution, as I know having worked at the next desk to the DTI's state aids unit. In 1998 John Prescott promulgated a generous regional support package designed, in part, to offset cuts to aid from Brussels, as assistance was switched to much more deprived areas of former Communist countries that were joining the EU. The area of the United Kingdom classified as 'assisted' was being reduced from 34 per cent to 28 per cent, and Prescott launched a scheme costing £3 billion over seven years to plug some of the gaps, under the EU treaties' provisions for 'regional selective assistance'. Unfortunately Brussels had not been thoroughly consulted, and after the scheme had been launched with a fanfare of trumpets it was vetoed by the European Commission as violating state aids guidelines.

The DTI, understandably, went into its shell. Having seen a high-profile state aid package from another department embarrassingly blocked, it felt obliged to warn firms applying for government assistance that they had to be very sure of their ground. Not surprisingly applications, and grants paid out, tailed off for a while; by 2010 the lion's share of regional grants from the UK government were going to firms headquartered on the Continent.

There have also been persistent complaints from British manufacturers and exporters that other member states interpret state aid regulations far less restrictively, or connive at abuses. It is an open secret that in Italy machine tools and other goods are made under subsidy in the assisted south, stored there for six months, then sold at a discount in the booming north. There are also important exemptions from the state aids regime: Germany is free to offer special incentives for firms to locate in the *Länder* of the former German Democratic Republic, these have led Rolls-Royce to relocate part of its R&D operations in Brandenburg rather than expanding further in Britain.

Another aspect of the Single Market is the Commission's commitment to achieve a 'level playing field' on procurement by public authorities, instead of each country simply awarding contracts to its traditional domestic suppliers. The vehicle for this is the Official Journal of the European Union (OJEU), launched under the 2003 Treaty of Nice, in which public sector bodies are expected to list available contracts so that interested companies across the EU can compete for them. Most British organisations required to advertise contracts in the OJEU do so, but again there are suspicions – and complaints – that public bodies in some member states habitually fail to do so, or make sure after conforming with the requirement to put a notice in the Journal that its traditional supplier wins the order. Again, such infractions are hard to prove unless taken all the way to the European Court, and much of the evidence is anecdotal.

EU procurement rules came under the spotlight in 2011 amid the political storm over the Department for Transport's award of the £1.4 billion contract to build and maintain 1,200 new carriages for the Thameslink route to Siemens, rather than Bombardier's plant in Derby. David Cameron blamed the previous Labour government for agreeing to strict rules in a directive on procurement that were have said to have left the DfT with no alternative but to award the contract to Siemens. Pressed in the Commons by furious Labour MPs, Cameron replied: 'We inherited the procurement process from the previous government. But we are now looking at all the procurement rules in Europe and making sure that better decisions are taken in the future.' However, had it chosen to, the DfT could apparently have specified that the winner should have the trains built in the United Kingdom; it also appeared that had the contract been for the trains alone, and not also a PFI-style deal for their maintenance, Siemens would not have been able to gain a decisive advantage through its superior connections with German banks. Again, it was not the EU's rules that had caused the problem, but the defensive way in which a British government had interpreted them.

Regulation is a fact of life in the 21st century: restrictions on anti-competitive practices, requirements for safety in the workplace, limits on working hours, controls on emissions. Parliament legislated in many of these areas before Britain joined the EEC, but the volume of regulation from Brussels has increased steadily despite a commitment since 1992 for matters to be left to member states wherever possible ('subsidiarity').

Much of the emphasis after Britain joined in 1973 was on standard specifications for products; intended to enable manufactured exports from any member state to penetrate import markets throughout the Community, they were widely seen within British industry as putting it at a disadvantage to its competitors. Not all such regulation came from Brussels: it was the US authorities who around 1970 handicapped British motorcycle exports by insisting that all machines sold there should have a Japanese-style gearshift and brake pedal. But it is Brussels that has become an engine for regulation, of varying degrees of helpfulness.

Overall, the conservative economic commentator Ruth Lea has calculated, regulation from Brussels (including standards that embrace existing UK legislation) accounts for 68.8 per cent of the cost of regulation to British business. Some regulation within the EU comes from the adoption of new areas of policy, like the Social

Chapter: the Working Time Directive of 2000 limiting most work-ers to 48 hours a week, which Britain did its best to stay out of; over its first 10 years it was claimed to have cost British employers £17.8 billion. Next most costly was a directive on vehicle emissions, on which a Eurosceptic think tank put a price tag of £10.4 billion over eight years. And a new directive giving agency workers the same rights to leave, holiday and sick pay as employees caused tension within the coalition in 2011 when the Lib Dem Business Secretary Vince Cable fought off an attempt by acolytes of David Cameron to have it implemented in the most restrictive way consistent with the law. Other new regulations have applied to the emergence of new technologies, or stem from public pressure for improved stand-ards, such as controlling timeshare selling or requiring 'sell by' dates on foodstuffs.

Directives have to be approved by ministerial councils with every member state represented, but they have their origins in the Commission; teams of civil servants beaver away at identifying issues on which they feel the EU should set a standard across all the member states, and recommending what those standards should be. It is clear that there is a mindset – particularly among some German and Benelux lawyers working for the Commission – that regulation should be used to diminish the power of national governments in the hope that they will eventually fade away. It is also fair to say that some member states, notably France, have regarded new directives as things to be encouraged provided that only the other member states actually implement them. But decisions in the ministerial councils are usually taken on practical grounds.

Take the case of the Bakery Jams Directive of 2001, relating to 'fruit jams, jellies and marmalades and sweet chestnut purée for human consumption'. The relevant directorate of the Commission had concluded that there was a need to set a standard determining what substances used as fillings in jam tarts, doughnuts and the like could be described as jam. The Belgian government argued, after lobbying from its bakery industry, that such fillings should not be classified as jam. This was a direct threat to the Jammie Dodger, which if the directive was approved would have to change its name or its recipe. When it got to the ministerial council (I was in the room), the British delegation convinced its counterparts that such a ruling would fly in the face of logic, and the Jammie Dodger was reprieved – a great relief to Burtons, who manufacture the biscuits at Cwmbran. Now, as then, the Jammie Dodger consists of shortbread, and plum jam. A few weeks later, a further initiative from the Commission that would have prevented Cadbury's marketing its products as chocolate because the recipe differed from that used by continental manufacturers was also dropped after objections from Britain.

It is easy to conclude from these episodes that much of the effort the Commission puts into regulating European industry and its products is a waste of time, energy and money. Every Eurosceptic website lists a host of perceived absurdities dreamed up in Brussels: a ban on the use of combine harvesters in the wet (few farmers would, so why legislate?); requiring yogurt sold in Britain to be renamed 'fermented milk' because it differs from Continental recipes; prohibiting the sale of 'imperfect fruit' like the legendary bent banana; the posting of warning signs in caves and on mountains. Manufacturers are most concerned with fresh attempts to legislate new rights and lavish social benefits for their employees by civil servants who do not have to foot the bill, or which hinder the operation of perfectly safe industrial processes or – worse still – require retooling or prohibit the sale of certain products when any risk is negligible.

Some of the lunacies from Brussels lovingly dwelt on in the tabloids turn out to be urban myths. Others again are the result of, local authority staff particularly, misunderstanding the directives that do exist or trying to justify their own existence when cuts are imminent. Some years ago there was a rash of stories in the press about councils insisting, on orders from Brussels, that playground swings must not be erected so that they face into the sun – the nonsense being that at some stage in the day they are bound to. I managed to track down the official in Brussels (a Scot) who was responsible to the directive, and it turned out to say nothing of the kind.

Nor does Whitehall necessarily help. Every department at one time or other has stood accused of 'gold-plating' EU regulations to place some further and unnecessary burden on business: MAFF's handling of a directive on abattoirs in a manner that forced dozens of small slaughterhouses out of business in the late 1990s is a case in point. And in the field of interpreting directives, the individual civil servant has an astonishing amount of power. In 1999 I wrote a feature for the *Daily Telegraph* on a DTI ruling that was forcing dentists to abandon a particular teeth-whitening treatment or face a possible prison sentence. Every other member state had approved the treatment under the Medicines Directive, but the DTI had concluded that it violated the separate Cosmetics Directive, so should be banned. Working at the DTI the following year, I met the civil servant who had taken the decision; she was unrepentant, declaring that the treatment was unsafe – though the only suggestion that it was came in one scientific paper from Japan which had been ignored even by the Japanese government. Brussels had nothing to do with this.

Issues have also arisen when EU regulations are set which are less exacting than those previously imposed from Whitehall. In the early 1990s, 99 per cent of safety footwear sold in the UK was British-made. The British standard was then replaced by a less demanding one covering the entire European Community which did not require products to be checked annually. Chinese manufacturers producing less robust safety boots and shoes targeted the British market, and by the early 2000s British manufacturers retained just 1 per cent of the market, with obvious repercussions for those companies and for jobs. The other side of the coin concerns Hanson's brickworks at Stewartby, Bedfordshire. The plant comfortably met EU regulations on sulphur emissions, but struggled to conform with tougher standards set by the Department of the Environment. Hanson responded by closing the Stewartby works (beside which was a model village built for its workers by London Brick), in 2008, concentrating brick production on sites around Peterborough. Again, a discrepancy in regulations – this time with London exerting tighter controls than Brussels – led to a loss of jobs.

Closer economic engagement with Europe has, over the first four decades of membership, refocused British trade – export, import and more recently invisibles – on the Continent and inevitably invited comparisons between the ethos under which British, German, French and other European business and industry operate. Despite the uniformities Brussels has attempted to impose – at times, where a freer market is concerned, with British support – strong cultural differences remain, leading to surprises and pitfalls. The risks of an Anglo-Dutch merger were only discovered after the event when the supervisory boards – a feature of that country's businesses – began tilting the strategies of Leyland DAF and Corus in favour of their Netherlands operations, at the expense of those in Britain. It remains a cause for bewilderment among British business leaders that Spain is able – apparently within European law – to offer its companies tax incentives to take over foreign firms. And the promulgation of the 'Loi Danone' not long before Kraft's unresisted (by government) takeover of Cadbury, was a reminder that while Britain's political leaders – since Margaret Thatcher – have seen our industries as assets to be sold off to the highest bidder no matter who that may be, France sees them as integral to the fabric of the nation. Germany, though less brazenly, feels much the same.

While Germany has been the clear winner, economically, from European union with France a close-ish second, was this the inevitable outcome? Could Britain, by joining the Common Market in 1958 rather than in 1973, have performed more strongly and emerged with its industries in better shape? The most likely answer is that we would have done better, but still have been outperformed in many sectors. The crucial impetus for both Germany and France was the need to make a fresh start after the war; Britain had no such incentive, carrying on with outdated plant and industrial structures and attitudes that militated against achieving higher economic growth. But by staying out of Europe for those crucial 15 years, Britain passed up the chance to share in the boom as a thriving market in consumer goods was created, losing out not only on a higher growth rate but on tariff-free access to Continental markets and paying the price for staying pat in a smaller home market.

Whether earlier or more enthusiastic membership of the EEC would have led to successive British governments making fewer poor decisions on the future of key industries can only be guessed. The likelihood is that we would have learned a little from the way our Continental partners and competitors do things, but not enough. It is hard to see how, for example, we could have devised a system as conducive to industrial stability and growth as Germany's, with its many large family-controlled firms supported by regional governments and banks. In Britain, the moment an investment bank gets close to a family-owned company it encourages it to float on the Stock Exchange, paying the way for a takeover by a foreign competitor – with the bankers taking a hefty commission from both transactions and the national interest the loser. Yet Germany's industrial culture is not entirely one of consensus: it has seen hostile takeovers – Krupp's of Hoesch in 1991, not to mention Vodafone's acquisition of Mannesmann – the near-bankruptcy of BMW and the collapse of AEG, and crippling strikes over a shorter working week in steel in 1978/9 and engineering in 1984.

France, too, has adopted strategies that have been more successful than Britain's: protectionist, but also pragmatic. Instead of the doctrinaire amalgamation of all its motor and aerospace companies into single nationalised industries, it allowed two or more competitors to continue on each sector under near or complete state-ownership. By fostering both Aerospatiale (now EADS) and Dassault, and both Renault and Peugeot Citroën, it prevented the situation where when a nationalised, then privatised monopoly lost interest in a particular product line, the only solution was to sell the capacity to a foreign competitor. And although Renault management took on the Communist CGT trade union with almost Thatcherite brutality as it paved the way for privatisation, the concept of privatisation to the French official mind is very different to ours. Around 2006 I attended a briefing from the French defence ministry on the privatisation of their naval shipyards – a truly radical measure that consisted of transferring a part-shareholding from one state-controlled company to another.

Yet state sponsorship of industry has not been totally successful for France. Its efforts to turn Machines Bull into a world-beater were in the end no more successful than Britain's promotion of ICL – though the French did not give up so easily. The efforts of Left-wing French governments from the 1980s to expand social provision at home, then work through Brussels to force other member states' economies to become equally uncompetitive, did not succeed; witness the desire of subsequent governments to roll back the 35-hour week granted by Lionel Jospin's socialist administration in 2000. This has yet to come about because France remains, in Nigel Lawson's memorable words, 'a democracy tempered by mob rule'. It is also still handicapped by a trade union movement split between Communist (CGT), socialist (CFDT) and Catholic (FO) unions; while British trade unionism has evolved, albeit clumsily, from its traditional fragmented craft base and Germany's benefited from being reorganised by industry after the war. No country's industrial base is free of problems – but we in Britain have been slower, and less successful, than our key competitors in overcoming ours.

8

WHATEVER HAPPENED TO...?

Over the past six decades, many companies and brands that were once household names have vanished as a result of takeovers, changes in public taste or straightforward corporate suicide. Others still exist, but with a lower profile or under new, and usually foreign, ownership. New ones have taken their place, but the vast majority are multinationals and global brands, rather than the homegrown and peculiarly British firms and products with which the post-war generation – and some since – grew up. Everyone will have their own favourites that have disappeared from view or have been reinvented, but here is a selection of twelve:

ACCLES & POLLOCK
Almost everybody in the 1950s had heard of Accles & Pollock, even if they were never likely to purchase the Dudley-based steel tube maker's products. The company had pioneered the steel golf club shaft, the tubular box spanner and tubular furniture (especially bus seats), and in 1963 made the world's smallest ever steel tube: an American firm sent over its smallest as a challenge, only for Accles & Pollock to return it with an even smaller one inside.

But what made Accles & Pollock a household word was its advertising. Customers often had problems with the company's name, and one day a letter arrived with an American stamp addressed to 'Speckles and Dollops Ltd, England'. Scrawled across it in Post Office blue pencil was the message: 'try Apples and Scollops, Oldbury.' Accles & Pollock's advertising agency got to work and before long adverts were appearing in newspapers and on Tube trains showing a baffled post-man scratching his head over letters addressed to the likes of 'Tickles & Wallop' and 'Ankles & Fetlock'.

While humour does not always give rise to orders, Accles & Pollock remained a niche producer of steel tubing until the turn of the century, under a series of owners: Tube Investments, Hay Hall Group, Senior Tube and Tyco Components. Accles & Pollock closed its stainless steel mill in 1999 and stopped manu-facturing tubes in 2001; it now specialises in the manipulation of tubing for aerospace and nuclear projects and has since 2004 been owned by Baron Swraj Paul's Caparo Group, which since its foundation in 1968 has developed into one of Britain's leading tube manufacturers.

ALBRIGHT & WILSON

A staple of the London stock market in the 1950s, Oldbury-based Albright & Wilson was Britain's second largest chemicals manu-facturer after ICI, though of nothing like its magnitude. A Quaker family-owned firm until its flotation in 1948, its speciality was phos-phorus; in 1951 it opened a new plant at Portishead and four years later took over the Marchon phosphorus-based detergent plant at Whitehaven.

Albright & Wilson diversified into silicones, detergents, food additives and chemicals based on chromium and strontium. In 1972 it moved production of 'white phosphorous' from Oldbury to Newfoundland – from where it was shipped to Britain by tanker – but the relocation was over-ambitious and ensuing technical and finan-cial problems led to Tenneco of America taking over the company in 1978 and selling off many subsidiaries.

Tenneco returned Albright & Wilson to the stock market in 1995, but its core businesses were under pressure, particularly phospho-rus detergents whose use had been curbed when they were found to be seriously polluting Britain's rivers and canals. The Portishead plant closed in 1989 and that at Whitehaven in 2003, by which time Albright & Wilson had been taken over by the French multinational

Rhodia – until 1998 a division of Rhone-Poulenc. Part of the Oldbury site remains in production, and since 2008 has added metal extraction to its range of activities.

BRYANT & MAY

Britain's most famous match maker was Bryant & May, both for its brands and for the London match girls' strike of 1888 which secured long overdue improvements in working conditions throughout the industry. By the 1950s Bryant & May – technically the British Match Corporation, a joint venture with Swedish Match since the 1920s – had absorbed most of its competitors, its brands ranging from Captain Webb and England's Glory to Swan Vestas.

In 1973 the British Match Corporation merged, bizarrely, with Wilkinson Sword, the company best known for its razor blades which since its foundation in 1772 had graduated from making swords to (briefly) motorcycles and more recently garden shears. The aim was to create a larger company with the resources to combat Wilkinson's giant American competitor Gillette, but there was little in this for the Match part of the combine.

Wilkinson Match was taken over in 1978 by Pittsburgh-based Allegheny Ludlum, after whose bankruptcy it was owned by the Stora metals group and, finally by Swedish Match. During this time the manufacture of matches in Britain came to an end: the original Bryant & May factory at Bow closed in 1979, its Glasgow and Gloucester plants in the 1980s and, finally in 1994, the Swan Vestas factory in Liverpool.

Wilkinson Sword gravitated to Pfizer, who in 2003 sold it to the American battery firm Energizer. Wilkinson's Acton sword factory ceased production in 2005, the equipment for producing ceremonial swords for the British and other armies passing to WKC of Solingen – Wilkinson's even more august German counterpart. Wilkinson Sword-branded razors are now also made in Germany, but production of Wilkinson garden tools continues at Bridgend, Glamorgan, under the ownership of the Finnish company Fiskars.

FERODO

Throughout the post-war decades, everyone knew about Ferodo brake linings even if they didn't drive a car. The company had negotiated a deal with the railways to emblazon those three words in letters 3ft high on their bridges over the busiest roads up and down the country; a few of these advertisements still survive.

Based at Chapel-en-le-Frith in Derbyshire, Ferodo – a play on its founder's surname of Froode – built a worldwide reputation between the wars making clutch and brake linings from the 'wonder material' of asbestos, by then as a subsidiary of Turner & Newall (T&N), Britain's largest manufacturer of asbestos products.

A new factory was opened at Caernarfon in 1962; T&N sold it as a going concern to Friction Dynamics in 1997. It closed ten years later after one of the longest industrial disputes in Welsh history, involving 86 workers who had won an unlawful dismissal claim after being sacked in 2003 by the plant's American owners for going on strike.

T&N, including Ferodo, was taken over by Federal-Mogul of America in 1998, just before the extent of its liabilities over asbestosis became evident. Federal-Mogul in turn got into financial difficulties as a result of asbestosis claims and had to file for Chapter 11 protection, its British businesses going into administration in 2001. But Federal-Mogul, and with it Ferodo, survived. Ferodo brake linings, still made at Chapel-en-le-Frith, are not only used in motor sports and by many vehicle manufacturers, but can be found on sale at Halfords – if no longer publicised on so many of the nation's railway bridges.

ILFORD

After Kodak, the biggest name in post-war Britain for photographic films was Ilford, the company which in 1902 had taken the name of the area of east London where its factory was sited. Its most successful camera was the 35mm Sportsman, launched in 1957, an import from Germany; far cheaper than the rival Kodak Retinette which for a time sold 40,000 a year. Eventually, though, the quality of Kodak and Agfa cameras prevailed.

Ilford gained a global market for its Ilfocolor films and the higher-quality Ilfochrome range that followed in 1962, and for its photographic papers and chemicals. A partnership with Ciba of Switzerland (later Ciba Geigy) promised much, but in the late 1960s Ilford moved out of colour film to concentrate on the high quality end of the black-and-white market.

The business was shrinking even before the advent of the digital camera. The company moved its manufacturing base to Cheshire in 1983, and in 1989 was taken over by America's International Paper, who merged Ilford with its graphic materials subsidiary Anitec. Ilford Anitec went into receivership in 2004, but its British operation emerged from a management buyout as Harman Technology; trading as Ilford Photo, it makes high-quality monochrome photographic products, including films. In 2009 it relaunched Ilford's long-discontinued mail order processing service as Ilford Lab Direct.

J LYONS & CO

There have been few more open-and-shut cases of corporate suicide than that of 'Joe Lyons'; during and after the years of rationing Britain's third largest baker, one of its two dominant ice-cream makers and the owner of its only national restaurant chain. Lyons in the 1950s was a national institution, even building its own pioneering computers; Margaret Thatcher worked for the company as a research chemist before reading for the Bar. By its demise in 1995, the company did not bake a single loaf or freeze a single ice lolly; and of all its brands, only Lyons Cakes is still in evidence – as part of Premier Foods.

Still controlled by the Salmon family who had founded the company in 1887, Lyons began losing ground in the 1960s when a wave of competition from new, less formal venues forced it to start closing its teashops. Standards had fallen; the smart waitresses known as 'nippies' were long since gone, and by 1967 the Ludgate Circus Lyons was dispensing tea which was bright purple. A few were modernised and rebranded Jolyon – in the wake of that year's blockbusting *Forsyte Saga* serialisation by the BBC. Lyons' Corner Houses, for decades *the* places – and almost the only places – for the middle classes to dine in London, were struggling too; the last Corner House closed in 1977 and the last teashop in 1981. In the meantime Lyons had moved into Wimpy bars, opening its first in 1953 but selling out in 1976.

Lyons's bakery business had continued to prosper, outgrowing its Cadby Hall headquarters in west London; the bread side was sold off in the mid-1960s, and at the end of the decade cake and biscuit production was transferred to a new factory near Barnsley. In 1978 the company merged with Allied Breweries to become Allied Lyons; momentum (and maybe interest) was lost as the brewery side predominated and the business again struggled. Lyons Maid ice cream, the principal rival to Wall's (owned today by Unilever) was sold to Nestlé in 1992; six years later the brand name was dropped. As Allied merged in 1994 with Pedro Domecq to become essentially a drinks company, Lyons Cakes was sold to RHM, taking its place alongside Mr Kipling. And finally Lyons Biscuits was disposed of to Hillsdown Holdings; after a spell under American ownership the business gravitated to Burton's, makers of the Jammie Dodger. Joe Lyons was no more.

MECCANO

Either side of the war Meccano Ltd, the company founded by Frank Hornby in Liverpool in 1908, was Britain's biggest toy maker, with its metal construction sets, die-cast Dinky Toys of cars and lorries, and Hornby trains. It held its position in the 1950s, though competition arrived from Corgi and Matchbox cars and from Triang and Trix model railways among others. Marketing its products through the *Meccano Magazine*, a must for every schoolboy, Hornby updated its Dinky range with the latest models on the road, and trains of the smaller oo gauge, electrically powered rather than clockwork.

One acquisition that might have worked was of Bayko, a construction toy produced since 1934 by Plimpton Engineering which had a 24-year start on the remarkably similar Lego. Meccano took over Bayko in 1960, just two years after the first Lego brick was cast in Denmark; it started making Bayko bricks in polystyrene instead of Bakelite, but Lego made an instant breakthrough and Bayko was dropped in 1967.

From the early 1960s, Hornby and its competitors came under threat from imports of (usually inferior but much cheaper) plastic toys, and while it began a shift from weighty metal to plastics, particularly on Hornby Dublo railways, it fell foul of changes in consumer taste. In 1964 Lines Brothers, the makers of Triang, who by then claimed to be the world's biggest toymaker with a strong line in tiny tricycles and the first Scalextric sets, took over Meccano. Triang's own less sophisticated model trains were rebranded as Hornby.

Triang in turn hit problems as its overseas operations lost money, and in 1971 the company went into voluntary liquidation. Hornby Railways and Scalextric were taken on by Dunbee-Combex-Marx, which moved manufacture to Margate, and when that company too hit the buffers in 1980 a management buyout as Hornby Hobbies restored its fortunes. Several European model train makers were taken over, as was the plastic kit maker Airfix in 2006, whose range has since been perpetuated.

There was an irony in this. Airfix in 1972 had ridden to the rescue of Hornby's Liverpool factory, continuing the production of Dinky Toys and Meccano. But demand for both was eroding, and in 1979 Airfix provoked a political backlash by closing the factory without notice. Meccano continued to be made by Meccano France, which passed into the control of America's General Mills, better known for its food products. Since 2000 Meccano has been manufactured in France and China – though with a very different feel to the original engineering-orientated product – by the Japanese company Nikko.

METAL BOX

Generations of Britons used Metal Box Company products every day without realising it; thanks in part to a pre-war agreement with America's Continental Can, Metal Box enjoyed a 90 per cent share of the UK's tin can market. By the 1960s it was also the leading supplier of packaging to companies including Unilever, Nestlé, Heinz, Imperial Tobacco, BAT, ICI, Hoechst and Shell.

The US Department of Justice forced Metal Box and Continental Can to curb their agreement, and in 1967 – when the company had

40 plants in the UK and 32 more in Africa, Asia, Italy and the West Indies – the Monopolies Commission ruled that it was operating a monopoly, though not a harmful one. Shrugging off a takeover attempt from American Continental Can's great competitor, Metal Box diversified in the 1970s, becoming a market leader with its Stelrad central heating radiators; it also opened a giant canning plant in California for Coca-Cola. Tiring of its original product, Metal Box – which had been hard hit by the recession of the early 1980s – changed its name to MB in 1988, and the following year reversed itself into the ambitious bathroom products conglomerate Caradon. Caradon went through a series of restructurings and the collapse of its doors and windows business, eventually admitting it now had 'no core business'; concentrating on building security and controls, it changed its name to Novar in 2001, hit the financial rocks and in 2005 was taken over by Honeywell of America.

MB-Caradon had sold its canning business in 1993 to the Brussels-based Carnaud SA. Carnaud Metalbox's manufacturing profile in Britain is greatly reduced, but its modern Shipley factory remains a world leader in making canning machinery, and in 2010 won a Queen's Award for Enterprise. The days are long gone, however, when Metal Box's British shareholders received a collapsible marquetry-pattern tinplate coffee table as a Christmas gift.

MORPHY-RICHARDS

Morphy-Richards, founded in 1937 by Donal Morphy and Charles Richards, became a household name in the 1950s selling millions of electric irons (one model becoming a design icon) and becoming Britain's market leader for hairdriers, electric toasters and electric blankets. But it suffered from the frequent upheavals as the UK white goods industry struggled to gain some sense of direction in the face of European competition, and survives as a niche manufacturer of small appliances and digital radios with markets across the Commonwealth. Its surviving British factory is at Swinton, South Yorkshire.

In the consumer boom of the 1950s Morphy-Richards – already a maker of irons, spin driers, refrigerators and floor scrubbers – added to its range a pioneering steam iron, convector heaters and electric blankets. Forty per cent of production from its factories in Kent and Scotland went for export. In 1960 it was taken over by EMI.

The following year Morphy-Richards opened a new factory in Dundee which made a quarter of the nation's refrigerators, and in 1964 absorbed EMI's record player division. It was employing around 4,000 people when, in 1966, EMI and AEI, the owner of Hotpoint, merged their white goods divisions to create British Domestic Appliances; GEC's subsequent takeover of AEI left it with a two-thirds stake in the operation.

In 1970 Morphy-Richards fridges were rebranded as Hotpoint; Morphy-Richards's original factory at St Mary Cray was closed, production of most small appliances moving to Swinton though another plant in Kent continued to make kettles and coffee percolators.

Morphy-Richards was sold in 1982 to Capital for Industry, under which it briefly made audio equipment and televisions, then in 1985 to the infant Irish electronics group Glen Dimplex. The new owners injected more advanced technology into its kettles, toaster, hairdryers and breadmakers, also developing digital radios.

Russell-Hobbs, the highly successful manufacturer of quality electric kettles and coffee makers, was founded in 1952 by two senior staff who had fallen out with Morphy and Richards. Taken over by Tube Investments in 1962, Russell-Hobbs has survived subsequent ownership by Polly Peck, Pifco and Salton Inc of Illinois, which in 2009 renamed itself Russell-Hobbs Inc. Russell-Hobbs products are now made in China, though an Isle of Man company, Strix, still makes the switches.

PYE

In the 1950s and 1960s Pye was a household word not only for the radio sets and televisions it produced, but for its record labels launched from 1953 which generated hit after hit for Petula Clark, Lonnie Donegan, the Kinks and, in the 1970s, the Brotherhood of Man. Founded in Cambridge in 1896 to make scientific instruments, Pye in the immediate post-war years was also Britain's leading producer of mobile radio equipment.

The struggles of Britain's radio and TV manufacturers have already been explored; Pye had to sell its Ekco factory in Southend in 1966, and that year Tony Benn allowed Philips to take a 60 per cent stake in the company provided televisions continued to be made at its other plant in Lowestoft (later taken over by Sanyo). Philips completed its takeover in 1976, Pye's rights to the record label expired in 1980 and the firm attracted unwelcome publicity over its supply of radios to Idi Amin's genocidal Public Safety Unit.

Philips moved the manufacture of Pye televisions to Singapore, and the brand enjoyed a resurgence in the 1980s with its music centres and, later, DVD recorders. Its final flourish in the mass media came with the launch in 1983 of TV-am, Britain's first specifically breakfast station, when a series of commercials were screened starring the zany Spike Milligan under the slogan: 'Wake up to what Pye is doing!'

RANK

The business empire headed by J. Arthur Rank not only gave Britain some of its greatest movies – *Brief Encounter, Great Expectations, The Red Shoes* and later the *Carry On* films – and a 650-cinema chain, but also a flour milling business, the manufacture of photocopiers, televisions and hi-fi equipment and a small but successful record label. In the austere 1950s, Rank's 'gongman' was one of the few corporate logos evoking instant recognition. Ironically for a business founded on the principles of Methodism, all that survives under the name is the Rank Group, which runs a chain of casinos and bingo clubs.

The flour business, sizeable and well run, was the lowest-profile part of Rank's portfolio. Under J. Arthur Rank as chairman from 1952 and his nephew Joseph from 1969, Rank injected technology into flour production and promoted agricultural research – leading in 1984 to the invention of the meat substitute Quorn in collaboration with ICI. Rank took over Hovis-McDougall in 1962 to expand into baking, and in 1968 Rank Hovis McDougall (RHM) acquired the world-wide Cerebos salt business. But the company lost its identity when in 1992 it was taken over by the conglomerate Tomkins. They sold it on to the London private equity firm Doughty Hanson, who in 2005 refloated RHM on the Stock Exchange. Its independence lasted just two years before it was snapped up by Premier Foods, who already owned Lyons Cakes.

Rank's involvement in non-food manufacturing began in earnest when in 1956 it formed a partnership with the Haloid Corporation to launch Rank Xerox, making photocopiers; its highest profile plant was at Mitcheldean in the Forest of Dean. In 1962 Rank Xerox formed a partnership with Fuji to break into the Japanese market and promote R&D. The Mitcheldean plant closed in the 1980s, and in 1997 the Xerox Corporation bought out Rank, discontinuing the Rank Xerox brand.

The Top Rank record label was launched in 1959, two years later notching up a number one hit with John Leyton's 'Johnny Remember Me'. Soon after, Top Rank was taken over by EMI. Rank was also Britain's fourth largest maker of televisions in the 1950s, later producing them in partnership with NEC of Japan, the sets being branded as Rank in European markets until the 1980s. It also made stereo music centres in the 1970s.

SLAZENGER

One feature of the past thirty years has been the swamping of highly regarded British brands of sports accessories by expensively-promoted global brands; in good measure because those brands, in sports like athletics, golf, football and tennis, have paid (mainly American) professional players handsomely to wear kit bearing their logos in international competition.

One British brand with a continuing claim to global reach is Slazenger, whose origins date back to 1810, but typically its manufacturing footprint in this country is greatly reduced. Slazenger is best known as the official tennis ball supplier for Wimbledon, having held the contract since 1902, but in the 1950s they also made rackets, cricket and golf equipment, and sportswear.

When Ralph Slazenger sold the business to Dunlop Rubber in 1959, it was making tennis balls at Barnsley, with five other factories in Yorkshire; four at Horbury and one at Normanton. But the rise of the metal and then the composite tennis racket put Slazenger's traditional wooden product under pressure. Against this background Dunlop Rubber was taken over by BTR in 1985, and the following year sold on for £300 million to a management buyout backed by the investment company Cinven (Coal Industry Nominees for Venture Capital – which also involved the British Rail and Barclays Bank pension funds). In 2004 Cinven sold Dunlop Slazenger – minus branding rights in key markets like Australia – to Mike Ashley's Sports Direct for an estimated £40 million.

During Cinven's ownership of Dunlop Slazenger the four Horbury factories closed, and in 2001 the works at Barnsley. Since then the iconic Slazenger Wimbledon tennis ball – 48,000 are used at each tournament – has been produced at a factory on the Bataan peninsula in the Philippines (better known for the wartime 'death march' by American prisoners of the Japanese), where workers are paid around £5 a day. The Bataan facility also houses a sophisticated ball testing laboratory. Shuttlecock production continues at Barnsley, former Slazenger workers having set up a new company, Echelon Sport, which makes 5 million a year for leading brands including Carlton.

9

COULD WE HAVE DONE BETTER?

British manufacturing industry enters the seventh decade of the new Elizabethan age with much to congratulate itself on: far higher quality, acceptance of revolutionary new working methods, a virtual end to strikes. Yet these achievements have been too little, too late in terms of maintaining leadership and market share, globally or at home; for by the time these improvements were made the game was already effectively lost. Britain is no longer a leader in the great post-war technologies of aerospace, nuclear energy or (except in its universities) computer development, and its strong position in pharmaceuticals is under constant challenge as patents expire. The loss of two million manufacturing jobs every decade has only been partly offset by higher productivity, and Britain's share of world export markets has slumped; it is four decades since anyone seriously expected our imports of goods to match our exports. Britain does retain a reputation for quality niche and branded products, but in all too many cases only the label is British, with the product manufactured abroad. Moreover, there are still issues of poor performance to tackle: watchers of the recent Channel 4 *Grand Designs* series could not help noticing that almost every time British glass was required for a project, it arrived late.

Many factors lie behind Britain's industrial decline over the past six decades, not least the steady erosion of the corporate and financial base once provided by a combination of family ownership and the existence and engagement of a healthy mix of individual and corporate shareholders. But it is possible to identify specific decisions – or failures to identify a course of action that needed to be taken – that proved pivotal in making matters worse. Most were the responsibility of government, but the leaders of particular industries, and in a few instances specific companies, have also been culpable. Among the most disastrous of these decisions and non-decisions (some of them mutually exclusive) have been:

Concentration of R&D funding by the immediate post-war governments on aircraft development to the exclusion of other promising sectors, notably electronics.

The failure of the Churchill/Eden/Macmillan government to negotiate to join the Common Market when it was formed in 1958, and of governments after Britain eventually joined in 1973 fully to engage so as to maximise the benefits and minimise the disadvantages.

The cancellation of the Blue Streak military rocket programme, by the Macmillan government, leading to Britain playing only a junior role in the European space programme after diverting R&D resources from aircraft development to rocketry.

The failure of Britain's shipyards to capitalise on the global boom in demand for oil tankers from the 1950s.

The separation from 1954 of civilian and military nuclear reactor development.

The separation from 1962 of UK academic, commercial and military computer development.

Courtaulds's over-investment in the 1960s in Lancashire's declining cotton industry.

Harold Wilson's refusal to devalue the pound on taking office in 1964, leading to recurring sterling crises – and pain for exporters – over the three years before Britain was eventually forced into devaluation.

The imposition of a Selective Employment Tax, by Wilson's first government, that was designed to shift labour from services into manufacturing, but which in practice was a disincentive to manufacturers to become more efficient.

The shotgun marriage of Leyland Motors with the British Motor Corporation in 1968, brokered by Tony Benn.

Britain's withdrawal from the Airbus consortium in 1969, handing the initiative to France and Germany – again Benn's decision, with Concorde seen as a higher priority.

Benn's decision that Britain should proceed with Concorde at the expense not only of Airbus but BAC's own Three-Eleven airliner, which airlines were ready to order and was several years ahead of what became the Airbus A-300.

ICL's decision, taken under pressure from Benn and Clive Jenkins to persevere with its 1900 range of computers, rather than switch to the technically superior and IBM-compatible System-4 inherited from English Electric Leo Marconi.

The failure of British Aerospace, when nationalised and after privatisation, to concentrate production on as few major centres as possible.

The failure of Margaret Thatcher's government, and the automotive industry, to anticipate and avert the collapse of HGV manufacture in Britain in the late 1980s.

The failure of that government and its successors to realise – or care – that bus and rail privatisation and deregulation, and clumsy intervention in rolling stock procurement, would deprive British manufacturers of the orders needed to stay in business.

Lucas's decision to merge into the much smaller American component maker Varity.

GEC's decisions under Lord Simpson to abandon its core activities in heavy electrical engineering to its French partner Alst(h)om and concentrate on defence – briefly – and modern communications, paying heavily over the odds for American acquisitions in the latter field.

ICI's abdication from the conservative field of bulk chemicals, for long its core business, into riskier higher-value specialities which did not mesh with the company and whose acquisition imposed financial strains that speeded its demise.

BMW's sale of MG Rover to the Phoenix Four rather than Alchemy Partners in response to local political pressure, maintaining jobs at Longbridge in the short term but almost guaranteeing the company's failure through the continuance of unsaleable models.

BAE Systems' unilateral withdrawal from Airbus in 2006, carried out in a way that stymied Tony Blair's government from maintaining its influence within the consortium.

In addition, a number of factors can be identified which have been decisive in accelerating the decline of British industry, which are the result not of one specific decision but of broader failures to grasp the nettle or appreciate the disastrous effects of policies being followed:

The debilitating effects on manufacturing industry – as a supplier and a victim – of the cycle of nationalisation and denationalisation under alternating Labour and Conservative governments from the 1940s to the 1980s.

The encouragement of immigration in the 1950s as a means of tackling labour shortages, rather than taking steps to increase productivity.

The unions' pursuit of – and management's capitulation into the 1980s to – wage demands not merited by increased productivity that made British manufacturing increasingly uncompetitive.

Failure by companies across the board to keep investing in giant plants opened between the wars, such as Dagenham, the Michelin plant at Stoke and the Guinness brewery at Park Royal, which became increasingly uneconomic or unsuited to new production methods.

The strikes at Ford and Vauxhall in the 1970s which forced these companies to import cars from Germany to Britain when previously they had exported – hastening the relocation of corporate decision-making from Britain to the Continent.

The absence, after the creation of British Aerospace, of a second force UK aircraft manufacturer, able to take on strategically important or commercially attractive projects – such as short-haul and corporate jets – following BAe/BAE Systems's lost interest.

The absence of a similar British-owned second force in motor manufacture, to maintain a viable product range as British Leyland concentrated on keeping volume car production at Longbridge afloat.

The persistence of self-made businessmen in the 1980s in launching takeovers in the United States when acquisitions within the EU would have contributed more to Britain's competitivess.

The weakness of British industry by the 1990s which prevented it adding to its capacity by opening new plants in eastern Europe to manufacture competitive exports, but instead encouraged it to transfer capacity and jobs from Britain to those same countries.

What lessons should we learn for the future? Is there any point in trying to reverse a decline that has already deprived Britain of most of its manufacturing base, and of control over much of what is still made here – that could very easily be moved somewhere cheaper? On the evidence of the failures of strategy, policy and nerve listed above, it is tempting to expect the decline to continue, with ever more British jobs and skills lost and with even less of what remains accountable even to the stock market.

Yet there are some causes for optimism. For every ten British manufacturers who have given up the ghost, there are a handful of new ones – smaller, but driven by a thirst for success. British companies now engaged in manufacturing are there out of choice, not inertia, there having been myriad opportunities for their owners to sell out. Moreover, the debilitating ideological argument over nationalisation that paralysed key sectors of British industry is now at an end, and the trade unions no longer see their role as forcing major employers to the verge of collapse. Against that, the reluctance of the banks to support any potentially productive venture when there are greater bonuses to be earned through the rashest forms of speculation remains a significant brake, not only on manufacturing companies' expansion but all too often on their survival. The insistence of British banks on encouraging family businesses to float, then engineering their sale to new and usually foreign owners has been particularly damaging. In 2012 the CBI's director-general John Cridland appealed to the banks to foster "patient capital"

Nevertheless, with the innovative spirit alive and well, there must be some hope not only that Britain's manufacturing workforce will not halve again over the next decade, but that when new technologies and products emerge, we will this time round be able to turn a respectable proportion of them into world-beaters ourselves, and start the long, strenuous process of rebuilding. But just think where we could have been had management, the unions and, above all, government got more of their decisions right.

Eric Schmidt, chairman of Google, declared at the 2011 Edinburgh Television Festival: 'The UK does a great job of backing small firms and cottage industries, but there's little point in getting a thousand seeds to sprout if they're then left to wither or get transplanted overseas.' This needs addressing. After Hewlett Packard's £7 billion bid at the same time for the British software company Autonomy, Labour's shadow Business Secretary John Denham summed up the broader challenge when he said: 'The economy needs a critical mass of clearly British-owned, domiciled and led companies.' We had them once; it will be hard to achieve it again, but surely we have to try.

INDEX

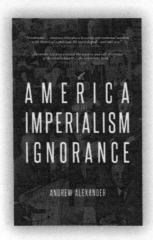

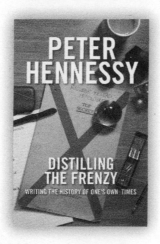

Available now from Biteback

STUMBLING OVER TRUTH

KEVIN MARSH

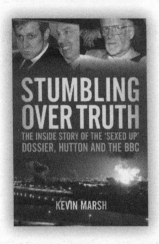

The 2004 report of the Hutton Inquiry created today's BBC. It cost the corporation its Chairman and Director General and seemed to many to usher in an age of self-doubt and caution. It was also the end of the most extraordinary experiment in news management Britain has ever seen – the decade of Alastair Campbell, Tony Blair's spin doctor, charged with delivering what Peter Mandelson described as New Labour's mission to 'create the truth'. *Stumbling Over Truth* is an important book for anyone who wants to understand the toe-to-toe confrontations between Tony Blair's government and the BBC, and the fight to resist unremitting government attempts to manipulate the media.

POLITICOS.co.uk
THE ONLINE POLITICAL BOOKSTORE

WE'RE BACK

BREAKDOWNS OF THE
BEST POLITICAL
LITERATURE ON
THE HORIZON

BE REWARDED FOR YOUR LOYALTY
WITH OUR POINTS SCHEME

AN ONLINE COMMUNITY OF
POLITICAL BOOK LOVERS

THE POLITICOS.CO.UK
TEAM ON HAND TO
OFFER YOU GUIDANCE
AND BESPOKE
BOOK SUGGESTIONS

TAILORED BESTSELLERS
LISTS FROM RECESS
READING TO POLITICAL
RESEARCH MATERIALS

WEEKLY POLITICAL
BOOK PODCASTS

SPECIALIST, CONSTANTLY UPDATED,
POLITICAL CONTENT

Politicos.co.uk is owned and managed by Biteback Publishing. @Politicos_co_uk